The Authors
Trained as a journalist, Nicholas Perry was
once a postulant in the Greek monastic
republic of Mount Athos and is now a full-
time writer. Loreto Echeverría, an historian
and former research assistant at the Catholic
University of Santiago (Chile), has since
1977 researched international politics and
contemporary society independently in
London and other centres. Both authors
travelled widely to prepare this book,
visiting shrines from Fatima in Portugal to
Copacabana in Bolivia.

UNDER THE HEEL OF MARY

UNDER THE HEEL OF MARY

NICHOLAS PERRY

and

LORETO ECHEVERRÍA

ROUTLEDGE

London and New York

First published 1988
by Routledge
11 New Fetter Lane, London EC4P 4EE
29 West 35th Street, New York NY 10001

Printed in Great Britain by
T.J. Press Ltd, Padstow

British Library Cataloguing in Publication Data

Perry Nicholas
Under the heel of Mary.
1. Great Britain. Mary, mother of Jesus
Christ. Worship. History.
I. Title.   II. Echeverría, Loreto.
232.91′0941

ISBN 0–415–01296–1

CONTENTS

Contents

Part II The Siècle de Marie

Contents

Part III Tiara et Fasces

Part IV Escalation of the Message of Fatima

Contents

ACKNOWLEDGEMENT

We wish to thank
Geoffrey and
Marigold Best for
their encouragement.

INTRODUCTION

On 24 March 1984 Pope John Paul II knelt before a white statuette of Our Lady of Fatima in St Peter's Square and, watched by a crowd of 150,000 and a potential television audience of one billion, dedicated the planet to the Immaculate Heart of Mary. Reading a formula in Italian and English, the Supreme Pontiff intoned: 'The power of this consecration lasts for all time and embraces all individuals, peoples and nations. It overcomes every evil that the spirit of darkness is able to awaken, and has in fact awakened in our times, in the heart of man and his history.'[1]

A year later, the temporal leader of the west – a 'born again' Christian – publicly associated himself with this solemn act. 'In the prayers of simple people everywhere, simple people like the children of Fatima,' President Reagan told the Portuguese parliament, 'there resides more power than in all the great armies and statesmen in the world . . . I would suggest to you that here is power, here is the final realization of life's meaning and history's purpose.'[2]

Notwithstanding the perhaps exaggerated nature of these claims, the apparitional cult of Mary, which culminates in Fatima, has certainly played a major role at all levels for centuries. The focus of this book is not on the complex *myth* of the Virgin – the subject of recent studies[3] – but on the development of Marianism in relation to power and the struggles of Rome. With the obvious exception of papal supremacy, no cult or devotion in Catholicism has contributed more to the consolidation of authority and institutional growth than the ever-expanding Marian faith. The apparition – the nucleus of Marianism in the absence of scriptural 'facts' – has invariably been an instrument of conquest, 'evangelization', revival and agitation.

1

Laying the foundations of a vast doctrinal edifice inimical to the potentially subversive Christ of the Gospels, visions of Mary infuse the Church with the zeal and asceticism needed to preserve the ecclesiastical order – monarchical and celibatarian. Shrines and pilgrimages, religious orders and confraternities (as much 'divisions of Mary' as of the pope), indulgences ('judicial forgiveness') and scapulars (a salvific device in her gift) have furnished the Roman priesthood with an indispensable means of control and with revenues.

As the New Israel,[4] Mother of the Eucharist, *Auxilium Christianorum* the Queen of Heaven and earth, Mary embodies the Church Militant and Triumphant. Ecclesiastical and pontifical authority was reasserted through the dogmas of the Immaculate Conception (1854) and the Assumption (1950). As the founder of Opus Dei eloquently said:

> Mary continually builds the Church and keeps it together. It is difficult to have devotion to Our Lady and not to feel closer to the other members of the mystical body and more united to its visible head, the Pope. That's why I like to repeat: All with Peter to Jesus through Mary![5]

An inexhaustible source of inspiration and strength against heresy and subversion, the cult of the Virgin also underlies dissent and schism. Because the organization and devotion of the Roman Church rest very largely on the figure of the heavenly Queen, resistance to the power of the keys generally takes the form of movements against the cluster of beliefs and practices associated with her cult.

Protectress of crusaders and conquistadores, patroness of inquisitors and counter-reformers, the Virgin became a central symbol in the seventeenth-century absolutist order, resurrected after the French Revolution along with the inextricable Sacred and Immaculate Hearts. As the nineteenth century opened with the annihilation of Jansenism – the oppositional force to Marian-Ignatian spirituality and papal absolutism – so the twentieth century began with the extirpation of the Modernist heresy (a rebellion comparable to the theology of liberation) and the identification of the 'captive' Church with the ideals of Action Française and *intégrisme*, preparing the terrain for Catholic collaboration in the twenties and thirties with fascism in a variety of national forms.

Votaries of the serpent-crushing 'exterminator of all heresies' were to lead the anti-intellectual, anti-Semitic mood. Today her zealots are a major force within the New Right, their apocalyptic views on nuclear war and their sexual politics virtually indistinguishable from those of Protestant fundamentalists. The Blue Army of Our Lady, official 'apostolate' of Fatima founded in the United States at the outset of the cold war, endeavours to defeat the Red Army by means of the rosary. The twenty-five million supporters claimed worldwide are fortified with indulgences and the Brown Scapular of Our Lady of Carmel, a devotion based on a vision in the Middle Ages.

We shall not attempt to summarize the prodigious historical development of Mary's role. The reader who requires a general picture of the phenomenon should see Part I and the 'overviews' of Parts II, III and IV. Because of the growing political importance of the cult, we have concentrated on the modern and contemporary periods.

Literally thousands of 'scientific' studies on Mary are produced every year and numerous libraries, academic centres and congresses are devoted to the subject. 'Apparitions,' we are told by a leading Mariologist, 'are rediscovering their meaning and their value.'[6] Yet militant Marianism has never been examined globally in its political – and geopolitical – context. The aim of our book is to begin, however inadequately, to close this historiographical gap.

Part I

ORIGINS OF MILITANT MARIANISM

1

GENESIS OF THE CULT UNDER BYZANTIUM AND ROME

Do thou hold the helm of the Church's hierarchy, and bring it to quiet harbours, sheltered from the breakers of heresy and scandal. . . . Guide the sceptre of the orthodox emperors who cling to thee . . . as to their diadem and royal robe. . . . Overthrow hostile, foreign peoples who blaspheme thee and the God born of thee, and stretch them prostrate at thy feet. In time of war help the army that always relies on thine assistance. Strengthen the subject people that they may persevere, as God commands, in the happy service of obedience.[1]

St Germanos 1, Patriarch of Constantinople (715–30)

The paucity of references to Mary in the New Testament[2] was compensated for early on by poetical, liturgical and iconographic developments fed by apparitions, miracles, legends and the transmutation of pagan myths.[3] Underlying nascent Marianism was a theocratic order based on a sacerdotal caste owning vast lands and controlling an intricate ritual without which there was no salvation. As the ministers of the altar – a place of 'terror and shuddering'[4] in the words of St John Chrysostom (d. 407) – became prominent, virginity gained a supreme, intrinsic value.

Even before the breakdown of the *Pax Augusta* a number of ideas and practices concomitant with the cult of Mary emerged among the Christian communities: veneration of images, belief in intercessors and in the malignant nature of the flesh. By the beginning of the third century images were consecrated and, to Tertullian's horror, the Church claimed the power to remit sins. Organized monasticism arose in Egypt during the second half of the century. The first recorded apparition of Mary occurred even before this, while Christianity was being savagely persecuted under Decius and Valerian. The seer was the Bishop of Neocaesarea, St Gregory Thaumaturgus (d.c. 270), a brilliant missionary who staged attractive religious festivals, instituted feasts in honour of the martyrs and performed marvels. St Gregory of Nyssa recounts in the next century that 'the Wonderworker' had received Trinitarian revelations from Mary and St John the Evangelist. These visions mark the beginning of Mary's role as the hierophantic voice of orthodoxy. She was thus set against the dualist and monarchian sects then in existence – Marcionites, Manichaeans, Montanists – which, although admitting of a Great Mother in their gnostical cosmology, denied the human nature of Christ and consequently ignored His 'mother'.[5]

In the final years of the Roman Empire Mary's jurisdiction expanded as Christianity was assimilated to the precarious order of a politically fragmented, barbarized and ruralized world – some parts of which still worshipped Isis and Kybele the Magna Mater.[6] The age of invasions – with the collapse of power structures, the economy reverting to the land, and the decay of classical scholarship – was propitious to the development of both priestly power and Marianism.

Theocracy, even in embryonic form, identified with the one who, chaste and chosen, was the 'type' of Mother Church. Not long after the heroic struggle for survival was over the see of Peter strove for supremacy. In 385 St Siricius, the first Bishop of Rome to be called Pope, claimed primacy over the universal Church. The first execution for heresy took place that year in Hispania.[7] Around the same time Siricius issued one of the first decretals imposing celibacy on the priesthood[8] – not without encountering some opposition.

Helvidius, Bishop of Sardica, denied the perpetual virginity of Mary, citing St Matthew; Jovinian, an 'apostate Milanese monk',[9] refuted the spiritual claims of sexual abstinence. Pope Siricius and two special councils condemned both critics. Jovinian and his numerous followers were expelled by St Ambrose (339–97), Bishop of Milan and the founder of western Mariology.[10] Active in Rome until at least 412, the heretics ended up scourged, exiled and scattered.[11] In Gaul Vigilantius, an influential reformer and missionary, vigorously attacked relics, shrines, maceration and compulsory celibacy. He seems to have been silenced by St Innocent 1 (401–17) and St Jerome (d. 420),[12] who wrote treatises in defence of relics and Mary's perpetual virginity. It was probably at around the time of this controversy and purge that the first apparitions of Mary occurred in the west. The visionary was the revered thaumaturge St Martin de Tours (d. 397), the founder of monasticism in Gaul, who thought marriage 'pardonable, virginity glorious'.[13]

The veneration of relics ('dust and ashes' according to Vigilantius) was an important aspect of the new devotionalism because it inculcated trust in mediators and the idea of sacredness in material things and places.[14] The cult of relics also complemented devotion to Christ's humanity, which in turn prepared the way to the worship of Mary, whose flesh and blood were shared with her Son.

By the second half of the fourth century the clergy began to wear elaborate vestments and celebrate with rich ornaments. The apostles' 'breaking of bread'[15] was assimilated to the new cult. In the words of St Ephraem the Syrian (d. 373), claimed by the west as a pioneer of the Immaculate Conception doctrine, the Eucharist was 'grape from Mary'[16] – a seminal idea of cardinal importance for modern Mariology. As Arianism – the belief that the Son is inferior in essence to the Father – persisted, exaltation of Mary became the hallmark of orthodoxy: 'If anyone does not accept the holy Mary as Theotokos', taught St Gregory of Nazianzus (d. 389), 'he is without the godhead.'[17]

Nestorios, Patriarch of Constantinople, and theologians at Antioch rejected the concept of Theotokos ('Mother of God'), preferring Christotokos. Nestorios was condemned by Pope Celestine in 430 and, despite the support of Emperor Theodosius II, excommunicated the following year by the Council of Ephesus – to the delight of the populace, who illuminated the town with flaming torches.[18] The Marian faction at Ephesus, which included the flourishing Egyptian monasticism, was headed by St Cyril, Patriarch of Alexandria, for whom Mary was 'crown of virginity, sceptre of Orthodoxy'. One of his companions was the abbot of the White Monastery at Athribisis on the Upper Nile, who governed a huge community of both sexes with an iron rule of flogging and 'written professions of obedience'.[19] in 435 Nestorios was banished to the desert and the emperors commanded that all Nestorian books be burned.[20] Yet Nestorianism rebuilt a base in Persia and spread through the east as far as Mongolia and China.

By mid-century, around the time that Rome was sacked by Vandals and threatened by Huns, the doctrine of Petrine primacy was consolidated in the pontificate of St Leo the Great (440–61), who initiated papal jurisdiction over bishops. Leo I taught, somewhat abstrusely, that 'there would be no hope of salvation for the human race if he had not been the Son of the Virgin who was the creator of the Mother.'[21] The Council of Chalcedon (451), under Leo's influence, reaffirmed Mary's prerogatives and condemned Nestorios once again.

In this tragic fifth century the first relics[22] and miraculous icons of the Virgin appeared in the east, while the west saw the first representations of St Peter holding the keys (frescos in the eighth century depicted the pope receiving his emblems of power from the Virgin).

The nexus of absolutism, a celibate hierarchy and the cult of Mary is clearly manifested in Byzantium the following century. Justinian I, whose monogram appeared on the first iconostasis and whose reign (527–65) – 'the high watermark of imperial influence in religious matters'[23] – was under the patronage of the Theotokos and St Michael the Archangel, gave the feast of Christ's conception a Marian emphasis and imposed clerical celibacy with harsh penalties for those who dared to infringe it.[24] He also restricted the civil rights of Jews and pagans, outlawed the reading of the Bible in Hebrew and closed down the Academy of Athens founded by Plato,[25] relentlessly persecuting all who opposed 'orthodoxy'.

The monothelete heresy (that Christ has two natures and one will) absorbed much of Rome's attention throughout the seventh century, during which a series of feasts of the Virgin were instituted: Purification, Assumption, Annunciation and her Nativity. These celebrations – established during Benedictine ascendancy and Muslim expansion – encouraged much fantasy and speculation about Mary. St Ildefonsus, Bishop of Toledo (d. 667), a great champion, against the Helvidians, of Mary's perpetual virginity, experienced the first recorded vision in Iberia. Our Lady appeared on his episcopal throne and handed him a chasuble to be worn on her feast days. In England St Egwin (d.c. 717), Bishop of Worcester, was moved to found the great Eversham monastery by a vision of Mary beside the river Avon.

The war against the use of images in the eighth and ninth centuries – in which iconodules and devotees of the Theotokos were one – was a violent struggle against the monasteries, possibly perceived to be manipulating the people through sacred likenesses which even today are hailed as 'carriers of all the power of the Virgin'.[26]

In 726, by the time the patriarchates of Antioch and Jerusalem were subjected to Islam, Leo the Isaurian issued his iconoclastic edict. Although challenged by the Patriarch of Constantinople and the pope (who never again paid taxes to Byzantium), the soldier-emperor, whose army had saved Constantinople from the Arabs in 718, was able to implement his reform. Some historians have pointed out that his policy – in agreement with the iconoclastic tendency of the army – was aimed at curbing the wealth and influence of monasteries,[27] which enjoyed the allegiance of the people through iconolatry.

Less attention has been given to the fact that Emperor Leo's assault coincided with the dawn of the new religion of Marianism. His two great opponents in the iconomachy were the outstanding Mariologists of the period: St Germanos, the eunuch patriarch, and St John of Damascus (d.c. 749), a monk declared Doctor of the Church in 1890 and considered – in Latin eyes – 'the St Thomas Aquinas of the East'. Through the work of both divines, in which poetry and doctrine intermingle, the Church reached a watershed after which the Mariological element has been indissoluble. 'God', says Germanos, 'obeys you through and in all things, as his true mother'.[28] He called himself a 'slave of Mary', who averts the wrath of God, is the refuge of sinners and partakes in our redemption. St John – a tactical advocate of papal authority[29] – also speaks of 'maternal authority', affirming Mary's Assumption, mediation and Immaculate Conception – because Joachim 'ejected an absolutely stainless sperm'.[30]

Leo's successor, Constantine V, was an extreme iconoclast who razed monasteries, forced monks and nuns to marry, destroyed relics and forbade prayers to the saints and Mary.[31] It was probably during his long reign (740–75) that Rome – now suzerain of extensive domains – produced the False Decretals, in which the Church is presented as 'controlling the gates of heaven and hell',[32] and the Donation of Constantine, the forgery legitimizing the temporal power of the papacy (a document unchallenged until the Renaissance).

As army power waned towards the end of the century iconolatry duly returned and was exalted at the Seventh Ecumenical Council (Nicea, 787) called by the Empress St Irene.[33] Iconoclasm, the Nicene fathers taught, was a Jewish, Islamic and Manichaean heresy.

Later developments in Byzantium left permanent testimony of the link between relics, images and the cult of Mary. When iconoclasm was finally eradicated, the Empress St Theodora, a good friend of the papacy, instituted the Festival of Orthodoxy (843), marking the restoration of the cults of both images and saints.[34] And in the following century, with the empire under external threat, the Theotokos appeared to St Andrew the Fool-in-Christ (d. 936) holding her veil – a Constantinopolitan relic – over the faithful. This apparition was the origin of the feast of the Protection of the Mother of God, still celebrated by the Orthodox Church.

2

THEOCRACY, THE RISE OF MARY, AND HOLY WAR

Italy, by a decree of Providence, possesses . . . superiority over all the lands of the earth. The font of the Christian religion is in Italy and in the primacy of the Apostolic See, the authority of the Empire and the priesthood are intertwined.[1]

Pope Innocent III (1198–1216)

Since early times the religious orders were instrumental in the process of strengthening Rome and Marianizing Christianity. Through them as repositories of learning, the Marian mysteries unfolded and a whole religious sensibility was cultivated. The monastic establishment, prop of a papacy beset with enemies, fought for papal supremacy and ecclesiastical discipline, producing at the same time a piety, liturgy, music and art enthralled by the figure of Mary. Affiliated to the great monastic centres were the military orders, another cornerstone of western theocracy. The knights, embracing celibacy, were equally enfeoffed to their celestial lady.

The advent of the Cluniac Congregation, which originated in the reformed Benedictine monastery founded at the beginning of the tenth century in Burgundy, was a landmark in the transformation both of the cult of Mary and the physiognomy of the papacy. There is an acknowledged link between the Marianism promoted by this 'vast ecclesiastical nexus'[2] with its dominance of pilgrimages to all the major Spanish shrines and the doctrine that the successors of Peter alone have the power to bind and to loose through Mary's intercessions.[3] The monks of Cluny exercised a decisive influence over St Leo IX, in whose reign (1049–54) the 'dark age of the papacy' ended. An enemy of clerical concubinage, simony and lay investiture, Pope Leo bestowed many privileges on Le Puy (Haute Loire), the most important Marian shrine in the west.[4] The long process of schism with the Byzantine Church reached a decisive climax at the end of his pontificate, which had also seen the legal edifice of Latin Christianity begin to take shape.

Under Hildebrand, Gregory VII (1073–85), the greatest pope of the Cluniac era, the Donation of Constantine was incorporated into canon law. Engaged in a deadly war against the Holy Roman Empire, feudal lords and a priesthood unwilling to conform to celibacy, Hildebrand forcefully stated the claims of Rome to infallibility and the unique power of the pope to call a general council and interpret canon law. As the *Dictatus Papae* – 27 dicta attributed to Hildebrand himself – has it, '. . . the Roman Church has never erred, nor ever, by the witness of Scripture, shall err to all eternity'.[5]

These unsurpassable claims were formulated when Mariology started to flourish in the west, in the very circle of Hildebrand. The reformer and ascetic St Peter Damian (d. 1072), a close friend of Hildebrand, taught that the Church sprang from Mary. He was also one of the first theologians to elaborate on the connection between the Eucharist and the Mother of God. Peter's brother, the Blessed Marino, was a forerunner of Marian slavery.[6] Among other supporters of the pope's reforms, the Benedictine Geoffrey of Vendôme (d. 1132) stressed the intercessional powers of the Virgin, and Bishop Bruno of Asti (d. 1123) considered her head of the Church after her Son.[7]

Notwithstanding the Hildebrandine dicta on the pope's supremacy over emperors, it was Emperor Henry IV who deposed him. New divisions and more propitious times were needed for the consolidation of papal power.

By the end of the eleventh century the great Christian offensive started. Toledo was reconquered in 1084; and on the day of the Assumption, 1095, the first crusade was led, even in the field, by the Bishop of Le Puy, who had received Pope Urban II when he came to the fortified 'Angelic Church' to entrust the glorious *peregrinatio* to Our Lady.[8] A Venetian battle early in the following century inaugurated an era of expansion and prosperity for the Italian peninsula.

In 1098, three years after the first crusaders had set out for the Holy Land, the motherhouse of the Cistercian family – another branch of the Benedictines – was founded in Burgundy by three saintly monks. Tradition says that the Virgin told one of them, St Alberic, to change the colour of their habit from black to white.

Since then the Cistercians have commemorated the Descent of the Blessed Virgin at Cîteaux. This legend is characteristic of the times, which grew more Mariolatrous as heresy spread, chiefly in the south of France and northern Italy. St Bernard (1090–1153), the greatest Cistercian, founder of Clairvaux and preacher of the second crusade, was a key figure of the period, canonized 21 years after his death. He taught devotion to the pope[9] and Mary, whose great intercessional power is like an aqueduct between mankind and God.

Some of St Bernard's contemporaries went further. The Benedictine abbot Arnold of Bonneval (d. c. 1156) asserted that Jesus and Mary had one will and one flesh, implying a hypostatic union between Mary and the Trinity. Another Benedictine abbot, Godfrey of Admont (d. 1165), maintained that the Church was founded on Mary and that she was 'the unique matter of all the sacraments'.[10]

These febrile speculations were complemented by visions, relics, and shrines multiplying everywhere in the custody of the orders. The exact measurements of the house of the Annunciation were supplied by Mary herself to the lady of the manor of Walsingham (England). This 'perfect copy' of the holy house erected in 'the Dowry of Mary' was entrusted to the Augustinian Canons in the latter half of the twelfth century and soon became a rich and popular place of pilgrimage until its destruction in the Dissolution (1538).

The struggle to impose celibacy on the priesthood and military orders lasted throughout the Middle Ages. Concubinage was rife nearly everywhere, despite the growing popularity of the Virgin's cult among monks and knights and despite all the miracles which proved the wickedness of unchaste clergy. In the second half of the twelfth century the canonist pope Alexander III unsuccessfully proposed to restore clerical marriage in order to end scandal and disorder. The political context of this unusual attempt to regularize the sexual life of priests is significant: Rome had to contend with, on the one hand, Emperor Frederick I and the antipopes dominated by him, and, on the other, the heretics (Albigenses and Waldenses) who were denouncing corruption and a lack of *vita apostolica* among ecclesiastics.

Lothaire dei Conti di Segni, crowned pope at 37 and reigning as Innocent III (1198–1216), styled himself Vicar of Christ on earth and resolved to crush heresy with military force. A few months after his elevation he sent a delegation to Toulouse, epicentre of Catharism, to take the necessary measures against the rebels, who already had bishops consecrated according to their rite.

Through their scholastic work and devotionalism the new orders thriving in the thirteenth century (Dominicans, Franciscans, Carmelites, Servants of Mary, Mercedarians) laid a solid, almost definitive, basis both for papal supremacy and Mary's aggrandizement.[11] Dominican and Franciscan engagement in the Inquisition was also crucial in the preservation of Roman autocracy under the changing historical conditions: growing urban populations and increase in trade and intellectual awakening. However, a fateful hiatus of 73 years came at the beginning of the fourteenth century with the fall of Rome as the see of the papacy.

*   *   *

The first canonization took place at the end of the tenth century[12] and the first indulgence was sold by the beginning of the eleventh – two landmarks in the history of Roman theocracy. Although these innovations did not immediately affect devotional life, the keys now possessed two fundamental means of fostering the type of piety on which Marianism is based.

In an age dominated by the fear of hell, Mary, as Co-Redemptrix with quasi-omnipotent mercy, had been paramount in the economy of salvation since early scholasticism. The Benedictine Eadmer (d. 1124), for example, thought that her merits always intercede – even undeservedly – and the influential Peter Damian (Doctor of the Church since 1828) also subscribed to the widespread belief that Mary placates the Judge. This postulate was the basis of the scapular devotion, later to take on, to a certain extent, a sacramental character.[13] The doctrine of purgatory and indulgences – a fruit of medieval scholasticism – is, like the scapular, related to the intercession of both Mary and the Church. Remission of the culpa and pena attached to sin is effected through the power of the keys, which can dispense of the 'treasure of the Church' deposited by the 'merits' of Christ, the Blessed Virgin and the saints. The Dominican St Albert the Great (d. 1280) asserted that 'every grace in the Church derives from Mary's merit'[14] and his pupil, St Thomas Aquinas (d. 1274), established the papal monopoly in indulgences.[15]

As a sort of tax on sin (forgiveness in exchange for alms or work) and a spiritual insurance for crusaders and pilgrims to Rome,[16] indulgences became a strategic device for the papacy from the end of the eleventh century. Both the shielding figure of Mary and the allure of indulgences were widely deployed in the crusades. When the first war against the infidels was launched from the shrine of Le Puy, Pope Urban granted remission of sins to those who fought and ordered Marian devotions on Saturdays (Our Lady's day) to obtain her help. Later on, papal largess was extended to those who assisted the crusaders with money or colonized land for Roman Catholicism.[17] Innocent III pardoned the sins (including those not yet committed) of anyone engaged in the internal crusade in Languedoc headed by the abbot of Citeaux. Military and religious orders were intertwined. In Castile, for example, the Knights of Calatrava wore Cistercian habit and followed the Benedictine rule adapted for a life of war.[18] These fighting orders, many of which were established during the twelfth century advance, were essentially Marian and aristocratic. King Alfonso the Wise, author of exquisite songs to Mary, founded one similar to the Calatravians: the Orden de Santa Maria de España, 'at the service of God and in honour of the holy Virgin Mary, His mother'.[19]

The great Christian victories in Iberia over the Muslim invaders were honoured by the construction of a shrine or church of Nuestra Señora. The oldest sanctuary in the peninsula is Covadonga in Asturias, founded at the beginning of the eighth century after Pelayo's victory. When James the Conqueror, 'apostle of the honour and glory of the Virgin',[20] seized Alicante, he ordered the 'purification' of the mosque, which became the church of Santa Maria, later the site of a thriving confraternity of the Immaculate Conception.

According to tradition, King James of Aragon was one of the three founders of the Order of Our Lady of Mercy or Ransom. The other two were St Pedro Nolasco ('a fugitive from the Albigenses')[21] and St Raymond of Peñaforte, master-general of the Dominicans and a great theoretician of the Inquisition. The 'Mercedarians' were established in 1218 in obedience to a command from the Virgin, whose radiant apparition amidst a host of angels[22] is still commemorated by the order every month.[23] By mid-century the Mercedarians took over the monastery of Our Lady of Puig, under whose protection King James had expelled the Moors from Valencia. Nuestra Señora de Puig – of apparitional origin – has been since then patroness of Valencia. The cult of the Patroness of Jaen (Andalusia) also dates from this period. A few years after St Ferdinand II of Castile conquered Seville (1248) 'the image of holy Mary appeared to a poor

Granadinian shepherd.'[24] The dark-featured image was enthroned in the famous shrine of Nuestra Señora de la Cabeza, from which dozens of confraternities sprang.

*   *   *

The whole Marian doctrine and the ecclesiastical machinery at the service of the cult have their roots and models in pre-Reformation times. Virtually every message and image of the Blessed Virgin and its analogous devotion has its origin in the Middle Ages. The seers of the last four centuries add little of substance to the old revelations. During the baroque period and later, the Church merely regurgitated the medieval pattern with modifications. For example, the Benedictine St Gertrude of Helfta (d. 1302), with her 'exercises in honour of the five wounds'[25] and exchange of hearts with Jesus, provided a paradigm of the Jesuitic devotionalism of the seventeenth century, which culminated in St Marguerite Marie Alacoque's visions of the Sacred Heart.[26] Like Sister Alacoque, Gertrude received revelations about Our Lady. God told her, 'Honour my Mother, who is seated at my side, and employ yourself in praising her.' Then the Blessed Virgin 'planted in her heart the different flowers of virtue – the rose of charity, the lily of chastity, the violet of humility.'[27]

The case of St Gertrude the Great (as she is known) is classified by William James as a very low example of 'theopathic saintliness'.[28] Yet the impact of some of these revelations on ecclesiastical tradition should not be underestimated. St Alphonsus Liguori, a Doctor of the Church and the most important founder in the eighteenth century, based much of his Mariology on them. St Francis de Sales (d. 1622), also *Doctor Ecclesiae* (and in the twentieth century, patron of writers), based his reflections on the Virgin's death partly on the experiences of St Mechtilde (d. 1298), another Benedictine of Helfta, who received communications from Mary and the Sacred Heart.[29] St Jean Eudes, seventeenth-century founder and apostle of the Immaculate Heart of Mary, saw in the visions of Mechtilde and Gertrude 'the beauties and mysteries of devotion'[30] to the Heart of the Mother.

Devotion to the humanity of Christ and the Passion led to the cult of Our Lady's compassion and her Seven Sorrows. This practice took an organized form and expanded through the Servants of Mary (Servites), an Italian mendicant order of the thirteenth century, whose founders the Virgin instructed to wear black in memory of the Crucifixion.

Marian piety, with its emphasis on the sins of the flesh and encouragement of passive virtues (obedience, humility, patience),[31] was the spontaneous manifestation of an age that saw concupiscence and pride as the roots of all evil.[32] But as new heresies spread, the hierarchy, fearful of losing control of its flock, came to rely even more on veneration of the Virgin as the touchstone of right belief. By the end of the twelfth century, when heresy was rampant, the Bishop of Paris instructed all priests of the diocese to urge their parishioners – from pulpit and confessional – to 'visit' Our Lady at least once a year.[33] Not long afterwards, as Catharism was extirpated, the synod of Paris added the Hail Mary to the Lord's Prayer and the Creed as a catechetical obligation. And when the walls of Toulouse were demolished (1229) and the French king extended his dominion over the region, the public penance inflicted on Count Raymond was none other than a whipping at the altar of Notre-Dame de Paris. In thanksgiving for his victory, Louis VII asked permission of the Holy See for nocturnal worship of the host, a practice intimately connected with worship of Our Lady[34] and one which has become widespread in modern times.

It has been pointed out that in opposition to the Catharist errors, 'the cult of the Virgin greatly grew in strength', forming, as it were, 'a secret link between the idea of the Virgin Mother and Catholic Orthodoxy'.[35] There is no doubt that the Albigensian threat, in the heart of Christendom, boosted Marianism, but the connection between this and Church authority is no 'secret'. The Cathars adhered to the ancient heresy that Christ had merely the appearance of human form (his real nature was seen at the Transfiguration). Hence they dismissed the role of Mary and the celebration of the Eucharist as irrelevant. Some, indeed, saw the Virgin as a symbol of the Catholic Church they so despised.[36] What is more, as believers in reincarnation, they denied the existence of hell and, as pacifists, the legitimacy of war.[37] The greatest efforts of St Bernard – like those of St Dominic, the Spanish founder and preacher (d. 1221, canonized 1234) – were directed against such enormities.

The Waldenses – voracious Bible readers – also rebelled against military service, the doctrine of purgatory, indulgences and images. By the end of the twelfth century, when both Cathars and Waldenses were extending their influence, Church legislation against heresy was introduced and, a few years later, the Inquisition was set up. Aquinas argued that heresy was a sin against the common good which deserved the death penalty. By the mid-thirteenth century torture was legalized in the pontificate of a great canonist, Innocent IV. But heresy and incredulity persisted and at the second council of Lyons (1274) it was deemed necessary to reaffirm transubstantiation, purgatory and the supreme authority of the Holy See.

Another of Rome's major objectives during the thirteenth century was the mass conversion of the Jews, undertaken mainly by Franciscans and Dominicans (founded in 1210 and 1216 respectively).[38] Aquinas was induced by St Raymond of Peñaforte to write *Summa Contra Gentiles*, completed in 1264. Soon afterwards, in the reign of Clement IV (1265–68), the powers of the Inquisition over false converts were augmented. Already obliged to wear distinctive clothes (a measure that met with St Thomas's approval), the Jews were subjected to an even closer vigilance. They were often accused of desecrating the host, and the Talmud was burned on several occasions.

It was in this context that the militant organization and devotions of the Church started to take their present shape. Lay divisions attached to the orders were formed. In 1264 the general of the Franciscans, St Bonaventura, founded at Rome one of the first Marian confraternities.[39] Great personages figured in these brotherhoods. St Louis, King of France (d. 1270, canonized 1297), belonged to the Servite confraternity, whose members, devotees of the sacrament of the altar, wore the Black Scapular of the Compassion.[40] The Third Order of St Francis played an important part in fostering orthodox mysticism. Among outstanding tertiaries was St Margaret of Cortona, a penitent favoured with visions of the Sacred Heart. Both canonist popes Gregory IX (1227–41) and Innocent IV (1243–54) rewarded the Franciscan Third Order with privileges for its work during times of crisis.

Sir Richard Southern has observed that 'the history of papal indulgences between 1095 and 1500 is an epitome of the history of the papacy during these centuries'.[41] We may add that the cult of Mary epitomizes both papacy and indulgences. Since the thirteenth century Marianism advanced in tandem with the system of indulgences, without which pope and orders would have been deprived of a vital source of sustenance and devotional leadership. The pardon granted by Clement IV in 1267 for contributions to the enlargement of a Mercedarian shrine is a typical example of the 'local' indulgence, a device which fostered devotion to specific places. The most conspicuous case in the thirteenth century was the 'Portiuncula', based on apparitions of Jesus and Mary to St Francis, in the chapel of St Mary of the Angels near Assisi – an indulgence which became a major asset for the Franciscans. The friars claimed their founder had been granted a generous indulgence (the first of its type) remitting all sins of those who confessed and visited the chapel of the apparitions at a given time of the year.[42] As a result of this concession – which unleashed an insatiable desire for similar privileges among rival orders – the Umbrian chapel was transformed into a leading Marian shrine by the end of the century.

Under Boniface VIII (1294–1303), who claimed universal sovereignty and disputed the taxes paid by the French clergy to Philip IV, another Italian shrine began to gain prominence: the Holy House of Nazareth – transported in stages by angels to papal territory. An official chronicler records that 'the great renown of Our Lady of Loreto dates from the jubilee of 1300, which had the effect of drawing to Rome and to Loreto representatives from all over Europe'.[43] This portentous symbol of the Temporal power – also to end in mendicant hands – would be greatly enriched with indulgences, its treasure secured by impressive fortifications.

All these extraordinary innovations marked the consolidation of a trend that would barely be moderated even in the face of the sharpest criticism and the eventual revolt of half of western Europe. On the contrary, the very dynamic of the Counter-Reformation and the overriding interests of the orders, papacy, and other crowns deriving power and prestige from the myth of Mary appear to have made the prodigious growth of the Marian devotional complex irreversible.

3

THE APOTHEOSIS OF MARY

Many who hold the faith of the son only build temples in the name of the mother.[1]

Leonardo da Vinci

LATE MIDDLE AGES

The inauguration of the Avignon papacy and the enigmatic exter-
mination of that most powerful order, the Templars (1312), were
followed by a long economic recession. A number of heretical
movements against theocracy accompanied this crisis (which was
particularly severe outside Italy).[2] Jacques Duèse of Cahors, reigning
as John XXII (1316–34), boosted Marian science and devotion, and
implacably opposed the current theories – which were that the general council of bishops had authority over the pope and the power of the
Empire came from God through the people. 'The greatest financial
organizer of the church',[3] John condemned 'abstract' mysticism and
evangelic poverty. In 1323 he declared the teachings of Franciscan
'Spirituals' heretical, and several were burned in southern France
for insisting that the Church should follow Christ's example of not
holding property.[4] A few years later, in 1329, shortly after his deposition by the Emperor (protector of the 'Spirituals'),[5] John issued a
bull against Meister Eckhart, whose mysticism – devoid of images,
doctrine and intercessors – was to remain suspect.[6] At the same
time Jacques of Cahors was sanctioning the fantasies of Franciscan
scholastics and he enriched the 'Ave Bells' with indulgences.[7] Like
his predecessors he surrounded himself with zealous Mariologists,
among them the Franciscans Peter Oriol and Francis of Mayronis,
followers of Duns Scotus, the 'Doctor Marianus' (d. 1308) who first
developed the doctrine of the Immaculate Conception. Oriol even
ventured that Mary is somehow 'the principle of the Holy Spirit',[8]

an idea that was to capture the imagination of some theologians and the 'charismatics' of our own age.

The Immaculate Conception controversy was full-blown by the second half of the fourteenth century, when scholasticism was in decline, the papacy still subjugated to the French crown, and plague and poverty had ravaged western Christendom.[9] The passionate devotion to the Immaculate Conception contrasted sharply with schism, dissension and ecclesiastical scandals. As the Holy See imposed heavy taxes[10] and the prestige of the 'captive Church' was shattered by interminable disputes and rivalries, Mary's deification was accomplished by means of fresh visions and revelations, new divisions, indulgences and such devotions as the cults of St Anne and St Joseph.

In the same way that the Servites claimed their order had been founded 'for her service, her glory and her glorification'.[11] John Baconthorp (d. 1348), the leading Carmelite and defender of the Immaculate Conception, established the filial relation between Mary and his fellow religious. In the year of Baconthorp's death, as the Black Death devastated Europe, the scapular revelation to the 'Brethren of the Blessed Virgin of Mount Carmel'[12] was disclosed by William of Coventry: Our Lady had appeared to the prior-general of the Carmelites, Simon Stock (d. 1265), and, in handing him the order's habit, declared, 'This shall be the privilege for thee and all Carmelites: whosoever dies in this shall not suffer eternal fire.'[13] This reassuring promise was the origin of the Brown Scapular, a device of great importance for centuries to come and one which still attracts indulgences.[14]

The Order of the Holy Saviour founded by a Franciscan tertiary, St Bridget of Sweden (1303–73), was another division pervaded with Marianism. One of the most colourful personalities of the century, St Bridget was a visionary of some influence at the papal court. Several Avignon popes (Clement VI, Urban V, Gregory XI) 'received the most urgent warnings'[15] from her and she begged them to return to the eternal city. Christ himself assured her of the sacredness of Rome and the convenience of papal pardons: 'The indulgences which the holy Pontiffs have merited by their prayers, and which may be gained in Rome, are a shorter way of getting to heaven.'[16] And at Assisi the authenticity of the Portiuncula indulgence was confirmed by Our Lady in person. These revelations – granted after the doctrine of the 'treasure' was officially formulated in 1343 by Clement VI on the occasion of the jubilee – indicate a growing scepticism about the power of the keys.

Mary's role in salvation was stressed by St Bridget, who had been told, 'My Son and I have redeemed the world as it were with one heart.'[17] This idea and image would be repeated with insistence down the centuries by visionaries and Mariologists alike. According to the Swedish mystic – canonized in a magnificent ceremony only 18 years after her death – our 'Salvatrix' was conceived without sin and taken to heaven in her glorious body.[18]

Another important seer of the period was the Dominican tertiary St Catherine of Sienna (d. 1380), who persuaded Gregory XI to return to Rome in 1377. She was also consulted by his successor, Urban VI, who reactivated the shrine of Loreto and approved St Bridget's writings. A mystical pioneer of the Sacred Heart devotion, St Catherine saw Dominican spirituality as founded on Mary,[19] although Our Lady herself informed her that, in accordance with Aquinas's teaching, she was not Immaculate. A few years after Catherine's canonization (1461) a Franciscan pope, Sixtus IV, denied her stigmata. Nevertheless, she remained an inspiration in Europe and South America for centuries, and was eventually declared a Doctor of the Church (1970).[20]

Aggravated by the Great Western Schism and amidst a torrent of visionary experiences,[21] the Immaculate Conception belief reached fever pitch in the 1380s. New Conceptionist waves swept orders and confraternities, courts and universities, absorbing a great deal of both the creative energy and repressive powers of Church and state, particularly in France. The Sorbonne expelled the refractory Dominicans by the end of the century, and Charles VI ordered the detention of all who refused to accept the Immaculate Conception.[22] His subject Clement VII (1378–94), the antipope in Avignon, declared these 'maculists' to be heretics. In 1402 the Confrèrie de la Passion set up the first public theatre in France, at which was staged the *Miracles de Notre-Dame*, a cycle of plays showing the merciful omnipotence of Mary.

Clear signs of radical revolt against the authority and doctrine of the Church are seen during the last years of the fourteenth century alongside the Devotio Moderna, a movement critical of devotional abuses and with an aversion to pilgrimages.[23] Although suppressed, these heresies, which had fundamental implications for the Marian cult, were to influence the reformers of the sixteenth century. The

Brethren of the Cross, for example, a secret sect that emerged in Thuringia and was ruthlessly eliminated in 1414, rejected absolution, clerical celibacy, image worship and all the other components of Marianism. In England, in a context of social upheaval, the radical postulates of Wyclif (d. 1384) pointed in the same direction: Wycliffites called the popes 'apostates', the mendicant orders 'heretics' and veneration of images 'idolatry'. They rejected Church ownership of property, priestly celibacy and the doctrine of transubstantiation, accepting the Bible as the only source of authority. The Lollards were to talk of 'the Witch of Walsingham', alleging in their *Conclusions* (1394) that Corpus Christi was 'full of false miracles'.[24] They denied, like the Cathars before them and the Anabaptists later, that Christ 'took flesh of the Virgin, since he possessed a celestial body'.[25]

Conceivably, this doctrine moved Gerson (d. 1429) to call the Virgin 'Mater Eucharistiae' and she who offered Christ as a victim for us[26] – an idea repeated by twentieth-century popes.

Meanwhile at Rome the Italian popes lavished the 'treasure' in exchange for Eucharistic and Marian worship. In 1389 Urban VI, on the occasion of a miracle and at the threshold of the Great Schism, offered a plenary indulgence to pilgrims to Loreto for the feast of Mary's nativity.[27] In the same year he granted an indulgence of 100 days to those who accompanied the Blessed Sacrament when taken to the sick.

THE RENAISSANCE

At the councils convoked in the fifteenth century to overcome schism and condemn heresy the Immaculate Conception was a central issue. Petitions for a Conceptionist declaration, as well as for a feast of St Joseph, were presented at Constance (1414–18), which had Wyclif's disciple the Bohemian John Huss burned. The fathers of Basle discussed and favourably resolved the Immaculate Conception question, but their dogmatic pronouncement made in the closing sessions (1438–39) under Duke Amadeus of Savoy (the antipope crowned the following year as Felix V) had no validity.

The Venetian pope Eugene IV managed to reassert his authority at the Council of Florence (1439–43), where the Greek Church, threatened by the Turk, submitted. Under the auspices of Cosmo de Medici, the pope's creditor, Florence reaffirmed the existence of hell and purgatory and the primacy of the Vicar of Christ over the general council. But an important discovery in those years cast a shadow over the Petrine claims: the spuriousness of the Donation of Constantine.

The end of the western schism – on Felix's abdication in 1449 – coincided with a period of general recovery in which Church and art glorified Mary in a magnificent way even though the papal coffers were almost empty. The Hussite heresy, the Ottoman peril, new learning, the Iberian expansion – all dominant factors during the fifteenth century – greatly stimulated the growth of Marianism, seen in the mushrooming of shrines and confraternities. Alongside mendicant influence,[28] an almost ostentacious showering of indulgences – already under attack in Germany[29] – prevailed.

Among the fifteenth-century devotional practices the most lastingly important was the rosary, conceived in 1470 by the Dominican Alain de la Roche 'from a vision', according to one authoritative opinion.[30] Roche's Universal Brotherhood of the Psalter of Our Lady was followed by countless other rosary confraternities throughout Christendom. Possessing an arsenal of indulgences and often subordinated to the orders, these brotherhoods epitomize the struggles of the Church Militant.[31]

Yet it was Franciscan doctrine and practice, characterized by an attachment to the Immaculate Conception, that pervaded the Quattrocento, just as the seventeenth century would be dominated by the not-so-different theology and devotionalism of the Society of Jesus.

By mid-century the old triad of Mary, holy war and indulgences revived trenchantly in the teeth of the Ottoman advance. St Bernardine of Sienna (d. 1444), a Franciscan active at the Council of Florence, was appointed by Eugene IV to preach the crusade against the Turks, in which a plenary indulgence was offered to financial backers. A great devotee of St Joseph, Bernardine was also an ardent defender of the divine nature of Mary: 'Only the Blessed Virgin Mary', he wrote, 'has done more for God, or just as much, as God has done for all mankind'.[32] Despite many of his views causing scandal at the University of Bologna, Bernardine was canonized during the splendid jubilee of 1450. He was closely associated with

St John of Capestrano, another Franciscan missionary, who was sent to extirpate the Hussites in 1451 and later to fight the Turks. Of the school of Bernardine of Sienna was Bernardine of Busti, the friar minor whose *Mariale* (c. 1478) expounded Mary's total monopoly of grace.[33]

Although not a canonical dogma, the belief that Mary had been conceived without sin was imposed in a number of ways. The Franciscan Sixtus IV (1471–84), who dedicated the Sistine Chapel to the mystery, issued a bull condemning those who dared to deny its truth. He authorized an effusive office for the feast of the Immaculate Conception and granted for its celebration the same indulgences his predecessors had bestowed on Corpus Christi.[34] In 1496 the Sorbonne approved a statute establishing an obligatory oath to defend the Immaculate Conception, stipulating expulsion and degradation of all who refused to accept this condition; in some parts of the Iberian world the custom persisted until recently.

Among the most significant foundations of the century were the French Order of the Blessed Virgin Mary or Annonciades and the Spanish Order of the Immaculate Conception or Franciscan Conceptionists, both devoted to the mystery of the Virgin's birth and the Eucharist. The Annonciades, who strove to imitate Mary, 'the very essence of the Rule', were established by the Franciscan Gabriel-Maria (d. 1532) and the mystical Joan of Valois (d. 1505), daughter of Louis XI of France. The Conceptionists were founded by the Blessed Beatriz de Silva (d. 1491), to whom Mary appeared while Beatriz was locked up in a chest.[35]

The intensity of the controversy over Mary's status is indicated by a bizarre conspiracy of 'maculist' Dominicans in Berne at the beginning of the sixteenth century. An apparition of Mary to a novice explained that she had been sanctified three hours after birth and that those who had taught the Immaculate Conception were now languishing in purgatory. The Black Friars were forced to admit the fraudulent nature of these claims – involving faked stigmata, bleeding hosts and such 'friarly toys' (John Foxe)[36] as a mechanical image which groaned and sweated – and several, including the Provincial, were put to the torch (1509).

Of all the Renaissance shrines none would surpass the Holy House of Mary near the prosperous Adriatic port of Ancona. The Santa Casa – 'a vital center of artistic activity during the fifteenth and sixteenth centuries'[37] – became immensely popular after the restoration of Roman hegemony. In an age when cities declared war over the possession of a relic of Mary,[38] the house of Nazareth was bound to capture the imagination in a way difficult for us to comprehend. Its fame was secured after 'the cure . . . through the intervention of Our Blessed Lady of Loreto, of two pontiffs in succession',[39] the impecunious Pius II (1458–64)[40] and the devout Paul II (1464–71). The latter claimed 'countless miracles wrought . . . in Our person'.[41] Under Paul II – whose mistrust of classical studies led to the closure of the Academy of Pomponius Laetus – the shrine of Loreto achieved a paramount position: he instituted feasts, granted a generous scheme of indulgences to pilgrims and ordered the construction of a basilica. During his reign the image of Our Lady of Good Counsel at Genazzano – also miraculously transported – became another source of indulgences and cures. Paul's successor, Sixtus IV, was a votary of both Genazzano and Loreto, granting the latter sanctuary the title of 'Alma Domus'.[42] During the subsequent pontificate of Innocent VIII – who, compelled to pawn his tiara,[43] issued even more indulgences – the Carmelites were appointed custodians of the Holy House (1489).

The formidable power of the friars – in charge of parishes, dioceses, shrines – advanced under Sixtus IV. Pilloried in 1476 by Masuccio di Salerno, the mendicant world was more thoroughly satirized by Erasmus, who advocated clerical marriage and ridiculed Marian piety and scholasticism.[44] He wrote 'an atrocious libel on the Franciscans' (as a twentieth-century friar viewed it)[45] and denounced the 'infernal machines of war'[46] and its profiteers, accusing the clergy of having turned 'the trumpet of the Gospel' into 'a trumpet of war'.[47] His pacifist work *Querela Pacis*, published in 1517 (the year of Luther's 95 theses), was burned by theologians of the Sorbonne and the Spanish Inquisition.

The socioeconomic and devotional framework in which the mendicant orders operated came under attack as a whole. In Calvin's view, the Marian cult was an 'execrable blasphemy'[48] and the institutionalization of mendicancy and alms-giving was 'spurious charity'.[49] Luther accused Rome and the friars of fostering a religiosity of idleness and dissoluteness with their pilgrimages and saints' days.[50] He denied that Mary possessed special merits and denounced the system of indulgences as economic exploitation.

The mendicant establishment responded swiftly. In 1520, when Giovanni de'Medici (Leo X) condemned Luther, the general of the

Franciscans commanded the training of 'special preachers to combat Lutheranism'; and 'prayers were ordered in particular to the Mother of God, the destroyer of all heresies'.[51]

In 1528, a year after the sack of Rome, Giulio de'Medici, Clement VII (1523–34), recognized a community of reformed Franciscans later known as Capuchins. Challenging humanists and Protestants, Rome clung desperately to the Marian cult, even embellishing the myth. In 1530, as the Augsburg Confession repudiated veneration of Mary and Charles V decided to convoke a council, the panicking Clement VII invoked the 'Sabbatine Privilege', becoming the first pope to countenance that great promise enjoyed by wearers of the Carmelite scapular.[52] A few months later he accepted the first official history of the Santa Casa as 'a faithful account of the acts of the Empress of the heavenly court'.[53]

HISPANIC CONQUEST

By the middle of the fifteenth century, as the Devotio Moderna spread in northern Europe, the cultured, aristocratic Order of St Jerome in Castile was nurturing, in Americo Castro's words, 'the idea of a universal, spiritual, interior and biblical Christianity'.[54] The conversos, who were awakening Christian humanism through their biblical scholarship, found in this order their 'most passionate defender'.[55] But by the end of the century – with the Spanish Inquisition in operation and discriminatory measures against new Christians in many guilds and confraternities – conversos were excluded by the Hieronymites, who wholly reverted to the old practices. The shrine in their custody, Our Lady of Guadalupe (between Cáceres and Toledo), flourished and by the following century was the most prominent in the region.

In the effort to organize the crusade against the Turk after the fall of Constantinople (1453) the Spanish pope Alonso de Borgia, Calixtus III (1455–8), also took an aggressive stance towards the Jews in his dominions, imposing special taxes and withdrawing some of their privileges. Soon after his accession he canonized the 'revivalist' Dominican preacher Vicente Ferrer (d. 1419), 'the Angel of the Judgement' and author of a sermon entitled *Contra Perfidiam Judaicam*. St Vincent's apocalyptic style, forcefully directed at Jews and Muslims, was permeated by an 'obsessive Marian peity'.[56] In the following year Calixtus issued the celebrated 'diploma' of the shrine of Our Lady of the Pillar which confirms the 'historical tradition'[57] of her journey 'in mortal flesh' and encounter with Santiago the Apostle (St James) in Saragossa. A few years later, the King of Aragon adopted Nuestra Señora del Pilar as his patroness, initiating a tradition that reached its acme during the fascist era.

By the end of the century the papal throne was occupied by another Spaniard, the nephew of Calixtus, Alexander VI (1492–1503), the first pope to apply indulgences to the souls in purgatory. A paradoxical figure interested in magic and Egyptian religion,[58] Rodrigo Borgia was a great promoter of the cults of St Anne and Mary, and he encouraged the rosary, restored the angelus and confirmed the Immaculate Conception bull of Sixtus IV.

Shortly after Columbus had set sail for the Indies (1492) in the caravel *Santa María* Pope Alexander divided the unknown New World between the crowns of Portugal and Spain.

In the very year of the discovery of America the 'Reyes Católicos' conquered the kingdom of Granada, the last Arab bastion in the peninsula. A few months later the monarchs entrusted the miraculous image of Santa María de la Victoria to the new Franciscan branch, the Minimi Fratres,[59] who established in the fallen Muslim kingdom a cult still flourishing today, that of Our Lady of Victory in Málaga. Mary's assistance in Spanish overseas expansion was no less efficacious. In 1495, two years after the conquest of the Canaries, the miracles of Nuestra Señora de la Candelaria, patroness of Santa Cruz de Tenerife, were registered before a public notary. Hernán Cortés, among others, carried the medal of her miraculous image.[60]

By the beginning of the sixteenth century, as the first voices of the reformers were raised against Rome, a movement against *ministerium mechanicum* can be detected in Spain. The most significant heterodox school was 'illuminism', practised by the sect called 'Alumbrados', which rejected images, corporal penance, meditation on the Passion, the doctrine of intercessors and the existence of hell.[61] The converso Juan de Valdés, who exalted the scriptures and denounced 'false worship of the Virgin' and 'false miracles',[62] was probably involved in this movement.[63]

Illuminism throve in the 1520s alongside Erasmianism but both were soon stamped out in Spain, where the mighty Holy Office would even challenge the Emperor. When Charles V's favourite preacher was gaoled for three years by the Spanish Inquisition on charges of 'Erasmian opinions', the Emperor's numerous letters of complaint were ignored by the Inquisitor-General.[64] In the third decade of the sixteenth century – when the shrines and statues of Mary were systematically destroyed in England and Scandinavia – all traces of Erasmianism had been eliminated in Spain. Staffed by Dominicans and Franciscans, the same machinery was already working with amazing effectiveness in the New World against Indians and 'the sects of Moses and Mahomet'.[65] Among the light penances prescribed by the Inquisition in Mexico was a pilgrimage to Our Lady of Remedios, the image enthroned by Hernán Cortés and rebaptized 'Victory'.

In a world revolutionized by printing, artillery, ocean navigation and new economic practices the broken power of Rome found vital compensation in the Iberian expansion and civilization – 'a particular variety of Western Civilization'.[66] Indeed it was in Spain and Portugal, and in their vast dominions that papal, and Jesuit, influence and the spirituality of visions reached their zenith.

The Mariocentric religiosity of the Counter-Reformation was also shaped by the dynamic of expansion and the missionary zeal of the age. The needs of the conqueror and general conditions of development in America favoured *ministerium mechanicum* and consolidated the anti-scriptural movement. Besides, the immediate consequences of European invasion were such that the cult of the Great Mother and Immaculate Protectress could not but thrive. For various reasons the native population was decimated during the first decades of Spanish settlement. Central Mexico, for example, went through the traumatic experience of seeing its people reduced from twenty-five million to one million during the course of the sixteenth century.[67]

The New World was soon teeming with Marian apparitions, miraculous images and wonders assimilated to the Iberian tradition, constituting the core of religious life in the empire. As a Jesuit has faithfully recorded, 'the continent was stamped with the imprint of Our Lady, with thousands of geographical names from her mysteries and dedications'.[68] Indeed, we can say that Hispanic colonization was Marian colonization.

4

IGNATIAN SPIRITUALITY AND COUNTER-REFORMATION

We must put aside all judgement of our own and keep the mind ever ready and prompt to obey in all things the true Spouse of Christ Our Lord, our holy Mother, the hierarchical Church.[1]

St Ignatius of Loyola

The Counter-Reformation was above all a movement to reassert Church authority, a monumental effort to impose astringent discipline as a defence against the inquisitive spirit of the age.

In 1542 the Roman Inquisition was set up by Alessandro Farnese (Paul III) and within a few years, under the 'intransigent warrior'[2] Giovanni Pietro Carafa (Paul IV), had become an awesome tribunal which employed torture and did not hesitate to arraign even the Spanish bishops.[3] The former Inquisitor-General St Pius V (1566–72) established the complementary Congregation of the Index, which would assiduously work on for centuries.

If the Church was to be reformed on Hildebrandic lines, celibacy and obedience were essential. For their enforcement – a difficult task in the dissolute sixteenth century – the agency of Mary Immaculate was required. The Society of Jesus, with its network of preachers and confessors, colleges and sodalities of Our Lady, chapels and shrines, was the chief architect of the reconstruction.

At the centre of the international scene was the Catholic King, the right hand of the Church, whose vast resources were invested in the Roman conquest and Habsburg expansion. Although politics and religion had become indissociable, the Gallican resistance to Hispano-papism (resulting in various alliances with Protestantism) and the papal revolts against Spanish domination of the Italian peninsula show that the confessional struggle was only one aspect of the intricate European conflicts of the sixteenth and seventeenth centuries.

Besides the politico-religious upheaval of Protestantism, a whole range of developments threatened the scholastic edifice: the new science (Copernicus' great work was published in 1543) no less than the reformist naturalism of the Renaissance with its epicurean ethic and magical practices as typified by Giordano Bruno (burned 1600).[4] Loyola's militia, conceived in the Virgin's chapel at Montmartre on the day of the Assumption, 1534, waged a relentless war against both rationalism and magic. Witch-hunters and demonologists, the Jesuits also became pioneers of 'scientific' Mariology.[5] Their ethos – like the mysticism of the founder, whose permanent state of chastity derived from a vision of Mary[6] – was deeply rooted in the Middle Ages. The Spiritual Exercises of Ignatius (published in Latin in 1548) are a perfect expression of western orthodox religiosity, framed in doctrine and sensual imagination. Loyola's Rules for Thinking with the Church are a crystalline echo of the Council of Trent (1545–63). Everything outside the scriptures which underlines Marianism and the ecclesiastical apparatus is categorically reaffirmed: pilgrimages, indulgences, images, virginity, continence and the religious state.

Defence of the Virgin's prerogatives forms a central plank in Tridentine doctrine. One of the first measures of the fathers of Trent, who renewed the dispositions of Sixtus IV on the Immaculate Conception, was to anathematize Erasmus' version of the New Testament in which important points concerning Mary and the authority of Jerome were at stake. After the Resurrection, says Ignatius, Christ appeared to the Virgin Mary, 'Though this is not mentioned explicitly in the Scripture it must be considered as stated when Scripture says that He appeared to many others.'[7] St Peter Canisius (d. 1597), a Doctor of the Church and one of the Society's greatest missionaries, made use of the apocryphal gospel of St James in his work on Mary; Francisco Suarez, SJ (d. 1617) – known as the father of scientific Mariology – quoted such imprudent enthusiasts as St Bernardine of Sienna.[8] Bernardine was almost surpassed by Quirino de Salazar, SJ (d. 1646), whose monumental work on the Co-redemptrix and all-powerful priestess is an important part of 'Spanish classical Mariology'.[9]

Counter-Reformation sermons harped on the power of Mary. Among the most inspired preachers were St Andrew Avellino (d. 1608), a prominent Theatine who called her the 'heavenly commissioner', St John Leonardi (d. 1609), founder of the Clerks Regular of the Mother of God, and St Lawrence of Brindisi (d. 1619;

Doctor of the Church since 1959), a Franciscan missionary to Jews and Lutherans who taught that 'her kingdom and empire is no less than the Kingdom of God and Empire of Christ'.[10]

Spurred on by the Calvinist doctrine denying the Real Presence in the Eucharist and the significance of the humanity of Christ and Mary, Perpetual Adoration of the host was systematically encouraged by the orders, particularly the Capuchins, in full expansion by the 1580s. The leading figures who spread the devotion in Italy included St Charles Borromeo (d. 1584) and St Philip Neri (d. 1595), founder of the Oratorians.

Mary's intercession was confirmed in private revelations too. St Catherine dei Ricci (d. 1590), a Dominican visionary who corresponded with Pius V, Neri and Borromeo, heard Jesus say, 'Oh my dear Mother, have I ever refused you anything and is not your heart the natural road that leads to my Heart?'[11]

As Catholicism resorted more and more to miracles and pageantry, Protestant iconoclasm became more entrenched. In England the royal injunctions execrated images and pilgrimages, striking a mortal blow at the cult of Mary. Spanish shrines were fair game for English sea-dogs. Our Lady of the Rosary, patroness of Cadiz, for example, was despoiled during Raleigh's famous sack in 1596. Iconoclast outbreaks played a significant part in uprisings on the continent. In 1562 the Huguenot armies made repeated but unsuccessful attacks on Le Puy. One of the most spectacular explosions of image hatred was seen a few years later in the Netherlands, in 1566, after which Philip II sent a mighty force led by the Duke of Alva, who established the dreaded Council of Disturbances.

Where Protestantism was essentially scriptural, the Counter-Reformation was plastic. The Society of Jesus, the first great teaching order, was the chief protagonist of the baroque, which Braudel calls 'a militant civilization' working 'through the power of the image'.[12]

By the second half of the sixteenth century many wonders ascribed to Our Lady were reported in various parts of the Papal States; a number of new devotional aids were introduced by the missionaries, such as the crib (a device of apparitional provenance)[13] and the coronation of Our Lady's images, a Capuchin innovation[14] whose utility would be paramount in modern times. The processional effigy of the Dolorosa with imperial crown was well-established in Spain by the end of the century. In the 1600s the hearts of the Dolorosas began to be pierced with one or seven swords in remembrance of Mary's sorrows; and the classic representation of the Sacred Heart with cross, wounds, thorns and flames was diffused by the Jesuits and the Visitation Order of Holy Mary. Another significant development was the monstrance in the form of Our Lady, the Blessed Sacrament held in her bosom, to be exposed for Perpetual Adoration or carried in Corpus Christi processions.

The dividing line between art, literature and devotions was almost as indistinct as it had been in the Middle Ages. The Jesuit drama, based in the Society's colleges and sodalities and initially often performed in churches,[15] provided an excellent vehicle for artistic expression, religious education and propaganda. In Spain pupils of the Society, as members of Marian confraternities, acted in plays written by Jesuits in honour of the Immaculate Conception 'represented in triumphal carriage'[16] or in colloquies – with dancing – between the Virgin and the Devil.[17] One of baroque theatre's most distinguished exponents was the Bavarian F. Lang (d. 1725), a moderator of a Marian sodality who put the Spiritual Exercises on the stage.[18]

The mystical life of Catholicism consequently remained shackled to the senses, emotions and dogmas. After the generalates of Mercurian (1573–80), who censored books of mystical theology, and Acquaviva (1581–1615), a no less vigilant superior in the field of humanities, the spiritual life of the Jesuits became highly regimented and restricted very much to the Ignatian exercises.

The subtle Teresa of Avila (d. 1582), a devotee of St Joseph who had experienced a vision of the Virgin,[19] understood that to flee from corporeal things in meditation was dangerous, leading to a rejection of the Blessed Sacrament devotion, the sacred humanity of Christ and his 'Madre Sacratísima.'[20]

*   *   *

The Society of Jesus – backed by the Spanish crown,[21] under the special protection of the Holy See, free of jurisdictional restraints, endowed with academic privileges – was also entrusted with the most strategic shrine: the Santa Casa of Loreto.[22] The cult of Virgo Lauretana soon became as international as the Jesuits themselves, who propagated her litany and enthroned replicas of her image throughout the world.

Menaced by bandits and mocked by Calvinists,[23] the richest Marian sanctuary was a place of almost compulsory pilgrimage during the Counter-Reformation and seems to have replaced the Holy Land. St Francis Borgia, the Jesuit general, visited the shrine once more shortly before his death in 1572 and was rewarded with a vision of Our Lady gathering the Society 'underneath her mantle'.[24] In 1579 St Charles Borromeo journeyed many miles on foot to the Santa Casa, where he celebrated Our Lady's Nativity. St. Francis de Sales, a great missionary to the Calvinists and founder of the Visitation Order, renewed his vow of celibacy there. Royalty and nobles showered the Holy House with precious and significant gifts. Christina of Sweden, for instance, after her conversion and abdication in 1654, presented her crown and sceptre to the image.

The Santa Casa was gradually transformed into a devotional-sacramental-educational-charity complex not unlike today's Opus Dei centre of Our Lady of Torreciudad in Aragón. Paul III (1534–49), initiator of the Counter-Reformation, opened a hospital at Loreto, and the shrine's official historians tell of important developments during the pontificate of Julius III (1550–5). He instituted a college of the Society 'with priests expert in foreign tongues'[25] and appointed Jesuits as penitentiaries to instruct 'rude people' and 'purge the souls of the pilgrims'.[26] Around this time an 'apparition of heavenly lights' occurred over the House and inside the church. Witnessed by several Jesuits, the phenomenon became known as the 'miracle of the flames' and was attributed to the presence of the Holy Spirit.[27]

While Pius V (1566–72) rid the Church of all sorts of abuses including some indulgences, he sanctioned an Agnus Dei stamped with a representation of the House of Mary.

Among the training centre for priests opened by the 'Jesuited' Gregory XIII (1572–85) was the Illyrian College at Loreto under Jesuit direction. Gregory – who extended the feast of St Anne to the universal Church – ordered the publication in eight languages of the official statement of belief in the miraculous origin of the shrine.[28] Loreto's main benefactor in the sixteenth century, however, was Sixtus V (1585–90), a shrewd manager of the papal states.[29] He raised the sanctuary to the status of a city and episcopal see, extended the fortifications to protect the treasury and founded the military Knights of Lauretani, the Ordo et Religio Equitum

Lauretanorium Pontificorum, to defend the holy place 'against pirates and brigands'.[30]

Elsewhere the Society of Jesus was attached to a prominent sanctuary or image of Our Lady: in Rome to the popular shrine of La Strada; in Luxemburg to the patroness of the duchy, Our Lady of the Afflicted; in Bavaria to Our Lady of Altötting, possibly the most important shrine in the German sphere. The Jesuits built numerous sanctuaries to the Virgin around Vienna, seeking her protection from plague and Turk.

The cornerstone of the Society's apostolate was the Sodality of Our Lady. The first – or Prima-Primaria – was that of the Annunciation, founded at the Roman College in 1563 'out of singular love for the Blessed Mother of God'.[31] The primary objectives of these brotherhoods – enriched with indulgences and extended throughout the world under the authority of the Jesuit general – were devotion to Mary, defence of the Holy See and good works (prison and hospital visiting, catechism, etc.). They played a vital part in the Catholic reconquest. The Citizens' Sodality of Cologne, for instance, busied itself with the destruction of heretical books in 1580, reciting 20,000 rosaries for the conversion of heretics. In Avignon by the turn of the century the Gentlemen's Sodality managed a fund to assist converts.[32]

The school sodality was selective: 'only the flower of the student body'[33] was recruited. And within the sodality were 'inner circles' composed of the pious elite. Sodality membership was a prerequisite for entry to the academies, Jesuit colleges for special training. As loyal sodalists, a large number of pupils remained linked to the Society all their lives. All the powers of Catholic Europe were connected with the Sodality of Our Lady: the kings of Portugal and Poland; the Duke of Bavaria and the Archduke of Austria. The supreme council of Castile was a corporate member. Many cardinals and bishops belonged, and the now permanent nuncios,[34] whose role had been a key one since the 1580s.

Retreats and exercises, recitation of the rosary, the Little Office of the Virgin, pilgrimages and celebration of Marian feasts were the standard devotions of the sodalists.[35] Rules were modified, however, according to circumstances. In the secret sodalities of the Jesuits' French colleges, for example, members attended a monthly 'Day of Recollection'.[36]

At the initiation ceremony – an act of consecration to Mary – the candidate received a medal with the inscription 'Regina, Advocata et Mater'. In the consecration formula, probably written by the Belgian Jean Leunis, [37] founder of the Prima-Primaria, we see a basis for the Marian slavery devotion and the *votum sanguinarium*, the oath signed in blood to defend the chief 'prerogative' of the Virgin; that she was conceived without sin.[38] The 'slavish movement', a perfect expression of baroque spirituality, spread to other orders[39] and by the mid-seventeenth century the Immaculate Conception vow was compulsory at universities in the Habsburg dominions.

Through the sodality and the slavery devotion the Society gave shape and direction to the militant Church. It moulded the 'mystical' sensibility and, more than any other order, inspired, promoted or supervised religious communities,[40] and apostles of Mary and the Holy See such as Cardinal Pierre de Bérulle, St Jean Eudes, St Louis Marie Grignion de Montfort, St Alphonsus de' Liguori.

The century of Habsburg and Bourbon absolutism was the age of Mary's queenship and Jesuit supremacy, of Marian slavery and Marian secret societies. The two great devotions persisting in modern times, the Immaculate Conception (celestially confirmed at Lourdes) and the Heart of Mary (revealed at Fatima) were already firmly established by the seventeenth century, likewise through 'locutions', visions and raptures. These cults were developed by the Society and the increasing number of divisions under its wing to combat Jansenism and quietism, Protestantism and Freemasonry, social upheavals and the nascent radical enlightenment, republican and pantheistic.[41]

5

SPANISH POWER AND MARIAN COLONIZATION

> The office of the Spanish . . . is to impugn heresy and their glory is to exalt the sceptre of the faith which is Mary, converting infidels.[1]
>
> Jacinto de Aranaz, O. Carm., H.M. Preacher, 1723

As Protestantism was deeply divided and lacked anything resembling the Society of Jesus, the Counter-Reformation forces made rapid strides among the rebels, mainly in the fragmented southern German-speaking lands, Bohemia, Poland, the southern Netherlands (Belgium) and France, a still divided kingdom with an exhausted and dwindling Calvinist population.[2] Some of Rome's imperial designs, however – shared by the Catholic King – failed. A 'still archaic power',[3] Spain was never to overcome the religious-political opposition of the strategic northern Netherlands. And England, challenging Iberian control of the Atlantic as early as the 1560s, finally shattered the myth of Spanish invulnerability with the defeat of the 'Armada Invencible' (1588).

As England feared a Spanish invasion, so Spain dreaded a Muslim one. After the Djerba disaster (1560) and the 1568–9 revolt in Granada (the Morisco problem persisted despite massive repression and deportations) it was imperative for Spain to recover control over the Mediterranean. The Holy League against Constantinople, solemnly proclaimed in St Peter's in 1571, led to that famous 'rosary victory' the Spanish needed so badly, Lepanto. Before the decisive encounter with the Turk beads were distributed to the combatants, who, harangued by Jesuits and friars, were ordered by Pius V to 'invoke the Blessed Trinity, and to salute the Virgin with the battle-cry: "Help of Christians, pray for us! Auxilium Christianorum, ora pro nobis" '.[4]

The conversion of the uprooted and floating Arab sub-proletariat (as the Muslim masses in Spain at that time have been described by modern historiography)[5] was another challenging mission for the Catholic King. A well-documented thesis has identified three great obstacles in the evangelization of Muslims: the concept of the Trinity, the figure of Christ, and the Church.[6] It is likely, in our view, that Mary served as a more natural vehicle for assimilation, for, unlike Christ, she is not a rival of the Prophet and the Koran accords her an honourable place.[7] If the colonized Moorish population rejected the Roman hierarchy, they were at least able to adopt its most cogent symbol, Nuestra Señora. There is no doubt that the most extravagant and 'extra-sacramental' forms of Marianism developed in Andalusia through the mystery of the Virgin's dolours. The cults of Nuestra Señora de Angustias, de Soledad and de Lágrimas may well be an expression of the torments suffered by Granada, a conquered and torn land. By the mid-sixteenth century the Franciscans were among the first to establish colourful confraternities and processions for Holy Week in meridional Spain – still a vibrant custom.

Andalusians (many falsely claiming the prerequisite *pureza de sangre*) crossed the Atlantic in droves. This fact, combined with the indigenous realities of America, helps to explain why the Andalusian cults of Mary (including the Inmaculada Concepción) took root so tenaciously in the New World, where she often intervened as Auxilium Christianorum. A famous apparition was that of Nuestra Señora de la Descención in Peru at the time of Pizarro.[8]

Highly stratified and unscriptural, the Church in America grew round the images of Our Lady. The hierarchical and semi-feudal system which Spain imposed on her colonial possessions required equally discriminatory ecclesiastical structures. Natives and mestizos were excluded from the priesthood at the first Council of Mexico (1555) and, a few years later, forbidden to read the scriptures. A lack of scriptural knowledge, however, was universal in the Hispanic world; the Inquisition's ban on lay reading of the Bible was not lifted until the end of the eighteenth century – only then did the first vernacular translation see the light of day (1790).

The numerous confraternities of Mary were organized according to caste. The most important Marian brotherhood in Lima – created in the mid-sixteenth century to worship an image of Our Lady of the Rosary brought over by the conquistadores – segregated members in three categories: Spanish, mestizo, and Indian.[9] Confraternities of the rosary were established early on in many cities, granted indulgences and run on the same principles. Some brotherhoods performed works of mercy. Indians belonging to a sodality of Our Lady in Lima were described as 'zealous in their care for the sick'.[10] Policies and customs were substantially the same in the Philippines, where a Jesuit supervised the foundation of the first female congregation in the islands, the Religious of the Virgin Mary.

As a 'civilizing' factor, the Marian cult was systematically encouraged. The Councils of Lima and Mexico in the 1580s (under strong Jesuit influence) prescribed a series of measures to foster filial love for the Great Mother.[11] Some of the new expressions of the cult, however, were seen by some as idolatry in disguise. Bernardino de Sahagun, the great Franciscan chronicler, opposed the syncretic cult of Guadalupe, inspired by the mother goddess Tonantzin of Tepeyac: 'It is clear that in their hearts the common people who go there on pilgrimages are moved only by their ancient religion.'[12] But the hierarchy was enthusiastic; in 1555, a few years after a devastating plague, the first basilica of Guadalupe was erected by the bishop who was soon to launch an inquiry into the miraculous image of the Immaculate of Tepeyac. By 1629 Guadalupe was acknowledged as 'principal patroness' of Mexico City against the frequent disaster of floods. Her cult, as well as that of St Thomas ('Quetzalcóatl', according to Mexican tradition the evangelist of America), flourished in the seventeenth century alongside the imperial cult of Our Lady of the Pillar and St James (Santiago the Apostle).[13] As Jacques Lafaye has shown in his erudite study, the legend of the apparition of the Virgin of Guadalupe was not publicized until 1648. It was consolidated in the next century under the leadership of local Jesuits as 'a creole response' to the myth of 'el Pilar'.[14] The dominant position of Guadalupe as Protectora Americana was firmly established after the epidemic of 1736–7, during which the images of both Our Lady of Remedios and Our Lady of Loreto proved ineffective.

Silver mines, like plagues and floods, also contributed to the development of Marian devotions. A striking case is that of Nuestra Señora de las Penas in Peru at the beginning of the seventeenth century. An Indian called up for the *mita* (forced labour) in Potosí ('the miner's purgatory')[15] was resolved to commit suicide, but Our Lady, wrapped in a blue mantle (the Immaculate), turned him from his course. 'Confused and repentant',[16] the seer went to confession and later became sacristan of the shrine built at the locus of the vision.

American 'mysticism' was no less subjugated to Mary. Saint Rosa de Santa María (d. 1617, canonized 1671), patroness of America and the Philippines, was an ascetic Dominican tertiary inspired by St Catherine of Sienna and deeply devoted to Our Lady of the Rosary in Lima. This 'unworthy slave of the Queen of the Angels' was wont to 'lose herself in divine colloquy'[17] before the famous image, which on Santa Rosa's death greeted the entry of her coffin with joyful rays of light.[18]

The other celebrated saint of the region is Mariana de Jesus, 'the Lily of Quito', who under Jesuit direction made a vow of chastity at the age of ten and, up to her premature death in 1645, subjected her body to the most terrible torments. An eremitical woman with a 'passion for vicarious suffering',[19] she was buried according to her wishes: beside the Compañía's altar to Our Lady of Loreto.

*　　　*　　　*

Spanish hegemony waned as heavy dependence on foreign manufactures, a precarious domestic industry and shrinking productive population fettered attempts to pursue an effective mercantilist policy. By the 1620s other powers had penetrated the Antilles and the Dutch were controlling Brazil. The decline in America's mineral output (1610–20) was followed by an inflationary phase lasting many years, by which time a new wave of disasters had hit Spain: the House of Bragança restored Portuguese independence (1640), Irish Catholic revolts failed (1641–9), the 'invincible' *tercios españoles* were defeated in Flanders (Recroi, 1643), rebellion shook the kingdom of Naples (1647) and finally, in 1648, came the 'iniquitous' Peace of Westphalia, as Innocent X called it.

Against this background of crumbling Spanish power exaltation of Mary, particularly under the title of Immaculate, knew no bounds. Spain's Golden Age, baroque and Jesuitical, gave free rein to the collective passion of Our Lady's chief prerogative. As lodestar of the Spanish and Portuguese crusades and empires, she had supplied a key component for early nationalism. *Limpieza de sangre*, 'purity of blood', and the mystery of the conception of Our Lady, *limpia* and *sin mancha*, 'pure and without stain', now became two great inextricable ideals in the Iberian ethos.

The Immaculist mass movement began with riots in Seville[20] in 1613, coinciding with the final years of the Morisco deportation (1609–14) instigated by the friars, who enlivened their arguments with evidence of miracles.[21]

It is scarcely an exaggeration to say that since 1617 the Catholic King had 'made the Immaculate Conception a matter of state policy'.[22] As the Inquisition began to move against Galileo (1616), Philip III sent the first 'Immaculist embassy' to Rome. The following year the Venerable Ursula Benincasa, foundress of the Theatine Sisters in Naples, received a vision of the Immaculate and the 'Blue Scapular' revelation. In September the Roman Inquisition imposed a ban on opinions contrary to the pious belief, a decree greeted euphorically in Andalusia, where the Real Junta de la Inmaculada Concepción had recently been established.

Spain then launched a theological crusade, headed by the monarch and the religious orders, for the dogmatization of the belief. The Hispanic world was flooded with campaign literature ranging from 'juridical reports' to 'allegorical dramas representing the triumph of Mary over the serpent'.[23] Diego Granado, the Jesuit chronicler of the feasts of the Immaculate, published a characteristic work asserting the classic argument: Mary's parents never experienced sexual pleasure and Joachim's semen was purified by God.[24]

Thousands of confraternities and 'Slaves of the Virgin' were mobilized.[25] In 1618 orders, cities, guilds and universities took the *votum sanguinarium*, which was followed by theatrical displays. Lope de Vega wrote *La Limpieza no manchada* ('Purity Untainted') for Salamanca (where the vow to defend the Immaculate Conception became a prerequisite for the doctoral degree). Feasts went on for days with allegorical processions and bull-fighting[26] (the splendid celebrations on Ignatius' canonization in 1622 – with literary contests and fireworks – lasted eight days).

Philip IV inaugurated his reign (1621) with the vows of his ministers, two years later Vitelleschi, the Jesuit general, ordered the Society to work for the Immaculate Conception declaration.[27] But the pontificate of Urban VIII (1623–44), an anti-Spanish and nepotic pope fond of magic, brought the Immaculist cause to a halt.

Around 1637, at a time when many in the Compañía had written or were writing erudite biographies of Our Lady[28] with exact chronologies and compilations of her miracles, the Franciscan Conceptionist Mary of Agreda (d. 1665) began her life of the Virgin Mary, later known as *The Mystical City of God*. Through her own visions and revelations (on occasions disrupted by Beelzebub) the abbess penetrated all mysteries. She learned of Joachim's imperviousness to pleasure, of Our Lady's journey to Spain in *carne mortal*, and of her authority in heaven as co-Judge. The 'Mistress of the Church' even deigned to defend her low profile in the Gospels: 'I myself commanded the Evangelists that they should say no more of my eminence and merits than was absolutely necessary for the Church at the time of its foundation. . . .'[29]

In May 1643 the Catholic King proclaimed Our Lady of Victories Patroness of the Royal Arms, giving orders for her feasts to be celebrated throughout his dominions. The Spanish army, however, suffered defeat in Flanders later that year – during which a prolix correspondence began between the monarch and the 'almost rustic'[30] Mary of Agreda. In November Philip avidly digested the first part of her revelations. The undesirable reign of Urban VIII ended shortly afterwards and the king could turn again towards Rome and the Immaculate Conception enterprise.

Portugal, in serious difficulties in the far east on the fall of Malacca (1641), was also mobilized in that fateful decade, when plague and poverty struck the *Compañía* in the peninsula. The Duke of Bragança, now King John IV, instituted a sodality of Our Lady at the court (1643) and in the following year cities, towns and villages took the Immaculate Conception as their patron. In 1646 the Cortes pronounced her patroness of the kingdom and overseas possessions; and the University of Coimbra, in plenary session, unanimously established the vow to defend her prerogatives.[31] Yet nothing could prevent the triumph of Protestantism: in 1654 it was Cromwell who dictated trade conditions for the impoverished Lusitanian land.

In 1656 (four years before Mary of Agreda completed the second version of her book)[32] Philip IV dispatched the great Immaculist embassy, graciously received by Alexander VII (1655–67), an enemy of France. Finally, in 1661, while the Jesuits of Clermont were defending papal infallibility, the bull *Sollicitudo* avouched that Mary was untouched by sin. Any opinion to the contrary was heresy. There was rejoicing in the thousands of Spanish monasteries and convents[33] and the image of the Immaculate processed triumphally throughout Iberia.

Not content with this doctrinal advance, Catholic King and Real Junta de la Inmaculada Concepción embarked on a fresh religious-diplomatic campaign – to rescue Mary of Agreda. The writings of the visionary – whose canonization process had opened under Clement X (1670–76) – were condemned by the Roman Inquisition in 1681 and on translation into French (1695) banned by the Sorbonne as well. Not unconnected with the struggle for Agreda's honour was the cult of Nuestra Señora del Pilar, whose feast was now fixed on 12 October, the date of the discovery of America.[34] In 1680 the Cortes of Aragon petitioned Rome for an appropriate office celebrating the Virgin's visitation to Saragossa (described in detail by Agreda) and the following year Carlos II put Francisco de Herrera the Younger to work on an ambitious project around the sacred pillar. The office was not granted until 1723, by which time *The Mystical City* had been removed from the Index. That same year the Carmelite Aranaz published *The Sceptre of the Orthodox Faith, Most Holy Mary in Her Angelic and Apostolic Temple of the Pillar*, dedicated to Queen Isabel Farnesio. In this extensive work the national myth was crystallized: 'In order to transfer the Kingdom of the Divine Faith from her ungrateful Hebrew People, the Exalted Lady chose happy Spain. . . .'[35] The primate excommunicated all who questioned this tradition.[36]

But as the weakened and bankrupt Spanish crown sought recognition for Marian cults and revelations in the kingdom, the City of London – motivated by both anti-popery and an expansionist, anti-Spanish policy[37] – was pouring funds into scientific research and education.

6

THE GRAND SIÈCLE

The Blessed Heart of the Queen of Heaven displays a perfect imitation of the plenitude and self-sufficiency of God.[1]

St Jean Eudes

Sacerdotal celibacy – never an easy matter[2] – and monastic revival were fundamental for mystical renewal and the restoration of ecclesiastical influence. By the beginning of the seventeenth century the weak French crown had need of a militant and prestigious Church to accomplish 'unification' – that is, the subjugation of the Fronde and the Huguenots. All the great French reformers and founders of the century, collaborating closely with the monarchy, embarked on the 'purification' of the clergy through Mary. The Oratorian general, Charles de Condren, spoke of an alliance between the Virgin and the priesthood 'in producing the Body of Christ'.[3]

The Huguenots – who formally declared the pope to be Antichrist – were eventually crushed in their strongholds of La Rochelle (1628) and in southern France (1629). Louis XIII then laid the foundation stone of Notre-Dame des Victoires in thanksgiving for the triumph over heresy and, a few years later, in 1638, in the midst of starvation and popular revolts, consecrated his kingdom to the Virgin.[4] According to the chronicles, this royal vow was inspired by the pious circle surrounding the Most Christian King: Cardinal Richelieu, the Jesuit Caussin, the Visitation nun Louise de la Fayette, and the Capuchin Joseph du Tremblay, the *éminence grise* who claimed to receive supernatural instructions via the nuns of Our Lady of Calvary, a congregation reformed by him in 1617.[5]

During the first decades of the century Catholic France displayed a remarkable missionary zeal. The foundation of the Order of the Visitation of Holy Mary (1610) was followed the next year by the French Oratory of Jesus and Mary, set up by Pierre de Bérulle (d. 1629), apostle of the Incarnate Word (and a diplomat). Cardinal Bérulle's doctrine on the interior life of the Virgin and the power she exercises over Jesus was seminal. With the crusade against Calvinism and the disruption and horrors of the Thirty Years War (1618–48), more divisions emerged. The great clerical reformer and sodalist St Vincent de Paul (d. 1660) founded the Congregation of the Mission or Lazarists (1625) and the Sisters of Charity (1633). Jean-Jacques Olier (d. 1657), for whom Mary was Queen of the Clergy 'reigning on the throne of God',[6] opened the Seminary of St Sulpice (1642). Olier – who had learned about consecration to the Virgin from the Dominican visionary Mother Agnes of Jesus[7] – asserted that Jesus is 'but one heart, one soul, one life with Mary'.[8] The cardio-Marian doctrine of total amalgamation of the two Hearts was evolved by St Jean Eudes (d. 1680), father, doctor and apostle of the Heart of Mary. Inspired by 'divine communications'[9] vouchsafed to one Marie des Vallées (previously a victim of demoniacal possession for 36 years),[10] Père Eudes composed the Office of the Holy Heart of Mary (1641). Around the same time he formed the Society of Our Lady of Charity and, shortly afterwards, the Congregation of Jesus and Mary, to promote devotion to the Heart of Our Lady, whose first feast was authorized in Autun cathedral in 1648.

A sodalist from his youth and priest of the Oratory until 1643, Eudes was to obtain a string of indulgences for the numerous confraternities he set up to honour Mary's heart. He distinguishes three dimensions in this object on which all his missions and scholastic endeavours were based: (a) the 'heart of flesh enclosed in her virginal breast'; (b) her spiritual heart 'made God-like'; (c) one which is 'divine and is truly God Himself, for it is none other than the love of God'.[11] At the same time Mary's heart is 'the heart of the Church Militant, suffering and triumphant';[12] and he also compares it to the throne of Solomon, temple of Jerusalem and fiery furnace of Babylon. Like other zealots of the times, Eudes signed a mystical marriage contract with Mary, a document which accompanied him to the grave.[13]

No cult is more revealing of the medieval spirit of the Counter-Reformation than that of the heart.[14] It had long been the custom to extract the hearts of popes, kings and saints on death and enshrine them – a practice echoed strikingly in the devotion to the hearts of flesh of Christ and Mary developed within the Jesuit school. Henry IV, shortly before his assassination (1610), expressed the wish for his heart to be entombed in the Jesuit college of La Flèche. By mid-century the hearts of the Bavarian princes were preserved in the lady chapel at Altötting, the ancient shrine by now under Jesuit administration. Another interesting case is that of the dethroned James II of England (d. 1701), also heavily under Jesuit influence, who left orders for his heart to be placed in the Visitation convent of Chaillot in the incorruptible company of the founders' hearts. The heart of St Francis de Sales oozed with a 'clear oil'[15] for years and the organ of his partner, St Jane de Chantal (d. 1641), served as a barometer during Church crises, sometimes swelling as though 'about to burst into groans'.[16] The heart of St Vincent de Paul – of which more later – remains incorrupt and is venerated in Paris today.

Alongside the foundations mentioned (still in existence) secret brotherhoods connected with the Society of Jesus and consecrated to Mary were operating. At a time when heretics were thought to possess esoteric knowledge and assemble in mysterious networks,[17] and witches, the worshippers of Satan, to organize themselves in mafias, the creation of clandestine groups under the seal of the exterminator of the serpent was a logical step.

The most remarkable of these underground circles was the so-called 'AA', which promoted mutual aid, fraternal communion and 'apostolic' (i.e. papal) zeal.[18] Its field of action ranged from missions among the peasantry to colonial expansion. 'The soul of the AA' was secrecy[19] and its distinctive practice Marian devotion. Physical mortification was stressed through mutual application of 'the discipline' or scourging. The slavery consecration was probably an integral part of the initiatory rites, as suggested by the book of a distinguished cleric and confrère, Henri-Marie Boudon: *Le Saint Esclavage à l'Admirable Mère de Dieu* (1668).

Recruited exclusively from the Sodality of Our Lady,[20] the AA sprang up in French Jesuit colleges by the third or fourth decade of the century,[21] carrying out a keen apostolate in that country ravaged by wars. Forming a network with other secret organizations, the AA groups exercised a formidable influence. The Paris AA (unmasked by Jansenists in a pamphlet of the 1650s) founded the Séminaire des Missions Étrangères (1664) with funds provided by the Compagnie du Saint Sacrement, another powerful and absolutely secret[22] confraternity linked to the Jesuits, the Oratory, St Sulpice and the monarchy.[23] As a propagator of the Immaculate Conception, it is highly likely the AA also championed papal infallibility.[24] A few of these cabals, mostly under Jesuit direction, survived the dissolution of the Society and the French Revolution.

JANSENISM AND ITS DIVINE ANTIDOTE

The political-ideological evolution of Jansenism – a movement inspired by the *Augustinus* of Cornelius Jansenius, Bishop of Ypres (d. 1638) – and its confrontation with the Society of Jesus profoundly influenced French politics from the mid-seventeenth century up to the Revolution, helping to determine the course of papal power and the cult of Mary. The theological subtleties of the controversy are beyond the scope of this book; suffice it to say that the war between Augustinians and Pelagians – between pessimistic rigorism and optimistic laxism – represented a second reformation and counter-reformation. Once again, the value of external devotions, indulgences and the power of intercessors were challenged; the need for scriptural knowledge also occupied a central place in the dispute. The reformers, accused of crypto-Calvinism and *raison géométrique*,[25] were to contend against French absolutism and a declining papacy still striving for supremacy.

Long before Jansenius began his voluminous work (published posthumously in 1640 and condemned two years later by Urban VIII), the Flemish theologian was a sworn enemy of the Society. In the 1620s he travelled twice to Spain to campaign for the curbing of Jesuit academic privileges. Although he failed in this task, his views, diffused by his collaborator, the Abbé de St Cyran (d. 1643), found favour in cultured circles in France.

In 1656 – after fresh papal anathemas – Pascal published anonymously the *Provincial Letters*, an out-and-out indictment of the moral-devotional system advocated by the Jesuits.[26] The Cartesian and Jansenist Antoine Arnauld (d. 1694) was expelled from the Sorbonne that year and the *Provinciales* were condemned and burned. Nevertheless, they made a great impact, and many rumours about Jansenism were now circulating. A tract published in London (1667) claimed that Jansenists considered indulgences, images and the worship of the Virgin and the saints 'human inventions' and thought bishops to be no lower than popes.[27]

The abbey of Port-Royal, stronghold of Jansenism, was to explore a mysticism somewhat removed from Roman orthodoxy. Mère Agnes Arnauld's reflections on the incomprehensibility of God have been called abstract, obscure and revealing of 'an indecisive theology inimical to the sweetness and familiarity of the relationship of the soul to God'.[28]

Also set apart from what Aldous Huxley called 'emotional Christianity'[29] was quietism, a movement led by Miguel Molinos, a Spanish priest condemned to life imprisonment by the Roman Inquisition in 1687. Molinos sought to free the mind from 'the operations of the imagination';[30] he taught 'the interior way', a 'mystical silence' leading to 'the perfect contemplation' – a state not subject to illusions and ecstasies. The nuns under his influence were accused of scorning indulgences, saints and the rosary;[31] an anonymous tract charged the quietists with conspiring against the religious orders themselves.

The Society of Jesus and its affiliates reacted strongly against both Jansenism and quietism by means of 'activism' and devotion to the Sacred Heart, 'the divine antidote prepared by God for the virus of the cunningly devised heresy.'[32] Such practices as the Rosary of the Heart[33] embellished the Sacred Heart cult, which later became emblematic of royal and temporalist forces. Enemies of the Society were identified as subversives early on. In France and Italy Jansenists and quietists found support among some Oratorians who, according to a confidential report of the Jesuit confessor of Louis XIV, were attracted to a republic and, consequently, 'bad subjects of kings'.[34] Perhaps no one was more representative of Oratorian rationalism than Malebranche (d. 1715), a Cartesian convinced that it was 'an act of piety to reduce the number of miracles'.[35]

As new devotions and wonders multiplied,[36] Jansenist critique continued to develop. *Moral Reflections on the New Testament* by the Oratorian Pasquier Quesnel (d. 1719), which appeared in Paris in 1671, was an assault on the Roman policy of promoting repentance by 'fear of punishment'[37] and the ban on lay study of the scriptures, especially by women.[38] Proposition 84 states defiantly: 'To withdraw the New Testament from the hands of Christians or to keep it closed to them and prevent them understanding it is to close the mouth of Christ to them.'[39] In November 1673, shortly after Louis XIV's invasion of Utrecht (which fired a Jesuit revival), the famous *Monita Salutaria BVM ad cultores suos indiscretos* was published with episcopal approval in Ghent. Denouncing a 'fantastick and foolish devotion'[40] towards Our Lady, the tract urges a return to the spirit of Christ, which 'should be the same with that of the Gospels'.[41] It warns against slavery to Mary and devotion to her holy Heart; and upbraids those who put their trust in images, blindly accepting 'everything that is told them of the revelations, apparitions and prerogatives of the Virgin'.[42] This 'cold and rigid opusculum'[43] was condemned by Rome as Jesuits staged processions in reparation.

At the Visitation convent of Paray-le-Monial in December 1673 – just a month after the publication of *Wholesome Advices* – Sister Marguerite Marie Alacoque (for whom no division existed between the Sacred Heart of Jesus and the Heart of Mary) experienced her first vision of Christ. Bleeding and covered in wounds,[44] his tone was bitter: 'They persecute me in secret. If they do not amend I will chastise them severely.'[45] The nun was visited the following year on several occasions, the Virgin promising protection[46] to 'her chosen daughter'.[47] On the feast of the Visitation of Our Lady in July (a month after Widenfelt's pamphlet was put on the Index) Marguerite Marie saw 'His five wounds shining like so many suns' and 'His adorable breast, which was like a furnace'.[48] The Second Person of the Trinity announced, 'I have a burning thirst to be honoured by men in the Blessed Sacrament'.[49] In 1675 the so-called Great Apparition took place, during which Christ complained of sacrileges and coldness, and demanded acts of reparation before the Eucharist and a feast day 'in honour of my Heart'.[50]

Sometime between late 1674 and early 1675 Claude de la Colombière,SJ, a director of sodalities, arrived at Paray to take charge of the spiritual guidance of the visionary, who was instructed to write down an account of the events. Soon afterwards, in the autumn of 1676, Fr Colombière was transferred to London as chaplain to Mary of Modena, Duchess of York and future Queen of England. Princess Mary, who remained intimately attached to the Society and the Visitation Order all her life,[51] was the first to hear of the Sacred Heart revelations. Fr Colombière's enthusiastic dissemination of the messages was interrupted by the Titus Oates 'Popish Plot' (September 1678) during which he was thrown into prison; and by early 1679 the 'destroyer of heresy', as Alacoque called her director, returned exhausted to Paray, where he was soon to die.

This setback did not impede the progress of the devotion during the 1680s and 90s, a period of wars and French expansion. In addition to her report on the apparitions, the Visitandine embarked on a letter-writing campaign which lasted until her death (1690), explaining the promises of the Sacred Heart (peace in families, comfort in afflictions, refuge in life and death) and demands: 'He assured me that He took a singular pleasure in being honoured under the figure of His Heart of flesh, the image of which He wished to be exposed in public.'[52] She introduced a scapular ('He wished me to wear this image òn my own heart')[53] and composed litanies for the Hearts of Jesus and Mary. The interdependence of the two hearts was firmly established.[54]

Opposition to the cult – superstitious and sensual in the 'gloomy' Jansenist view – failed. Quesnel was expelled from the Oratory and went into exile in 1685, the year Molinos was arrested[55] and the Edict of Nantes revoked (a measure welcomed by James II of England). It was also the year in which Paray-le-Monial first paid public homage to the Sacred Heart and the visionary declared that a new era had opened: that of the Sacred Heart mediation.[56]

In July 1688 – a few months before the flight of King James and Queen Mary into the arms of Louis XIV – the saint received a fresh vision: the Heart of Jesus now appeared with the founder of the Visitation Order, St Francis de Sales, as well as with the late Colombière and the Virgin, who appointed the Society of Jesus and the Visitandines as 'guardians' of the Sacred Heart cult, commanding them to 'enrich the world with it'.[57] In 1689, year of the Grand Protestant Alliance led by William of Orange, Sister Alacoque transmitted via the Visitation convent at Chaillot (under the patronage of Mary of Modena) her last messages, this time dictated by Christ to Louis XIV: the King should consecrate himself to the Sacred Heart, render it public homage, build a chapel in its honour and incorporate the symbol into the royal coat of arms.[58] As far as we know, the Sun King did not follow any of this advice – and in 1692 the French navy was destroyed and the invasion of Ireland failed once more.

When the Peace of Ryswick (disadvantageous to France) came in 1697, Mary of Modena presented, without success, the first official petition for the establishment of the Sacred Heart feast. The Jesuit general T. González (1687–1705), who, together with Innocent XI (1676–89), was sympathetic to Jansenist criticism of probabilism, had little enthusiasm for Paray-le-Monial and its friends.[59] In his plans for reform, however, González was isolated [60] and the political effervescence following England's Glorious Revolution (1688) and Louis XIV's disastrous campaigns made the Society even less open to self-criticism and change.

By the turn of the century revolutionary ideologies were crystallizing in the Anglo-Dutch sphere, where Huguenots were to play a prominent and vengeful part within Freemasonry. At the Hague, English radicals and French refugees (writers, publishers, artists) formed a significant pantheistic and Masonic society, the Knights of Jubilation.[61] Anti-monarchist and anti-absolutist, they stood in direct opposition to Catholic theocracy. Republican circles of intellectuals were also emerging in France; Jansenism, increasingly drawn to Presbyterianism, was growing more hostile to royal despotism day by day.

To counter these developments, the Jesuits launched the anti-philosophic *Journal de Trévoux* in 1701 with funding from a son of Louis XIV. Two years later Quesnel was arrested in Brussels. In the meantime Clement XI (1700–21), who ignored González's proposals for a compromise between rigorism and laxism, began a merciless campaign against Jansenism. In 1708 he commanded the universal celebration of the Immaculate Conception and shortly afterwards, as a new wave of famine devastated France, the nuns of Port-Royal were forcibly dispersed. The abbey was obliterated and the bones buried there exhumed. Finally, on 8 September, the day of Our Lady's nativity, 1713, Rome issued the bull *Unigenitus* anathematizing *Moral Reflections* (republished in 1699 with the approval of Cardinal de Noailles of Paris).

The bull, which met with great resistance, effectively gave a platform to the forces struggling against 'Jesuitism'. Far removed from deistic French philosophy, eighteenth-century Jansenism derived strength from the Catholic Enlightenment, which was epitomized by Ludovico Antonio Muratori (d. 1750), the founder of modern Italian historiography. A few months after *Unigenitus*, Fr Muratori published in Paris *The Science of Rational Devotion*,[62] in which he laments the trust placed in 'fictitious legends' about Our Lady contradicted by 'the certain and infallible truth of the Holy Scriptures'.[63] In his view, 'indiscreet modes of devotion' towards Mary are deleterious to true spirituality: 'the incommunicable majesty and attributes of God are horribly violated'.[64]

The following year, 1715, saw the death of Louis XIV – none other than Antichrist and the Whore of Babylon in Newton's Anglican eyes.[65] This event signalled the gradual ascendancy of Jansenism through Gallicanism and the Parlements.

The official existence of the cardio-Marian devotions would become precarious and not even the Sacred Heart campaign launched around 1725 by Philip V and the now Bourbon court of Madrid would obtain a definitive pronouncement from the Holy See.[66]

MONTFORTIAN SLAVERY AND THE SECOND COMING

The most prominent Marian apostle in France by the turn of the century was St Louis-Marie Grignion de Montfort (1673–1716). A Breton called to the priesthood by a talking image of Our Lady,[67] and formed by the Society of Jesus and at St Sulpice, Louis-Marie was an ardent sodalist, preacher and champion of 'popular spirituality'. At a time when heretical and clandestine literature was mushrooming, Montfort made pyres of books topped by an effigy of the devil. Rejected by Jansenist prelates in various parts, he somehow managed to 'evangelize' a few places, including La Vendée. He erected numerous rosary confraternities and founded two congregations: the Daughters of Wisdom (1702), a teaching and nursing order, and the Company of Mary (1705), later known as the Montfort Fathers. In 1706 Pope Clement granted him the title of 'missionary apostolic'.

Central to his apostolate was the 'holy slavery of love', expounded in *The Secret of the Rosary* and *The Secret of Mary*. Montfort taught that consecration[68] or surrender to Mary was the key to heaven; he called the Ave Maria 'the melody of the predestinate'[69] as love of Mary was a sign of predestination.[70] He wore instruments of torture 'as the sign of loving bondage'[71] and, in his quest for self-abnegation, swopped underclothes with beggars.[72]

Montfort's view of Mary and the Trinity, which derives from the Bérullian school, is devastatingly simple: they are not only united but practically equal. 'God has graciously deigned to give her such high authority that she appears to enjoy the same power as God'.[73] The divinity's access to man, however, depends on Mary's agency, even in the Eucharist. What is more, the Blessed Virgin can 'produce another Divine Person' – unlike the Holy Ghost, who 'remains sterile'.[74]

It is Mary, 'the exterminator of the enemies of God',[75] who will 'produce the great events which will mark the ending of time'.[76] In the meantime, 'we must perform our actions in Mary' and 'for Mary'.[77]

Rediscovered in the nineteenth century,[78] the figure of Montfort attained a supreme place in the apocalyptic Marianism that followed World War II. Pius XII raised him to the altars in 1947, considering his doctrine equal to that of the Doctors of the Church;[79] and John Paul II has said reading *The True Devotion* was a 'turning point' in his life.[80]

7

MARIAN CRISIS AND JESUIT COLLAPSE

[the deist] laughs at Loretto and Mecca, but he helps the poor
and he defends the oppressed.[1]

Voltaire

We are friends to all the world except to the Jesuits, whom not
one master of a lodge would receive in our order.[2]

Jean Rousset de Missy (d. 1762)
(leading figure in Dutch Freemasonry)

By the second half of the seventeenth century the papacy no
longer enjoyed a commanding position in international affairs and
the backwardness of Iberia and the Mediterranean sphere under
Spanish influence had become painfully apparent. The fall of the last
English Catholic king and the accession of William of Orange (1688)
consolidated Protestantism, Freemasonry and what has been called
the Newtonian Enlightenment.[3] The English financial revolution
also began in this period. In 1705 Britain captured Gibraltar and
by 1713 was penetrating the market of the Spanish empire. British
supremacy seemed unstoppable.

The new science and political thinking which unfolded throughout the seventeenth and eighteenth centuries created an almost
permanent crisis and eventual rupture of the theocratic order,
accomplished by the dissolution of the Society of Jesus (1773) and
the French Revolution (1789).

The anticelibatarian movement, springing from the newborn
naturalism, and the revival of the scriptures undermined theocracy
and the cult of the Virgin. A tendency to demystify Mary and
rebuff papal claims – those two major features of eighteenth-century
Jansenism and Catholic Enlightenment – bear out our contention:
devotionalism and politics are inseparable.

Some strategic Marian shrines were called into question by

the Catholic Enlightenment, prompting the Jesuit general, F. Retz (1730–50) to demand the Bollandists' absolute silence on the miraculous translation of the Santa Casa of Loreto, in the custody of the Jesuits. Apparitions officially recognized or sanctioned by tradition ground to a halt in the 1700s. One exception was the 1733 Sacred Heart revelation to the Venerable Bernardo de Hoyos,[4] which was to play so prominent a part in modern National Catholicism. This visionary, and other eighteenth-century Spanish missionaries of the Sacred Heart (for example the Jesuits P.A. Calatayud and Juan de Loyola) worked 'indefatigably to propagate devotion to the Heart of Mary uniting it to that of the Heart of Jesus'.[5] This binary cult suffered a serious blow, however, in the expulsion of the Society from Spanish dominions (1767).

As witchcraft expired, its 'antidotes' (scapulars, Agnus Dei, devotion to Mary) were devalued. Latin lost its magic and importance, and the intellectual prestige of scholastics and demonologists – among whom the Jesuits were outstanding – suffered irreparably. D'Alembert was surely not alone in labelling Jesuit thinking 'religious madness with a method'.[6]

Yet resistance to post-Aristotelian knowledge persisted in some quarters, notably in Spain, where the vow to defend the Immaculate Conception was embraced by the Royal Academy of History (founded in 1735).[7] Jesuit doctrine was to survive the blows of the Enlightenment in the guise of 'Liguorianism', the teachings of St Alphonsus de' Liguori (1696–1787), the greatest eighteenth-century Mariologist and unsurpassed apologist of papal infallibility.[8] It is significant that this 'true knight of Mary',[9] a thoroughly medieval personality who covered his body with cilices[10] and lived tormented by the fear of hell,[11] hailed from the pauperized kingdom of Naples, where – as in some areas of the Spanish empire – serfdom was still operating in the eighteenth century.[12]

A patrician and former barrister, Liguori became the great defender of Jesuits and of probabilism through yet another scholastic doctrine, equiprobabilism.[13] The Redemptorist Order he founded (not without visionary assistance)[14] became on occasions instrumental in the maintenance or restoration of Rome's influence, and his prolific pen was providential. The first major work of this Doctor Ecclesiae was the most complete vindication of the cult, *The Glories of Mary* (1750). In this she is not only reinstated as Queen of Heaven but recognized as 'also Queen of hell and all evil spirits'.[15] It was

Mary who, shortly before the Assumption, conferred supremacy on Peter. The apostles 'were miraculously assembled in Mary's room', when 'she called St Peter to her, and as the head of the Church and Vicar of her Son, recommended to him in a particular manner the propagation of the faith, promising him . . . her special protection in heaven'.[16] Having reasserted both Mary's divine status and Peter's sacredness, St Alphonsus turns to practical advice on the value of indulgences in exchange for little devotions,[17] the use of Marian scapulars[18] and the importance of belonging to sodalities: 'O, with what terrible chastisements has Our Lord punished those who have abandoned the confraternity of Our Blessed Lady.'[19] But 'the brothers who persevere have both their temporal and spiritual wants provided for by Mary.'[20]

Jansenist sources indicate that St Alphonsus was also a great propagator of *Alacoquisme*. Together with the Venerable Maria Celeste Crostarosa he founded the Redemptoristines, whose habit bore the Sacred Heart emblem.[21] The Liguorian missions, however, were centred on ancient Neapolitan images of Mary, which had been known to sparkle as the founder levitated in ecstasy.[22] On one occasion, in the disorderly Apulian town of Foggia, the effects of this 'divine intervention' were striking, as recorded by his biographer: 'Once more did the Immaculate Virgin crush the serpent under her heel, women of evil life were seen publicly confessing their sins. . . .'[23]

In that year, 1745, the Redemptorists took over a property given on condition that they adopt an abandoned fifteenth-century image in Iliceto, Santa Maria della Consolazione.[24] The young community of missionaries based on this resurrected shrine concentrated their efforts on the peasants of Apulia.

Despite the anticlericalism of the government, which did not recognize the Order in Liguori's lifetime, the Redemptorists were allowed to carry out their prodigious apostolate and even given a modicum of help. Perhaps this was because by this time in Naples, as Braudel observes, 'social disobedience was growing to near epidemic proportions'.[25]

*　　　*　　　*

As Jansenism mustered the Appellants in defiance of *Unigenitus* and consecrated its own Bishop of Utrecht in 1723 (the cause of yet another schism), Freemasonry was introduced into France and other countries.[26] Despite imprecations and penal threats, particularly from the Inquisition in Spain and Portugal, the Craft, entangled with Jansenism and the Enlightenment, advanced steadily.[27] The Marian associations of the Jesuits and their affiliates were challenged as never before.

In 1732 *Nouvelles Ecclésiastiques* (the Jansenist weekly founded in 1728) unmasked and mocked the AA of Orleans. A Knight of Jubilation, the philosopher Charles Levier, composed the satire *Histoire de l'Admirable Don Inigo de Guipuscoa, Chevalier de la Vierge* (the Hague, 1736).[28] Meanwhile the pupils of the Jesuits were staging parodies of Masonic initiation ceremonies.

The secret societies, which harboured many clerics,[29] stimulated the taste for reparation. St Leonard of Port Maurice, leading sodalist and one of the most remarkable missionaries of the century, through whom baroque religiosity was energetically revived, told Benedict XIV in 1751 of his desire for self-immolation – 'to extirpate this evil weed which has spread all over Italy'.[30] St Leonard was alluding to the Liberi Muratori, a Masonic sect erroneously identified with the historian, who had published in 1748 a new critical book touching on Marian devotionalism.[31] Labouring under this misapprehension, a Spanish friar published a tirade punningly entitled *Muro invencible mariano contra los tiros de un murador disfrazado*.[32]

In *The Glories of Mary* (published in reply to Muratori) St Alphonsus exhorts the reader to join Our Lady's confraternities, in which 'many weapons of defence against hell' are obtained. 'It would be of the greatest advantage to introduce in honour of the Divine Mother herself, the secret congregation, composed of the more fervent brethren'.[33] And he goes on to describe the traditional regime of the secret sodality.

But Jansenism and the Enlightenment, in full swing by mid-century, had driven the Jesuit establishment and its Marian networks into a corner. Liguori's *Dissertation on the Prohibition and Destruction of Bad Books* (1759) was of no avail. There was already an almost universal agreement that the moral-devotional system upheld by the Society fomented corruption and superstition. The Jesuits' grip on education was believed to be causing the stagnation of the arts and science, and their loyalty to the papacy weakening the crown. The Spain of Carlos III (1759–88), striving for modernization, declared the Jesuit presence an impediment to 'the public happiness'.[34]

In Portugal persecution of Jesuits reached its climax early with their expulsion as traitors in 1759 by the Marquis of Pombal (initiated as a Mason in 1744). In 1761 – as Seville began three years of frenetic celebrations of the official patronage of the Immaculate Conception over Spain and the Indies declared by the bull *Quantum Ornamenti* – the renowned Portuguese missionary Fr Malagrida was publicly strangled and burned on charges of heresy brought by Pombal's brother, the lay Inquisitor-General.[35]

'The revenge of Port-Royal' came at the same time. The Parlement of Paris suppressed the sodalities in Jesuit colleges (1760),[36] a measure extended to the dioceses where Jansenism was strong.[37] In 1762 an official report justified the removal of all magistrates who belonged to the Sodality of Our Lady, now seen as a menace to royal interests. After Louis XV's ordinance had sealed the fate of the Jesuits in France (1764), the pope issued a bull supporting the Order as well as a decree which finally established the Sacred Heart feast requested by Poland and Bavaria. With the approval of general Ricci (1758–73), the Society henceforth regarded the Sacred Heart as their badge and banner.

The 1765 decree on the Sacred Heart was followed by *Christianae Reipublicae*, an acrimonious encyclical in response to Febronius' assault on papal power.[38] 'Accursed men', fulminates Clement XIII, 'from all sides vomit the poison of serpents from their hearts for the ruin of the Christian people by the contagious plague of books.' Particular targets of papal bile are the 'presumptuous theologians' who dare to examine 'the hidden mysteries of faith' and 'ridicule the faith of simple people'.[39] The letter ends by reminding the bishops of their duty to destroy bad books. This outburst was soon reinforced by another Liguorian dissertation against Febronius and on the need for an infallible head.[40] The international campaign against the Society and ultramontanism, however, continued relentlessly. In 1767 the Jesuits were evicted and their property confiscated in Spain and her dominions as well as in Naples, Parma and even Malta. Ten years later, a papacy neither feared nor respected was forced to disband its greatest division and imprison the general.

After the suppression (July 1773) the Jesuits were also expelled from the Austrian lands, but found refuge in Orthodox Russia and Protestant Prussia.

The Redemptorists in the meantime – threatened by anticlericals in Naples who accused them of excessive wealth and of being Jesuits in disguise – established a foothold in the Papal States in 1777. In Frosimone they adopted Our Lady of Graces, a miraculous image, and in Benevento took over a Jesuit school, also assuming the devotional functions of the Society.[41]

The pontificate of Pius VI (1775–99) opened with thunder against 'men maddened by a monstrous desire of innovation'. Without even mentioning Christ, the pope invoked 'the merits of the Most Holy Mary, Mother of God, Our Special Patroness', as well as 'the protection and defence of St Peter the Apostle'.[42] Nowhere in Catholic Europe was this innovatory mood more articulate than in the Austrian Empire. Here Jansenism blended with Febronianism and enlightened depotism in the formula known as Josephinism. The transformation advocated by Emperor Joseph II and his brother Leopold, Grand Duke of Tuscany, was possibly the most comprehensive programme to challenge Marian theocracy since the Reformation.

The strong movement against scholasticism went hand in hand with an attempt to improve the education of the clergy. A new curriculum with an emphasis on the study of history and the scriptures was introduced at Vienna and other centres. At Pavia University, within the Austrian ambit, Jansenist thought flourished under the leadership of Pietro Tamburini.

Jesuit devotionalism was no less under attack. The emperor suppressed the cult of the Sacred Heart, discouraged relics like the robe of Our Lady in Aachen cathedral, and sought to control pilgrimages[43] and end the sale of indulgences. A large number of convents of contemplatives were closed down during Joseph's reign and many other ecclesiastical interests were damaged. Pius VI's journey to Vienna in 1782 failed to mollify the imperial policies. The following year brotherhoods were abolished and, to the curia's horror, sacerdotal marriage was officially commended on the grounds that compulsory clerical celibacy was unscriptural.[44]

The see of Pistoia and Prato in Tuscany, long under Jansenist sway, was filled in 1780 by the Florentine Scipione de Ricci (d. 1809), a reformer destined to preside over that most radical synod, held in the city in September 1786. A disciple of Quesnel and of Muratori, whose books he diligently diffused, Ricci fought the Sacred Heart cult (*cardiolatria*) and the veneration of images, particularly that of the Madonna dell'Umiltà. He taught that 'it is not rosaries, not novenas, not enrolments in confraternities, that make us holy but the practice of Christian virtues'.[45] In his conflict with the orders and brotherhoods Ricci received ducal support. As Ricci's pastoral on the need for religious instruction and knowledge of the scriptures circulated to his brother bishops in the empire, the Duke abolished festivals and confraternities on the grounds that they fomented idleness and political agitation.[46] Finally, Leopold convoked the synod of Pistoia, whose objective was, in Ricci's words, 'to combat in detail that diabolical and anti-Christian invention – the ancient machine of papal monarchy'.[47]

With relentless coherence the synod assailed papal infallibility, scholasticism, indulgences and the divisions: all orders should be dissolved and reorganized according to Benedictine rule and the spirit of Port-Royal. The role of the laity and episcopal authority were upheld, with the parish and scriptures as the centre of religious life. The legends still printed in missals and breviaries, and external devotions attached to images, were condemned:

1 Let there be removed from the churches all images that either present false dogmas, as those of the Human Heart of Jesus, or give an occasion of error to the uneducated. . . .
2 Let there be removed alike those images in which it would seem that the people have special faith. . . .
3 the Holy Synod wills to abolish the pernicious custom of distinguishing certain images, especially of the Virgin, with particular titles and names for the most part vain and puerile.[48]

A few months after the publication of the synod's acts and decrees, riots – probably incited by friars and ex-Jesuits – broke out at Prato (May 1787). The clients of Mary were mobilized by the fear that her girdle was threatened. Jansenist books were burned and the discarded statues returned to their niches.

8

MARIAN RESISTANCE IN THE REVOLUTION AND FIRST EMPIRE

Pardon, O Mary, a thousand thousand pardons for all the
excesses of fury and rage committed of late by France.[1]

Fr Marie Joseph Coudrin

In 1788, a year before the fall of the Bastille and a time of wretched
harvests and widespread misery, Madame Elizabeth asked her
brother Louis XVI to dedicate his kingdom to the Sacred Heart and
the Virgin according to her own formula: 'Heart of Jesus, we offer
thee our whole country and the hearts of all thy children. O blessed
Virgin, they are now in thy hands; we have delivered them to thee
by dedicating ourselves to thee as our protectress and our mother.'[2]
The king did not acquiesce, but as late as February 1790 (when the
monastic orders were suppressed) he made a solemn consecration at
Notre-Dame de Paris.[3]

Targets of Jacobinical hatred and a source of counter-revolutionary inspiration, the figure of Mary and emblem of the Sacred Hearts
became even more central in the years of international convulsion.
A typical move was Pius VI's granting permission from captivity
for a special office and mass for the feast of Mary's Heart. The
new liturgy was celebrated at Palermo in 1799 shortly after the
Parthenopean Republic had been proclaimed in Naples. But there
is no space here to expatiate on the Marian and anti-Marian events
of the Revolution, which were set against diverse and complex
scenarios of the Napoleonic empire. Our scope must be limited to
the reconstruction of Mary's divisions, which formed the basis of
the Restoration.

Auctorem Fidei, the bull anathematizing Pistoia, was issued eight
years after the Jansenist synod and at the time of the Jacobins' fall
(August 1794). Repudiated from Lisbon to Vienna, the papal edict

may have marked the return of Jesuit ascendancy – that is, the victory of zelanti over regalisti in the Roman curia. In fact, Jesuit influence had never ceased. Prominent ex-members of the Society remained active and were often to be found in positions of command. F.A. Zaccaria (d. 1795), for example, the distinguished apologist of priestly celibacy and papal power, directed the Accademia dei Nobili Ecclesiastici under Pius VI. A. Muzzarelli (d. 1813), papal penitentiary, remained spokesman on indulgences and his *Emile Undeceived* (1782) secured his place among leading anti-naturalists. Like many Jesuits of the time, both Zaccaria and Muzzarelli wrote effusively on the Sacred Hearts.

The Sodality of Our Lady, a separate 'moral entity', was untouched by the brief of suppression and, while the Prima-Primaria sank into a rather torpid existence, it retained its privileges and indulgences, which were confirmed. Nor did Marian secret societies linked to ex-Jesuits die out. The AA des Messieurs de Toulouse was refounded shortly after the fall of the Jesuits in France, and during the Revolution formed a group of reparators called the *Saint Militia*.

An important clandestine leader was the ex-Jesuit Nicholas de Diesbach (d. 1798), who after the synod of Pistoia set up two secret societies in Turin to fight Jansenist and Masonic influence: Amicizia Cristiana and Amicizia Sacerdotale. These brotherhoods, founded between 1778 and 1782, circulated 'good books' and worked towards the creation of a new elite moulded by Ignatian spirituality and Liguorian doctrine. Diesbach's principal disciple was the Venerable Bruno Lanteri (d. 1830), a forerunner of Catholic Action and 'great apostle of the religious revival in Piedmont'.[4] Lanteri was instrumental in spreading the networks throughout central Europe and, on returning to Turin from gaol and exile, he founded the Oblates of the Blessed Virgin Mary (1815).

The Sulpicians in Paris operated a sort of AA in the early 1780s. Superior-general Jacques Emery (d. 1811), anti-Jansenist reformer of the seminary, played a major part in the revitalizing of the cardio-devotions and formed new inner circles, the nurseries of founders and future Jesuits.

Many ex-Jesuits sought affiliation to the vestigial body in Russia (composed mainly of Poles passionately devoted to the Sacred Hearts) and worked through new communities and underground groups for the restoration of the Society. This objective was set by the

Society of the Sacred Heart, formed by an aristocratic coterie at St Sulpice, and the Society of the Faith of Jesus, or Paccanarists. These two congregations amalgamated at the beginning of the Consulate in 1799. A female branch of the Jesuits opened the following year: Ladies of the Sacred Heart. This important teaching order was founded by St Madelaine Sophie Barat (d. 1865) and Joseph Varin,SJ (d. 1850), a pillar of the resistance. Many confraternities, particularly in the Midi, sprang to life around this time.[5]

The year of Rome's concordat with Napoleon, 1801, proved to be crucial. The Jesuits in Russia received formal papal approval and, as Pius VII crowned the recently-liberated statue of Our Lady of Loreto[6] (February), the most powerful of all secret divisions was formed in Paris: La Congrégation de Sancta Maria, Auxilium Christianorum. The mysterious Congregation evolved from a kernel of students directed by Père J.B. Delpuits (d. 1811), an ex-Jesuit. It very soon gained members in the upper echelons of the law, army and Church (including nuncios), with branches in the provinces and abroad. One of its activities was a clandestine courier service for the exiled pope. Initiation, in the traditional way, took the form of personal consecration to Mary. 'The Holy Virgin protects those chaps', said Fr Delpuits, 'she covers them with her mantle.'[7]

The first cell of another division, inspired by Our Lady's Sodality, met in February 1801 (at the very same hour as the Congrégation, so it is said) in western France. The founder of what would grow into the Marianist Family was Joseph Chaminade (1761–1850), author of *Manuel de Serviteur de Marie* and architect of 'a plan for the moral and social reconstruction of the social order':[8] the Marianist Social System and Marianist Ascetical Method (see below). Called by interior voices to found religious societies while at the shrine of the Pillar in Sargossa during his exile (1797–9), Chaminade organized the Sodality of the Blessed Mary at Bordeaux, the first sodality to obtain official approval after the Revolution.

The congrégation was personally blessed by Pius VII when he was in Paris in 1804; Delpuits received many indulgences and the right to found associate sodalities all over the country.[9] That same year the Jesuit Order in Russia (now activated by Count de Maistre, the great ideologue of the counter-revolution)[10] was also granted powers to aggregate sodalities to a new head association.

A pontifical decree the year before had declared the corpus of Liguori (a 'venerable' since 1796) *nil censura dignum*, free of all error.

His teachings were thus hallowed as the framework needed for the reconstruction of the Church. Hell-fire was fanned[11] and devotions galvanized, particularly the Sacred Hearts and Christ's flesh and blood – coalescent with Mary Immaculate.[12] The new devotion of the Precious Blood was instituted in the Papal States during the Napoleonic invasion. In 1808, shortly before the conqueror declared Rome a 'free city', Francesco Albertini founded, on the feast day of the Immaculate Conception, the Archconfraternity of the Precious Blood. And in Rome two years later, when Pius VII was a prisoner, Giacomo Sinibaldi set up the Nocturnal Adoration Society.

In France no devotion flourished like the Immaculate Heart. In the forefront of the cardio-Marian apostolate was P.J. Picot de Clorivière (d. 1820), an ex-Jesuit from Brittany for whom devotion to Mary was 'the essence of Christianity'.[13] Author of a biography of Grignion de Montfort (1785) and an unpublished defence of Mary of Agreda, de Clorivière founded two congregations while the Civil Constitution of the Clergy was demanding oaths of loyalty and coercing priests into marriage: Daughters of the Heart of Mary (1790) and the Institute of the Heart of Jesus (1791). Two years later, during the brutal de-christianization campaigns which followed massacres and the execution of the monarchs, he composed an act of reparation to the Virgin.

Fr Marie-Joseph Coudrin (d. 1837) was equally committed to Marian reparation and inspired by Montfort. Belonging to a secret society in the seminary of Poitiers, he was secretly ordained during the Terror (1792) and soon afterwards founded the nucleus of the Picpus Fathers, the Congregation of the Sacred Hearts of Jesus and Mary of the Perpetual Adoration of the Most Holy Sacrament of the Altar. Countess Henrietta Aymer de la Chevalerie, on her release from prison, founded with Coudrin the Picpus Sisters, a teaching congregation worshipping the Hearts and the Host. Both male and female Picpus branches grew rapidly, despite the hostility of the Napoleonic police, and obtained full approval in 1817.

After the bull of excommunication *Against the Robbers of St Peter's Heritage* (1809) the Congrégation and the Sulpicians were dissolved.[14] An even more secret group – one destined to be a ruling cabal – rose almost instantly from the ashes: Chevaliers de la Foi, founded by Count Ferdinand de Bertier, a Congréganiste. The Knights – who infiltrated the bureaucracy and worked for the return of the legitimate monarchy – blended Masonic organization and ritual with chivalric ideas from the Middle Ages. Holders of the supreme grade, 'Knights of the Faith',[15] carried a rosary with a silver cross as their sign of mutual recognition.

Part II

THE SIÈCLE DE MARIE

9

OVERVIEW

This century, which has succeeded that of the encyclopedists, may, by virtue of the admirable reaction of which we are the witnesses, be fitly christened the 'century of Mary'.[1]

Louis Veuillot

It seems that, exiled from her native Judea, which crucified her Son, Mary has made France her second fatherland. . . .[2]

Count Lafond

BACKGROUND

On Ferdinand VII's restoration to the Spanish throne (1814), Jesuits and inquisitors returned and the Society of the Exterminating Angel was free to pursue its secret, terrorist and absolutist activities. Sir John Bowring has left an angry account of the persecution of Freemasons, 'despotism exercised over authors and publishers', 'ridiculous trash' in the Spanish press about Our Lady's apparitions and miracles, and the large profits amassed by the 'guardian friars' of Marian shrines.[3] The revolts against the Marian-Inquisitional order which broke out in Iberia (1820), and their suppression, set the violent pattern of political and religious conflict in both Spain and Portugal, which persisted up to the final triumph of fascism.

The independence movement in South America – harshly condemned by Rome – also suffered defeat at the Restoration. But 'the damnable weeds of sedition' (Pius VII) continued sprouting and the colonies eventually threw off Spanish rule (1824). From Mexico to Chile local patronesses were engaged in the wars of independence, during which an anomalous alliance was forged between Freemasonry and Marianism. As 'Generala' of the patriotic armies and protectress of caudillos, Mary's miraculous assistance was solemnly attested at the birth of each Latin American republic. Her queenship of these conflictive post-colonial societies was to leave indelible marks – as contemporary military Marianism shows.

The blueprint of modern militant Catholicism, though, was provided by Rome's 'Eldest Daughter' (France), still cornerstone of the papacy. All the seminal apparitions – with their messages of submission to the Holy See, politicized pilgrimages, rejuvenated devotion to the rosary, scapulars, and indulgences – were French. A large majority of key ideologists, saints and publicists, new or restored congregations (many based on Ignatian principles and ultimately controlled by the Society), of schools and missions (domestic, colonial, international) came from France. The model of Marian counter-Masonry was a French creation, likewise a new form of lay activism inspired by it, which would eventually lay claim to Christian Democracy.

The magical religiosity based on Mary's power and sponsored by the royalist party (temporalist and infallibilist) was paralleled in France by an anti-hierarchical, revolutionary religious movement. The egalitarian figure of a proletarian Jesus – central to the romanticism of the *démocrates-socialistes* in the mid-nineteenth century – threatened the Catholic order no less than bourgeois secularism did. As a recent study points out, 'in banishing Jesus from its discourse, the clergy implicitly acknowledged that Jesus had become the symbol of a nascent egalitarianism'.[4] The response to the Christocentric, radical anticlericalism of 1848 – itself part of a Protestant revival – was an intensification of the monarchical cults of pope and Mother of God, intertwined devotions which culminated in the dogmas of the Immaculate Conception (1854) and papal infallibility (1870). Christ's inconvenient teaching of fraternal love here and now was to be supplanted by the messages of a flowery Janus who, with one face, exemplified obedience, resignation and celibacy, echoing the instructions of the Holy Father in Rome; and with the other – no less Roman – promised to destroy all the 'enemies of the Church' from Freemasons to the hired labourers who ploughed their own plots on Sunday.

Significant reverberations of the nineteenth-century revival were felt in the 'Anglo' world. By mid-century England was a priority target for Catholic missions, and in the United States 'Romanism' grew bold for the first time.[5] But Catholic expansion met with the violent hostility of American Nativism, an early form of Anglo-Saxon Protestant supremacy. In 1846 – a year after the Native American Party had emerged to challenge Catholic power in Maryland – the sixth provincial synod of Baltimore, representing the national episcopate, declared the Immaculate Conception patroness of the USA.

Although reported apparitions (none 'authenticated') and miracles were rare in the US,[6] devotion to the Sacred Heart and the Virgin was marked in the second half of the century as a considerable number of French congregations – some displaced by persecution – gained a foothold across the Atlantic.[7] After the massive immigration which followed the civil war (1861–5), especially from Ireland and Germany (later from eastern and southern Europe), American Catholicism was established as a flourishing sector with an extensive educational network.[8] In 1866 the National Labour Union was formed at Baltimore, to be succeeded by the Knights of Labor (1869) under Catholic leadership. These movements were shadowed by the Invisible Empire, Knights of the Ku Klux Klan (1867) – anti-Catholic as well as racist. The most successful Catholic secret society to respond to the plethora of mutual aid networks was the Knights of Columbus (1882).

DEVOTIONS AND DIVISIONS

Ignatian spirituality, triumphant over Jansenist 'gloom' and 'abstract' mysticism, found fertile soil in the romantic revival. Both apocalyptic and maternal, the Virgin was the alpha and omega of the revival, the one through whom all actions were to be performed. She was defended with scourge and rosary, hyped by a nascent Catholic press, saluted by the phalanxes of Catholic Action, engraved on a billion amulets and marketed with 'holy pardons'. Bejewelled and surrounded by her 'slaves', the Queen of Heaven and earth was enthroned in canonical coronations from Poland to Mexico as an object lesson in temporalism, her shrines a fount of honour and vital source of income.

Saints Joseph and Anne regained their eminence. As mother of the Mother, St Anne, Patroness of Brittany, was crowned in a great basilica built in her honour at Vannes (1868). Medals were struck and litanies composed for St Joseph, the 'august Spouse'. Catholicism, according to its critics, had become 'polythéisme anthropomorphique' (A. Debidour).

Ultramontanes, in search of a corporative order, turned to scholasticism and Mariology. In an age of change and dissent the supreme Marian virtues of humility and chastity were held up more than ever as the keys to salvation. Pride (the demon that forms a critical mind) and lust (enjoyment of the senses) were identified as the roots of all contemporary ills. Behind the anathemas against 'modern civilization' (*Syllabus of Errors*, 1864), the religious pluralism and social involvement of 'Americanism' (*Testem Benevolentiae*, 1899) and 'Modernism' (*Pascendi*, 1907) is Mary, whose magic blue mantle protects all who obey. The merciful and shielding Consolatrix Afflictorum, with her intercessional power as Queen and Mother over Christ's throne of judgment balances the threat of hell. Never absent from the teaching of her apostles, hellfire kept burning in Mary's century, creating an insatiable desire for scapulars and indulgences. 'Never', noted Mgr Lépicier with satisfaction, 'was such a prodigality witnessed in ages past. New grants come out every day.'[9]

Marian devotionalism remained linked to various forms of fetishistic worship: the cults of the Sacred Hearts, devotion to the Precious Blood, adoration of the Host. Mariologists stressed the mystical bond between Virgin and Mother Church, the Immaculate and the Eucharist.[10] The Real Presence, called down by priestly power, was also Mary's presence. The cult of the Blessed Sacrament soared after the 1848 revolution during a growth period of both Marianism and ecclesiastical authoritarianism. Although Christ and Mary were considered one heart and flesh (the belief underpinning the Assumptionist and Immaculist movements), the Church curbed certain developments in this exuberant century, strongly censuring devotion to the Very Pure Blood of Our Lady (1875).[11] But new titles with far-reaching implications were accepted, such as Our Lady of the Atonement, who 'wears a red mantle, symbolizing the Precious Blood of the Atonement of which she is the Immaculate source and by which men are united to God'.[12]

The populist cult of the pope, which was fully developed by Leo's reign (1878–1903), began to take an organized form after the mid-century revolutions. 'Peter's Pence' – now a voluntary collection by the 'divisions' – was reintroduced in 1860 to compensate for the loss of territory in the Papal States and the cost of the war. The litanies of St Peter, enriched with indulgences, were recited everywhere for the 'liberation' of the infallible chief. St Peter's miraculous chains gave birth to a prosperous confraternity (1866) and the reactivated Santa Casa of Loreto could count on 7,000 confrères by 1895.

Religious congregations and their lay subsidiaries formed the backbone of reconstituted papal power. Grand Almoners of the Roman treasure of indulgences and scapulars, these Marian satellites of the Holy See were also guardians of shrines and stewards of a new type of pilgrimage, clerically controlled and politically motivated. Deprived of its coercive and penal powers, and of much of its wealth and privileges, the Church deployed these cohorts – and their ultimate model, the Society of Jesus – in a fight for survival amidst growing Christian communism, Jewish emancipation, Protestant expansion and Masonic networks.

As growth and urbanization accelerated, pursuit of the 'conversion of sinners' through the established devotional system became more centralized and international. Numerous sodalities armed with the spirit of crusade and expiation, like the Pious Work of St Francis de Sales (Paris, 1857) and the Association of St Francis Xavier (Brussels, 1854), spread to many countries. The Sodality of Our Lady, 'a bulwark against secret societies',[13] also grew considerably: 16,674 sodalities, involved in a wide range of works, affiliated to the Prima-Primaria in Rome between 1829 and 1892. The Sacred Hearts cult was disseminated through a vast worldwide network of congregations and associations.

European imperialism beat a path for cardio-Marian missions in new territories. The Society of the Immaculate Heart of Mary, founded in 1841 by the Venerable F.M.P. Libermann (d. 1852), a Jewish convert, aimed 'to bring the faith to the Negro race'.[14] Guided by Libermann's anti-Jansenist spirituality 'characterized by concreteness',[15] the new congregation reached out to Africa and the Caribbean.[16] The Sons of the Sacred Heart were established in Verona as a secular institute for African missions in 1867 by the learned Bishop Daniele Comboni (d. 1881), who was appointed vicar-apostolic for central Africa (Sudan, Nubia and the region south of the Great Lakes) ten years later. In 1910 the Verona Fathers (transformed into a religious congregation under Jesuit direction in

1885) were taking the Sacred Heart to the kingdom of Ethiopia (an Italian protectorate) and on to Uganda and Mozambique. Missions conducted by the Jesuits and new apostolic orders of Ignatian rule like the White Fathers and White Sisters under Cardinal Lavigerie (French 'Primate of Africa') penetrated the Algerian Sahara and other regions in the wake of the colonial scramble.

The Portuguese Church, in contrast to those of other colonial powers, remained in a state of decadence and dependence. In a context of widespread illiteracy (over 75 per cent, according to the 1911 census), Portugal was barely able to provide priests; the Church, oppressed by intermittent liberal regimes, lacked enterprising and charismatic figures. The majority of missionaries in Portuguese Africa were French. And in Goa attempts to Romanize the Malabar Christians by transferring churches 'with unscrupulous violence to the patronage chiefly of Mary' (according to the official voice of British Methodism)[17] made little headway. With the exception of the military Order of Our Lady of Conception of Vila Viçosa (founded in 1818 by King John VI, a confrère of the Slaves of the Conception), practically no new congregation appeared in Portugal throughout this expansionist century, which produced most of the more than 700 Marian orders launched since 1837.[18]

PARADIGM OF A MODERN APPARITION OF THE VIRGIN MARY

Background: Social upheaval, economic crisis and political conflict; the Catholic Church persecuted, its power threatened. Centuries-old tradition of 'visitations' in the region, usually an underdeveloped, rural or isolated province.

Seer: Backward peasant girl, illiterate and of the poorest family. Religiously precocious and acquainted with past official apparitions. Member of a Marian association.

Vision: Heralded by a flash of lightning, a 'lady' who 'glows more brilliantly than the sun', her clothes the last word in regal couture. She may float, grow or weep. Reveals herself as the Virgin under a specific title.

Message: Apocalyptic. Transmitted to the Vatican on the orders of the pope. Parts of it may be strategically released some time in the future. An ultimate 'secret', however, is kept by the seer. Support is given for a doctrine currently promoted by Rome. Lax and liberal priests are warned they are driving people from the Church. Disobedience and sins of the flesh are emphasized. Penance, fasting and the rosary are the only ways to avert divine wrath – expressed in wars, disease, famine, revolutions and natural disasters. Mary asks for a chapel to be built on the spot as a new centre for processions and pilgrimages.

Miracles: Physical cures are effected by a miraculous spring indicated by the apparition. Abundant 'conversions' and an amelioration of local moral standards (i.e., eradication of drinking, dancing and lascivious courting) are noted. The visitations are confirmed to large crowds by 'public miracles', especially irregular solar phenomena (e.g., the sun spins like a Catherine-wheel or 'falls from the sky'). Sacred objects – rosaries, scapulars, crucifixes – presented to the Lady on behalf of pilgrims absorb magical powers of protection for their owners.

Reactions: Embarrassed relatives initially disavow the seer's claims and the parish priest shows little interest, but all are later persuaded of the veracity of the stories. Many local Catholics remain incredulous, some sectors of the community are hostile to the point of violence (from face-slapping to destruction of makeshift altars). Civil authorities, suspecting anti-social or clericalist motives, attempt to intimidate the seer and discover her 'secret'. Upper-class/subversive elements come to the rescue. Large crowds flock to the site but are driven back by troops or police. Economic and political pressures dissuade the government from its policy of repression, even though the national hierarchy may be divided in its response to the supernatural events. Opponents appeal to the Vatican, which adopts a circumspect approach. Legal battles over property and marketing rights flare up as commercialization of the shrine gets under way.

Ecclesiastical action: The local bishop, in consultation with Rome, chairs an inquiry while the seer is put under monastic discipline and indoctrination. Her communications with the outside world are strictly controlled for the rest of her life. A number of secular priests attempt to prevent development of the cult but are silenced by superiors. On canonical approval, masses are said at the locus, where foundations are laid for a sanctuary and church which will later be raised to the rank of basilica. Religious orders and lay associations are launched to promote the new cult. Step by step, the pope grants indulgences and other privileges to the shrine's organizations, gives permission for a feast day of the vision to be celebrated, sends a high official to crown a statue depicting the apparition, and makes references to the new title of Our Lady, which will boost the Marian networks throughout the world. His successors will visit the shrine in person – stimulating its revenues – and, after a lengthy and highly secretive process, canonize the seer (whose 'incorrupt' body is now also an object of veneration).

10

RESTORATION AND THE MYSTICISM OF AUTHORITY

Princes should see that in strengthening religion the Jesuits
strengthen their thrones at the same time.[1]

Cardinal Consalvi, Secretary of State to Pius VII

She loved the sick lamb, the Sacred Heart pierced with sharp
arrows, and poor Jesus falling beneath His cross. To mortify the
flesh, she tried to go a whole day without food; and she puzzled
her head for some vow to accomplish.[2]

Madame Bovary

The watchword of the romantic revival was self-immolation. 'Guards
of honour' in the new congregations led reparation to the Hearts of
Jesus and Mary. An apostolate of sacrifice would appease God's
anger and lead to conversions.

The expiatory spirit of the century is illustrated early on by the life
and visions of the stigmatic Anne Catherine Emmerich (1774–1824),
an Augustinian nun of Westphalia, whose large Catholic population
fell under Protestant Prussia at the Congress of Vienna (1814–15).
Living in a period of acute conflict and confusion, she embodied
the suffering and militant Church and was in constant communication with the supernatural. One of her first visions (1802) was
clearly an indictment of Jansenism: St Augustine 'had shown her
his heart burning with love'.[3]

Very like Mary of Agreda, Sister Emmerich travelled through
the ages, contemplating the entire history of redemption 'in pictures'
and receiving revelations, especially from Our Lady, of all mysteries.
She had the power to verify true relics (which often induced her
raptures), experienced visions of visions, heard purgatorial voices
and moved in spirit to every corner of Europe to spy sinister men
plotting against the pope: 'I saw the Holy Father surrounded by
traitors ... the destroyers attacking the Church of Peter, Mary

standing with her mantle over it, and the enemies of God put to flight. . . . I saw throughout the whole country a chain of secret societies. . . .[4]

Her whole mind and body, which, according to her confessor, 'never experienced a movement of sensuality',[5] were devoted to vicarious suffering and atonement for the beleaguered Church. During a crisis in 1820, for example, when the anti-celibatarians were on the offensive in Germany, she fell critically ill, her body presenting an unbearable sight.

Among the remarkable revelations she dictated from her bed of agony to the poet Brentano was *The Life of the Virgin Mary*, published a few years later (and still being reprinted today). Emmerich's complete biography was published by the Redemptorists at the beginning of the *Kulturkampf*; and soon afterwards Pope Leo XIII opened her beatification process.

The call to self-immolation was also a call to political submissiveness. Towering intellectually over the Catholic revival was the Count de Maistre, for whom Protestantism was 'the great enemy of Europe . . . the fatal ulcer that attaches itself to all the sovereignties and continually consumes them, the Son of Pride, the Father of anarchy, the universal dissolvement. . . .' Protestantism was 'not only a religious heresy but a civil heresy'. In 'freeing people from the yoke of obedience' it had 'unchained pride against authority and put discussion in the place of obedience'.[6] Conversely, the essence of Catholicism was subjugation to the feudal-sacerdotal order: '. . . the real lax doctrine in the Catholic Church is disobedience. One who does not know how to submit to its authority ceases to belong to it.'[7]

De Maistre's reactionary masterpiece *Du Pape* was published, not without difficulty, in 1819. Here ultramontanism found its highest expression. The eternal city is exalted ('Thou has been for eighteen hundred years the centre of truth'),[8] papal infallibility upheld ('Infallibility in the spiritual order of things and sovereignty in the temporal order are two words perfectly synonymous')[9] and the Immaculate Virgin and saints glorified. Impervious to charges of paganism, the jubilant closing paragraphs proclaim, 'All the Saints in the place of all the Gods! . . . the Divine Mary ascends the altar of Pandemick Venus'.[10] The universal character of the Church – 'the number of subjects and the geographical extent of the Empire' – demands a monarchy. 'The rule of the Church is monarchical, but sufficiently tempered with aristocracy to be the best and most perfect of governments'.[11]

On Napoleon's defeat the exiled Pius VII returned to Rome (May 1814) and was paraded on his triumphal *sedia* by the noble youths of the city. On 7 August, two days after the King of France had re-established the processional vow to Mary introduced by Louis XIII, the pope restored the Jesuits, those 'vigorous and experienced rowers' of the 'bark of Peter, tossed and assailed by continuous storms.'[12] This move, which Thomas Jefferson thought 'a retrograde step from light towards darkness',[13] was followed by a Draconian edict against secret societies and their infernal conventicles, which undermined throne and altar. Freemasons were imprisoned by the Roman government and Catholic brotherhoods reactivated.

In 1815, in memory of his suffering during captivity, the pope extended the feast of the Seven Sorrows of Mary to the universal Church and crowned the statue of the Madonna di Misericordia (Savona). The following year he instituted the feast of Our Lady, Help of Christians; and Alphonsus de' Liguori, 'chosen by God to be a new star in the firmament of the Church Militant',[14] was beatified. His relics were exposed for veneration and his picture encircled with rays.

In the meantime future saints were forging careers in the eternal city, reintroducing Marian devotions and purifying customs. In a mood that recalls the Rome of the Counter-Reformation, the Unio Antidaemoniaca was set up 'to act with greatest determination against every work of art in the city that offended one's sense of modesty'.[15] Backed by the celebrated Passionist missionary and bishop, St Vicenzo Maria Strambi (1745–1824), this 'Alliance against the Devil' received papal approbation in 1818. That year the young St Vincent Pallotti (1795–1850), whose recent ordination had featured a vow to defend the Immaculate Conception, wrote: 'Please let us honour and love Mary, let us save souls . . . into the fire with these objectionable images, paintings and books! Death and destruction to the immoral statues!'[16]

Pallotti was a typical spiritual athlete of the age: passionately devoted to Mary,[17] rigorous in his practice of self-flogging and a heroic pastor during the cholera epidemic. An important founder (see below), he was also a great propagator of the Month of Mary and Marian brotherhoods for priests.

Part of the labours of St Gaspare del Bufalo (1786–1836), a Roman missionary associated with Pallotti, was the burning of offensive images and writings. A disciple of Albertini, Bufalo conceived of a new congregation during his exile (1810–14): the Society of the Precious Blood, which gave birth to an archconfraternity and, later on, to several sisterhoods.[18] St Gaspare was encouraged by Pius VII, eager to see these new zealots active among the bandits on the rampage from Rome to Naples.

The Vienna Congress left the greater part of northern Italy to the absolutist rule of Austria, where St Clement Mary Hofbaufer (d. 1820) and his band of Redemptorists carried out a prodigious work of Romanization. Piedmont (now a larger, and Mediterranean, state through the acquisition of Genoa) also came under strong Liguorian influence through the apostolate of 'Pio Bruno' Lanteri, who believed the author of *The Glories of Mary* had saved thousands of souls from the 'sorrow and despair' of Jansenism.[19] Lanteri's Oblates of the Blessed Virgin Mary, a congregation of priests (Turin, 1815) who specialized in retreats and Spiritual Exercises, were involved in the Amicizia Sacerdotale and the Pastoral College for Secular Clergy. In 1817 Lanteri established La Amicizia Cattolica to 'counteract the Protestant Biblical Societies of London'.[20]

Fear of the advancing 'principle of discussion' on which, in de Maistre's view, Protestantism is based, fuelled the battle over Bible reading. On General Brzozowski's refusal in 1812 to collaborate with the scriptural movement sponsored by British and Russian societies, the Jesuits were viewed with mounting hostility by the Russian government. And while the Society was rehabilitated in the west, it was now expelled from St Petersburg (1815), where Freemasonry, it seems, was enjoying the imperial favour.[21]

Of all the traditional enemies of ultramontanism – regalism, 'encyclopedism', Jansenism (now underground and linked to repub-licanism), Waldensianism, etc. – none was more central than Free-masonry, that international vehicle of political subversion accused of fomenting a *cultus diabolicus*. In execrating the most feared of the sects, the mysterious Carbonari, Pius VII spoke in 1821 of 'sacrilegious ceremonies [based on] the Passion of Christ'.[22] This allegation was repeated later in the century by the Catholic historian Cesare Cantù, who also complained that the Carbonari had transformed Christ into a symbol of liberty, equality and fraternity.[23] The radical political theology attributed to the 'charcoal-burners' is strikingly similar to the religiosity of the *démocrates-socialistes* and Louis Blanc, for whom

Jesus is 'the sublime master of all socialists'.[24] Anticlerical and egalitarian, the 'good cousins', as the sectaries called themselves, seem to have worshipped Christ as 'the great Carbonaro', a victim of tyranny, and vowed to destroy his enemies, symbolized by Caesar, Herod and Judas.

The accession in 1824 of Charles X, the last Bourbon to occupy the throne of France, inaugurated a period of ultra-clericalism and 'Jesuitism', while at Rome the election of Leo XII (1823–9) marked the triumph of the Zelanti faction.

In 1824 Leo returned the Sodality of Our Lady of the Annunciation (the Prima-Primaria of Rome) and 2,476 associated sodalities to the Jesuits, granting the general the following year the privilege of aggregating non-Jesuit sodalities to the Prima-Primaria. Marguerite Marie Alacoque was given the title of Venerable (March 1824) and Leo ordered a 'canonical inquiry' to examine her writings.

Pope Leo reimposed the medieval custom of university teaching in Latin only and conducted a bitter campaign against the increasing private perusal of the Gospels:

> You have noticed a society, commonly called the Bible Society, boldly spreading throughout the whole world. Rejecting the traditions of the Holy Fathers and infringing the well-known decree of the Council of Trent, it works by every means to have the Holy Bible translated, or rather mistranslated, into the ordinary languages of every nation. There are good reasons to fear that . . . they will produce a gospel of men, or what is worse, a gospel of the devil![25]

Strict decrees against the theatre and the tavern were issued in Leo XII's reign, the torture chambers of the Inquisition were reopened and the property rights of Jews revoked. This tyrannical attempt to rebuild Catholic power should be seen in the context of heavy economic losses suffered by the orders and the ecclesiastical establishment. The 'seamless robe of Jesus Christ' – the pope's 'indivisible' territory of some three million subjects in the northern Romagna or 'legations', the eastern Marches, Umbria and the Patrimony of Peter surrounding Rome – had, with the neighbouring kingdom of Naples, the most primitive economy in Italy. The Papal States had a very backward infrastructure, little industry, and inefficient mechanisms of commerce. The artisan class was in steep decline due to the industrial revolution north of the Alps. The countryside, parcelled into great estates owned by absentee prelates and nobles, was extremely unproductive, forcing the papacy to raise loans from foreign bankers to import food.

Even the significant revenues traditionally provided by pilgrimages plummeted in 1825, when the 'sacerdotal trumpet sounding the sacred jubilee to the people of god'[26] drew only a small number of pilgrims to Rome and Loreto. This first pontifical jubilee of the century, held amidst pauperism and violence (the Roman Jews were forced to put back the gates of their ghetto and the bodies of Carbonari rotted on the gibbets of Ravenna) was a failure despite the allure of indulgences.[27] Promulgating the extension of the jubilee, the pope reminded the bishops:

> You must make sure that [the laity] understand and believe that Christ left the inexhaustible treasury of his merits to the Church, that this treasure was enriched with the merits of the Blessed Virgin and all the saints, and that the distribution of these riches to men is in the hands of Him whom Christ makes the visible head for Himself of the invisible Church.[28]

Although the jubilee dragged Rome deeper into debt, it closed with a miracle: a gigantic luminous cross appeared in the air to 3,000 parishioners at Migne (Poitiers). Leo authenticated this marvel by a brief of April 1827.[29]

*   *   *

Catholicism was once more the state religion in France, 'servile' work was forbidden on Sundays, priests' salaries were raised and money poured into the reconstruction of the Church's infrastructure. Missionary societies burgeoned, propagating *dévotions nouvelles* and *confréries de pénitents*.

The penitents, devotees of Our Lady and recruited mainly from the disenchanted peasantry and artisanate in a still overwhelmingly rural France, were royalist and allied to the nobility, which, refusing to die out, regained some popularity and strength, especially in the south and in isolated regions. In the Midi during the White Terror the aristocratic-peasant alliance liquidated several hundred Protestants, including capitalists who had benefited from the Revolution. Populist anti-capitalism cloaked itself in piety, turning Catholic festivals into anti-Protestant riots.[30] Religious processions, complete with military bands, and ceremonies of atonement, were staged for the crimes of the Revolution;[31] wandering preachers erected prominent iron crosses on which hearts were engraved, each one inscribed with the name of a potential convert.[32]

A host of crusade organizations – similar to the Liguorian campaigns of the previous century in Naples – pullulated during the Restoration. The most important of these were either founded or taken over by Congréganistes: the Association for the Defence of the Catholic Religion, the Society of Good Works, the Society of Good Studies, the Society of Good Books – to stem the 'terrible torrent of filth . . . caused by the books issued by the diabolical worships of wicked men'.[33] These organizations were complemented by a large number of teaching orders, many of which extended overseas and whose founders would be canonized.[34]

The most remarkable aspect of the revival was the proliferation and scope of organizations consecrated to Notre-Dame and offering boundless allegiance to the infallible pontiff. The impact of their manifold activities (education, missions, pilgrimages, retreats) on contemporary struggles should not be underestimated. Recipients of the munificence of aristocratic benefactors, these foundations constituted a fundamental part of the framework that would sustain the apparitions and subsequent devotions, Marian 'science' and papal dogmas. Through them millions were conditioned to an obedient life 'under her mantle' and found consolation amidst the miseries of the age. Refuge of Sinners, Mother of Mercy, Suppliant Omnipotent, Mary stood in diametrical opposition to Marianne, the allegorical figure who simultaneously personified the republic and was the mother of it. 'Virgin of Liberty, deliver us from King and Popes! Virgin of Equality, deliver us from aristocrats!' Shamelessly parodying the Ave Maria, revolutionaries sang, 'Hail Marianne, full of strength, the People are with thee, Blessed is the fruit of thy womb, the Republic!'[35]

Just as Montfort had fought 'conceited scholars of hard and sceptical minds'[36] with rosary campaigns, penance, and book-burning, so Joseph Chaminade, founder of the Marianist Family, challenged religious indifference and 'philosophism' in every town, village and hamlet, heart and mind,[37] through schools and sodalities, Mariological studies and the 'Marianist Ascetical Method'.[38]

Chaminade's Daughters of Mary Immaculate and the Society of Mary, founded in 1816 and 1817 respectively, had the purpose of 'glorifying Mary'[39] with 'a family spirit and the spirit of humility'.[40] These congregations were organized under a rule based on 'filial piety towards Mary', an open profession of faith in the doctrine of her Immaculate Conception and consecration in her service, sealed with a fourth vow and symbolized by a gold ring worn on the right hand. Adherents form part of the 'Family of Mary' composed of 'pious societies' and 'holy militia'.[41] The covenant with Mary is consummated through a 'familistic' (corporate) and rigidly hierarchical order, whose members, clerical and lay, act as her apostolic sons and daughters, for Mary is 'the Conquering Woman to whom is reserved total and final victory over evil'.[42]

Managed by a secret central committee known as 'the State',[43] this 'vast network'[44] of institutions had as its aim nothing less than the 'total re-Christianization, not only of France, but of the whole world'.[45] As a reward for their work in the Restoration the Marianists were given control of state schools by the French government, which also subsidized their own private schools. These privileges were lost in the 1830 revolution.[46]

While the Marianist congregations based at Bordeaux thrived, the various branches of the 'Marist Family' developed no less successfully in eastern France: Sisters of Mary, Little Brothers of Mary and the Society of Mary. Backed by Pius VII, this conglomerate traces its origins to the solemn consecration to the Virgin of a group of seminarists at Lyons in 1816. The Marists, who revere as founders St Jean Claude Colin (1780–1875) and the Blessed Mercellin Champagnat (1789–1840), were imbued with 'the spirit of the Blessed Virgin, a spirit of humility, self-denial and unwavering loyalty to the Holy See'.[47]

We learn from a first-hand account[48] how Champagnat's Little Brothers renewed their vows and consecration to the tender Mother on each of her five principal feasts; how daily life, particularly Saturday, was dedicated to her as a way of gaining her protection and acquiring the virtue of purity; and how Marian exercises – the Salve Regina, recitation of the Ave Maria each hour of the day, the Month of Mary and so on – dominated the devotional life of these communities. Unlike the Jesuit practice at the time, compulsory flagellation was not part of the rule, but Fr Champagnat (who held the Montfortian view that devotion to Mary is a sign of predestination) 'looked upon his body as his greatest enemy' and 'ceased not to torment it'.[49]

All this seems an expression of 'semi-erotic mysticism',[50] a fairly widespread tendency during the revival and concomitant with unquestioned obedience to the Holy See. Champagnat – for whom popes were 'divine oracles'[51] – made the Brothers stand, as though for the Gospels, while reading an encyclical of Leo XII on bad books. In 1836, obeying the 'voice of Rome',[52] Colin and Champagnat sent missionaries to Oceania, where they reaped glorious martyrdom.[53] With the help of rich nobles like the Count and Countess de la Grandville, the Marists played a major role in French education, particularly among the lower classes, and they prospered during the Second Empire.

Charles Eugene de Mazenod (1782–1861), a former exile of noble descent and Congréganiste, future Bishop of Marseilles (1837) and a symbol of the Restoration's spirit of reconquest, was engaged both in popular missions (Missionaries of Provence) and elite groups (Congrégation de la Jeunesse Chrétienne, an aristocratic secular institute in Aix). Formed 'to repair the havoc caused by the Revolution',[54] the Provençal missionaries (later to be the Oblates of Mary Immaculate) worked in the poorest parishes of Marseilles, managing to placate the 'fiery and turbulent masses'.[55]

Mazenod erected Liguori's first altar on French soil (Aix, 1818) and adopted his theology as the Oblates' official teaching.[56] Like the Redemptorists, they attempted to 'revive the spirit of faith among rural and industrial populations'[57] through missions, retreats and devotion to Mary and the Sacred Hearts – 'a supernatural means of regeneration'.[58] They took a leading role in the domestication of rustic worship, especially by eliminating cults of unofficial saints including Jansenists; and ran sanctuaries and pilgrimages not only all over France but also from Ceylon to Canada. Among the greatest missionaries of the age, the Oblate Fathers undertook the heroic evangelization of the icy coast of Labrador in the 1840s and in 1863 they established a settlement among the Sotho in Southern Africa called Motse oa' M'a Jesu (Village of the Mother of Jesus, later known simply as Roma).[59] The great chief Moshoeshoe was persuaded to consecrate his territory to the Virgin and the Vatican.

In addition to the stewardship of miraculous places, the Oblates (priests as well as brothers) busied themselves with catechism, reformatories, practical instruction on farms and in workshops, and the supervision of young men's societies and Catholic clubs.

Like many other orders, they suffered intermittent persecution and expulsions.

The post-1789 foundations centred on the Hearts of Jesus and Mary mostly prospered, and old Marian congregations were resuscitated. Both wings of the missionary Company of Mary – the Montfort Fathers and the Daughters of Wisdom – were reorganized in 1820–1 by the fructuous Fr Deschayes. But the order remained relatively unimportant until the founder was accorded the title of Venerable in 1838 and his manuscript of *The True Devotion* was authenticated four years later. The fortunes of the Company, a pontifical congregation since 1835, then began to improve and its representatives reached Haiti during the Second Empire.

The Congregation of Jesus and Mary ('Eudists') based in Brittany did not manage to recover fully until the 1820s. Eudist teachings were to be widely disseminated under the direction of Ange le Doré (1870–1916), a crusader against the Third Republic.

The Jesuits and their affiliates were the lifeblood of the French Restoration (as was the case throughout Europe). The Congrégation – openly regrouped in 1814 by Père Ronsin,SJ (d. 1846) – came to power under Charles X[60] principally through chief minister Vièle (1822–7), foreign minister the Duke Mathieu de Montmorency, police chiefs Franchet d'Esperey and de Delavau, and Prince Jules de Polignac, appointed President of the Council in 1829.[61] Since 1814 Congréganistes had dominated the Treasury and were highly influential in the legal system. Between 1821 and the final dissolution in 1830, no less than 36 bishops, including three nuncios, became members.[62]

A large number of nuns' sodalities were associated with the Prima-Primaria; new congregations and confraternities espousing the cults of the Sacred Heart, the Virgin and the Blessed Sacrament were either directly inspired or erected by Jesuits. Fr Louis de Bussy (d. 1821), the great champion of Mary's Month in France, founded a sodality of the Virgin at Saint-Acheul in 1814; he later launched another one for children, La Congrégation de Saints Anges. The important sodality of the Children of Mary of the Sacred Heart was founded in 1818 by St Madelaine Sophie Barat and Fr Varin,SJ. The main aim was 'to love and serve the Immaculate Heart of Mary by imitating her virtues, above all, her fortitude and spotless purity'.[63] Fr Debross,SJ (d. 1848), who was responsible for the Library of Good Books at Paray, created another major confraternity based on Alacoque's revelations of the Holy Hour. The public practice of this devotion – which 'should take place preferably before the Blessed Sacrament'[64] – was generously indulgenced and became very popular.

In Dauphiné, the apostolate to pilgrims visiting the relics of the Jesuit missionary St Jean-François Regis gave birth in the 1820s to the Contemplative Religious of the Cenacle,[65] who adopted Perpetual Adoration as their devotional aim along with Ignatian rule and Jesuit guidance. The Congregation of Our Lady of the Retreat in the Cenacle offered catechetical instruction and spiritual retreats – characteristic functions of the new foundations.

The Jesuits also influenced independent figures like Mlle Pauline Marie Jaricot (1799–1862), foundress of the Society for the Propagation of the Faith (1822). One of the outstanding characters of the revival and a protégée of the Count and Countess of Bremond, Jaricot enjoyed the admiration of Gregory XVI, who personally congratulated her on 'the heroic example she was giving of faith in the intercession of the saints'.[66] Obsessed by 'bad books' and the wickedness of the times (especially as perpetrated by 'the iniquities of the Jews' and the 'social and religious peril of the monopoly of wealth by masonic impiety'),[67] Pauline set out to build 'a strong rampart of mutual prayer' through 'an association accessible to all': the Living Rosary, 'the best means of regeneration and the most powerful prayer to obtain mercy'.[68] Put under the management of the Dominican general and canonically erected in 1832, this association was one of the landmarks in devotion to Our Lady and would very soon have branches all over the world.

As the major promoter in France of the cult of Saint Philomena – whose historical existence was denied by the Vatican in 1904 and whose Neapolitan shrine closed in 1961 – Mlle Jaricot was closely associated with the famous ascetic St Jean-Marie Vianney (1786–1859), otherwise known as the Curé of Ars. Great crowds were drawn to this remote village in the district of Trévoux by Philomena's bones,[69] and the Curé's fervent preaching and thaumaturgical power were such that the railway company issued an eight-day excursion ticket.[70]

An enthusiast for Marian apparitions (as will be seen later) and confraternities, the Curé engaged the devil in a lifelong physical struggle during which the fiend often soiled a picture of the Virgin. Supported by the lady of the manor and her brother the Viscount d'Ars, Vianney rid the village of *cabarets*,[71] along with drinking, music and dancing. He harboured a peculiar hostility towards nature, which he continues to defy: like several other saints of the century,[72] his body is incorrupt.

11

THE MIRACULOUS MEDAL

Indifferent Christians and hardened sinners, Protestants, unbe-
lievers, the Jews themselves, beg for it, receive it with delight, and
wear it with devotion.[1]

Fr Aladel, confessor of St Catherine Labouré

The context of the first major modern apparition was, characteristically, one of political turmoil, anticlericalism and social unrest.
Demands for reform seemed irrepressible and a new wave of
attacks hit the Church – in particular the Society of Jesus, whose
contingents were again depleted. A number of key elements in the
Vincentian visions of 1830 recall the experiences of Marguerite
Marie Alacoque. In both cases the dead founder of the order and
the Blessed Virgin appeared as mediators, giving instructions of a
disciplinary and devotional nature, messages of reassurance for the
community, promises of missionary success, and a specific reference
to the Catholic faith in France and the king.[2] The wounded heart of
Christ was replaced by the 'deeply-afflicted heart' of St Vincent de
Paul, whose 'family' would grow and prosper in the years to come.
The confessors of both seers were missionaries with a boundless zeal
for the Sacred Heart.

  The immediate background to this 'Mariophany'[3] at the end of
the Restoration was the extravagant translation of the remains of St
Vincent, 'Father of the Poor', from Notre-Dame to the Vincentian
chapel of St Lazare in Paris on 25 April 1830. A military band and
companies of guards and policemen accompanied the reliquary,
which cost 40,000 gold francs.[4] Charles X, who had reintroduced the
'royal touch' for scrofula sufferers at his annointing, went in person
to venerate the relics. In the crowd was farmer's daughter Catherine
Labouré, a 24-year-old postulant of the Sisters of Charity. The night
after the ceremony, Catherine saw the founder's heart[5] hovering
above a case containing his 'small relics' at the mother-house in the
rue de Bac, Paris:

It appeared to me, at three different times, three days running: white, colour of flesh, announcing peace, calm, innocence and unity. Then I saw red like fire: which must light the flame of charity in people's hearts. It seemed to me that the whole Community should renew itself and spread to the farthest points of the world. And then I saw red-black, which brought sadness to my heart. . . . I did not know why, or how, this suffering had to do with the change of government.[6]

The organ appeared once more in a light shade of red and 'an interior voice' declared, 'The heart of St Vincent is a little consoled. He has obtained from God, through the intercession of Mary, that his two families shall not perish in the midst of these calamities, and that God will make use of them to revive the faith in France.'[7]

Christ appeared to the postulant as a king in the early summer of 1830 as she took Holy Communion. His form, seen through the Host as it was held out to her lips, turned black on 6 June, filling her with forebodings of the dethronement of King Charles.

On 18 July the visionary went to bed hoping that 'that very night I would see my Blessed Mother'.[8] To induce the visitation she ate a piece of the founder's surplice.[9] Sometime before midnight she was woken by her guardian angel in the form of a golden-haired little boy, who led her downstairs to the chapel. She had not been waiting long when she heard 'a faint rustling as of a silk gown' and 'looking up she saw a lady of wondrous beauty enter the sanctuary and sit down in the director's chair'.[10]

In addition to a secret, which Catherine never revealed throughout a long life, Mary told her, 'Misfortunes will come crashing down on France. The throne will be toppled.' Breaking down, the Virgin sobbed, 'There will be victims in other communities . . . the Archbishop will die . . . the cross will be despised and trodden underfoot; the side of Our Lord will be pierced anew; and streets will run with blood. . . .'[11]

As for the state of St Vincent's foundations, Mary was far from pleased: 'There are great abuses in regularity. The rules are not being observed. There is a great laxity in both the Communities.'[12] Not all was doom, however, for Catherine's confessor (Fr Aladel, a Priest of the Mission) founded the Association of the Children of Mary, and there were celebrations 'with great pomp' of the Month of Mary and widespread adoration of the Sacred Heart. The latter cult, in fact, received an immediate boost when, on 22 July 1830, the relics of Sister Alacoque were exhumed and carried in procession, working a miraculous cure in at least one nun, Marie Thérèse Petit.

Days later, Charles X abdicated in favour of his grandson, the Duke of Bordeaux, and revolutionaries sacked episcopal palaces throughout the country. On 7 August Louis-Philippe, Duke of Orleans, was proclaimed 'King of the French'. The Most Christian Monarchy of the Bourbons was never to return. A few months later, on 27 November, Catherine was summoned to the chapel to receive plans for a major Marian campaign.

Mary made her appearance at 5.30 p.m. wearing a white silk robe, her fingers covered with rings which emitted beams of light. 'These rays', she explained, 'are a symbol of the graces which I obtain for those who ask them of me.'[13] She stood on a globe, which, in her own words, 'represents the whole world, and France in particular, and everyone in it'.[14]

The Virgin then stretched out her arms in the stance that traditionally represents the Immaculate Conception; and an oval frame formed round her on which was written in golden letters: 'O Mary, conceived without sin, pray for us who have recourse to thee.' The 'picture' swivelled round to reveal on the other side a large letter 'M' surmounted by a cross and below, two hearts, one encircled by thorns (Jesus') and the other pierced by a sword (Mary's). A voice instructed Sister Catherine: 'Have a medal struck according to this pattern. Those who shall wear that medal when it is indulgenced will receive great graces, especially if they wear it round their necks.'[15]

Once more, in December 1830, Catherine heard that exquisite rustle of silk and saw the Virgin in a high-necked dress with her hair centre-parted and tied with a band of lace. 'You will not see me anymore', said the visitor, 'but you will hear my voice during your prayers.'[16]

By 1830–1, revolutionary movements and secret societies came back into action, demanding an end of the temporal power and pressing for constitutions and liberalization in the central duchies and the kingdom of Naples. On 8 February 1831 – just a few days after the election of Pope Gregory XVI – the philo-Carbonari government of Bologna[17] boasted that it had 'broken every link which made us subject to the Roman Pontiff'.[18] The papal legate was imprisoned and the port of Ancona seized. Other cities fell to the rebels.[19] But Austrian troops soon intervened and the old order was once more restored in the peninsula. In the lands subjected to the tiara those pontifical Tontons Macoutes, the Centurioni, who numbered around 50,000 in 1832, inflicted yet another white terror.[20]

With this scenario and a severe cholera epidemic that struck Europe in the 1830s, the Miraculous Medal met with a resounding success. Mass production began on the approval of Archbishop de Quélen in 1832;[21] the children of Louis-Philippe were soon wearing it, and within seven years ten million copies were in circulation as far afield as the USA, China, Russia and Abyssinia.[22]

The thaumaturgic reputation of the Marian amulet rested initially on a number of cures during the plague. The French colonization of Africa[23] subsequently did much to 'militarize' it. 'Marshal Bugeaud wore it during his eighteen campaigns . . . after his death the little medal . . . was set in gold and laid at the feet of the Madonna of the Church of Notre-Dame d'Afrique.'[24] As military nurses in the Crimea, Papal States, United States, Mexico, Austria, Prussia and France,[25] the Sisters of Charity surreptitiously slipped it into the bandages of wounded apostates who subsequently confessed and met 'edifying deaths'. Pressed onto 'obstinate Jews', 'bigoted Protestants', Freemasons, and actresses who miraculously submitted to Rome, the medal was worn by 'every devout Catholic'[26] and 'kissed by dying lips'[27] from Naples to Nanking. Above all, the charm inculcated a belief in the Immaculate Conception through 'the prayer which Mary herself had dictated',[28] providing a major stimulus to the revival.

Instability at home offered new openings. During the Lyons insurrection in November 1834 associates of the Living Rosary organized an 'ambush' of rebels, scattering Miraculous Medals on the road together with 'a lot of little papers bearing the words "Mary was conceived without sin" '.[29]

Following a now familiar pattern of graduated approval by Rome through associations set up to promote the new devotion, the Medal burst the billion-copy barrier in Labouré's own lifetime.[30] According to her confessor, 'Nor is it propagated in France alone: it has spread rapidly over Switzerland, Italy, Spain, Belgium, England, America, the East. . . . In Naples . . . the king had a number struck in silver for himself and his court and family, and ordered a million for distribution during the outbreak of cholera. . . . In Rome the Generals of the religious orders took active part in the propaganda, while the Holy Father himself placed the medal at the foot of his crucifix as a special token of his blessing.'[31]

Fr Jean-Baptiste Etienne, superior-general of Catherine's order, found that 'after this apparition of Mary Immaculate, everything changed its face. . . . Already in 1831, colonies of missionaries inspired with the purest and most ardent zeal crossed the seas and went into the Levant and into China to forge with our overseas missions new links for the chain of generations that the Revolution had broken.'[32]

Details of the visions on which this revival was based were not published until 1834 and then anonymously in the *Mois de Marie* magazine. In 1841 the visionary put pen to paper 'under obedience' to Fr Aladel, who promptly brought out a book that sold 130,000 copies within eight years. Further testimonies were given by the nun in 1856 and 1876, the year of her death. Although the Virgin appeared again on 17 August 1835 to a member of the community of Our Lady of Einsiedeln in Switzerland – urging her to wear the Medal 'and try to make others wear it too'[33] – the ecclesiastical commission which approved the practice in 1836 declined to pass judgement on the apparitions.

The doctrinal message engraved on every copy was repeated in 1840 to Sister Bisqueburu, a fellow novice at the rue du Bac. On this occasion Mary demonstrated another way of disseminating the future dogma: the Green Scapular, for those who prefer cloth to metal. The new product was approved by Pius IX in 1863. The Red Scapular – depicting the instruments of the Passion and Sacred Hearts with the legend 'Holy Hearts of Jesus and Mary, save us!'[34] was unveiled to yet another Sister of Charity (Apolline Andreveau) in a vision in 1846. Fr Etienne pleaded Sister's cause in Rome the following year, obtaining immediate papal authorization.[35] The distribution of the Red Scapular (also known as the scapular of the Passion) was entrusted to the Priests of the Mission by Pius IX, who granted an indulgence of 200 days 'every time it is kissed'.[36]

The Children of Mary, who already existed in the 1820s, were officially constituted under the Sisters of Charity in 1840. Members (girls and young women) were invested with the blue ribbon and medal, enjoyed automatic membership of the Sodality of the Living Rosary and benefited from a generous system of indulgences.[37] A manual reminds the Child of Mary that the theatre, balls, novels and 'doubtful assemblies' are to be avoided by 'persons consecrated to the

Queen of All Virtues'.[38] Also of great importance in the distribution of the Miraculous Medal was the Archconfraternity of Notre-Dame des Victoires, whose associates (there were eleven million all over the world in 1847)[39] had to wear it. Cardinal John Henry Newman, leader of the Oxford Movement, was among the celebrities who received the charm from the founder himself.

The Medal's most celebrated 'catch' – which led to renewed efforts in the Catholic mission to the Jews – was Alphonse Ratisbonne, carefree son of a Strasburg banker. Reluctantly accepting a medal from friends in Rome, Ratisbonne experienced a vision of Mary, and was 'in one instant changed from a Jew to a Christian, from a hater of the Catholic Church to one of her most faithful sons'.[40] In William James's view, the case strongly suggests 'an epileptoid seizure'.[41] Baptized in the (Jesuit) Church of the Jesù, the convert was backed by Pope Gregory in his foundation of the Congregation of Our Lady of Sion.[42]

Throughout the intense promotion of the vision and its product – 'the graphic expression of the conceptionist dogma'[43] – the seer continued to look after the henhouse in the Enghien Hospice at Reuilly outside Paris.[44] She was visited by an aristocratic circle that included the wife of Marshal MacMahon, president of the French Republic (Madame MacMahon inherited Catherine's own copper medal and set it in gold), the daughter of the last Emperor of Brazil and, oddly, the Shah of Persia.[45]

In 1894 Pope Leo XIII granted the Medal its own mass and office; two years later, Catherine Labouré's 'ordinary process of canonization' was opened in Paris.

12

CATHOLIC ACTION, MARIAN ACTION

Now . . . that an ever-increasing pauperism stands face to face in rage and desperation with a monied aristocracy, whose bowels of mercy have grown hardened, it is well that there should be found mediators who may prevent a collision.[1]

Frédéric Ozanam, founder of the Society of St Vincent de Paul

The July Revolution (1830) once more dislocated the clerical, aristocratic order[2] and the forces that sustained it: the Society of Jesus and the Congrégation. The Orleanist regime – which included both Voltaireans and Protestants[3] – drastically reduced the clergy's role in education, promised to put 'a school in every village', redeemed, on conservative lines, the revolution's Académie de Sciences Morales et Politiques and purged the Université of Ultramontanists.

Catholicism was again in disarray. Two months after the fall of the last Most Christian King, Abbé F.R. de Lamennais (d. 1854), a charismatic leader among Catholic elites, launched the newspaper *L'Avenir* under the mast-head 'God and Liberty' to persuade believers to put their trust in the pope rather than the king. To his unsolicited promotion of papal populism (a strategy to be adopted by Pius IX and Leo XIII) Lamennais added an incongruous element of liberalism by supporting religious tolerance.

In condemning the fiery Breton in 1832, Gregory XVI (1831–46) called liberty of conscience an 'absurd and erroneous proposition'.[4] The following year the pope assailed liberal Catholics in Germany who had questioned the power of the keys to remit 'temporal pains of sin'.[5] The intransigence of Rome jarred provocatively with the new politico-religious ideology born of dramatic changes in the spheres of labour, capital, culture and communications.[6]

Around 1820 artisans in the major French cities had begun to frequent *cabinets de lecture* well-stocked with radical material inspired by the Gospels and centred on Jesus.[7] This growing Christian socialist movement irredeemably hostile to the hierarchical Church[8] may have had an impact on Lamennais himself, who eventually concluded that Christianity and capitalism are incompatible. His writing, in turn, had an enormous influence on workers for the rest of the century.

In response to the emerging 'social question' and the movement inspired by Jesus the Carpenter, a lay crusade – obsessed by socialism[9] and linked to the Jesuits – began to take shape: the Society of St Vincent de Paul. The first *conférence*, as local cells were called, was assembled in 1833 by Frédéric Ozanam (1813–53), future Sorbonne professor of literature and one of the first intellectuals to wear the recently-struck Miraculous Medal.[10] This 'network of charity',[11] under the patronage of the Blessed Virgin[12] and endowed with a complex system of indulgences,[13] can be regarded as a continuation of the banned Congrégation.[14] Its declared objective was to reduce class conflict in the smouldering 'bourgeois monarchy' of Louis-Philippe. Ozanam, whose cause for beatification was introduced in 1923, 'felt strongly that the spirit of class hatred, or the revolt of Labour against Capital, could only be combated by a revival of Religion, and by the personal visits to the poor at their homes by educated Catholics who would fraternize with the workmen and advise them.'[15]

Working closely with the Sodality of Our Lady[16] and enjoying the patronage of the episcopate and Rome (a Cardinal Protector was appointed in 1851), the network became the most powerful lay association in the land[17] and was soon to be captured by legitimists who, forbidden by the pretender to hold public office, exercised pressure through the *confréries*. Vincentians dominated these whether mutual aid societies, works for the regularization of marriages, sabbatarian vigilantes or anti-Protestant propagandists. The conferences allowed followers of the Count de Chambord 'to safeguard and to increase their social influence, and thus open up paths to political action'.[18]

In addition to over 1,000 conferences in France,[19] there were by August 1848 some 400 groups of 'Brothers' operating in England, Holland, Ireland and Canada. A prominent Vincentian Brother (until 1843) was Louis Veuillot, vitriolic editor of the *Univers* and key publicist in the Immaculate Conception and infallibility campaigns, for whom the pope was simply 'Christ on earth'.[20]

The July Revolution brought a wave of lesser, though super-naturally inspired, foundations such as the Congregation of the Saviour and Our Lady. Sensitive, as always, to the needs of the time, the Virgin told the foundress, Mother Marie du Bourg (d. 1862), in August: 'I want to make use of you to found a new congregation, destined to help the poor, care for the sick and instruct youth. . . .'[21]

Mlle Jaricot was also to receive a call from heaven. 'If you cannot enter the Society of Jesus', an incorporeal voice asked, 'can you not form the Society of Mary?'[22] And after a retreat under Fr Renault, SJ, Pauline founded at the feet of Notre-Dame de Fourvière (1830) a lay society devoted to the Immaculate Conception and reparation through the Eucharist, the Filles de Marie.

In Italy, too, a number of new institutes sprang from the embers of revolution. In Bergamo the Daughters of the Sacred Heart – formed immediately after the 1830 upheavals by the Blessed Teresa Verzeri – aspired 'to revive the faith and reduce social conflicts by means of feminine education'. Also in Lombardy Saints Bartolomea Capitanio and Vincentia Gerosa established the Sisters of the Infant Mary (Suore di Carita o di Maria Bambina, 1832).[23] In Rome St Vincent Pallotti, 'a forerunner of Catholic Action' (Pius XI), formed the Society of the Catholic Apostolate, composed of clerics and laypeople. Approved in 1835, this new foundation, put under the patronage of Our Lady, Queen of the Apostles, was to 'operate through Mary'.[24] Closely linked to the Roman College and the Society of the Precious Blood, the Pallottine Fathers and Sisters pursued a wide-ranging, international apostolate, opening orphanages and schools for young workers.

Pallotti, who has been compared with the Curé of Ars for his thaumaturgic powers in life and incorruptibility in death, felt that characteristic nostalgia for artisan guilds and longed for the conversion of England, whither he sent missionaries after Catholic Emancipation.

*   *   *

In these early years of the international movement which would later be known as Catholic Action the new cardio-Marian confraternities of global dimensions complemented the social apostolate under Mary's banner. In Paris the 'passionately monarchical'[25] Abbé Dufriche-Desgenettes, on hearing in 1836 an interior voice saying,

'Consecrate your parish to the most Holy and Immaculate Heart of Mary', launched the flourishing Confraternity of Notre-Dame des Victoires.

The Paris headquarters of the association (raised to the rank of archconfraternity in 1838 at the request of Princess Borghese) was endowed by pilgrims from all over the Catholic world, making it one of the richest temples outside Rome. A major objective of this brotherhood, which ran to thousands of branches and a membership of many millions,[26] was the conversion of Albion. In 1841 Benedictine nuns near Rugby established an association of the Immaculate Heart linked to the Paris archconfraternity.

The most centralized and widespread lay network of devotional and political action was founded by the Jesuits at Vals (France) in 1844: the Apostleship of Prayer.[27] 'A league of prayer and sacrifice for the glory of God and the salvation of souls in union with the Sacred Heart',[28] the Apostleship invited its members to a life of reparation 'through the Immaculate Heart of Mary' and in 'close union with the Pope'.[29] Associates would be urged to enrol in Catholic Action and recite the rosary daily as a 'token of filial confidence' in the Mother.[30] Enriched with indulgences and privileges, the association – a thriving enterprise by 1861 – was active in all spheres including schools, where pupils formed 'Pope's Militias'.

According to its great architect, Fr Henri Ramière, SJ (1821–84), the Apostleship was to employ the 'power of association' to counter 'sacrilegious projects' of the 'favourites of Satan' in the 'lodges'.[31] Ramière's scenario was one of 'evil struggling against good, darkness against light, vice against virtue, death against life, Hell against Heaven, Satan against God. It is the terrible battle which began at the fall of the rebel angels.'[32] Society would be rescued by restoring 'the fatherly devotedness of superiors, the cordial subordination of inferiors'.[33] And the 'balance of the world's destiny' is to be recovered by awakening devotion to the Divine Mother.[34] 'Spiritual individualism', that great enemy of the Church, would perish through the cults of the Sacred Heart, Mary and Joseph. The apostleship of Prayer 'is the apostleship of the Blessed Virgin too', for her intercession is 'the infallible means of obtaining everything from Jesus.'[35]

Ramière increased the potential of his division by association with the Living Rosary and, together with the monthly *Messenger of the Sacred Heart*, he edited the bulletin *Petit Messager du Coeur de Marie*. A professor of theology and philosophy, he taught that Catholics are 'in communion' with the Sacred Heart through the heart of the pope: '. . . the divine life, whose source is the heart of Jesus, is diffused in the heart of the Roman Pontiff, who communicates it to the bishops and through them to the priests and through the priests to the universality of the faithful.'[36]

13

LA SALETTE: MODEL OF THE MODERN SHRINE

Help of the Church Militant,
Advocate of the Church Triumphant.
By thy apparitions and thy miracles,
revive the faith of thy people.
By thy mysterious looks towards Rome
make us more and more devoted to the Holy See.[1]
Prayer of the Archconfraternity of Notre-Dame de la Salette

Three months after Pius IX had mounted the fisherman's throne, the Virgin visited the French Alps. Archbishop Ullathorne, who ascended the 'Holy Mountain' of La Salette near Grenoble to pray for the conversion of England, wrote: 'And who that studies God's ways sees not how, as error thickens, and the devil gains power, his adversary, THE WOMAN, extends her power more and more within the Church.'[2]

The first major shrine of the romantic reaction, La Salette brought to the familiar elements of the Sacred Heart and Miraculous Medal apparitions an important new emphasis: a prophecy of global destruction. The 'warning' produced mass pilgrimages, overseas missions, commercial enterprise, a national focus for revival – and boosted the cult of the pope.

On 19 September 1846 the cowherds Mélanie Mathieu (15) and Maximin Giraud (11) were pasturing their animals when they saw a giantess sitting on a rock and weeping profusely. 'The brow of the august Queen was encircled with a crown of white, red and blue roses and a glittering diadem of stars surmounted by a high and luminous *coiffure* slightly falling forward. A white tissue, also adorned with a garland of roses, covered her bosom. Under a golden apron shone a starry gown, studded with pearls . . . right down to her white shoes she was covered with roses of various colours; and in the midst of all the roses came a sort of flame that burned like incense and mixed with the radiant light by which Mary was surrounded.'[3]

Switching to patois when the seers failed to understand French, Mary delivered herself of the public message, imparted 'secrets' and indicated a miraculous spring.

The background to the visions was a severe economic crisis within the prolonged period of general depression in agriculture and industry that led to the 1846–7 famine and precipitated the 1848–9 revolutions. Although unions had not yet developed, socialist thought thrived in a situation of widespread poverty contrasting with the ostentatious lifestyle of the few. The Church, under attack and demoralized, was mounting a campaign against Sunday work – a frequent cause of friction between *curés* and hired labourers for whom the Lord's Day provided the only opportunity to cultivate their own plots.[4]

These social realities were reflected in the message. According to Mélanie, the Virgin complained that 'only a few old women come to the Mass and the others work on Sunday all summer. . . . During Lent people go to the butchers like dogs.' Provoked by the blasphemous language of cart-drivers, she was 'forced to let go of my Son's arm' with the result that a great famine would strike the region (all crops would fail) and children under seven would 'tremble and die in the arms of those who hold them'.[5]

Aware of a centuries-old local tradition of apparitions to shepherds, the police accused the two of disturbing the peace. Thousands of lapsed Catholics throughout the Midi returned to the fold as news of the visions spread. Up to 60,000 pilgrims a day were soon gathering at the mountain site to implore deliverance from the impending cataclysm. But the majority of clergy who had studied the case rejected its supernatural claims despite the 'huge profits which the influx of pilgrims and the sale of La Salette water . . . assured to certain priests and to the whole diocese'.[6]

The first of a series of articles by Louis Veuillot cautiously promoting the 'miracles' appeared in the *Univers* in February 1847, while the (Catholic) *Gazette de Lyon* took a less enthusiastic line. The national and provincial non-Catholic newspapers – republican and royalist – launched a scathing attack. For the pro-government Paris *Constitutionnel,* the panic caused by the apparition at such a moment of crisis qualified it as 'a crime'. To fight it was in the 'real interest' of religion.[7] The republican *National* spoke of the 'thirty miracles of

1846' of which La Salette was merely the latest.[8] And the local *Patriote des Alpes* (Grenoble) considered the events a 'stupid invention swallowed by the imbecility of some, exploited by the brazen-faced charlatanism of others'.[9]

Defying outraged educated opinion and mounting hostility among moderate clergy, the octogenarian Bishop of Grenoble, Mgr Philibert de Bruillard, an ex-Congréganiste, backed the erection in May 1848 – less than three months after the revolution – of the Archconfraternity of Notre-Dame de la Salette. The new division soon counted on 80,000 members to fight 'blasphemy, the profanation of the Lord's Day, intemperance, neglect of penance and prayer'.[10]

In consultation with Rome in September 1851 Mgr Bruillard declared the apparitions worthy of belief. The following year Pius IX indulgenced the archconfraternity and sanctuary, where the Bishop laid the foundation stone of a basilica that would cost $700,000.[11] That year also saw the foundation in Grenoble of a new congregation: Missionaries of Our Lady of La Salette, which by the turn of the century was training priests in the United States.[12] By 1854 there were 800 monuments to the Virgin of the Alps in France, Spain and Italy, with sanctuaries of La Salette throughout the world. Even Dahomey – 'one of the darkest spots of the Black Continent'[13] – had its own replica of the Alpine shrine.

Controversy within the French Church, however, did not evaporate. Oddly, opponents were able to cite the Curé of Ars – the very man who used to carry around 'a piece of the rock on which the Blessed Virgin stood'[14] and had distributed pictures of Our Lady of La Salette by the thousand. Vianney's ardour for the Madonna of the Alps cooled in 1849 after an interview with Maximin Giraud, who admitted he had 'seen nothing' but refused to withdraw his false testimony on the grounds that 'it does good. Many people have been converted.'[15] The saint reverted to the cult eight years later, having supplicated successfully for a 'temporal favour' to the Virgin under her title of La Salette.[16]

In 1852 another version of the events appeared in *Valley of Lies*, a pamphlet by local curés Déléon and Cartellier, who repeated their allegations of a conspiracy in a memorandum to the pope in 1854 signed by 54 priests of the Grenoble diocese. The sceptics claimed that an eccentric ex-nun, Mlle Constance Saint-Ferréol de la Merlière, convinced of her mission to save France, had played the role of the Virgin in the Alpine meadow. Her attempts to sue for libel were impeded by local magistrates who considered the shrine 'the work of the fanaticism, credulity or the cupidity of certain priests'.[17]

In the meantime Mgr Ginouilhac succeeded de Bruillard in the see of Grenoble and at first attempted to silence the affair, expelling Maximin from the seminary for lying.[18] But before long the bishop was obliged to accept the economic benefits of the sanctuary, and in 1866 he opposed an episcopal nomination on the grounds of the candidate's 'obstinate incredulity to the miracles of La Salette, which is at once a source of embarrassment and wealth.'[19] Ginouilhac was supported by papal secretary of state Antonelli, who used his veto against the nominee (Gérin of Grenoble), citing the latter's lack of respect for his local Marian shrine and the temporal power.

What went wrong with La Salette – dismissed by today's Catholic scholars as a 'turbid uncertainty'[20] – was the failure of the Church to control the seers. At first they cooperated, sending details of their 'secrets' in episcopally-sealed envelopes to the curious Pius IX in 1851. The gist of these was leaked when Mélanie asked how to spell 'Antichrist' and what 'infallibility' meant.[21] Yet neither child embraced a role proper to one who had beheld the Blessed Virgin. Maximin, whose 'manners, gestures, look – his whole exterior in fact' was 'repulsive' to the Bishop of Orleans,[22] ended up bankrupt after launching a drink called 'Salettine'.[23] As a wandering Carmelite released from her vows, Mélanie caused an even worse sensation. In 1879 – the year of the statue's pontifical coronation – she decided to publish the secret (on which the Virgin had unaccountably placed an embargo until 1858). Its contents heaped obloquy on the French clergy.[24]

Mary had told Mélanie that the 'ministers of my Son, the priests, by their bad life, by their irreverences and their impiety in celebrating the holy mysteries, by the love of money, the love of honours and pleasures, the priests have become cloacae of impurity. Yes, the priests invite vengeance and vengeance is held over their heads.'

The nemesis to which the Virgin refers is nothing less than Antichrist's installation in Rome and the end of the world. The apocalyptic picture embraces every major feature of the vision of St John the Divine: famine, earthquakes, meteorological irregularities, 'contagious diseases', persecution, revolutions and wars in which 'the world will become like a desert'. Added to the scriptural model are maledictions on Napoleon III, secularism, materialism, atheism and bad books. Neither the *patrie* nor the family are cherished. The spirit of evil will enter the cardinals and convents ('putrified flowers of the Church') as 'in the year 1884, Lucifer with a great number of demons will detach themselves from hell' and obliterate the faith on earth. In spite of everything, the pope will persevere, with Mary's support: 'The Holy Father will suffer much. I shall be with him to the end. . . .' Mary's tender prerogative of pardon in the heavenly judiciary will be sustained.

Mélanie passionately concludes: 'The Holy Virgin was crying almost all the time she spoke to me. Her tears flowed slowly one after another as far as her knees; then, like sparks of light, they disappeared. They were brilliant and full of love . . . the tears of our tender Mother, far from diminishing her air of majesty, of Queen and Mistress, seemed, on the contrary, to beautify her, to render her more lovable, more beautiful, more powerful, more full of love, more maternal, more ravishing; and I would have eaten her tears, which made my heart leap with compassion and love. . . .'

The backward girls who formed subsequent links in the apparitional chain were not the only ones whose imagination was fired by Mélanie's description. Writers like Joris-Karl Huysmans and Léon Bloy were drawn to the 'mystery' of La Salette.[25] And for the rest of the century the shrine was a centre of romantic reaction – not without some sinister associations.[26]

14

REVOLUTION AND COALITION

Socialism is an angel that has descended to earth from the heavens in order to relieve and to heal the ills and sufferings of humanity.[1]

The republican press, 1849

The precarious order of the Congress of Vienna, shaken by the events of 1830–1, was again under siege. The tidal wave of revolution that passed from Sicily to Berlin at the end of the 1840s was more intense, complex and multifarious. The socioeconomic transformations of the last decades had generated frustrations and contradictions which exploded in the revolts of peasants, proletarians and artisans (anti-usury riots, occupation of land, destruction of machinery, tax-strikes), and in the bourgeoisie's nationalist-liberal rebellion against the Rome-Vienna axis and remnants of 'feudalism'. Anticlericalism was, of course, a central feature of the revolt, though less so than in 1830, starting with the sectarian civil war in Switzerland. Clashes between Protestant and Catholic cantons resulted in the expulsion of Jesuits and their 'affiliates', Liguorians, Marianists and the Sisters of St Vincent de Paul. The assassination in Rome of the pope's minister followed in 1848, while religious orders – especially the Society of Jesus – suffered attacks from 'the mob' in Loreto,[2] Lyons, Turin, Milan, Vienna, Naples and other cities, as well as the loss of many of their privileges.

The papal and Habsburg courts fled, and laic constitutions were proclaimed in both centres, emancipating Protestants and Jews. The 'sect' led by Mazzini and other patriots was now in charge of the eternal city.[3] For a while fraternities and democratic clubs also controlled Venice, Tuscany and Lombardy. In France the February Revolution (1848) overthrew the House of Orleans and the Second Republic was proclaimed.

Although possibly fuelled by the recently-translated *Communist Manifesto*, which reached Paris in the summer of 1848, the French insurrections and revolutionary programme of these years were, to a great extent, responding to strong and articulate Christian convictions, as recent studies have conclusively shown.[4] 'The French Communists,' said Engels in 1843, 'belonging to a nation well-known for its unbelief, are themselves Christians. One of their favourite maxims is "Christianity equals Communism", and with the help of the Bible they seek to demonstrate the truth of this. . . .'[5] In fact, the Gospels and the ideal of evangelic freedom and simplicity provided a platform for political action. After Louis-Philippe's flight, demonstrators in Paris were chanting, 'Long live the true Republic . . . of Christ!'[6] *Le Christ Républicain*, a broadsheet which appeared around this time, poured scorn on the god of 'vestry tartuffes', devotees, beati and monks.[7]

The acclamation of Christ as a model for peasants and craftsmen was commonplace. Statues of Christ the Worker were erected and Jesus the Carpenter was adopted by many trade organizations. Seen as 'the first communist' and an exemplary figure of fraternal love, he was often pictured as a revolutionary hero. His portrait, with a caption taken from Lamennais, replaced the traditional image of the Virgin in a Corpus Christi procession. No less significant were lithographs of Marianne, the republican goddess, as 'the gateway to the heavenly city'.[8]

The Paris insurrection led by Blanqui was effectively repressed (June 1848) and the Solidarité Républicaine outlawed in January 1849. During the summer of that year Napoleon sent troops against Rome, bringing about – in combination with Austrian and Neapolitan forces – the fall of the Second Republic (July 1849). French protests against this betrayal led to further repression and banishments. The Voltairean-Gallican bourgeoisie was now closing ranks with its former ultramontane enemies to constitute a formidable coalition – the Party of Order – which enabled the Church to regain much of the power and wealth lost during the Orleanist régime.[9] About one-third of the predominantly rural electorate was disenfranchised in 1850[10] and, in the same year, the *Loi Falloux* restored clerical privileges in education. The Little Brothers of Mary, for example, eventually obtained (June 1851) the long-desired decree whereby they were allowed to acquire property without restrictions and were exempted from military service. 'Sceptical' teachers were blamed for much of the chaos, and a purge of the education system followed. The education budget fell by two million francs between 1852 and 1859 while allocations to the Catholic clergy rose by nearly six million, the final figure representing more than twice what was spent on education.[11]

The bloody coup d'état of Louis Napoleon (December 1851) brought a great uprising organized by hundreds of secret societies operating mainly in the centre and south of the country. Demonstrations replete with symbolism were seen once again. In Provence crowds with red flags were led by the evocative figure of the 'goddess of liberty' – a beautiful woman clad, like Mary Immaculate, in a blue cloak, albeit with a red lining.[12]

The French army, said Pius IX, had saved France and Europe from 'fatal and bloody riots hatched by the men of anarchy'.[13] And in 1853 his legate placed a crown studded with diamonds and emeralds on the statue of Notre-Dame des Victoires.

The alliance between Church and Empire[14] thrived by and large during the boom of the 1850s, despite tensions and cracks. An interesting manifestation of the 'coalition of guardroom and sacristy' (Montalembert) was the baptism of the Prince Imperial in 1856, at which the French hierarchy represented the pope as godfather. The occasion was marked by the extension of the feast of the Sacred Heart to the universal Church.[15]

When the Crimean War (1854–6) took fire from a monks' row over the Holy Places, Napoleon III championed Catholicism against the Orthodox 'schismatics', sending a picture of the Immaculate (glorified by the recent dogma) as a standard for the fleet in the Black Sea.[16]

Images of the Blessed Virgin destroyed during the revolution – such as the ancient wooden statue at Chartres and the Madonna of Le Puy – were re-erected with enthusiastic government help. 'Our Lady of France', a colossus fashioned from the molten steel of 213 captured Russian cannons, was entrusted to the Bishop of Le Puy on imperial orders.[17] Standing on a globe, the statue is crowned with stars and bears the inscription 'Salve Regina!' The serpent under her heel measures seventeen metres.[18]

15

SECOND REVIVAL:
MARY IN THE EUCHARIST

We shall honour Mary under the title of Our Lady of the Blessed
Sacrament.[1]

St Pierre Julien Eymard (d. 1868), founder and Mariologist

Faced with the horrors of revolution, Pius IX instituted the feast of
the Most Precious Blood (1848) and, on the day of the Immaculate,
1849, ordered the Italian episcopate to step up missions and Spiritual
Exercises. In Spain some bishops called for the restoration of the
Inquisition; and the Assumptionist campaign – soon to become a
right royal enterprise – was launched in June 1849. The following
month, St Antonio Maria Claret (1807–70), illustrious propagator of
all Marian devotions and future confessor to Isabel II,[2] founded in
Catalonia the most important Spanish congregation of the century,
the Sons of the Immaculate Heart of Mary. Pilgrimages and
processions, rosary campaigns and indulgences,[3] were reactivated all
over Europe, including Germany, where the number of supplicants
at Kevelaer rose noticeably.[4] The free communication now permitted
between Rome and her subjects in France and Germany enhanced
the presence and prestige of both pontiff and orders, now seen
through new eyes. After the revolution even the Düsseldorf police
printed and distributed Jesuit sermons in 1851 'to help restore law
and order in a city which had been a centre of radical democracy
during 1848–9'.[5]

This was the conjuncture Rome took to open the final debate on
the Virgin's birth – a matter central for 'scientific Mariology'. The
Immaculate Conception declaration (1854) laid a sound basis for the
renewal of ecclesiastical authority and militant Marianism.

After 1853 the Society of Jesus grew steadily, its influence
spread by satellite congregations and the proliferation of sodalities
and institutes of education[6] and charity such as the Sisters of the
Sacred Heart of Mary. This congregation, with Ignatian rule and

the motto 'All for Jesus through Mary', appeared in 1849 in Beziers, the Communist stronghold of Languedoc. Leading the legitimist party, the Jesuits were particularly powerful in the Midi (Marseilles and Toulouse) acting through their own organizations, the press and the conferences of St Vincent de Paul. In Provence they controlled education as well as the *confréries de pénitents* and *sociétés de secours mutuels*.[7] At Le Puy they formed the Labourer Brothers of St Jean-Francois Regis (1850), who ran 'model farms for the education of poor children'.[8] In mid-century the Society in many German cities organized 'Marianic' confraternities strictly on class lines to fight subversive ideas.[9] These brotherhoods, occupied with devotion to Mary and prefiguring corporativism, were somewhat akin to Masonic lodges, and with their emphasis on chastity, temperance and renunciation created an atmosphere not unlike that provided by the Protestant ethic.[10]

Mary and the Church were still more closely associated through the Eucharist, and the spirit of expiation returned with a vengeance, particularly in France, where countless divisions emerged. In Paris in 1848 Christ commanded Théodelinde Dubouché (Marie-Thérèse du Coeur de Jésus, d. 1863) to found the Congrégation de l'Adoration Réparatrice. The following year, at Villefranche-sur-Saône, Caroline Lioger (Mère Marie Véronique, d. 1883) was called from the tabernacle to a life as 'victim'. Guided by a Sulpician, she typified the revamped seventeenth-century French mysticism. Consecrated to the Immaculate Conception, she founded on 8 December 1856 – with a vow of self-immolation – the Institut de Victimes du Sacré Coeur de Jésus. After the creation of the Institute ('under the maternal protection of the august Queen'), Mother Marie Véronique took a mystical trip to Nazareth, where Our Lady instructed her in the mysteries of love, and she obtained a miraculous cure through the intercession of Notre-Dame de la Salette.[11] The foundress was encouraged by Pius IX and Fr Giraud, superior of the Missionaries of Our Lady of La Salette (1852), a man no less driven by the spirit of self-immolation. Lighting this stony path was the 'dispensatrice des grâces'.[12] As Marie Véronique declared, 'The Victim Soul cannot live without union with Mary'.[13] 'Mystically crucified' with Christ, Mary supplies the very substance of the Eucharist: as 'Vierge Prêtre' who offered Jesus as 'a perfect holocaust', she represents the suffering Church.[14]

The dominant force behind the cardio-Marian-Eucharistic cult during the revolution was, predictably, the Society of Jesus. At Vals in 1848 Fr Lyonnard founded the Archconfraternity of the Agonizing Heart of Jesus and the Compassionate Heart of Mary for the Salvation of the Dying. In 1854 Fr Drevon formed the Association of the Communion of Reparation, canonically erected some years later in Paray-le-Monial and eventually absorbed by the fast-growing Apostleship of Prayer. The Communion of Reparation set out to console the Heart of Jesus 'in union with the Blessed Virgin',[15] pray for the pope and obtain conversions.

After a Eucharistic rapture in Paris in 1847 the Spanish viscountess Micaela Desmaisières López (d. 1865, canonized 1934) founded, under Jesuit guidance, the Congregación de Adoratrices Esclavas del Santísimo Sacramento (1856).[16] The Belgian baroness Emilie d'Hooghvorst (d. 1878), who experienced an inner vision on the day of the proclamation of the Immaculate Conception,[17] founded three years later the Society of Mary Reparatrix, orientated to worship of the Host. The director was Fr Paul Ginhac (d. 1895), a saintly Jesuit who supervised another congregation under Ignatian rule, the Society of Marie Auxiliatrice.[18]

A Romantic propagator of the Blessed Sacrament devotion was the former concert pianist Hermann Cohen (1821–70), rescued by Mary from 'the darkness of the synagogue'.[19] The pupil of Liszt, friend of George Sand, and darling of artistic high society was transformed into one of the century's most active Marian preachers through a mystical experience – of a Eucharistic nature. Cohen's fealty to Mary – 'Ark of my covenant' and 'Mother of the Eucharist' – was absolute.[20] He attributed his recovery from an eye condition to the mediation of Our Lady of Lourdes and also energetically promoted La Salette. The celebrated convert joined the Vincentian conferences in 1847 and the following year he founded, in the church of Notre-Dame des Victoires, the Association of Nocturnal Adoration (an archconfraternity since 1858). A few months later he entered the Carmelites – 'an Order of true Israelites'[21] – as Fr Marie-Augustin of the Most Blessed Sacrament.

An even more important champion of the devotion was Cohen's director, the Marist St Pierre Julien Eymard (1811-68), whose writings on Mary and the Eucharist represented a Mariological breakthrough.[22] Eymard created the Third Order of Mary within the Marist conglomerate and after a 'triple apparition'[23] at the shrine of Fourvière in 1851 he formed in Paris two congregations (fathers and sisters), a league of priests and a flourishing confraternity devoted to Mary and Eucharistic adoration. He also directed Mme Emilie Tamisier in her labours to prepare 'the social reign of Christ through the Eucharist'.[24] A friend of the Curé of Ars whose body had similarly evaded decomposition, Eymard prophesied that 'devotion to Our Lady of the Blessed Sacrament will grow with the worship of the Eucharist'.[25]

'A special devotion to the Blessed Sacrament and to the Blessed Virgin; zeal for the triumph of the Church . . .'[26] were equally fundamental to the rule of the most significant missionary institution to develop during the Second Empire: the Augustinian Congregation of the Assumption, whose members first took vows in 1850. The Assumptionists, who were to provide the organizational and propaganda framework for mass pilgrimages against the Third Republic and later to spearhead anti-Semitic agitation, grew from the aristocratic College of the Assumption founded at Nîmes by Père Emmanuel d'Alzon in 1843.

D'Alzon's devotional approach – the so-called Assumptionist spirituality – hardly differs from Ignatian piety and counsel. As a youth he dreamt of 'a kind of religious militia'[27] and of the 'complete diffusion of Catholic truth'.[28] The Assumptionist spirit must be fired with a fearless, supernatural zeal and 'absolute submission in both actions and judgments to the directions of the Holy See'.[29] A believer in 'the fertile power of virginity', d'Alzon recommended chastity 'in defiance of the modern spirit of paganism'.[30]

His male and female congregations operated as newspaper and book publishers, teachers, and missionaries. Close collaborators of the Society of St Vincent de Paul, the Assumptionists opened numerous workmen's clubs and 'alumnats', seminaries for poor boys. As one of the main objects of the Order was to heal the schism in the east, Assumptionists were sent by the pope to Constantinople in 1863.[31] Several other foundations later sprang from d'Alzon's work, with numerous subsidiary lay associations, spreading devotion to Our Lady from Turkey to Chile.

Many of the old divisions crossed the Channel after the revolution. In 1850 the Catholic hierarchy was re-established in England, and three years later in Holland. Several major congregations were attracted to England by hopes of bringing back 'the strayed children of the mighty Mother'.[32] The Servants of Mary arrived in

1850, the year Mazenod visited London for the first time and his Oblates restored the pre-Reformation shrine of Our Lady of Grace on Tower Hill.[33] Passionists and Redemptorists also came to the dowry of Mary. Ousted by the revolution, the sons of Liguori (whose works were soon to be translated into English) opened a second house in England in 1851, angering Protestants by the sale of 'popish mummeries'.[34] It was also in this 'second spring' (Cardinal Newman) that the Venerable Hermann Cohen travelled to London with the blessing of Pius IX to found a Carmel as well as confraternities of the Holy Scapular and Nocturnal Adoration.[35]

16

TRIUMPH OF THE IMMACULATE CONCEPTION

Great indeed is Our trust in Mary . . . Her foot has crushed
the head of Satan. Set up between Christ and His Church, Mary,
ever lovable and full of grace, always has delivered the Christian
people from their greatest calamities. . . .[1]

Pope Pius IX in exile

During the longest pontificate in history (1846–78), Count Giovanni
Maria Mastai-Ferreti, who took the name Pius IX, endorsed four
apparitions in France. He declared Mary was conceived, like Christ,
without sin. He was chased out of Rome by Italian patriots and
proclaimed himself infallible.

Pio Nono started out on a reformist tack, introducing a sham
constitution[2] and flirting with the liberal Catholic dream of an Italian
confederation under the presidency of the pope; emptying the political
dungeons, excusing the Jews from sermons, installing street lighting
and laying railway lines. However, within weeks of being 'placed
inscrutably by God upon this Chair of Truth',[3] he acknowledged
the ultramontane claims about his 'living infallible authority'[4] and
condemned the 'filthy medley of errors which creeps in from every
side, and as the result of the unbridled licence to think, speak
and write'.[5] He invoked the Immaculate against 'the unspeakable
doctrine of Communism' and 'those secret sects who have come forth
from the darkness to destroy and desolate both the sacred and the
civil commonwealth.'[6]

After the 1848 revolution, the assassination of his minister, and
a humiliating flight to the kingdom of Naples, Mastai found his
'barque' would not respond in heavy 'seas of error' to anything
but the oars long wielded by the stalwarts of Ignatius. He would
return to Rome bitterly opposed to all political change and
determined that Mary and his own office be exalted to even
greater heights.

While Mazzini administered the Second Roman Republic, the exiled pope took 'refuge in the glory of Mary, seeking only her glory, completely forgetful of self'.[7] He urgently consulted the world's bishops in 1849 on the ancient Marian issue, for

> there was in the entire Catholic world a most ardent and wondrous revival of the desire that the most holy Mother of God – the beloved Mother of us all, the Immaculate Virgin Mary – be finally declared by a solemn definition of the Church to have been conceived without stain of original sin.[8]

On the feast of the Immaculate Conception that year, he issued another Marian encyclical from Gaeta: only she could smite the enemy, the 'sects' and 'pernicious fictions of Socialism and Communism', for 'her powerful patronage with God obtains what she asks for and [she] cannot be denied'.[9] Pius IX goes on to fulminate against the circulation of vernacular translations of the holy scriptures, popular with some revolutionaries (see chapter 14).

> Since these infringe the Church's rules they are consequently subverted and most daringly given a vile meaning. So you realize very well what vigilant and careful efforts you must make to inspire in your faithful people an utter horror of reading these pestilential books.[10]

The bishops responded almost unanimously in favour of the definition.[11] Not a single member of the Ibero-American episcopates was opposed. The whole siege-works of Marianism was wheeled out, especially in Italy, France and Spain, to campaign towards the glorious goal. On the pope's restoration to his throne (moved from the Quirinal to the fortified Vatican) in 1850, the Ignatian armies began to prepare the way for the declaration through the key Roman organ *Civiltà Cattolica*[12] and by means of their vast devotional network.[13] The curial commission which drew up the dogma included the vicar-general of the Redemptorists but its dominant minds were the Italian Jesuits Giovanni Peronne, who was also to shape the definition of papal infallibility, and Carlo Passaglia (who defected in 1859).[14]

Under the Society's protection, the Holy House of Our Lady of Loreto played an important part in the battle against 'the deadly virus of indifferentism and incredulity'[15] which could impede the dogma. It was in the Santa Casa that, as a dangerously ill officer of the Noble Guard, Pius had vowed to take holy orders if he was cured;[16] as pope, he visited no less than seven times the place where 'the most holy Virgin, predestined from all eternity and perfectly exempt from original sin, was conceived'.[17] Loreto also served to justify the temporal rule. 'Is it not by an unparalleled miracle', Pio Nono asked, 'that this Holy House was brought over land and sea from Galilee into Italy? By a supreme act of benevolence on the part of the God of all mercy it has been placed in our pontifical domain, where for so many centuries, it has become the object of the veneration of all the nations of the world and is resplendent with incessant miracles'.[18] With the 'intent of making the holiness of the spotless Virgin and devotion towards Our Lady of Loreto flourish from one end of the world to the other', Pius guaranteed all the indulgences granted by past popes and the confrères of the Universal Congregation of the Holy House were consecrated to Mary under her favourite title of Immaculate.[19]

Two years later a magnificent procession of cardinals, bishops, and the heads of orders assembled in St Peter's; the pope on the *sedia gestatoria* was surrounded by papal soldiers and the Swiss and Noble Guards. Overcome by emotion,[20] Pius 'burst into tears'[21] and as 'the tears ran down his cheeks'[22] read out the dogma, which, though biologically vague, left no doubt about the fate awaiting those who failed to acknowledge its truth:

> We, with the authority of our Lord Jesus Christ, the blessed
> Apostles Peter and Paul, and with Our own, do declare,
> pronounce and define that the doctrine which holds that the
> Virgin Mary was, in the first instant of her conception, preserved
> untouched by any taint of original guilt . . . was revealed by God
> and therefore is to be firmly and steadfastly believed by all the
> faithful. Wherefore if any shall presume (which God forbid) to
> think in their hearts anything to the contrary to this definition of
> Ours, let them realize and know well that they are condemned by
> their own judgment, have suffered shipwreck concerning the faith
> and have revolted from the unity of the Church, and that besides
> this they do by this subject themselves to the lawful penalties if
> they dare to signify, by word or writing or any other external
> means, what they think in their hearts.[23]

Many prelates also 'wept like children'[24] as the bells of Rome rang out and the cannon of Fort Sant Angelo thundered. It seemed to

Bishop Mazenod that 'heaven was opened over our heads and that the Church Triumphant was sharing in the transports of joy of the Church Militant.'[25] Next day the founder of the Oblates of Mary Immaculate, together with 200 other witnesses of the declaration, received a medal bearing the image of the Virgin freshly minted from a pile of Australian gold recently given to the pope.[26]

A remarkable precedent had been set which would boost the cause of papal infallibility: the dogma was declared on the pope's sole authority, demonstrating that he was the fount of truth. This 'coup d'état', as Sabatier calls it,[27] led to schism. The so-called Old Catholics, who broke with Rome in 1871, rejected the Immaculate Conception no less than the 'last straw' of infallibility.

The Immaculate Conception definition was of the essence of counter-revolution. In the opinion of a Jesuit writing a century later, the French Revolution, the upheavals of the nineteenth century and 'growing irreligiosity' convinced Rome of 'the need to proclaim the Marian dogma as a means of fostering piety among the faithful'.[28] The declaration assumed, as Croce wrote, 'a reactionary tinge almost by way of exchange for the help given by the Madonna against the recent and successfully suppressed revolutions'.[29] Seen by some as the triumph of irrationality, the definition is acknowledged by its supporters in more recent times as a master-stroke in the struggle against secular thought. 'The dogma of the Immaculate Conception killed the false optimism of the inevitable and necessary progress of man without God,' wrote Archbishop Fulton Sheen. 'Humbled in his Darwinian-Marxian-Millian pride, modern man saw his doctrine of progress evaporate.'[30] This view is not without foundation: during the year the dogma was ratified by the Virgin in person at Lourdes (1858), Darwin published *On the Origin of Species by Natural Selection*, Marx his *Critique of Political Economy* and John Stuart Mill the *Essay on Liberty*.

17

LOURDES: THE SEAL OF PAPAL INFALLIBILITY

It seems that the Blessed Virgin herself decided to confirm,
so to say, in an astounding way the judgment given, with
the applause of the whole Church, by her Divine Son's Vicar
on earth.[1]

Pope Pius XII

Marie-Bernarde Soubirous was brought up in utter poverty. The
damp, fetid slum that was her home no doubt contributed to an
early death at 35; her father was accused of stealing firewood
and flour, her mother was a drunkard.[2] To the investigative
novelist Émile Zola, the future saint seemed 'an exceptional case
of hysteria, afflicted with a degenerate heredity and lapsing into
infancy'.[3] Yet religion still had a place in the family's room in a
derelict prison overlooking an open sewer. Here they prayed the
'Our Father', 'Hail Mary', the Creed and the recent invocation
of the Miraculous Medal alluding to the Immaculate Conception.
Gaining work as a shepherdess, Bernadette carried her rosary to
pass the time.

Her visions in the grotto of Massabielle beside the river Gave
between 11 February and 16 July 1858 were of 'a beautiful lady in
white' with yellow rosary, blue sash and yellow roses adorning her
naked feet. The apparition's long white dress resembled those worn
by the Children of Mary and she held her hands, in Bernadette's
words, 'in the position of those of Our Lady on the Miraculous
Medal'.[4] Both vision and fourteen-year-old visionary made the sign
of the cross and prayed the rosary.

For centuries local shepherdesses had been boasting of encounters
with the Virgin,[5] and *curé* Peyramale ignored the girl until he learned
that the sixteenth apparition had announced in dialect, 'Que soi
l'Immaculado Councepciou'.[6] However, the young Abbé Pomian,
to whom Bernadette confessed immediately after the visions,[7] was

suspected by the police of conspiring with his sister and the sacristan to provoke a clerical sensation.[8]

News of the visions sparked off a national commotion as ultra-montanes clashed with officials who, according to the historian Maurain, were 'good Catholics' who 'found the credulity of the pilgrims ridiculous and considered prevention of the development of this devotion to be necessary in the interests of religion'.[9] The local authorities were on the point of committing Bernadette to a madhouse. Crowds converging on the grotto were turned back by troops and policemen, who cleared the makeshift shrine of its already numerous ex-votos. Among those arrested for 'trespassing' were the governess of the Prince Imperial and the redoubt-able Veuillot, whose articles did much to promote the appa-ritions.[10]

By late February the seer's ecstasies were conducted in front of thousands as she received the Lady kneeling between two soldiers – their swords drawn like archangels – and surrounded by policemen, councillors and the local branch of the Children of Mary. Candle flames burnt down between her fingers without harming her and she received the gift of supernatural speed, racing up the hill 'on winged feet'. On one occasion she 'kissed the muddy earth and ate the grass', apparently on the suggestion of the Virgin.[11] The crowd had swelled to 20,000 by early March.

Breaking her mysterious silence, the 'Blessed Evangelist of the Immaculate Conception'[12] reported that the apparition had said, 'Repentance! Repentance! Repentance!', asked for a chapel to be built on the spot and for processions to be made to it, and indicated the hidden thaumaturgic spring (on which the town's future prosperity rested).[13]

In answer to derision and opposition, 'a shower of grace and cures descended on Lourdes'.[14] A blind labourer recovered his sight by washing in the muddy waters and a mother revived her dying baby by plunging it into that icy spring. In the autumn Louis Napoleon himself intervened on the side of the Church, ordering that the grotto be kept open and pilgrimages allowed. An ecclesiastical committee of inquiry was set up, and in February 1862 the Bishop of Tarbes formally declared that the Immaculate 'truly appeared to Bernadette Soubirous ... to the number of eighteen times'. The faithful therefore could believe in the visions 'with complete confidence'.[15]

Unseemly rows broke out in the new 'City of Mary' over the exploitation of this 'second Mount Tabor' as religious authorities, political interests and property claims clashed. Less explicable is what Fr Martindale calls 'a whole series of hysterical and pathological occurrences'. Girls heard

> hidden voices, or angelic ones, proceeding from or hovering round the grotto. A perfect epidemic of visions of all the saints in turn broke out. All manner of boys and girls fell into fits and convulsions of the most violent kinds.[16]

The sickly 'witness of Mary',[17] pursued by women 'surreptitiously rubbing some medal against her dress' (Zola),[18] joined the Sisters of Charity in the nearby town of Nevers. Mgr Mérode, war minister of Piux IX, attended her clothing in 1866. Refusing to reveal the threefold 'secret' entrusted to her by Mary, she died thirteen years later clutching a certificate of plenary indulgence made out to her personally by the pope.

Miracles immediately 'sprang up around her tomb and her body as plentifully as primroses among the grass in spring'.[19] There was a great demand for relics, with requests coming from the Countess de Chambord and Their Catholic Majesties in Spain.

The strategic significance of Bernadette's revelations was obviously related to papal supremacy. 'The thread of Heaven's dealing with earth in the form of supernatural communications', (as a pious writer calls the nineteenth-century apparitions)[20] led directly from Lourdes to that other mystery of the age: papal infallibility. The link between the Immaculate Conception and infallibility is not, of course, the mere fact that Pius IX dogmatized both or that the definitions were prepared and promoted by the same faction. Far from having a coincidental gestation, the dogmas are reinforcing and complementary. They are the consummation of an alliance between Rome and 'Mary' since earliest times. As the invisible maternal supervisor of the Church becomes equal to God – or as 'pure' as the Second Person of the Trinity – so her visible paternal counterpart makes a commensurate advance. When the world questions the Chair of Peter and its prerogatives, celestial confirmation is required. In turn, this supernatural factor can be ratified only by an incontrovertible, superhuman voice: that of infallibility.

The ultramontane Count Lafond concurs:

The two dogmas of the Immaculate Conception and of Pontifical Infallibility were echoed on earth; one seems to be the reward of the other. . . . Pius IX said to the Mother of God, 'You are Immaculate of your Conception', and the Mother of God said to Pius IX: 'You are the Infallible Vicar of Truth'.[21]

In the view of a Sister of Charity, Mary's return was 'to announce to the whole earth that the definition of her Son's Vicar is the truth inscribed from all eternity, thereby crowning the august Pontiff with the diadem of infallibility.'[22] And while the trend today is towards obscuring the nexus, the original understanding was frankly admitted not so long ago. In 1948 a Jesuit authority declared that 'from her seat in Lourdes, the Virgin-Mother still confirms the dogma and the infallibility, for all who have eyes to see and ears to hear and a heart to understand.'[23]

18

INFALLIBILITY: DEATH-KNELL OF COALITION AND TEMPORALISM

there is a very close connection between the Temporal Power and the Spiritual Primacy.[1]

Cardinal Pecci (the future Leo XIII), 1860

In November 1854, as the dogma of the Immaculate Conception was about to be proclaimed in Rome, an act of the Turin parliament suppressed two thirds of the religious congregations. The formerly clericalist Piedmont was now a haven for plotters and troops loyal to Mazzini and Garibaldi, whose warcry 'Rome or Death!' was rapidly becoming the dominant slogan of the Risorgimento.

European theocracy prepared its last stand. 'Our duty is to fight . . . by the arms we have, some by speeches, others by the pen, everyone by prayer and almsgiving to St Peter's Pence. I come, said Jesus Christ, not to bring peace but a sword.'[2] One of the 'swords' used was excommunication, applied to all who attacked the God-given civil power of the pontiff.[3] The other was the papal army, the reorganization of which was undertaken by Archbishop Xavier de Mérode, a former Belgian army officer.

The 4,000 Swiss Guards and regular French troops stationed in Rome were swelled to a force of around 15,000 by volunteers from Austria, Ireland, France, Belgium, Spain, Portugal and Poland. The social elite served in the Tirailleurs Franco-Belges, known since 1861 as the Zouaves pontificaux. The legitimist nobility was massively represented among these 'new crusaders', who established the Congregation of the Holy Virgin of the Zouaves, dedicated to the Immaculate Conception.[4] The regiment was commanded by Count de Becdelièvre and Baron de Charette (the standard of the latter, grandson of the Duke de Berry, was the Sacred Heart on a white field).[5] Fellow officers included the Marquis de Pimodan (posthumously created Duke de Castelfidardo by Pius IX) and scions of the Chevigné and Bourbon-Chalus families. Léon de Lamoricière, veteran of the French army in Africa, had overall command of the papal forces.[6] The secret societies were accused of mining the Zouaves' barracks.[7] 'We must make war on the traitors within our walls', General Lamoricière wrote to the pope on 7 September 1860.[8]

The first 'martyr' in the disastrous battle of Castelfidardo, fought within sight of the Santa Casa on 18 September 1860, was a member of the Society of St Vincent de Paul, 'voluntarily offered to God on the altar of Our Lady of Loreto'.[9] Hopelessly outnumbered by Piedmontese invaders, the Zouaves were routed after putting up a heroic resistance. The month before, Lamoricière had knelt before the image of the Madonna in the Holy House, imploring her to bless his sword.[10] Earlier, the Zouaves presented the pope with a banner of Our Lady of Victories, each receiving in exchange a Miraculous Medal.[11] The night before the battle they took Holy Communion at the shrine; and 'having the image of the Virgin in their hearts' and wearing the scapular, 'that buckler of the children of Mary',[12] ran upon the enemy shouting 'Jésus! Marie! Vive le Pape! Vive la France!'[13] Two thirds of the tiny corps perished, falling with their gaze on the dome of the sanctuary.[14] A survivor wrote, 'It was sweet to think, my good Mother, that a ball could perhaps put me with you in five minutes.'[15] The wounded were cared for inside the sanctuary by the Sisters of Charity. 'It was not without a great plan of God', commented Lamoricière, 'that Christian blood ran down the walls of the Holy House of Loreto.'[16]

Although Napoleon III kept on the garrison at Rome for strategic purposes, his coalition with the French clerical party had begun to break up by 1859. The astonishing growth of lay associations and congregations, particularly the enlargement of the Jesuit and Vincentian spheres of influence, alarmed the government, which started to implement measures to counter this rebuilt political muscle. Press censorship was relaxed, exiles allowed to return and rights of assembly and strike granted.

In 1860 a memorandum by Rouland (then minister of religion) denounced the power wielded by the papacy: 'Rome rules the clergy and the Church of France, and through the clergy and the Church she intends to rule the country'.[17] Indeed, this tendency to dominate was 'the inevitable result of the transformation of a man, the pope, into the infallible and absolute vicar of Jesus Christ on earth.'[18] To Rouland's mind, the congregation and charitable institutes had become a sort of freemasonry which linked up the whole spectrum of society. Shortly after this broadside, the *conférences* of St Vincent de Paul, along with the Masonic lodges, were obliged to apply for authorization and accept imperial appointment of their president. The *conseil général* refused to submit and was consequently outlawed in January 1862. The *Univers* was also suppressed.

As minister of public instruction in 1865, Rouland proposed the disclericalization of primary schools, for, in his view, Catholicism was hindering the development of modern education. Reflecting widespread fears of the 'secret control' exercised on women by priests, Rouland was eager to break the clerical grip on girls' education. His alternative programme was fiercely attacked by the hierarchy as likely to despoil French womanhood of its chastity and piety. It was around this time that the Sisters of the Holy Humility of Mary were refused teaching diplomas and prevented from opening schools.[19]

The resurgent anticlericalism of the government was met with an even more fervent public devotionalism and material support for the beleaguered pope. Processions – now encountering impediments – were transformed into legitimist demonstrations,[20] visions were officially endorsed,[21] long-forgotten relics paraded through the streets,[22] and more sodalities of expiation canonically erected.[23] Lourdes and the messages of Mary were again a focus of resistance and agitation. In May 1866 thousands of pilgrims gathered for the blessing of a new church at the Pyrenean sanctuary. 'Triumphal arches' spanned the streets and everywhere 'the eye encountered inscriptions in honour of Mary'.[24] Cannons roared as the bishop made his appearance and there were resounding shouts of 'Long live Our Lady of Lourdes!'[25]

Enthusiasm for the Temporal cause was renewed by Castelfidardo, especially in France, where national pride was at stake. Under the protection of the archangel, the Confraternity of St Michael was founded in Vienna in 1860 'to collect gifts as Peter's Pence for the oppressed pope'.[26] The Roman Archconfraternity of St Peter's Chains was formed to instil veneration for the apostle's fetters and loyalty to the pope, who offered indulgences to those who raised funds for military purposes.[27] In 1867 the re-equipped and augmented Zouaves contributed to a major victory over the Garibaldians at Mentana. But piece by piece the pontifical domains were liberated either by the Red Shirts (given to the destruction of images and relics)[28] or the soldiers of Victor-Emmanuel, whose capital was now at Florence. Only the tiny Patrimony of St Peter remained.

While the spirited resistance of the last autarch of Rome did not disappoint many of his followers, leading moderates like the Count de Montalembert were trying to avoid conflict with the new claims of the state and its citizens by asserting – at the Catholic congress at Malines in August 1863 – that liberty of conscience was 'most precious, sacred, legitimate and necessary'.[29] Rome's response to the reformers was the devastating *Quanta Cura* – issued, significantly, on the feast day of the Immaculate Conception, 1864 – condemning the insanity (*deliramentum*) of 'liberty of conscience and worship' and the 'mischievous vanity' of free discussion.

The encyclical – accompanied by the *Syllabus of Errors* with its repudiation of 'progress, liberalism and modern civilization'[30] – invoked the Mediatrix, 'who has destroyed all heresies throughout the world'. The Vatican initiative of publishing a comprehensive list of ideological heresies was launched in the year of the Immaculate Conception declaration (1854), when an ad hoc commission was appointed. An independent condemnation of modern thought by the Bishop of Perpignan in 1860 gave the theologians a greater sense of urgency, but it was not until Montalembert's highly popular speech in Belgium – and the convention signed by Napoleon III and the Italian crown (September 1864) – that the pope gave orders for immediate action; 1864 was also the year in which the First Communist International met in London and the legal right to strike was won in France.

Apart from the central issue of religious tolerance, other 'errors' in the Syllabus included the 'pests' of 'socialism, communism, secret societies, biblical societies, clerico-liberal societies'.[31] The principles and methods of scholasticism and Church privileges in education were reasserted, separation of Church and state condemned and civil divorce rejected. As the papal army regrouped after Castelfidardo, the right to use force in defence of the Temporal power – inessential according to Montalembert – was upheld.

The culmination of this regression was the Vatican Council (1869–70), the first event of its kind since Trent (1545–63). In the judgment of an eminent Lutheran historian, 'It was an act of isolation and hostility; the theory on which the modern state . . . rests was to be destroyed'.[32]

Since the pope announced in 1864 (the year of the Syllabus) his intention of calling an 'ecumenical council', devotionalist pressure groups, organized around religious congregations and the hierarchy itself, intensified their campaigns. Among the more popular issues were the Assumption of the Blessed Virgin (petitioned by 200 bishops) and the consecration of the world to the Sacred Heart – sponsored by the Apostleship of Prayer and 272 bishops. The Marian belief, however, was not put on the agenda and deliberations on the Sacred Heart were interrupted by the Franco-German war and the Italian invasion of Rome. A postulatum signed by 510 Fathers calling on the Jewish people to acknowledge Jesus as the Messiah was also shelved.

A compensatory measure taken on the demise of Temporal power, the declaration of papal infallibility had wide implications. Ecclesiastical power, the Fathers taught, is exercised 'not only in the realm of conscience . . . and [is] sacramental, but external and public – it is absolute and entire, namely, legislative, judicial and coercive. The Pastors have this power from Christ, and they exercise it freely and independently of any secular domination.'[33] The final constitution speaks not only of the pope's infallibility *ex cathedra* in 'defining doctrines concerning faith and morals' – the vague phrase stressed today – but 'also in those things which belong to the discipline and government of the Church spread throughout the world'.[34]

The theory of this massive power in the hands of one man was based on the writings of Aquinas, who, as Professor Küng has shown, made out his case for the Petrine primacy in 'a work that positively teems with quotations from forged documents'.[35] Infallibility has been called the 'triumph of Jesuitism'[36] and Giovanni Perrone, professor of dogmatic theology at the Roman College, is acknowledged as the leading 'father' of the definition.

Liguorianism made a lesser-known contribution: a volume prepared by the Redemptorists on their founder's teachings on the supremacy and infallibility of the pontiff. St Alphonsus, 'whose devotion to the Holy See was so conspicuous' (Pius IX),[37] was accorded the title *Doctor Ecclesiae* a few months later, on 7 July 1871. Liguori's elevation infuriated the great German theologian and historian Fr Ignaz von Döllinger, who labelled the saint's writings 'a magazine of lies'.[38] As for the dogma itself, it had destroyed 'the ancient Church Episcopate in its innermost essence'.[39]

The Catholic press – overwhelmingly ultramontane – made strenuous efforts to influence the secret proceedings. Civiltà Cattolica suggested that the Assumption be proclaimed at the same time, and Louis Veuillot opened a Roman salon to leak information favourable to the infallibilist cause.[40]

Initially, opposition was particularly strong among the majority of German bishops. Although unwilling to step openly out of line, the German, Austrian and Hungarian episcopates privately begged the pope not to declare himself infallible. The French hierarchy were divided into three groups: outright supporters, a small group of opponents and a larger number of 'inopportunists', who believed that the pope was infallible but they did not wish to say so at that moment. The vast majority of the 272 Italians who made up over one third of the council were in favour of the proclamation, and the 41 Spanish prelates were behind the pope to a man.[41] Chief whip of the infallibilists was Cardinal Manning of Westminster, who believed that 'visions, if true, are at all times acts of omnipotence and no human intelligence can prescribe limits to their effect'.[42]

Resistance to the pope's wishes was effectively met with intimidation: dismissals of curial staff, the destruction of documents and the threat of episcopal deposition.[43] The final vote was 451 in favour, 62 conditionally so, and 80 against. Out-of-step bishops were required to submit later in writing and promulgate the declaration in their diocese. Everyone did so.

The pope's authority was now independent of the whole body of believers. His definitions, 'of themselves – and not by virtue of the consent of the Church', were 'irreformable'.[44] And 'if anyone shall presume (which God forbid!) to contradict this Our definition, let him be anathema!'[45] Denied access to the Catholic press, the dying Montalembert wrote to a friend that 'justice and truth, reason and history' had been sacrificed 'as a holocaust to the idol that has been set up in the Vatican'.[46]

The issue of infallibility was, together with the Immaculate Conception, the flashpoint for a revolt led by Catholics in the recently united Germany. The Austrian government's immediate abrogation of the concordat (on the grounds that the nature of the papacy had been essentially altered)[47] was followed by the secession of the Old Catholics at their Munich congress of 1871. These 'schismatics' eventually comprised a communion of small churches in Germany, Switzerland; the Netherlands (incorporating the Jansenist 'Chapter of Utrecht'), Austria, Czechoslavakia, Poland and Croatia. In Germany, where they were predominantly bourgeois with a leadership of higher academics and bureaucrats, the neo-Protestants condemned 'abuses . . . in the granting of indulgences, veneration of the saints, use of scapular medallions. . . .'[48] Violent clashes occurred when a law passed during Bismarck's *Kulturkampf* gave Old Catholics right of access to their former co-religionists' churches.[49]

Excommunicated for his popular articles against infallibility, Döllinger led international Old Catholic congresses which attracted unprecedented ecumenical participation, especially from Anglicans and the Eastern Orthodox.[50]

The discord, schism and diplomatic rifts brought about by the declaration of papal infallibility were offset by its immense disciplinary and devotional potential. The dogma enhanced the universal role of the Church and fuelled the cult of Mary and her counterpart on earth. 'The Pope', Count Paganuzzi could confidently tell Italian Catholic Action in 1897, 'is, by Divine institution, the infallible guide of the human race . . . the Divine pilot of the barque of humanity.'[51]

*   *   *

Military efforts to shore up the pope's kingdom and authority were supported by new waves of piety intermingled with social and political initiatives as the 'social question' began to loom large in the peninsula. In 1865 the first step towards the creation of Catholic Action was taken in Bologna (since 1859 no longer papal territory) with the formation of a society for the defence of the Church in Italy. This ephemeral organization was succeeded in the same city by the Association of Italian Catholic Youth, founded by Counts Mario Fani and Giovanni Acquaderni in June 1867. This 'nucleus out of which Catholic Action developed'[52] was dedicated to resisting the unification of Italy with Rome as the capital and to restoring the triple crown in lands already liberated. Granted indulgences in 1868, the Association opened youth clubs throughout the peninsula. Similar initiatives in Rome were the Society of Veterans of Wars of the Holy See, associations of artisans and workers, the Pious Union of Catholic Ladies and the Sodality for the Care of Domestic Servants.

By far the most enterprising champion of Marian Catholic Action and the pope's prerogatives was the Turin-based St John

Bosco (1815–88). A fierce opponent of Jewish and Waldensian emancipation, and leading Temporalist for whom Mary represented 'a special auxiliatrice of kings and Catholic peoples all over the world',[53] Bosco was confirmed in his vocation at the age of nine by a vision of 'a lady of noble bearing' surrounded by lambs.[54]

When the Piedmontese government declared war on Church privileges in 1850, Don Bosco, who enjoyed the patronage of the nobility, founded the first association of Catholic workmen in the kingdom: the Society of Mutual Succour. The Society of St Francis de Sales followed (1859) – the germ of one of the most successful Marian educational and missionary conglomerates. The struggle escalated when dissenters within the Church, reacting to Mariocentric Roman absolutism, formed in 1862 the Società Emancipatrice e di Mutuo Soccorso del Sacerdozio Italiano. This Jansenist-inspired group supported free circulation of the scriptures in Italian, opposed 'irresponsible autocracy'[55] and demanded the abolition of compulsory confession and celibacy.

In May that year Bosco was granted the 'dream of two pillars', a vision of epic proportions in which the pontiff commanded his barque against the fleet of Antichrist. Two massive columns arose from the waves, one supporting a gigantic Host and the other, Mary Immaculate with the inscription 'Auxilium Christianorum'.[56] She appeared in the same month and under the same title at the Umbrian city of Spoleto in the Papal States. With Bosco's approval, the apparitions were promoted by the Osservatore Romano as an assurance of 'the triumph of the Church and her august Head' in the defence of Temporalism.[57] Gold, silver and bronze medallions of Our Lady of Spoleto were struck, which proclaimed 'Pius IX Pont Max. Romae'.[58]

The cult of Mary Auxiliatrice – to whom Bosco erected a basilica in Turin in 1868 – was similar to the Redemptorists' cult of Our Lady of Perpetual Succour, whose miraculous icon in Rome was entrusted to them by Pius IX in 1865. Devotions under both titles were spread throughout the world in a few years by the two orders and their sodalities. In 1870 Don Bosco set up the Archconfraternity of Our Lady Auxiliatrice to promote veneration of Mary (as helper of Christians) and the Eucharist. Two years later he co-founded, with St Maria Domenica Mazzarello (1837–81), the Institute of the Daughters of Mary, Help of Christians (the first missionary group of 'Salesian Sisters' left for South America in 1877). The male Salesians (priests and lay brothers) numbered over 1,000 on the founder's death, with 57 houses in Italy, Spain, France, England, Argentina, Uruguay and Brazil.

Bosco's associate the Blessed Leonardo Murialdo set up the Turin Workers' Unions in 1871. Murialdo was also active in the Opera dei Congressi, founded for the defence of the Holy See in 1874 after the first Italian parliament's sweeping anticlerical legislation. The Opera, whose president was appointed by the pope, constituted the backbone of Azione Cattolica; it endeavoured to save the working-class from 'irreligion and pauperism' through a chain of Catholic banks and mutual aid societies. Proposals for corporativist unions were made two years later at the Bergamo congress – a policy complemented by the Vatican's ban on Catholic participation in parliamentary elections (the *non-expedit* of March 1871).

Devotion to St Joseph the Worker – declared Patron of the Church in 1871 – was greatly encouraged by the Social Catholics. The 'delay that has taken place in the revelation of his glory' was caused, according to *The Messenger of the Sacred Heart*, by the patriarch's humility 'as well as the work of God's wisdom'.[59]

19

THE NATIONAL VOW AND MARIAN CORPORATIVISM

O Mary! conceived without sin, look on France, pray for France, save France. . . . Speak a word to Jesus, resting in thine arms, and France will be saved. O Jesus, once subject to Mary, save France.[1]

Daily prayer of Pope Pius IX

THE PILGRIMAGES MOVEMENT

On the pope's surrender to the Italians, Colonel de Charette of the Zouaves embarked for France, where he led the Western Volunteers against the Prussians, his standard of the Sacred Heart winning glory at Patay, Loigny and Mans. 'God requires victims', said Bernadette of Lourdes on hearing of the heavy loss of life.[2] The national humiliation of eventual defeat was followed by the Commune's assault on religion. Some 70 hostages including the Archbishop of Paris were shot in reprisal for the executions of 15,000 communards by Versailles. Pilgrims returning from Lourdes were attacked and churches desecrated. Notre-Dame des Victoires – Paris headquarters of the famous archconfraternity frequented by Princess Clotilde Bonaparte and the Empress Eugénie – was taken over by a battalion of 'Avengers of the Republic'. Revolutionaries disported themselves in sacramental robes and paraded the remains of Abbé Desgenettes' head in the streets on a pole.[3]

In May 1871 the royalist-dominated national assembly voted to offer up public prayers and 'reparation' for the evils that had befallen France, thus launching the National Vow movement. Its political aim was the restoration not only of the Most Christian Monarchy of the Bourbons but also the Temporal power in Rome through a war with the kingdom of Italy.[4] A committee was formed with branches in the provinces to promote the cause of the pope – a network enhanced in 1873 by a 'central committee'.[5]

The next step in the royalist/Temporalist campaign was the unofficial consecration of the French nation to the Sacred Heart of Jesus as requested in the vision of the Blessed Marguerite Marie. The ceremony, at Paray-le-Monial on 29 June 1871, was attended by 50 deputies, with the adherence of 150 more.[6] The third step – also in accordance with the visionary's wishes – was taken three weeks later when the national assembly voted by 389 to 146 to build the shrine of the Sacré Coeur on Loyola's hill of Montmartre in honour of the martyrs of 1871. The dispossessed pope contributed 50,000 francs towards the project.[7]

In January 1872 all Jesuit provinces were consecrated to the Sacred Heart. The ritual would be repeated for countless dioceses, institutions, families, individuals and nations in a battle against the 'apostasy of modern society'[8] master-minded by the Freemasons – or, in Pio Nono's phrase, the 'Synagogue of Satan'.[9] The bicentenary of the 'Great Apparition' in 1874 was an opportunity to recirculate Christ's message to the French king; the following year the Apostleship of Prayer handed the pope a petition signed by 535 bishops asking him to consecrate Rome and the world to the Sacred Heart, with appropriate indulgences.[10]

In 1877 a new archconfraternity of the Sacred Heart was formed at Montmartre 'to pray for the freedom of the Pope and the salvation of human society'[11] and Ramière obtained indulgences for a badge with the inscription 'Thy Kingdom Come'.[12] Over the next decade, with full support from Rome,[13] the Apostleship of Prayer launched a programme of consecration of families. The formula read: 'In order to hasten in our dear country the reign of thy adorable Heart, O Jesus, we consecrate under the protection of the Immaculate Heart of Mary and under the patronage of Saint Joseph, our whole family.'

Millions followed the urgent call, filling innumerable volumes of the 'golden books of the Sacred Heart'.[14]

Integral to the National Vow movement were the mass pilgrimages organized by the Assumptionist Order, the nobility and the demobbed officers under the white flag of the Count de Chambord, the legitimist pretender. Recent extensions of the railways and excursion tickets – as well as highly centralized backing and publicity for new and rejuvenated apparitional destinations – made possible a revival of unprecedented dimensions of the ancient custom of visiting shrines. The pilgrimages were undertaken, wrote Count Lafond, 'in the midst of our patriotic woes, for the health of France and the deliverance of the Pope, for we have two terrestrial fatherlands . . . France and Rome'.[15] The official prayer of the national pilgrimages stated that 'because the Sovereign Pontiff, head and infallible doctor of the Church, holds on earth the place of Jesus Christ, we submit entirely to him in the moral order as in our public and social life'.[16]

In 1871 the Assumptionist superior, Fr Picard, set up the Association of Our Lady of Salvation, which included 'members of the oldest families in France'[17] as stewards of the pilgrimages. The declared aim of the Association was 'the salvation of France by prayer and by the return of the working classes to Catholic morality. Although it does not neglect the material lot of the working man, the principal means employed are supernatural.'[18] Established in 80 dioceses, the Association encouraged 'social and national expiation' and opposed 'social apostasy and isolation in piety'.[19] Fr Picard also formed in 1872 a 'General Council of Pilgrimages', with such personages as the Duke de Chaulnes and Viscount de Damas, who received 'many precious indulgences' to fortify them for their task after a meeting in Rome with Pius IX.[20] The Council's weekly, the *Pèlerin*, had 80,000 subscribers.[21]

The first national pilgrimage – to La Salette in 1872 – drew 375 priests and their flocks.[22] In October 'vassals of Mary' from all over France gathered at Lourdes to proclaim 'Regnum Galliae, Regnum Mariae'.[23] The following year, the organizing committees mobilized over three million pilgrims, including 250,000 at Lourdes, where prayers were offered for the restoration of the monarchy and Temporal power;[24] messages were sent to Rome in support of the Syllabus of Errors and infallibility.[25]

Hymns sung at Lourdes were rousing: 'Rome groans under an oppressive yoke! But we shall see the sect annihilated. . . . Let us, Sacred Heart Soldiers, all arise. . . . Let us save Rome and France. . . . Let us pray to the Virgin. She is the deliverance; she aids the avengers of the King-Pontiff!'[26]

Coronations of images highlighted the link between Mario-papalism and the monarchism for which the pilgrims were agitating. In July 1876 the papal legate, assisted by 34 bishops, crowned the statue in the Pyrenean sanctuary.[27] Soon after the coronation of Our Lady of Lourdes the Bishop of Grenoble hastened to Rome on behalf of La Salette with the crown 'that the Pope is to hallow . . . having £1,781 worth of precious stones in it'.[28] In 1879 Leo XIII delegated to Cardinal Guibert (an Oblate of Mary Immaculate) the pontifical coronation of a statue of the lachrymose Virgin before a crowd of 25,000 votaries, among them ten archbishops. As the legate lowered the crown on the 'Reconciler of Sinners' cannons roared and there were 'three cheers' for the pope.[29]

The Breton shrine at Pontmain was a typical instrument of the National Vow, built on visions that spelt out a message born of military defeat. In January 1871 the young Barbedette brothers, both of whom became priests (one an Oblate of Mary), saw a beautiful woman floating above the roof of a cottage. She was dressed, according to a contemporary account, in 'a blue robe covered with golden stars, without a belt or waistline, like a sacerdotal alb. . . . Her shoes were blue like the robe and, in the middle, a ribbon of gold made a bow in the form of a rose.'[30] Mary took up the Immaculate Conception pose (arms outstretched) and, as at La Salette, swelled to double her initial size. The Prussian withdrawal of troops from the area was attributed to this intervention.[31]

A local priest and the Sisters of Charity organized rosary vigils and took down a celestial dictation as the children 'saw' the golden letters appear one after another. The final transcript read: 'But pray, my children. God will soon answer your prayers. My Son allows Himself to be moved by compassion.'[32]

Before the year was out, royalists had presented an image of 'Our Lady of Hope of Pontmain' to Chambord,[33] and in 1873 the cult was authorized by the Bishop of Laval. Among the 100,000 visitors that year was the recently promoted General de Charette, whose banner was now a familiar sight at pilgrimages throughout the country.[34] Pius IX gave the Pontmain association for children the rank of archconfraternity, and the parish was entrusted to the Oblates of Mary Immaculate – an order already controlling scores of sanctuaries of Our Lady and of the Sacred Heart in France and in many other parts of the world.

Mary's apparitions in occupied eastern France – with a message of liberation from the Protestant yoke – drew large pilgrimages, which were broken up by the Prussian army.[35]

Her last publicized visit to France of any significance was five years later, in 1876, when a new piece of devotional equipment was launched: the scapular of the Sacred Heart. The visionary

135

of Pellevoisin, a small town in the north, was Estelle Faguette, 32-year-old consumptive servant of the Count and Countess de la Rochefoucauld. Her visions of the Virgin on receiving the last sacraments effected a cure. She was entrusted with a 'secret' and, several months later, the new scapular was revealed: a red heart in relief with a figure of the 'Mother of Mercy' on the other side – a pattern not radically different from the Green and Red Scapulars or the Miraculous Medal, which as a Child of Mary Estelle already wore.

The Missionaries of Our Lady of the Sacred Heart of Issoudun adopted Estelle's salvific device to express 'the idea of Mary's empire over the Heart of Jesus',[36] a Eudist concept. And the Cardinal Archbishop of Bourges, Prince de la Tour d'Auvergne – leader of the French infallibilists at the Vatican Council – founded the Confraternity of Our Lady of Pellevoisin to 'radiate devotion to the Sacred heart through the newly-designed scapular'.[37] Among the first members was Mgr Chigi, the papal legate. Permission to distribute the charm was later extended to the Priests of the Sacred Heart (see below) and to the Oblates of Mary Immaculate.

Accompanied to Rome in 1900 by the Duchess d'Estissac, Estelle was received by Leo XIII, who awarded an indulgence of 200 days for a prayer to the Virgin of Pellevoisin.

Gradually passing into obscurity, the shrine had a reputation in its day for curing demoniacal possession.[38] Scandals surrounding the seer – herself subject to diabolic visions[39] – moved the Vatican to deny any official belief in the apparitions in 1904 and 1907. Nevertheless, indulgences attached to the scapular of Pellevoisin were at the same time confirmed,[40] and pilgrimages continued.

With the *Kulturkampf* under way, Mary was reported to have communicated with children in half a dozen places in Germany in 1876–7. The visions drew large crowds and their promoters were prosecuted while gendarmes sealed off the abortive shrines. When the Bavarian hierarchy condemned one of these new pilgrimages, to Mettenbuch, villagers were angry at the loss of economic benefits.[41] Introducing herself as 'the Blessed Virgin, conceived without sin', Mary favoured four 'poor and very innocent young girls' in Prussian Poland in 1877.[42]

Two years later, phantasmagoric lights on a church wall in County Mayo challenged English Protestant campaigns and gave moral support to the Irish National Land League in its battle against Protestant landlords. Accompanied by St Joseph and St John the Evangelist (the latter in pontificals), Mary appeared to 15 witnesses at Archdeacon Cavanagh's church in the village of Knock. The following February a press campaign was launched to promote the visions.[43] Articles of Knock were juxtaposed with news of the Land League week after week until the end of October 1880. 'Mother we pray thee to intercede for the patriot chief' (i.e., Parnell) began one poem in praise of Our Lady of Knock.[44] Despite theories that the phenomena were caused by magic lanterns,[45] the apparitions continued and a solution of cement chipped from Knock church wall cured illnesses from Arabia to Newfoundland.[46]

THE 'SOCIAL CATHOLICS'

Closely allied to the National Vow and the pilgrimages movement were the so-called 'Social Catholics', whose aim of supplanting suffrage by a system of medieval-type guilds or 'corporations' adumbrated the fascist state. Mary, Joseph and European aristocracy played key parts in propagating this romantic alternative both to liberal capitalism and socialism. Under Mary's patronage, wrote Pius IX

> it was decided to gather together a congress of these Societies whose special purpose is to devote themselves to the interests of the workers. This Mother . . . sees the contribution which wicked men hope from them in their work of overturning public order. She has long since been trying to draw them to herself by a long and splendid series of favours and by innumerable miracles.[47]

Following the lead of Baron von Kettler, Bishop of Mainz, 'Workers' Circles' – to promote Marian corporativism – were set up under Count Albert de Mun and the Marquis de la Tour du Pin Chambly in France in 1872[48] (with Chambord's approval of their political doctrine), the Prince de Caraman Chimay in Belgium, Duke Salviati in Italy, the Prince of Liechtenstein and Baron von Vogelsang in Austria. As Leo XIII wrote to Count Balbo, president of the Piedmont Committee for the Promotion of Workingmen's Associations, 'We too believe that in this age there is no other way to fight that poison called Socialism'.[49] For Pope Leo, it seemed 'expedient to encourage associations for craftsmen and working men, which, placed under the sheltering care of religion, may render the members content with their lot and resigned to toil, inducing them to lead a peaceful and tranquil life'.[50]

One of de Mun's senior collaborators in the *oeuvre des cercles* was Fr Léon Gustave Dehon (1843–1925), founder of the Priests of the Sacred Heart of Jesus, a congregation with lay extensions dedicated to reparation, foreign missions, and social work. Currently a candidate for beatification, Dehon was an expert in social and devotional problems and consultant to the Index.

Outstanding among industrialists in the movement were Léon Harmel, author of *Essay on the Christian Corporation* (1877) and owner of a 'Christian factory'; and the philanthropist Philibert Féron-Vrau, whose ambition was to turn Lille into a 'holy city'.[51]

Harmel was keen on working-class leadership, a concept rejected by his noble associates. His spinning factory near Reims, where he was addressed as 'Father', offered an impressive range of facilities from pension schemes to a guild of the Blessed Sacrament and a branch of the Apostleship of Prayer.[52] Féron-Vrau, whose beatification process opened in 1914, supported nocturnal adoration and financed the first Eucharistic congress, at Lille in 1881. President of the Lille *conférence* of St Vincent de Paul and founder of the city's Catholic university, he was also active in the establishment of Catholic schools and newspapers.

Although the *cercles* leaders advocated worker protection (such as fixed hours of work and elimination of child labour), political discussion was forbidden among the working-class members, who were offered rest and recreation in a puritanical atmosphere[53] as well as a group identity, carrying their banner in processions and pilgrimages. Their devotions were dominated by the patroness, with chapels set aside for club use at her festivals and regular recitation of the rosary. All members wore the Miraculous Medal of the Immaculate Conception.[54]

20

POPE OF THE ROSARY AND THE SOCIAL QUESTION

Under thy virginal heel
Crushing the serpent of old
Ah! to thy servant reveal
Power of the prophets foretold:
Then shall my spirit, tho' weak,
Only of victory speak![1]

Pope Leo XIII

Spurning the royal and diplomatic privileges contained in the
Italian Law of Guarantees (1871), the politically shell-shocked
Pio Nono isolated himself from the new state whose sovereign was
now ensconced in the Quirinal. As 'the prisoner in the Vatican', he
witnessed the accession to power of the Masonic left (1876) under
Agostino Depretis. Religious processions were banned, congregations and Catholic congresses suppressed, and clergy drafted into
the army. The Romans' feelings towards the pontiff – whose rule they
had restrospectively condemned by a referendum vote of 133, 681
to 1,507 – surfaced shockingly on 12 July 1881 when the nocturnal
cortège translating his mortal remains to the church of San Lorenzo
Fuori le Mura was bombarded with stones, mud and phlegm while
the police stood by apathetically.[2]

Elected in captivity, as it were, Count Giovanni Pecci, who reigned
as Leo XIII (1878–1903), presided over a good part of the transition
from total boycott of the democratic process (in 1866 Catholics were
forbidden to vote even in municipal elections) to direct intervention
in national politics through the Partito Popolare (1919). Educated
by Jesuits at the Accademia dei Nobili Ecclesiastici, Pecci served
as chief of police in Benevento, nuncio at Brussels, and governor of
Perugia before receiving the pallium there in 1846.

Optimistic by nature, Leo's philosophy was most opposed to
'gloomy Jansenism'. From his perspective, science and faith need

not present contradictions. With due cooperation between the ecclesiastical and civil powers even the sciences, 'through that truth of which the Church is mistress, would rise speedily to a higher excellence'.[3] And the following words – addressed to the Eldest Daughter – would seem to suggest that there could be no real conflict between God and Caesar either: 'God, who is the Father of nature, from whom States receive on earth the reward of their virtues and good deeds, has conferred much prosperity on France, fame in war, the arts of peace, national glory and imperial power.'[4] Confident that the restoration of the Temporal power was divine will, the pope told ex-Zouaves and other pontifical veterans who had presented him with a diamond-studded inkstand on the occasion of his sacerdotal jubilee in 1887, 'I shall use this inkstand the day I write the decree for the reorganization of my army'.[5] Two years later, however, Leo fasted in protest as thousands marched in Rome to commemorate the 'martyrdom' of Giordano Bruno, hero of freethinkers and Masons.[6]

As pope, he is remembered for his vast contribution to the *magisterium*,[7] especially through the systematic encouragement of scholasticism[8] and Ignatian/Franciscan devotionalism. Pecci's intense Marianism covered every conceivable area: liturgical innovations like the mass of Our Lady of the Miraculous Medal,[9] the beatification of such figures as Louis de Montfort, 'slave of Mary',[10] canonical coronations from Poland to Mexico, Marian congresses,[11] Mariological studies,[12] and the teachings that have given him the popular title of 'Pope of the Rosary'. These two major aspects of his pontificate – scholasticism and Marianism – are rarely connected, though both were crystallized in the hierarchical, coporativist model.

The ideological framework on which Leo's statecraft rests is found in twelve social encyclicals known as the 'Leonine Corpus'. These teachings – 'the Church's complete answer to *Das Kapital* of Marx and, indeed, to Communism and Socialism in whatever forms'[13] – laid the foundations of state corporativism, providing an alternative to the workers' independent organizations.

Fearing secularization and pluralism, Leo also condemned 'Americanism',[14] a heresy which advocated the adaptation of Catholicism to modern American life and preferred active virtues (humanitarianism, democratic fellowship) to passive ones (humility, obedience, resignation). Americanism was clearly a tendency detrimental to traditional (Marian) devotionalism.

A tertiary himself and an ardent supporter of the Franciscan revival,[15] Leo found doctrinal inspiration in 'Franciscan spirituality' with its 'love of poverty' and 'respect for the private property of others'.[16]

In a period of industrial development and proletarian unrest Leo's utterances on social and labour relations – anticipated long ago by the Social Catholics – consolidated the work of Catholic Action, sodalities, and workingmen's clubs. The social lubricant of the rosary was to be applied mainly through these lay associations:

> battalions which fight the battle of Christ, armed with his sacred mysteries and under the banner and guidance of the heavenly Queen. How faithfully her intercession is exercised in response to their prayers, processions and solemnities, is written in the whole experience of the Church not less than in the splendour of the victory of Lepanto.[17]

The papal reading of history remained fundamentally Maistrian:[18] 'It is religion', pleads Leo in a message clearly directed at the Italian government, 'which gives rulers feelings of justice and love towards their subjects . . . which makes the poor respect the property of others; and causes the rich to make a right use of their wealth.'[19] Laws are not made 'according to the delusive caprices and opinions of the mass of the People, but by truth and justice; the ruling powers are invested with a sacredness more than human . . . public authority should be constantly and faithfully obeyed.'[20] Moreover, 'the authority of the husband is conformed to the pattern afforded by the authority of God.'[21]

Leo's strictly hierarchical, static and sacred order is certainly medieval. So was the inspiration of Professor Giuseppe Toniolo (1845–1918), founder of Christian Democracy and probably one of the ghosts of *Rerum novarum* (1891). Deeply devout – and now in the process of being beatified – Toniolo was under the spell of neo-Thomism, neo-Guelphism and the Tuscan economic order of the Middle Ages, in which he was an expert. His vision and doctrine – rejecting any form of compromise with modern capitalist society – epitomize the Leonine intelligentsia. Under Pecci, Christian Democracy was not to be given a 'political meaning'[22] and there was 'no question of fostering under this name of Christian Democracy any intention of diminishing the spirit of obedience'.[23]

Catholic Action – now gradually becoming a blanket term for all centralized social initiatives – was, according to its ultimate master, 'a powerful conservative force'[24] and 'a bulwark against the subversive theories of socialism and anarchism'.[25] Nevertheless, the movement was to keep

> outside politics, concentrated upon social and religious work, and [it] looks to raise the people by rendering them obedient to the Church and her Head . . . by inculcating respect for the principle of authority, and by lightening their load of poverty by the manifold works of Christian charity.[26]

In Spain, the Jesuit and sociologist Antonio Vicent (1837–1912) and his close associate Claudio López Bru, Marquis de Comillas (1853–1925), excelled in this task. These apostles of the gospel of Leo - the 'Patriarch of Social Catholicism'[27] and the 'Model Marquis'[28] – were the originators of modern Catholic Action in the peninsula through the systematic foundation of schools, workers' circles and propaganda. Their life mission was to fight anarchism and create an alternative labour movement based on papal teachings, with the pope as 'father of the workers'. In 1894, when the National Council of Catholic Corporations for Rural and Urban Workers was constituted in Spain, Fr Vicent organized workers' pilgrimages to the holy city, using vessels of the Marquis's line.[29]

That year labourers from all over Europe gathered in Rome to acclaim the author of *Rerum novarum*, whom the 8,000–strong Spanish contingent called the 'víctima de la perfidia de los sectarios de Satán'.[30] After recitations of the rosary at the beatification ceremony for Juan de Avila, 'Apostle of Andalusia', the pilgrims shouted 'Long live the Pope-King!' as Leo was carried around St Peter's in the gestatorial chair.[31] But attacks in Rome on trains bringing 20,000 Catholic workers from France obliged the pope to call the festivities to a premature close.

Leo's patronage of the Social Catholic movement extended to rural savings banks, cooperatives, allotments, cheap bakeries and information 'Bureaux of the People' set up to counter exploitation. He also engaged in the anti-slavery campaign, promoting for the first time pilgrimages to the Vatican for blacks and Arabs – received in audience in the Sala Ducale in 1888.[32]

The rosary, on which Pecci issued no less than ten encyclicals, is integral to his corporativism, 'For We are convinced that the Rosary, if devoutly used, is bound to benefit not only the individual but society at large.'[33] He cites three evils responsible for the 'downgrade movement of society'. They are: 'first, distaste for a simple life of labour; second, repugnance to suffering of any kind; third, forgetfulness of the future life.' The effect of the first tendency on the worker is 'to fix his gaze on things that are above him, and to look forward with unthinking hopefulness to some future equalization of property' with the result that 'the equilibrium between classes of the community is being destroyed, everything becomes unsettled, men's minds become a prey to jealousy and corroding envy. . . . For evils such as these let us seek a remedy in the Rosary'.[34]

The propitiatory rosary is also a way of physical salvation. Leo declared in 1884,

> With respect to Italy, it is now most necessary to implore the intercession of the most powerful Virgin through the medium of the Rosary. . . . Asiatic cholera, having, under God's will, crossed the boundary within which nature seemed to have confined it . . . to Mary, therefore, we must fly.[35]

In the land of the successors of Peter, Mary put in rare and fleeting appearances.[36] Some hoped the series of visions in 1888 at Castel Petroso would blossom as a 'Lourdes of Italy . . . victim of the modern heresy of liberalism'.[37] Although experienced first by peasants and then by several notables (including a bishop who testified that he had seen the Virgin of Dolours) and encouraged by the Servites,[38] the apparitions did not bear fruit.

Shortly afterwards, in 1891, papal legate Cardinal La Valetta consecrated the basilica of Pompeii, the Santuario della Madonna del Rosario. This Neapolitan shrine has its origin around 1870 in a supernatural communication to the lawyer and Assumption campaigner Bartolo Longo. Rambling on the property of his wife, the Countess of Fusco, in the valley of Pompeii (a region 'riddled with superstition and fear of the evil-eye'),[39] Longo heard a voice whisper, 'If you seek salvation, promulgate the Rosary. This is Mary's own promise'.[40]

Alongside the rosary devotion, indulgences and scapulars were central to Leonine piety. During his sacerdotal jubilee (1887–8) Pecci granted a plenary indulgence to those who came to Rome 'to offer him due honour and obedience',[41] and in 1891, the 'Leo Association' (an American confraternity engaged in prayers for the 'freedom' of the eponym) received two plenaries a year. Equally significant are two scapulars approved under Leo bearing symbols of the papacy. The scapular of St Joseph bears the image of the tiara and dove – 'The spirit of the Lord is his guide', while the scapular of the Mother of Good Counsel shows the tiara and keys, with the inscription: 'Son, follow her Counsel. Leo XIII.' Pope Leo also indulgenced new scapulars of the Immaculate Heart of Mary, the Sacred Hearts of Jesus and Mary, and the Sacred Heart (the 'scapular of Pellevoisin').

The most striking feature of the pontificate was the public projection of the cult of Mary and of Leo himself. Splendid coronations,[42] jubilees and congresses (dealing mainly with Catholic Action and the Sodality of Our Lady) were held all over the world, particularly in Italy and the Iberian sphere from the 1880s onwards. Papal and social propaganda – central aspects of Marian festivities – were emphasized. On his episcopal jubilee (1892) Leo proclaimed an anti-Masonic Holy Year[43] and granted indulgences to those who visited the Holy House of Loreto during the sixth centenary of the miraculous translation (1895). This had the double advantage of boosting revenues through alms giving and providing an object lesson in poverty:

> We gladly embrace this occasion to stir up the devotion of all the faithful towards the earthly home of the Holy Family. . . . Amid the poverty of this retired dwelling there lived those models of domestic life and harmony . . . to which we Ourselves have more than once endeavoured to recall and conform all families.[44]

After a magnificent pilgrimage in Saragossa (momentarily disrupted by a 'satanic' bomb), the image of Our Lady of the Pillar was presented with a precious chasuble bearing the pontifical arms – a personal gift from Pecci.[45] The following year (1881), as the Anarchist Workers Federation was formed in Catalonia, the Virgin of Montserrat was crowned, and proclaimed Patroness of the Catalans by Leo himself. The first of such ceremonies in Hispanic America was staged in Mexico in 1886, opening the era of Mary's official 'queenship' of the continent. The twentieth century began with the striking of new medals and numerous celebrations. In the Basque country, for instance, the Virgin of Begoña, crowned amidst flag-waving crowds and arcs of triumph, was sent a rosary of gold by Pecci bearing the effigy of the 'immortal Pontiff'.[46] The Catalonian

Mare de Deu de Misericordia received thousands of pilgrims in her shrine at Reus (1904), where the needy were fed bread and rice.[47]

After the great Milan insurrection of 1898 and the destruction of the Spanish fleet by the United States, devotion to the Sacred Heart reached its apogee: on 11 June 1899 – the day before the 'Masonic' proclamation of Philippine Independence – Leo consecrated the human race to the Sacred Heart. What had recently served as a Temporalist oriflamme was now offered to states as a 'blessed and heavenly token',[48] a new symbol of collaboration superseding Constantine's vision of the cross in the sky.[49] The highest Vatican sources averred that this solemn act was the result of a letter-writing campaign by the visionary Countess Droste zu Vischering – in religion Sister Mary of the Divine Heart, mother-superior of the Eudist convent of the Good Shepherd in Oporto.[50] Thirty years later, we shall see, an even more influential nun[51] was similarly moved to write to the pope, urging him to consecrate the world to the Immaculate Heart of Mary.

21

JEWS, PROTESTANTS AND MASONS: 'ENEMIES OF OUR LADY'

Noble Spain . . . sheltered under her regal mantle, fear not thine enemies . . . invoke Mary . . . then shalt thou be glorious again and reign over other peoples.[1]

Revista Católica de Filipinas, 1889

The war between Church and 'sect' continued to shape Catholic devotionalism, fuelling the corporative and crusading spirit that drove the Marian machinery. In 1884 the Jesuit general recommended the Sodality of Our Lady as 'a bulwark against secret societies'[2] and Leo XIII called for the expansion of the Third Order of St Francis as a way of 'crushing the power of the sects'.[3] Along with associations dedicated to charity and the defence of the papacy like the Society of St Vincent de Paul, the pope urged the re-establishment of workmen's guilds under the auspices of the bishops as another means of breaking the Masonic grip. The faithful were to invoke Mary, 'so that she, who from the moment of her conception overcame Satan, may show her power over these evil sects, in which is revived the contumacious spirit of the demon'.[4]

Leo's conviction that Freemasonry was the cause of all society's ills[5] was as strong as his belief that Mary would restore the natural order of things. Through 'conspiracies, corruption and violences', the Craft had, in the pope's view, 'come to dominate Italy and even Rome'.[6] Its power was expressed in 'a daily contempt for Our person',[7] its diabolic character shown by its 'naturalism' – the heresy which scorns divine revelation and dogma, and proclaims the sovereignty of the people.[8]

The Apostolate of Suffering, like the Apostleship of Prayer, was an anti-Masonic battalion, practising 'perpetual supplication' to the Virgin.[9] Ask Our Lord with insistence, taught one of its Jesuit

commanders, 'for the humiliation of the enemies of the Church
... ask for the extirpation of secret societies, of Freemasonry and
other anti-Catholic associations ... whose purpose is the complete
destruction of the reign of Jesus Christ on earth.'[10] A remarkable
counter-Masonic phalanx, the Knights of Columbus, was founded
in 1882 by Irish immigrants in Connecticut. Combining Masonic
structures and ceremonial with naval ranks and symbolism,[11] the
Knights were to play an important role in the Marian crusades of
the next century.

As secularism and Jewish emancipation advanced and the Protestant world became more powerful, devotion to the pontiff ('the
Lieutenant of Our Lord')[12] increased in the old world as in the
new. Nowhere was this loyalty so strong as in Spain, where
a letter to the queen regent from the episcopate during the
second national Catholic congress (Saragossa, 1890) denounced the
'diabolic machinations of the sects' and begged her majesty to fight
for the restoration of Temporalism.[13]

An indulgenced prayer composed for Leo's proclamation of the
Immaculate Conception as principal patroness of Latin America
(1899) presents Mary once again as intercessor of her people:

> free our peoples from the poisonous darts of the impious and
> heretical. Thou who hast raised and educated our peoples in
> the faith of thy most beloved Son, be now their Guardian, Avenger
> and Defender. Thine we are and thine we wish to be, show that
> thou art our Mother and Patroness.[14]

The notions expressed here adumbrate 'Hispanidad', a world-view
which originated in clerical Spain and spread among the oligarchies
of the former colonies. Faced with a hostile world, and committed
to Rome and 'tradition', Hispanidad invokes Mary, an ever-present
figure in decisive battles of conquest and colonization. Mystical
inspiration of imperial Spain, the Virgin provides a totemic, unifying
factor in the struggle against 'alien' and subversive elements. One of
the main purposes of crowning the Virgin of Guadalupe (1895) was,
as an episcopal pastoral puts it, to consolidate the 'true fraternity
that should exist between the different peoples of the New World
and Mexico'.[15]

The Filipino-Spanish confrontation at the end of the century
saw an alignment of revolutionary Masonic forces[16] with the
anti-Marian/anti-papalist movement which resisted the 'feudal'

order of Catholic crown and European friars. The latter denounced the 'baleful influence' of 'bible scatterers',[17] diffusion of 'practical Jansenism' and the 'work of Masonic lodges', and propagation of 'politico-religious errors imported from Europe'.[18] The Independent Philippines Church was formed by native clergy in 1902 on converse principles to Roman-Spanish Catholicism. The pope, declared Isabelo Reyes, is 'the caudillo of our eternal enemies the friars'.[19]

This repudiation, Obispo Maximo Aglipay explained, was 'precisely because he placed the saints above the true God . . . hiding the Sacred Book of the Bible'.[20] Among major points which established 'the heretical character of the new church' was its 'anti-Marianism'.[21] A striking feature of the rebels' doctrine was their distaste for the rosary: 'a tedious and useless repetition of Ave Marias which misleads the imagination.'[22] And while the Virgin Birth was upheld, Mary's divine maternity was denied: 'God has no mother because He would not be eternal if He had.'[23]

In Europe during Leo's reign political conflict was perceived by many as a war between good and evil, progress and retrogression. In 1882 M. Regnier, a Freemason, declared in Lyons:

> It should not be ignored, what is no longer a mystery, that for a long time the struggle has actually opened in France, in Italy, in Belgium and in Spain between light and ignorance, and that one will overcome the other. Now, you must know that the general staff, the commanders of these armies, are, on the one hand, the Jesuits, on the other, the Freemasons.[24]

The late nineteenth century saw a Masonic renaissance in France that sacralized the culture and ideology of the republican forces as well as providing congenial networks for discussion, intelligence-gathering and political action. Forming elites, particularly from the lower middle-classes, the lodges set up 'fronts' like the Ligue de l'Enseignement (1866), which mobilized teachers against the Catholic monopoly of education. The clerical hold was weakened by the 1880 law of Camille Sec (a Jewish Freemason) which provided state lycées for middle-class girls, hitherto taught by the congregations. Under the liberal Empire, the growth of Masonry had been 'rapid and powerful';[25] by 1896 there were some 24,000 lodge-members, mostly 'obedient' to the Grand Orient.

Catholic fears were aroused by militant atheism in socialist circles and the disavowal of the Great Architect by French Masonry in 1877. The vitality of the lodges was shown by their 'sacramental' development. Marriages and funerals were celebrated according to the Masonic rite, but more alarming were the alleged 'pompous ceremonies invented by the Freemasons to replace Catholic Baptism and First Communion'.[26] Children of an age for the latter mysteries (six to seven) 'wear black veils, on which are inscribed the words Misery, Ignorance and Fanaticism. These veils are torn from their heads with many emphatic speeches.'[27] Everywhere the 'militant civic burial'[28] for freethinkers eroded the Church's monopoly of ritual. And a Masonic congress in Paris celebrating the centenary of the French Revolution triggered off consecrations of families and institutions to the Sacred Heart.

Against a background of flourishing capitalism with financial rivalry between Catholic and protestant/Jewish groups,[29] the government of the Mason and Positivist Jules Ferry introduced radical anti-Catholic policies, particularly through the 'Ferry Laws' on education (1879–86). Protestants were appointed to key positions in the administration in order to laicize state schools and withdraw Church rights in higher education. Primary schools were made free and compulsory (in defiance of Catholic protests) and religious instruction was banned during normal lesson hours. Severe restrictions were placed on teaching orders. The Jesuits were expelled from the country and the police battered down the doors of fourteen defiant Redemptorist communities.[30] Some priests publicly burnt the new 'moral and civic instruction' textbooks which had been placed on the Index by Rome.[31] Disclericalization went far beyond education. Nuns were gradually replaced in hospitals, military chaplains were discharged, cemeteries secularized, public prayers banned, crucifixes removed from courtrooms and divorce legalized.

Catholic resistance did not restrict itself to a war against Freemasonry but denounced the two elements seen as united in the 'sect'. For Édouard Drumont, whose bestseller *La France juive* appeared in 1886, Freemasonry was the 'natural compound' of Protestantism and Judaism, which wanted to 'demolish the body and soul of France'.[32] In a later work, he complains that 'The Virgin is covered with indecencies . . . the development of an abject calumny of the Talmud.'[33]

Mgr Ernest Jouin (1844–1932), president of the Free-Catholic League and founder of *Revue Internationale de Sociétés Secrètes* (1912) – who 'personified the Church's fight against Judaeo-Masonry'[34] –

also claimed that the Talmud refers to Mary as 'excrement'.[35] A propagator of Sister Alacoque's message of 1689, Mgr Jouin wrote poems in honour of Our Lady of Lourdes, religious-patriotic plays about Bernadette and Joan of Arc, and tracts like *Sacred Heart and Masonic Heart: The Two Standards* (1919) and *Lourdes, Freemasonry and Bernadette* (1925). In an introduction to *The Protocols of Zion*, he accuses Judaism, Protestantism, Freemasonry and their affiliates (i.e., The League of Human Rights, pacifist and anti-militarist groups) of spreading 'the virus of liberalism' responsible for Americanism, Modernism and laicism.[36] Monseigneur's view of the political alternatives was stark: 'the choice is simple: either the Catholic supergovernment for the conversion of France or the Jewish supergovernment for the absorption of the symbolic serpent.'[37]

This perception of Jews as the 'absolute masters of Freemasonry'[38] prevailed among Catholic anti-Semites. Yet the Anti-Semitic League of France, which affirmed 'absolute liberty of conscience' and scorned association with 'clerical demonstrations',[39] apparently had some supporters in the lodges.[40] Towards the end of the century, episcopal pastorals accusing Freemasonry of devil-worship were widespread. Archbishop Meurin's *La Franc-Maçonnerie – Synagogue de Satan*, a classic of the world conspiracy doctrine, was first published in Paris in 1893.[41] According to the mitred Jesuit, the cabbala is the 'dogmatic base of Freemasonry'[42] and 'Jews form a masonry within masonry, just as masonry forms a State within a State'.[43] The aim of Freemasons is to 'put the kingdom of the world under the heel of the Jew',[44] to which end Lucifer himself has appeared at lodge meetings.[45]

Belief in the diabolic nature of Freemasonry was fed by the fantastic propaganda of renegade Masons like 'Dr Bataille' (author of *The Devil in the Nineteenth Century*)[46] and 'Leo Taxil', whose scurrilous production before his dubious conversion to Rome included *The Secret Loves of Pius IX* and *The Poisoner Leo XIII*. Among other targets of his pen were Lourdes water and Mary's apparition to Liguori.[47]

A professional anticlerical whose real name was Gabriel Jogand-Pagès, Taxil 'exposed' the lodges in 1885–6 with equally far-fetched tales about the beautiful high priestess of the Craft, 'Miss Diana Vaughan' – rescued from damnation through her fascination for Joan of Arc and supplications to Our Ladies of Lourdes, of Victoires and of the Sacré Coeur.[48] Mgr Meurin's theories were partly based on the defector's 'revelations'.[49] The contrite Taxil was star guest at a ten-day international anti-Masonic congress at Trent in September 1896 under the leadership of Prince Karl von Löwenstein, Cardinal Parocchi and 36 bishops (Leo cabled his support). It was unanimously declared that 'Freemasonry is the synagogue of Satan and Freemasons confess Lucifer as God'.[50] Taxil agreed to organize a universal anti-Masonic league but the following April he confessed that 'Diana Vaughan' was but a figment of his imagination.

At the time of the anti-Masonic congress, Civiltà Cattolica accused 'the synagogue' of putting the 'God-man' on the cross and of controlling 'half of Bohemia' through the Rothschilds.[51] In turn, Zola castigated the 'shady Catholicism of sectarians' who saw in that great banking family 'the descendants of Judas who delivered up and crucified his God'.[52]

The simmering anti-Semitism that boiled over in the Dreyfus affair (1894) permeated the Social Catholics, who invited Drumont to their Lyons congress.[53] With notable exceptions like the poet Charles Péguy, Catholics were solidly anti-Dreyfusard. Unsurprisingly, the French Jesuits, who had educated many army officers, were implicated in the conspiracy.[54] Hatred spluttered over the pages of Drumont's *Libre Parole* and *La Croix*, the high circulation daily of the Assumptionists.[55] *La Croix's* editor Fr Vincent de Paul Bailly (an epigone in the school of Veuillot) denounced Zola's *Lourdes*, published in the year of the Captain's arrest. For Bailly, the real culprit in the affair was 'free thought . . . defender of Jews, Protestants and all the enemies of the Church'.[56]

The Virgin Mary, caught in the cross-fire between anti-clericals and anti-Semites, absorbed a great deal of Zola's creative energy. His insight was given full rein in the proto-Freudian treatment of 'Abbé Mouret's' Mariolatry.[57] And the novelist was 'stupefied by the spectacle of that world of hallucinating believers'[58] when he happened to pass through Lourdes in 1892. '. . . the Grotto, the cures, the miracles, are indeed, the creation of that need of the Lie, and that necessity for credulity, which is a characteristic of human nature.'[59]

The cult of the visionary Joan of Arc – 'not an altogether healthy business' in the view of Simone Veil[60] – appeared forcefully during the Third Republic with the backing of Catholics and anti-Catholics.[61] Demands for the restoration of her feast day were made by the Catholic Association of French Youth, and student demonstrations were marshalled by the Abbé Garnier. Fearing the instrumentalization of this symbol of 'patriotic élan and national independence',[62] Masonic circles including Jules Ferry developed a parallel cult of a laic Joan complete with statues divested of 'all divine association'.[63] In contrast, the sculptor Real del Sarte, president of the Camelots du Roi (royalist toughs of the Action Française) represented her as the 'Mother of Mercy'.

Declared Venerable in 1894 and beatified fifteen years later amidst shouts in St Peter's for God and France, Joan's posthumous career would reach its apogee under Pétain as an anti-Masonic figure parallel to Mary.[64] In 1910 – a year after Joan's beatification – the Anglo-Italian mayor of Rome, Ernesto Nathan, created an international incident over his 'violent tirade against many of the doctrines of the Roman Catholic religion'.[65] Speaking at the fortieth anniversary celebrations of the liberation of the eternal city, the founder of the 'Giordano Bruno' lodge and ex-manager of Mazzini's newspaper *Roma del Popolo* called papal infallibility 'the reverse of the Biblical revelation of the Son of God made man on earth; it was the son of man made God on earth!'[66]

Pius X protested in a letter to the cardinal vicar of Rome which mentioned the Syndico's Jewishness and Masonic membership. Even less restrained were the public demonstrations in Austria and Germany against 'the outrageous insults to the Virgin Mary pronounced by the Jewish Freemason Nathan'.[67] The whole rumpus brought into focus the role of Mary – who has 'exterminated all heresies in the world'[68] – as the scourge of Jews and Masons.

22

THE MODERNIST HERESY

The tendency of modern Catholicism is to salvation neither by
faith nor by works but by machinery.[1]

Fr George Tyrrell, ex-SJ

Yet another wave of anticlericalism swept France when the Drey-
fusards came to power. The Assumptionists were suppressed in 1900
by the government of Waldeck-Rousseau.[2] The following year the
Jesuits were forced to close their 24 colleges and the Marists, Picpus
Fathers (Congregation of the Sacred Hearts of Jesus and Mary) and
the Company of Mary were removed from their posts in seminaries;
the Missionaries of the Immaculate Conception were driven from
Lourdes ('another proof of the diabolical intentions of an infidel
government').[3] In 1902 the ghost of the assassinated Ferry was
raised by the premiership of Dr Émile Combes, a former theologian
who admitted he had taken office to demolish the religious orders.[4]
Combes personally supervised the repudiation of the Napoleonic
concordat, the expulsion – even at bayonet point – of the majority
of religious from their communities and shrines, the closure of up to
10,000 Catholic schools, confiscation of ecclesiastical property worth
over a billion francs, and the final separation of Church and State
– 'a most pernicious error'[5] exacerbated by revelations in 1904 of
preferment in the war office for those loyal to the Grand Orient.

The persecution brought forth pontifical appeals to 'the intercession of Mary Immaculate'[6] and, according to a Jesuit authority,
stimulated 'prophetic imaginations'.[7] Visionaries 'felt themselves
impelled to go to the Holy Father to confide to him their predictions
and secrets'.[8] The message of La Salette was recycled by the
anti-Semitic press with a 'Judaeo-masonic' slant.[9] The 'noisy and
provocative pilgrimages reappeared'.[10] At Lourdes 60,000 pilgrims
heard the Jesuit Coubé 'make a violent call to the "electoral sword"
and transform his chief the Virgin Mary into a martial Virgin able,
like Joan of Arc, to lead the faithful to victory. "To battle,"

urged Fr Coubé, "under the *labarum* of the Sacred Heart!" '[11] Millions flocked to Lourdes;[12] its threatened closure was not only a political and religious matter: the shrine's defenders pleaded that such a move would 'throw the railway companies into a deplorable economic crisis'.[13]

Soon after these dramatic events in France – and the total eclipse of the Catholic Spanish Empire – came another severe blow for the Church: the bloody peasant-secularist Mexican revolution of 1910.[14] The great political and economic transformations at the beginning of the century were paralleled by a scientific and intellectual revolution of terrifying dimensions.[15] A new crisis arose within the Church, comparable in some aspects to Jansenism or, in our own times, the theology of liberation: 'Modernism'. A complex international movement, it challenged infallibility of Church and scripture, denounced the 'swarming legion of lies' of 'our falsified histories, our forged decretals, our spurious relics',[16] and demanded universal separation of Church and State with a democratic overhaul of the former's constitution. Catholic scientists meeting at Munich in 1900 were exhorted by Fr Hartmann Grisar,SJ, to 'rid the Church of some of the embarrassing legends'[17] including that of the Santa Casa. The 'New Theology' of the Reverend R.J. Campbell of the City Temple and the work of the Protestant theologian Sabatier in France reinforced the rebellion.

Modernism – that 'morbid state of conscience among Catholics and especially young Catholics',[18] as Abbate Cavallanti defined it – became the single most powerful force to oppose the Marian cult. 'Many of the central activities around Marian congresses that by then started to be celebrated ... failed because of the nascent modernist spirit,' a leading Mariologist complained years later.[19] In the words of its detractors, the movement was above all 'a system of criticism' that would bring about 'the destruction of all certainty in knowledge';[20] it preached the subversive belief that 'authority comes from below and not from God'.[21] 'Social Modernists', led by Murri, Fogazzaro and Buonaiuti in Italy, sought the removal of the *non-expedit* preventing Catholics from engaging in politics;[22] 'scriptural Modernists' like the Abbé Loisy (1857–1940) applied historical methods based on German scholarship that contradicted the inerrancy of the Bible; 'theological Modernists' like the Anglo-Irishman George Tyrrell (1861–1909), an ex-Jesuit whose views were equally relevant in the social, ecclesiastical and hermeneutic fields, denied the 'historic truth'[23] of the Virgin Birth, declared a belief in continuing revelation and called for the dismantling of 'the present highly centralized ecclesiastical empire'.[24]

In their demand that science be free from religious supervision and that the Church submit to scientific analysis of its structures and beliefs, the Modernists felt identified with Copernicus, Kepler, Galileo (not removed from the Index until 1835) and other intellectual victims of 'Roman autocracy'. Standards of truth in the Church were savagely questioned. Tyrrell was very close to the 'Solitaries' of Port-Royal when he attacked 'this decadent and enervating casuistry of the pulpit and confessional which is never weary of insisting on the merely venial character of untruthfulnesss and of relegating veracity to the very inferior rank of natural or pagan virtues.'[25] The year after the publication of this scathing criticism, a Vienna congress 'urged upon sodalists the duty of combating worldly ideals and prejudices hostile to the Church'.[26]

The well-oiled apparatus of Marian devotionalism under the thaumaturgic St Pius X (1903–14)[27] intensified the conflict. In an American tract entitled *Letters to His Holiness Pius X by a Modernist*[28] we read that 'not within the memory of living men have indulgences been so bewildering and meaningless in their prodigality as under your regime' – an accusation not without justification.[29]

The 'poisonous doctrines' of Modernism were anathematized in two papal documents: *Lamentabili sane,* issued by the Holy Roman and Universal Inquisition (sic) in July 1907, and *Pascendi Dominici gregis* (September 1907), drafted by Fr Joseph Lemius, an Oblate of Mary Immaculate. In August the Picpus priest Mateo Crawley Boevey – 'after the favour of a cure'[30] in the Chapel of the Apparitions at Paray-le-Monial – felt that 'Our Lord charged him with the mission of conquering the whole world, family by family, for the Sacred Heart'.[31] When he presented to the pope his plan for a social crusade, Pius X commanded him to dedicate his life to that work, which, according to the Catechism of the Enthronement, strives to establish 'the reign of the Divine Heart in the family, in order to prepare in this way the social reign of Our Saviour; to cause Him to rule over the whole society'.[32]

An Anglo-Peruvian educated in Chile, Fr Mateo (1875–1960) was the great modern apostle of the Sacred Heart and a pioneer in the lay movement. He worked closely with the recently restructured Catholic Action in Italy and with the Jesuits,[33] the leading force in the anti-Modernist crusade, whose Sodality of Our Lady became more dynamic and international: 'new bonds of union have been established among sodalities, by means of congresses, confederation and sodality newspapers and periodicals.'[34]

The son of a local government official of the lowest rank, Giuseppe Sarto – the only canonized pope since the Counter-Reformation – differed little politically from his high-born predecessors. 'Rich and poor, learned and ignorant, nobles and plebians' were, in Papa Sarto's view, part of the order constituted by God.[35] Under the slogan 'Restore all things in Christ' Pius X set out to 're-establish the principle that human authority represents that of God'.[36] In this increasingly difficult task the Virgin Mary was at his side. On the jubilee of the Immaculate Conception in 1904 he informed the faithful,

> Christ is seated at the right hand of Divine Majesty; but Mary stands at his right hand as queen, the surest and most faithful help of all in danger, so that there is nothing to fear and no reason to despair under her guidance, her leadership, her favour, her protection.[37]

Granting a plenary indulgence during the jubilee for prayers offered for the extirpation of heresies, Sarto observed that the 'manifestations' at Lourdes 'furnish splendid arguments against the incredulity of our days'.[38] He enlarged the miniature grotto Pius IX had built in the Vatican gardens, as his own 'little corner of France' and wrote to the Bishop of Tarbes (Lourdes) that under the protection of Our Lady 'your country will emerge victorious over all the evils that assail her'.[39] In spite of everything, France remained 'part of God's designs' – a fact avouched by apparitions. For there was 'but one Paray-le-Monial, but one Lourdes, and both are in France'.[40]

Yet it was Spain that rendered invaluable service to the Marian crusade against Modernism and, later on, through a victorious holy war, provided a 'modern' alternative to the Society of Jesus. Under the vigorous generalate of the Spaniard Luis Martin (1892–1906) and the royal protection of the pious Alfonso XIII, both the Jesuits and the Church in Spain seem to have revived, infusing new energies into a papacy abandoned by its 'Eldest Daughter'. Signs of this vitality were new foundations centred on Mary (see p.160, n71) and the rules of the Sodality of Our Lady drawn up in 1910 from an exemplary Catalan sodality.[41] The new rules emphasized 'zeal for the souls of others' and established defence of the Holy Church as a fundamental part of apostolic work,[42] exhorting sodalists to imitate Mary's 'splendid virtues, place all confidence in her and urge one another to love and serve her with filial devotedness'.[43]

There was great rejoicing throughout the Hispanic world in 1904 when Spain reactivated the Assumptionist campaign, mainly through the first Spanish-American Marian Congress in Barcelona.[44] The foundation of sodalities in 'the great centres of secondary teaching'[45] and sodality publications to fight blasphemy was also discussed at this memorable meeting. The Commonwealth of the Immaculate Conception throbbed with pilgrimages, literary contests, the erection of monuments and inaugurations of votive temples.[46]

In response to Pius X's call to honour Mary in her shrines, Catholic Spain was mobilized the following year (1905) for the great coronation of Nuestra Señora del Pilar. In an impassioned exhortation, the Archbishop of Saragossa declared,

> The Virgin of the Pillar is the Spanish Virgin, the Queen of
> Spain . . . she who has rescued us from the shades of paganism,
> she who has saved us from the Moor, she who has saved us from
> the domination and hated yoke of the French encyclopedists, she
> who will save us, and is now beginning to save us, from the
> errors of modern naturalism which so endanger the divine faith
> and permanent interests of social concord.[47]

Like many similar events of the past and in the years to come, the coronation and fiestas surrounding it had a distinctive military and aristocratic character. Regimental bands played 'marches and tunes suitable for the Holy Rosary'[48] and the nobility gave their enthusiastic support. Workers' confraternities also participated in these national celebrations, though a few ominous protests were seen.

Anticlericalism was, in fact, rife. As ministers 'followed one another like figures in a magic lantern',[49] the whole social edifice was shaken by financial scandals, strikes, poverty, terrorism and repression. Against this background and in the face of the threat of secularization, the Virgin appeared in Granada in 1906, creating yet another shrine: Nuestra Señora del Espino.[50] That year Catholic Action held its first course on the 'social question'.

In 1908 the Spanish national shrine at Saragossa was the venue of an international Marian congress, the principal objective of which was to fight Modernism – '*suma y compendio de todas las herejías*'.[51] As the general promoter of the Marian congresses expressed it at the time, 'Mary must crush the head of all [heresies], crushing the serpent of Modernism and thus reign in the world as Queen of the Universe'.[52] The congress issued statements defending the 'dogmatic and historical relations between Mary and the Pontiff' and the beliefs of divine maternity, Immaculate Conception and bodily Assumption against the objection of 'Modernists'.[53]

One of Sarto's first measures as pope was the swift dissolution of the Opera dei Congressi after its president, Count Grosoli, had complained that Catholics were 'anxious that the work of the living should not be impeded by dead issues'.[54] Determined, however, to make the anti-Modernist crusade effective, the pope soon replaced the Opera with three different bodies, including the Unione Popolare, devoted to 'pious activities and propaganda'.[55]

In the year that Modernism was condemned, the feast of the Appearance of the Virgin was extended to the Universal Church and the Congregation of Rites approved the scapular of the Immaculate Heart of Mary. The enthronement of the Heart of Jesus 'in the home' spread everywhere as 'the most appropriate means for the sanctification of the family and through the family, of the whole of society'.[56] The 'Councils of Vigilance' were also set up in 1907 to protect 'the pious traditions of different places'.[57] In response to a less than credulous work on the Santa Casa of Our Lady of Loreto by Canon Ulysse Chevalier in 1906,[58] a 'college of writers in defence of the Holy House' was formed, which, according to the cardinal secretary of state, would shield the shrine from 'insidious modern criticism'.[59] And in 1910 a solemn oath against Modernism (not rescinded until 1967) was demanded by Pius of all new preachers and seminary professors. Two years later, an encyclical called for reparation to the Holy Heart of Mary, and soon afterwards, the Holy Office approved the liturgical usage of the phrase 'Mary, our Co-Redemptrix'.[60]

The enemies of Modernism were favoured by the rise of the proto-fascist Action Française and the ideological influence achieved on an international scale by its leader, Charles Maurras – an agnostic who said he had 'entered politics like a religion'.[61] Author of *Le Bienheureux Pie X, Sauveur de la France* and benefactor of a chair of the Syllabus at the party college, Maurras enjoyed the support of St Pius, who called him 'a good defender of the Holy See and the Church'[62] and committed French dioceses to royalists. For Maurras, the achievement of the Catholic Church was in 'moderating the destructive content of the message of the "Hebrew Christ" through wisdom derived from ancient Rome'.[63] As Ernst Nolte has pointed out, Maurras admired the Church's 'hierarchical system of mediators'.[64]

Maurras coined the term *intégrisme* to describe his ideal of making traditional institutions like the Catholic Church integral to the state. Subsequently – around 1907 – the dominant faction in the Vatican launched within the Church an integralist and neo-Thomist movement that created a network of secret groups known as the Sodalitium Pianum (Sodality of Pius V) to root out Modernists from positions of responsibility in education, the orders, the Catholic press and the bureaucracy. Assumptionists and Jesuits were prominent in French integralist journals, while the Action Française daily and Drumont's *Libre Parole* championed the Vatican in its war against Modernism and other forms of Christian reformism.

Action Française was closely linked to members of the shadowy Sodality including its mastermind Mgr Umberto Benigni, an official of the Vatican press office and founder of *Correspondance de Rome*, key organ in the battle.[65] The president of the Ligue Franc-Catholique, Mgr Jouin, was accused of being 'the pope of Action Française' and chief of the *Sapinière*[66] (or 'firwood' as the Sodalitium was known in France).

While secretly encouraging the Action Française, Pius X ordered the dissolution of its rival the Sillon, a Christian republican group tinged with socialism. The condemnation, in August 1910, came just a week before the *motu proprio Sacrorum antis titum* establishing the anti-Modernist oath. Sarto complained, 'there is no hierarchy of government in the Sillon . . . its study groups are veritable intellectual cooperative societies.'[67] Sillonists divided Catholics, drawing priests and seminarists away from Catholic Action.[68] In contrast, the Catholic Association of French Youth, official expression of Catholic Action, was praised for 'the exact obedience with which you follow the directives of the Roman Pontiff'.[69] Created in 1886 to serve the spiritual needs of the upper class, the ACJF had become a mass movement with over 100,000 members, controlled by the Jesuits and with the motto 'Prayer, Study and Action'.

In Spain, too, integralism was primarily a Jesuit concern. The main organ, *Razón y Fe*, was founded by superior-general Martín in 1901[70] and the key integralist organization, the powerful *Asociación Católica Nacional de Jovenes Propagandistas*, sprang from a select sodality of Our Lady directed by Angel Ayala, a leading Jesuit in the Assumptionist campaign. This secretive network – officially consecrated by the nuncio in 1909 – represented the *crème de la crème* of Catholic Spain. Source of all major projects of Catholic Action, the *Propagandistas* formed the front-line against Modernism and Communism. Their apostolate of the press and social programme of co-operatives and savings banks for the working class complemented charitable and missionary work by a variety of recently-established divisions.[71]

Among the new foundations were *Damas Catequistas*, a lay institute for the 'promotion of workers' formed at the turn of the century; and the Ave María Schools, opened in 1888 by Padre Andrés Manjón (1846–1923) under the motto *'Religión y Patria'* and with the explicit aim of propagating Marian virtues and devotion.[72] The 'Schools of the Virgin'[73] were seen as the answer to the secularist, 'Masonic' tendencies in education, and they were soon to spread all over Spain.

Part III

TIARA ET FASCES

23

OVERVIEW

One could finally be both a good Italian, which is synonymous
with Fascist, and a good Catholic. . .[1]

Benito Mussolini

Her fiestas are the fiestas of the Empire. Without her we could
not have won the laurels of triumph, nor could we have liberated
the Fatherland. . .[2]

Francisco Franco

Our Lady is a great friend of mine[3]

Antonio de Oliveira Salazar

BACKGROUND

The years between the beginning of the First World War and
the end of the Second saw a marked militarization of the cult
of the Virgin Mary, whose dire warnings and expiatory demands
continued to influence events in many countries. Catholic eyes saw
her banner in the thick of most great struggles of the time. In
1937, for instance, when the popular fronts of France and Spain
were threatening Church power, Pius XI – 'as in the times of the
crusades' – called for a united Europe: 'let men implore from the
Mother of God that the subverters of Christian and human society
may be put to flight'.[4]

While the main dramas of militant Marianism were played out
in the Iberian peninsula, France and Belgium made substantial
contributions to an increasingly politicized myth.[5] In Italy the
figure of the pontiff seems once again to have eclipsed that of
the Madonna. Rome, however, was enthralled by Portuguese
revelations of the Immaculate Heart – a devotion which had a
preponderate influence on the policies of the papacy both in this
period and later.

If fascism was attempting to bring 'peace between employers and employees, between landlords and peasants'[6] and was understood by its founder as the antithesis of democracy, plutocracy, Freemasonry and the immortal principles of 1789, the Roman Church was bound to find it a natural and immediate refuge from the great post-war storms. Fascism provided the Church with a suitable vehicle for fighting her enemies and realizing, partially, geopolitical designs. In the Balkans and eastern Mediterranean, where Catholic missionaries were officially regarded as harbingers of Latin civilization, splinter Uniat churches formed a cultural bridgehead. The Vatican's centuries-old dream of 'Romanizing' the Orthodox – achieved in token by accommodation to the Greek, Russian and oriental rite – was given fresh hopes by the overthrow of tsarism and the near destruction of the Holy Orthodox Church. Even the terrifying events of 'October' did not prevent an attempt to succeed to the Third Rome. Two old realities seem to have continued shaping the Roman strategy: that of Mary as the theological bridge, and Poland as the political door, to the eastern empire.

Rome's politico-devotional programme was fuelled by the visions at Fatima, which – skilfully manipulated by Catholic Action and the Jesuits' Apostleship of Prayer – had made a significant contribution to the 1917 military coup. Under the godfatherly eye of Dr Salazar (a 'lay saint'[7] whose position as dictator was consolidated by his leadership of a secretive Marian network), the sanctuary became the supreme patriotic symbol and a major tool in combating the enemies of the Church.

In Spain Mary became equally central, sponsored first by Primo de Rivera's dictatorship, later by the Falangists. Her cult – papistical and ascetic – was of the essence of Opus Dei and its forerunner, the Jesuitic ACN de P. A bridge between the Iberian regimes under her title of Fatima, Mary was also the linchpin of the Hispanidad ideology through which Franco hoped to create a new commonwealth of the Immaculate embracing a Latin America that would abjure the 'gloomy Masonic works'[8] of the USA and look once again to Catholic Spain for leadership.

During the 1920s the Marian revival of National Catholicism (of great consequence for the years to come) was experienced throughout the Ibero-American world. Feasts and coronations were staged at major shrines as far afield as the Andes. In Cuzco, among the resolutions of the First Congress of Social Action (May 1920) were the erection of a commemorative monument to Our Lady of Descension (see Part I) and a petition to the Holy Father asking for the extension of the feast to the whole of Peru.[9] In Lima a few years later (1927) the image of Our Lady of the Rosary was canonically crowned in a solemn tribute to *patria* and religion, and covered with a rich mantle and emeralds bestowed by the aristocracy.[10] In Bolivia in 1925 La Mamita was proclaimed 'Queen of the Nation' at Copacabana.[11] The following year in Chile – four years after the foundation of the Communist Party – a 'grand historical-patriotic parade' organized by Catholic Action and the collapsing oligarchy culminated in the coronation of the Virgin Patroness of the Armed Forces by the papal legate.[12] During the Great Depression[13] new *ceremonias cívico-religiosas* were staged. In 1930 the 'patronage' of the Virgin was sworn in all three republics of the river Plate: Argentina, Paraguay and Uruguay.[14] During the same year in Brazil the Virgin of Aparecida was proclaimed patroness of the nation by pontifical decree.[15]

But nowhere in Latin America did Nuestra Señora serve fiercer political ends than in Mexico during the anticlerical regime of Calles (1924–35), holder of the Masonic Medal of Merit. Hundreds of local Knights of Columbus fell in the Cristero wars[16] (1926–9) or were executed, 'their rosary in their hands and the name of Christ the King on their lips'.[17] An army of 50,000 peasants, the Cristeros charged government troops with the cry, 'Long live Christ the King! Long live the Virgin of Guadalupe!'[18] Her shrine was the scene of anti-government demonstrations and official attempts to debunk the cult failed dismally as combatants on both sides claimed visions of Mary.[19]

The no less turbulent thirties saw the last Marian apparitions to be unequivocally recognized by the Catholic Church. The Belgian Rexists (future Nazi collaborationists who, like the Cristeros, took their name from 'Christus Rex') played a leading part in promoting the visions at Beauraing (1932–3), which were immediately followed, against a background of massive unemployment and economic collapse, by the appearance at Banneaux of the Virgin of the Poor.

The French crisis of the late 1930s triggered a new Marian offensive. Soon after the electoral victory of the left in France and the outbreak of civil war in Spain, a special jubilee was granted to the Eldest Daughter and her colonies to mark the tricentenary of the consecration of the kingdom to the holy Virgin by Louis XIII (August 1937–August 1938). As the French government faced violent opposition and diplomatic hostility,[20] the world's largest statue of Our Lady was erected near Lyons. Masonry was labelled the 'anti-Church' and the *vocation mariale de la France* proclaimed once more.[21] Three months after Blum's fall the royal vow jubilee closed with a splendid Marian congress at Boulogne. Over 2,000 children took part in a pageant starting with the papal march, and delegates asserted that 'under the care of Mary, model for mothers and wives', the French family could 'regain its impetus'.[22]

Lourdes was still the chief destination of pilgrims, as much for the universal Church as for France. The 'most extraordinary' Holy Year of 1933–4 in commemoration of the nineteenth centennial of the Crucifixion closed at the Pyrenean shrine with prayers for peace. Millions went there in response to a campaign of reparation for 'godlessness' and to stem the rising tide of 'neo-paganism'. Well inside the philo-Nazi zone in World War II, the world's most thaumaturgical spa was transformed into a centre of Pétainiste militarism.

Neither the Belgian visions nor the tradition of Lourdes deflected Fatima from its theurgical course. In 1929 the Pontifical Russian College (the 'Russicum') was founded for the training of priests for Orthodox/communist lands, and the surviving Portuguese seer was granted her 'Great Apparition'. The cult of Our Lady of Fatima was canonically approved the following year and in St Peter's the Vatican launched an indulgenced anti-Soviet campaign with a mass of reparation to the Divine Heart.[23]

The aggrandizement of the cult of the Immaculate Heart continued unabated during World War II as Sister Lucia sent letters to Rome describing her latest experiences. When Hitler invaded Russia in June 1941, Polish and German Jesuits were waiting in the wings to Catholicize the defeated 'schismatics'. It was at this moment that, apparently to encourage Catholic soldiers fighting alongside the Axis forces, the Vatican released the Carmelite's 'secret message' from the Virgin about Russia's conversion. Pius XII's 'paradoxical silence'[24] during the Jewish holocaust and other atrocities is consistent with this decision.

Fed on the anti-pacifist, anti-Modernist diet of the Fascist era, Our Lady of Fatima would pass confidently into the cold war – regnant and virtually unchallenged.

DEVOTIONS AND DIVISIONS

The cult of the Sacred Heart of Jesus – destined to be totally eclipsed by the Immaculate Heart of Mary – found new and diverse outlets, with consecrations of families, brotherhoods, whole nations. During the Great War 'splendid ceremonies took place in which units of various dimensions participated'.[25] The pious ambition persisted in France of substituting the royalist flag of the Sacred Heart for the tricolour.[26] A generous package of indulgences was granted to 'those who publicly consecrated their homes to the Sacred Heart'.[27] Zealously promoted by Fr Crawley Boevey, this ritual spread throughout the world. The example of King Alfonso XIII's consecration in 1919 of Spain was followed by Nicaragua, Poland (1920), Costa Rica (1921), Brazil (1922), Bolivia (1925) and Portugal (1928). Equivalent ceremonies sanctified Catholic corporativism. French railwaymen, for example, were entrusted to the Sacré Coeur on Loyola's hill of martyrs in 1924 after a night of adoration before the Blessed Sacrament.[28] By the 1940s a wave of consecrations to the Immaculate Heart, especially in the Iberian world, followed in the wake of the Fatima message.

The Eucharistic-Marian congresses movement was firmly established during the fascist era. In 1929 the French hierarchy set up an organization to coordinate Marian congresses on the same lines as the earlier Eucharistic body; the following year the tenth Italian Eucharistic Congress was held at Loreto. The first national Marian congress in the United States met in 1934 at Portland, Oregon.

The Immaculate Conception and 'cardio-Marian' devotions were boosted by the cult of new saints. The cause for the beatification of Padre Hoyos, SJ, pioneer of the Heart devotions, was introduced in 1914, and in 1920 the silver trumpets sounded for St Marguerite Marie Alacoque. Among the 31 souls canonized by Pius XI were Bernadette Soubirous, Jean Eudes, Madelaine Sophie Barat and Don Bosco. Prominent beati (Pope Ratti created no less than 531) included Antonio Maria Claret, Catherine Labouré, Fr Aladel (Alacoque's confessor) and Mgr Mazenod. The martyrs of the French Revolution were declared 'intercessors' (1925).

Theologians continued to theorize about the 'spiritual treasure' dispensed by the successor of Peter, indulgences. The standard manual of the 'illustrious Mariologist'[29] Mgr Alexis Marie Lépicier, now prior-general of the Servants of Mary, was enlarged and reprinted in English in 1928. The power of the keys – 'the power of admitting men into heaven or of excluding them therefrom' – stood defiantly against Modernist criticism.

Mary's intercession via the rosary was sought with Leonine insistence as 'a most powerful weapon to overcome the devil'.[30] During the French jubilee and Spanish civil war the pope launched a new rosary campaign, reminding the Catholic world that 'the powerful patronage of the Virgin Mother of God is bound up with all the glorious history of Christendom'.[31] Such pious practices of the past as sacrifices for Mary in May were encouraged. 'You will give yourself and all your prayer, alms and mortifications to her.'[32] Indeed, 'by doing something daily in honour of Our Blessed Lady you can gain an indulgence'.[33]

The relationship between Our Lady and the Eucharist deepened. 'We owe to Our Lady's mediation the institution of the Most Precious Sacrament,' Mgr Lépicier reminded the faithful.[34] A 'method of hearing holy Mass in union with Mary Immaculate'[35] was devised as well as ways of receiving Holy Communion 'in company' with her.[36] In 1938 adoration of the Eucharist, often performed with 'pious hymns in honour of Our Blessed Lady',[37] attracted a plenary indulgence when the rosary was recited simultaneously.

The Miraculous Medal – whose centenary was closed by Ratti on the feast of St Vincent de Paul in 1931 – and the Brown Scapular were widely distributed. A 'perpetual novena' in honour of the medal originated in 1930 at the Central Shrine of Our Lady of the Miraculous Medal in Germantown, Pennsylvania and spread to Canada, Britain, Ireland, India and China.

The Spiritual Exercises – impregnated with Marian devotions – remained a basic tool. In 1936 alone the Jesuits gave 18,940 retreats[38] and in Spain, soon after the nationalist victory, 5,000 miners from rebellious Asturias underwent Loyola's exercises in three years.[39]

Marian training was especially applicable to girls, who might aspire to be more 'Mary-like'.[40] Obedience was still the watchword, for 'Always and everywhere, Mary obeys'.[41]

The new mass media was a major conduit for the Marian campaigns. The first film about Lourdes was made in 1919, with five more versions released between 1925 and 1934.[42] Bishop Fulton Sheen began his radio 'Catholic Hour' in 1930 to win American souls for Mary and expose the evils of communism.[43] Five years later, the Franciscan Friars of the Atonement pioneered religious radio plays on their *Ave Marie Hour*. In October 1938 the Holy Father's 'intention', as relayed by the Apostleship of Prayer, was an entreaty 'through the most pure Heart of Mary' for 'all workers in the Catholic press, radio and films'.[44]

Supplementing the media apostolate was an ambitious programme of censorship. In Ireland a boycott of library books by 'anti-Catholic and pagan authors' was enjoined on the faithful;[45] and in Spain and Portugal, Balzac's 'amatorial' novels were among many works placed on the Index.

Developments in the ecclesiastical structure kept pace with the expansionist mood. Nearly 100 diocesan sees were created during Pius XI's pontificate (53 of them in South America) and 88 new missionary bishoprics were established, mostly in Africa and China. The Scientific Institute of Mission was opened in Rome (1932) with chairs of 'missiology' at Louvain, Paris and Lille.

During the period in question (1914–49) Catholic Action reached its zenith, older associations flourished and a variety of new divisions joined the serried ranks of Mary. The Society of St Vincent de Paul swelled to around 133,000 members in the 1930s as an 'antidote to the poison of socialism'[46] from Switzerland to Singapore, Santa Lucia to Shanghai. There were almost as many Brothers in the United States (23,849) as in France (24,793), with large numbers in Brazil (20,500) and Italy (14,266).[47] Don Bosco's Salesian Cooperators had half a million members.[48] The Apostleship of Prayer claimed 28 million members in 127,682 centres by the end of World War II.

Alongside new Franciscan congregations centred on the Sacred Heart and Immaculate Conception,[49] and many others of a traditionalist nature, a series of innovatory bodies sprang up: uncompromisingly anti-communist, anti-Protestant, anti-Masonic and permeated by the cults of Our Lady and Christ's Vicar. The populist Militia Immaculatae (1917) successfully exploited mass media and branched out far beyond its native Poland. Among divisions of an elitist, secretive character are the Opus Dei (1928) – which developed alongside the ACN de P – and the Knights of St Columbanus. The latter, an offshoot of the Knights of Columbus, exemplifies counter-Masonry in contemporary times. Founded in 1909 and transformed six years later by Fr James K. O'Neill of the Society of St Vincent de Paul, the Irish Knights aimed to confront 'Orange Ascendancy and British Socialism' in Belfast through 'sound and consolidated Catholic Action'.[50] Based, like their American model, on Masonic rituals and a strict code of secrecy,[51] the Knights of St Columbanus created a network of committees to secure 'nominations and appointments for Catholics in key positions'.[52] They embraced the 'vocationalism' (corporativism) of *Quadragesimo anno* (1931), setting up workingmen's clubs to 'stave off the dangers of communism'[53] and organized boycotts of Jewish businesses.[54] Canonically approved in 1934, the Knights forged strong links at home with the Legion of Mary (see below) and set up sister organizations in England and Scotland. The Order was consecrated to the Immaculate Heart of Mary in 1942 at the suggestion of Archbishop McQuaid of Dublin.

Of all the mass Marian organizations, the most notable also has Irish Vincentian roots. Appealing largely to lower middle-class women, the Legion of Mary grew out of a Dublin meeting of the Society of St Vincent in 1921. The Legion's leader was Frank Duff (1889–1980), a civil servant heavily influenced by Grignion de Montfort and W.J. Chaminade[55] who wanted to see five new Marian 'mysteries' added to the rosary.[56] Duff branded anti-Marian theologians as 'Jansenists', 'Modernists', even 'teddy boys'.[57]

Obsession with secrecy,[58] hierarchy, obedience and a vengeful Montfortian Virgin characterize the Legio Mariae. Nomenclature is borrowed from the Roman Legion. The *praesidium* is the basic unit or cell and the supreme governing body is the *Concilium*, which meets at De Montfort House, Dublin. An elite group, 'the Patricians', is charged with 'mass-mobilizing of the Catholics'.[59] The *Vexillum Legionis* depicts the Immaculate Conception and substitutes a dove for the Roman eagle. Legionaries assemble in military formation at an annual consecration to the 'general of the armies of God'.[60] Mary's authority (even Jesus 'obeyed His Mother')[61] devolves on the leadership: 'It is a natural step from the Queen to her special council . . . which would represent her visibly and share her superintendence of all the other Legionary governing bodies.'[62]

By the thirties a network of *praesidia* was established throughout Ireland and Britain, the USA, Mexico and Central America, Australia and New Zealand, India, Burma and China.[63] The Legion's 'conquest' of Africa began in 1934, when the prefect-apostolic of Calabar (Nigeria) organized the burning of rival idols and put Africans 'like clay into Mary's hands', teaching them to 'rely entirely' on her.[64] In Kenya Archbishop Riberi, apostolic delegate to missionary Africa, declared, 'The Legion of Mary is Catholic Action decked out in attractive and alluring form'.[65]

At the junior level the Legion shared a membership of millions with the Children of Mary, whose centenary in 1932 was celebrated 'in a fervent, worldwide union of spirit'.[66] Youth participation in international Catholic Action was largely channelled through Our Lady's sodalities, still the basic parish organization with its nerve-centre in the Roman College. The growing Marian network in the United States was streamlined in 1925 by Fr Daniel A. Lord,SJ, in 'The Queen's Work', an apostolate in which 'the modern girl is asked to follow Mary in a generation infatuated with the latest harlot of the screen'.[67] In 1931 Lord organized the Summer Schools of Catholic Action, where a horror of sex was combined with virulent anti-communism.

Youth was also a key field of activism for the Knights of Columbus, who numbered a million members in 1937, among them 'every archbishop in the US'.[68] A 'squires' and 'squirettes' centre catered for adolescents. Between 1922 and 1935 some 75,000 potential youth leaders attended ten-day courses at 'Boyology Institutes' across North America.[69] Catholic scouts and guides everywhere imbibed the Marian code. Youth was now under the universal patronage of the Passionist Gabriel Possenti of the Sorrowful Virgin (d. 1862), who was canonized in 1920 – the same year that the Maid of Orleans (another model of youthful virtue)[70] was raised to the altars in the presence of 60 French senators and 10,000 exuberant pilgrims. At Lourdes under Vichy boys paraded before the Céleste Maman, vowing to combat 'indifference, neglect of duty, egotism and cowardice'.[71]

The relative decline of the Society of Jesus[72] did not hinder the Mariological advance. The simultaneous canonization and enrolment of Albert the Great as a Doctor of the Church in 1931 was a landmark comparable with the exaltation of the infallibilist Liguori in the previous century. The *Mariale Super Missus Est* of Albertus Magnus (found to be spurious 21 years later) asserts that Mary's body was taken up into the 'heaven of the Trinity'.[73] Another supposititious work of St Albert, *De Laudibus Sanctae Mariae*, concludes that 'She gave her only begotten Son for the salvation of the world',[74] that 'the power of the Mother and the Son are one and the same'[75] and 'in the sacrament of her Son we also eat and drink her flesh and blood'.[76]

Liguorian Mariology was stimulated and spread by propagandists like the Redemptorist Dillenschneider.[77] Eudism, ten years after the founder's canonization, also flourished, and the Sodality of the Heart of the Mother Most Admirable had 25,000 members.[78]

The progress of Marian 'science' is demonstrated by new academic ventures: the *Société d'Études Mariales* was established in 1934 and by the end of the decade, *Revue Marianum*, the most important journal of Marian theology, was launched in Rome by the Servants of Mary. *Estudios Marianos* (1942), organ of the Spanish Mariological Society (formed at the feet of Our Lady of the Pillar after the Nationalist victory) nurtured those great Iberian enterprises: the cult of Fatima and the dogma of Our Lady's Assumption.

24

ROME RESURRECTED

The universality of the papacy, heir of the universality of the
Roman Empire, represents the greatest glory of Italian history
and tradition.[1]
> Benito Mussolini on the election of Pius XI

We have given God back to Italy and Italy back to God.[2]
> Pope Pius XI on the Lateran agreement with Mussolini

The acute economic and financial crisis in Italy brought about
by the Great War radicalized an expanding working class filled
with hope after the Russian revolution. Anti-war demonstrations
and battles between army and workers took place in the industrial
north. Lenin described the Turin uprising of 1918 as part of 'the
development of the World Revolution'.[3] The demographic bases of
the Church, the central and northern peasantry ('directly organized
by Catholic Action and the Church apparatus')[4] were being undermined. Large numbers of rural workers joined the socialist ranks
and day labourers occupied estates in a 'peasant tyranny' against
which squads were launched in 1919 – the year fascism emerged
and Catholics formed their first political party, Partito Popolare
Italiano (PPI).

The Vatican's début in parliamentary politics was presided
over by Benedict XV (1914–22). The incarnation of aristocratic
paternalism and generosity,[5] Papa Della Chiesa saw the direction of
Catholic Action (whose political arm was the PPI)[6] as 'the special
province of the Nobility'.[7]

During his short but combative reign significant expressions of
Marianism are seen. When Italy entered the war in 1915, Benedict
invoked Mary as 'Regina Pacis'[8] and in the dramatic year of 1918
he assured her clients of assistance at the hour of death.[9] In the
same document she is effectively declared Co-redemptrix by virtue
of her suffering at the foot of the cross: 'She redeemed the human
race together with Christ.'

A few months after the Italians went to the front, Della Chiesa reiterated the belief that the birthplace of the Virgin was transported 'by the ministry of angels from the Holy Land of Palestine'[10] and extended the office of Our Lady of Loreto to all Italy. On 24 March 1920, the Sacred Congregation of Rites announced that 'our most Holy Lord Pope Benedict XV' had appointed the Blessed Virgin 'under her title of Loreto, to be the Chief Patron before God of all aviators'.[11] Dubbed 'Pope of the universal mediation of Mary',[12] Benedict's glorification of her victorious rosary[13] complemented condemnations of 'exotic and barbarous dances recently imported into fashionable circles'[14] and stern warnings against 'the sects, enemies of religion'.[15]

A staunch supporter of Mgr Jouin,[16] Della Chiesa engaged the Church in fresh battles against secret societies. The new code of canon law (1917) imposed excommunication for all lodge members. Youth missions were stepped up and the cults of the Sacred and Immaculate Hearts reached new peaks through expanding divisions and canonizations (see previous chapter).

In 1917, the pope formally approved the Enthronement of the Sacred Heart as conceived by Fr Crawley Boevey, who formed that year, in close collaboration with Catholic Action, the Society of Youthful Enthronement Apostles. Shortly after the war, the Family of Franciscan Tertiaries for Promoting the Social Reign of the Sacred Heart was established in Assisi. Although bound by monastic vows, the members of this new female division wore no habit, lived independently of each other and were 'not publicly known as missionaries'.[17] A secular institute discreetly devoted to the service of the Church through Catholic Action, the Tertiaries have the specific mission of spreading Christ's kingdom in universities. It was founded by a 'devout client of the Sacred Heart',[18] Armida Barelli and the scientist Agostino Gemelli, OFM (1878–1959), a convert from socialism and sworn enemy of psychoanalysis (a method which violated the secrecy of the confessional).[19]

The attempt by Professor Toniolo to create a model Catholic university succeeded in 1921, when on the eve of the Immaculate Conception feast, the University of the Sacred Heart was opened by Cardinal Ratti in Milan, with Barelli as fund-raiser and Gemelli as intellectual overlord. Recognized by Mussolini's government in 1924, the university received active support from the Franciscan Tertiaries and was associated with the 'Maria Immacolata' institute for training secondary school teachers. A centre of clerico-fascism financed mainly by bankers and industrialists,[20] the Sacred Heart University set out to produce an elite to spearhead the Catholic reconquest of society.

Fr Agostino was also the architect of the International Federation of Catholic Universities (formed in 1924 to combat secularism in the academic sphere throughout the world) and headed the Papal Academy of Science after its resuscitation in 1936.

Pope Benedict found in Gemelli an able ally in his rejection of the Modernists' presentation of St Francis as a man 'guarded in his obedience to the Apostolic See, a specimen of a vague and vain religiosity'.[21] Della Chiesa, in defiance of all historical criticism,[22] confirmed the indulgence of St Mary of Portiuncula: Gemelli, following the scholastic tradition, depicted the Poverello as 'the Cavalier of the Madonna'.[23]

Another expression of the post-war Franciscan revival in Italy was the visionary Padre Pio (1887–1968), a Neopolitan Capuchin who in 1918 became the first priest to receive the stigmata (St Francis was never ordained).

The ancient image in the Santa Casa (now a triple symbol of Mary, papacy and airforce) was destroyed by fire in 1921. The following September – a few weeks before the March on Rome – a new statue carved from a cedar grown in Vatican soil was solemnly crowned and carried triumphally from the eternal city to the shrine in Ancona as a fly-past honoured *la celeste Patrona degli Aviatore*.[24] Music and speeches filled the air, flags waved and an official banquet with numerous representatives of the armed forces concluded the festivities. The *Osservatore Romano* pointed out that such devotions showed Rome to be once more the centre of the faith.[25] Religious feelings, unlike politics, united everyone in 'a single heartbeat'.[26]

The 'choreographic parade'[27] of October 1922 (led by a man who once called priests 'black microbes'[28] and the monarchy, army and war 'three absurdities')[29] brought about spectacular reversals both for the crown's and the Church's declining power and prestige. 'Religion', wrote an apologist of fascism not long afterwards, 'has been reinstated to a place of honour in State functions. Religious processions, as in the good old days, go unmolested through the streets amid a reverent populace.'[30] The people also enthusiastically followed the glorious anniversaries of the kingdom, learning that the monarch – symbol of unity and '*Potenza della Patria*' – promised a higher destiny.[31]

Freemasonry as an anticlerical force and Jews as 'alien elements' soon fell out of favour.[32] Modernism in all its forms and expressions felt the papal lash, together with even heavier strokes from the dictatorship. The mysterious Sodalitium Pianum (see Chapter 22), temporarily disbanded on the death of Pius X, continued working more clandestinely under the Sacred Congregation of the Council.[33] It is said that after its official suppression (though perhaps not complete disappearance) in 1921, the founder of this curialist network, Mgr Benigni, transferred his intelligence services to Mussolini.[34]

Benedict's successor, Pius XI (1922–39) or 'the Pope of Catholic Action', as Achille Ratti himself wished to be remembered, was a Lombard of petty-bourgeois origin, an historian and librarian who fulfilled his pastoral duties as chaplain to the Milan Cenacle for nearly 30 years, preaching the Months of Mary and the Sacred Heart.[35]

Characteristic of the triumphalist 'barque' of which Ratti had taken the helm was a *motu proprio* issued a few days after his accession declaring Our Lady of the Assumption principal patroness of the Eldest Daughter of the Church.[36] No less revealing is his early call on Catholic Action, worldwide lay associations of the Blessed Sacrament, and of the Virgin to fight a 'holy battle' for 'divinely given rights over education'.[37] The Spiritual Exercises movement was boosted in the ranks of Catholic Action, restructured in 1923 on similar lines to the fascist movements.

An active member of the Archconfraternity of the Immaculate Heart of Mary, the Franciscan Third Order and the Militia of St Thomas Aquinas, Ratti called on the Angelic Doctor early in his reign to preserve chastity in priests and deliver young men from 'the quicksands of passion'.[38] As a weapon against Modernism, the Militia received a complex series of indulgences (to be administered by the Dominicans) and a new medal of St Thomas with a picture of the Queen of the Most Holy Rosary on the reverse. In December 1922, castigating 'moral, legal and social Modernism' as well as the theological type, Pius XI spoke of Mary's 'veritable triumph' in having her new statue of Loreto blessed and crowned 'by Our own hands'.[39]

The Holy Year of 1925 marked a turning point both for Ratti's pontificate and the Duce's regime. Through the Leggi di Difesa (a corpus juris on national security) and a renewed agreement with the Holy See, the fascist state was greatly consolidated. An overhaul of ecclesiastical legislation began to tackle the 'Roman Question' and a new press law banned 'vilification of religion'. Freemasonry, the 'antithesis of the new Italy' representing the 'pacifist danger',[40] was ruthlessly suppressed,[41] and the corporative state and Fascist Grand Council strengthened.

Parallel to these developments, 1925 saw Vatican missionary exhibition, the jubilee of the apparition of the Queen of the Rosary (with processions to her shrine at Pompeii), pilgrimages to the eternal city for the beatification of numerous figures like the apostle of the Immaculate Heart of Mary, Jean Eudes, and the patroness of all the missions and Russia, Thérèse de Lisieux. The glory of Rome presented in these magnificent events was hailed as a 'return to the past' by the *Idea Nazionale*, a Roman daily which accused Freemasonry of sabotaging the Holy Year.[42]

In December, the encyclical *Quas Primas* instituted the feast of Christ the King and called for the restoration of 'the Empire of Our Lord'. Through the renewed consecration of mankind to the Sacred Heart, nations would be reminded that ruler and subject 'are bound to give public honour and obedience to Christ' and that the Church 'cannot be subject to any external power'. Church festivities and liturgical honours – especially those that venerate Mary – have produced such wonderful fruits as 'the perfect and perpetual immunity of the Church from error and heresy'.[43]

A distinctive form of clerico-fascism had now crystallized. In August 1926, Gramsci reported to the Italian Communist Party that Catholic Action 'today represents an integral part of fascism'.[44] The military mass in honour of Our Lady attended by the war minister later that year on Mount Grapa, north of Venice, was illustrative of the new Church-state collaboration.

The number of religious and members of Azione Cattolica rose steeply and Sacred Heart associations expanded and grew even more centralized. In 1928 Gemelli formed another group, the Men's Institute of Missionaries of the Kingship of Christ, which was put under the jurisdiction of Cardinal Schuster, Archbishop of Milan. That year the pope himself became spiritual director of the Family of Franciscan Tertiaries for Promoting the Social Reign of the Sacred Heart, which he renamed 'The Pious Association of Missionaries of the Kingship of Christ'.

A new encyclical on the Sacred Heart was issued later that year, calling for expiation and fulminating against sensuality and heresy (the very nidus of revolution): '. . . We purpose to expiate immodesty and shamelessness in behaviour and dress . . . the horrible blasphemies uttered against thee and thy saints, the revilings flung at thy vicar on earth and at thy priesthood. . . .'[45] The Virgin (whose cult of Fatima was soon to receive authorization) was invoked as 'mother of Reparation', for she it was who had 'offered Him a victim for our sins'.[46]

Mary's prerogatives and the pope's inerrancy remained signs of the elect: 'All true followers of Christ', wrote Pius in 1928, 'will believe the dogma of the Immaculate Conception of the Mother of God with the same faith as they believe the mystery of the august Trinity, the infallibility of the Roman Pontiff and the Incarnation.[47]

The date of the *conciliazione*, 11 February 1929, felicitously coincided with the feast of Our Lady of Lourdes, protectress of the Holy See, as Cardinal Gasparri did not fail to inform the Cavaliere Mussolini in the Lateran Palace.[48] The treaty recognized the absolute sovereignty of the pope in his 'Vatican City State' and Catholicism as the sole state religion.[49] The person of the Supreme Pontiff was 'sacred and inviolable', protected from 'public insults and offences made on Italian territory'.[50] The concordat guaranteed the 'sacred character of the Eternal City' as a 'goal of pilgrimages'.[51] The Santa Casa at Loreto was returned to papal jurisdiction.[52] The role of military chaplains was enhanced[53] and religious instruction made compulsory for elementary and secondary schools.[54]

Despite clear guidelines, conflict soon arose in the strategic field of education. The minister, Gentile, banned religious instruction in secondary schools in the belief that dogma was useful only for immature minds.[55] Ten months after the reconciliation, the pope was calling on Azione Cattolica to 'agitate' against the devaluation of Latin and 'pedagogic naturalism' founded on a denial of original sin. Sex instruction (an 'ugly term' to Ratti's mind) and co-education were considered illegitimate because they brought promiscuity and equality to the training of the sexes, exposing youth to 'the dangers of sensuality'.[56] Violence broke out between fascist youth and Catholic Action. The pope complained of 'rough hands upon the sodalities of the Children of Mary' and fascists' scorn for what they regarded as 'a swarm of "rabbits" only fit to carry candles and recite rosaries in sacred processions'.[57]

Facing a world recession of unprecedented dimensions, secretary of state Pacelli[58] and Fr Tacchi-Venturi, secretary-general of the Jesuits and an intimate of the Duce, achieved what amounted almost to a second reconciliation by September 1931: the *Acordo per l'Azione Cattolica*. The apostolate was now purged of officials who had belonged to 'parties hostile to the regime'[59] and was confined to activities of a purely religious character. 'I do not see', Pius XI is reported to have said in 1932, 'in the whole of Fascist doctrine – with its affirmation of the principles of order, authority and discipline – anything contrary to Catholic conceptions.'[60]

Yet another call for reparation to the Sacred Heart in 1932 seems calculated to assuage social discontent. Invoking the 'powerful patronage of the Blessed Virgin Mary, Mediatrix of all Graces', Ratti counselled 'holy austerity' and acceptance 'from the hand of God the effects of poverty'.[61] No weapon was to be resorted to in the 'hard trial of unemployment and scarcity of food' but prayer and penance, enhanced by that Marian virtue par excellence: humility.[62]

The same year saw the appearance in Venice under patriarchal approval of the 'Marian expiatory practice': exercises during the Month of Mary of reparation for blasphemy and the denial of her 'privileges'.

The auriferous Santa Casa became even more active as a national centre. Crowds flocked to the shrine to receive the sacraments on the Nativity of Mary and other festivals. Squadrons of the Royal Italian Airforce escorted her statue. On the *Festa della translazione* in 1934, Pius XI called Loreto '*il primo santuario mariano del mondo*'[63] and in 1936 he granted the same indulgences for visiting Mary's winged house as enjoyed by Lourdes and Palestine.

Mussolini's imperial dreams, rooted in a mythical Rome,[64] were shared by a papacy eager to assert itself after decades of political blockade and mortal danger. The 'glorious Pope of the Missions' had proclaimed in his first encyclical (1922) that Rome

> being the capital of the wonderful Roman Empire, was made by Him [God] the capital of the whole world, because He made it the seat of a sovereignty which, since it extends beyond the confines of nations and States, embraces within itself the Peoples of the whole world.[65]

The mystical nature of Rome was the basis of 'Latinity' – an ideology common to Church and state and one which naturally gave sustenance to the Christian goddess who had succeeded to Minerva's patronage of the eternal city. During celebrations in 1937 of the second millenium of the reign of Augustus, Cardinal Schuster compared the emperor with the Duce, finding a profound religious significance in the festivities.[66]

Capital of fascism and Catholicism, Rome was seen as the power most able to contend victoriously with the Reds in the east and the liberals in the west. As a leading Spanish Falangist wrote, 'The Church marches towards the restoration of Rome in the world, guided by Fascism. The Church is beginning to see in Fascism her new salvation.'[67]

A third front was to be opened to crusade and empire: Africa. The invasion of Ethiopia – aimed, in part, at the control of the Red Sea and the future of Palestine – was justified in 1935 by Action Française (see chapter 22) as the struggle of civilization against barbarism.[68] When in that year economic sanctions were imposed on Italy by the League of Nations (*Torre di Babele* of Freemasonry, Bolshevism and Anglicanism)[69] and while she was still fighting with poison gas to capture Addis Ababa, bishops called on the '*cuore della Dolcissima Madre Nostra*'[70] to protect the soldier-pioneers of Italian civilization, assuring the faithful that the war would 'smooth the way for the missionary of the Gospel';[71] the conquest of the 'barbarous Ethiopian empire' would free 'the slaves of the monophysite heresy'.[72] Religion and Patria, as in fascist Spain, had become one and the same thing. Italy, '*terra predilleta da Dio*[73] and her national flag were divinely favoured in this 'providential historic mission of Roman Christian Civilization'.[74] The glory of Jerusalem transferred to Rome through Peter belonged to the Holy See, whose custody was the 'exclusive privilege of the Italian people'.[75]

Ratti's support for the imperial designs of 'a great and good people'[76] (as he described the victors in Africa) was confirmed in 1937 by the bestowal of the Golden Rose – an honour given to Marian shrines – on Queen Elena as Empress of Abyssinia.

25

PATRONESS OF THE ESTADO NÔVO: OUR LADY OF FATIMA AND DR SALAZAR

Just a word, ladies and gentlemen, there can be no doubt about it, we are indestructible because Providence has willed it so, and you on earth also desire it.[1]

Antonio de Oliveira Salazar,
on surviving an assassination attempt

I never speak or write anything at all that comes from myself alone. I have to thank God for the assistance of the Divine Holy Spirit, whom I feel within me, suggesting to me what I am to write or say.[2]

Sister Mary Lucia of the Immaculate Heart,
the seer of Fatima

'MASONIC STATE' AND LUSITANIAN 'REGRESSION'

Led by Italian Jesuits, the orders began to return to Portugal from 1850 onwards but they were never to recover their prosperity. By far the most important lay association was the Apostleship of Prayer, organized in Portugal by Fr Antonio Marcocci,SJ, in 1864. By 1909, it could claim to have 1,505 branches with two million members – a staggering 34 per cent of the total population.[3] This potential for mobilizing the rural masses under the banners of the Sacred Heart and Immaculate Conception made Portugal, in the judgement of future prime minister Afonso Costa, 'a dependency of Jesuitism, which dominated King Manuel'.[4] The country was designated a Jesuit province in 1880 and the Portuguese College opened in Rome in

1898 to raise the level of the clergy, lampooned for decades in the liberal press.

Relentless forces were closing in on the Church in Portugal. Most of the lodges – the subversive machinery of liberalism as in France, Italy and Spain – were centralized in the United Lusitanian Grand Orient in 1869, and in 1871 a branch of the First International opened. Benefiting from the monarchy's extravagance, personality disorders and political interventions[5] against a background of extreme poverty and economic stagnation, the Republican Party (founded in 1876) began planning a revolution through the network of Masonic lodges and *ventes* of the Carbonaria,[6] two of whose members assassinated Carlos I and the crown prince in 1908. The Republic was declared on 5 October 1910 after a three-day battle.

The provisional government took anti-clerical measures whose ferocity has been compared to that experienced in Russia in 1917 and Spain in 1931.[7] Within three days of the proclamation of the Republic, Costa, as minister of justice, banned the orders, expelled the Jesuits and the papal nuncio, and seized all ecclesiastical property, including seminaries and episcopal residences. Clergy were forbidden to teach and religious instruction was abolished in state schools. The latter task was supervised by the Lusitanian Grand Master, Dr Sebastião Magalhaes-Lima[8] – a minister of education committed to fighting 'the spirit of hatred spread by religions'.[9]

Divorce was duly introduced and church marriages divested of legal status. Priests – now permitted to marry, thus ending their practice of 'concubinage' – were forbidden to wear robes in public. The military chaplain corps was disbanded and the army forbidden to attend religious ceremonies. Twenty-six Catholic holidays were given back to production and Christmas was renamed 'Day of the Family'. The Patriarch of Lisbon, the Archbishops of Braga, Guarda and Portalegre, and the Bishops of Oporto and Beja were exiled and many priests gaoled in degrading conditions.[10]

By an act of separation the following year, the Church was stripped of all financial privileges. Worship was strictly controlled by local boards of laymen, not necessarily Catholics. Only Portuguese priests who had studied in the country were allowed to officiate and non-religious missions were sent to Africa 'to spread Portuguese civilization, give prestige to the Fatherland and nationalize the indigenous population.'[11]

During the next seven turbulent years Costa served three times as prime minister. His claims to democratic socialism did not prevent the suppression of rural strikes with exceptional brutality and in 1913 his government disenfranchised 77 per cent of the population: illiterates, women (the latter on the grounds that they were controlled by their confessors), and serving members of the army, whose reply was the 'Movement of Swords' coup in January 1915 (reversed by Carbonario action in May). Costa's boast in Braga that the country would see 'the annihilation of Catholicism in two generations' (1911)[12] already seemed empty.

As the prime minister raged against the altar in the 'Portuguese Rome', an avowedly 'reactionary'[13] movement began to take shape among law students at Coimbra: Lusitanian Integralism. The apostle of integralism in Iberia was the 'fervent Catholic'[14] and monarchist Antonio Sardinha (1887-1925), author of *La Alianza Peninsular*, viewed in Spain as the 'capital work of Hispanidad'.[15]

The cornerstone of Sardinha's philosophy was 'regression': Iberia had to regress to its 'natural conditions'[16] of development, and Europe to the 'living sources' of scholasticism,[17] the only way of salvation. Even Portugal's 'rebuked unadaptability'[18] to modernity seemed to him the soundest guarantee of a positive western 'transfiguration'.[19] Heavily influenced by Maurras, Sardinha called for the rejection of 'philosophical individualism' and 'economic theories manifestly of Judaic roots'.[20] His teaching and motto 'Re-Portuguize'[21] found immediate resonance with Catholic corporativism, inspiring both Salazar and Caetano.[22]

Salazar entered the law faculty in 1910 – the year before Sardinha received his doctorate – and worked with Manuel Gonçalves Cerejeira, the future primate, to revive a counter-Masonic network that was to play a 'preponderate role in the government of the country':[23] Centro Academico de Democracia Cristã. An extension of the Academic Congregation of the Sons of Mary (1878),[24] the CADC was founded in 1901 by absolutists to undermine the lodges' influence at Coimbra. The future dictator, who had headed his seminary's sodality of Our Lady, became secretary of the CADC and his flatmate Cerejeira edited its journal *Imparcial*. With the motto 'Piety, Study, Action'[25] – emulative of the Catholic Association of French Youth – the CADC was to provide the National Dictatorship with a steady supply of ministers, university professors and bishops. Several members of this clique including Salazar himself were under the personal guidance of Fr Crawley Boevey. CADC sponsored 'Marian Weeks'[26] in its Lisbon headquarters and dominated the Society of St Vincent de Paul.

APPARITIONS AND COUP D'ETAT

In 1915 Lucia dos Santos, an eight-year-old shepherdess of Fatima, some 80 miles north of Lisbon, was sitting on a hillside praying the rosary when she saw a figure floating over the trees. Her first vision met with disbelief and scorn, even from a pious mother.

The seventh child of a drunken smallholder, Lucia's illiteracy was compensated by psittacine powers in learning prayers and stories: she knew all about the visits of Nossa Senhora to Lourdes and La Salette.[27] An early first communion was at first refused her but a timely intervention by Fr Francisco da Cruz, national director of the Apostleship of Prayer, persuaded the *cura* that her catechetical knowledge was outstanding.[28]

By Lucia's next supernatural encounter, Portugal had been forced to accept further loans from Britain and enter the world war as her ally (March 1916). 'The Angel of Peace', a beautiful adolescent, told Lucia and her younger cousins Francisco and Jacinta Marto that the hearts of Jesus and Mary were 'attentive to your supplications'.[29] In the summer of that year, he presented himself as 'the Angel of Portugal'. By that time, disastrous military expeditions weighed heavily against an unpopular regime. The Angel told the children to 'bear with submission the suffering which the Lord will send you';[30] he taught them prayers of adoration and dispensed the Eucharist from a chalice suspended in the air.

Thus heralded, the Virgin appeared in the Cova da Iria, a remote wooded spot near Fatima, the following year on 13 May – the month bread riots broke out in Lisbon. '. . . there before us on a small holmoak, we beheld a Lady all dressed in white. She was more brilliant than the sun.'[31]

She returned regularly on the thirteenth of the month until October. The children were asked if they were ready to suffer for the conversion of sinners and told to recite the rosary daily 'in order to obtain peace for the world and the end of the war'. The apparition demanded expiation in 'reparation of sins committed against the Immaculate Heart of Mary'.

For the *cura* of Fatima – transferred shortly afterwards – 'the finger of the demon' could be discerned in the stories.[32] Fr Cruz, who had narrowly escaped with his life during the republican revolution,[33] became one of the children's spiritual directors. News of the apparitions spread like wildfire and in July 4,000 pilgrims converged on the Cova. On 13 August the district administrator – 'an ambitious young freemason'[34] – imprisoned the seers (already mortifying themselves with nettle-stings and tight belts) and threatened to boil them in oil unless they revealed the secret message. Meanwhile, the government denounced the visions as 'a Jesuitical farce'[35] and sent troops to cut off approaches to Fatima. These measures did not prevent 100,000 people gathering there on 13 October 1917, when Nossa Senhora performed a public miracle: 'the sun appeared to whirl in the sky, throwing off shafts of coloured lights'[36] like a Catherine wheel.

The embryonic cult continued to mobilize popular support for an uprising. On 8 November the daily *A Monarquia* splashed Sardinha's claim that the case had 'turned the official mentality of the regime upside down'. On 6 December, a military coup ended the persecution of the Church. A front page story three days later leaves no doubt as to the politicization of the apparitions from the beginning:

> The maternal assistance of the Virgin to our dear Fatherland
> has revealed itself once again, and marvellously . . . Portuguese
> Jacobinism encountered its Thermidor in the end, precisely on
> the day of the Patroness of Portugal. . . . The Virgin spoke on the
> heath of Fatima to three innocent shepherds, pledging her blessing
> on the unhappy land of Portugal . . . the history of Portugal is the
> history of the cult of Mary. Once more the Virgin has crushed
> the serpent.[37]

THE ESTABLISHMENT OF FATIMA UNDER MILITARY DICTATORSHIP

Devotion to the Blesssed Virgin revived dramatically, with many families signing the diocesan 'golden book' promising to recite the rosary every day at home.[38] Church privileges were gradually restored, for the new rulers were not militantly Catholic. Their leader, Major Sidonio Paes (assassinated December 1918) was a 'moderate Mason';[39] another junta member was Machado Santos, Carbonario 'Founder of the Republic'. The Catholic Centre Party, which Salazar had helped to found, gained in strength and in 1918 relations with the Vatican were restored. Benedict XV spoke of new hope 'founded above all on the ardent devotion of your people for the Immaculate Virgin. Such a devotion merited the exceptional help on the part of the Mother of God.'[40]

During the fifteen years between the Fatima coup and the assumption of the premiership by Salazar in 1932, the country saw 39 governments, frequent riots, bombings, assassinations, bankruptcies and a brief civil war when attempts to restore the monarchy found support in the clericalist north. Meanwhile, the cult of Fatima moved steadily towards its destiny – in the eyes of Portuguese Jesuits – as 'the centre of the world' and 'capital of the empire'.[41]

The first moves of the ecclesiastical machine were routine and precautionary. The territory was brought under special supervision by a papal decree restoring the ancient diocese of Leiria-Fatima and Bishop Jose Alves Correia da Silva chaired a canonical inquiry lasting nearly eight years. By the beginning of 1920 the Marto children had died of pneumonia and tuberculosis. Their deaths facilitated control of the cult as well as contributing to its appeal: the authorities could concentrate on a single mouthpiece (Lucia) while building a picture of two potential saints from the same captive source in order to create boy and girl models for later programmes of juvenile identification.[42] Each child was allocated a sphere of spiritual influence in the didactic package of Fatima.[43]

In June 1921, as the investigation of the events in the Cova got under way, the fourteen-year-old Lucia was placed under the protection of the Bishop of Leiria, who sent her to a private school run by the Dorotheans[44] outside Oporto. In the same year diocesan permission was granted to celebrate mass in the 'Chapel of the Apparitions' built next to the holmoak; and the Rev Dr Manuel Nunes Formigão, known in print as 'The Viscount of Montelo', published the first book on the subject, *The Marvellous Episodes of Fatima.*[45]

A bomb destroyed the shrine in March 1922. The integralists blamed the Freemasons, 'who foment all these ignoble sacrileges'.[46] The CADC headquarters were also bombed in 1923 and 1924. As the inquiry laboriously collected statements with the aid of Fr Cruz and 'Viscount' Formigão, the beautiful countryside of the Cova was bulldozed to make way for a vast site for national worship.

In 1925 Lucia was installed in a Dorothean convent at Pontevedra, just across the border in Galicia. Shortly after entering the novitiate, she was visited by the Virgin and Child. Placing one hand on Lucia's shoulder and holding a thorn-encircled heart in the other, the Mother promised

> to assist at the hour of death, with the graces necessary
> for salvation, all those who, on the first Saturday of five
> consecutive months, shall confess, receive Holy Communion,
> recite five decades of the Rosary, and keep me company
> for fifteen minutes while meditating on the fifteen mysteries
> of the Rosary, with the intention of making reparation
> to me.[47]

On 28 May 1926 came what has also been claimed as a Marian coup. Drawing his sword in Braga, General Gomes da Costa made the verbose *pronunciamento* that marked the beginning of western Europe's longest dictatorship. Troops of the eighth infantry regiment were given moral support by a Marian congress then in session: demonstrations of military strength coincided with a procession in honour of the Immaculate Conception – one explanation for the bloodless and successful outcome of the uprising.[48] The officers were also backed by the more mundane Union of Economic Interests (representing capitalists and landowners).

Professor Salazar was already established as the 'undisputed spiritual leader of the Portuguese Right',[49] having starred at a Eucharistic congress the year before in 'this holy city of our national revolution'.[50] In 1928 he was appointed finance minister and swiftly drew in the reins of power, General Carmona accepting a ceremonial role as president. Salazar's minister of justice was Mario de Figueiredo, a fellow CADC members and ex-seminarist. Archbishop Cerejeira became cardinal primate.

Nearly half a million pilgrims visited Fatima in 1928 – the year Portugal was consecrated to the Sacred Heart – while foundations of the basilica were laid. Dr Formigão wrote to the Bishop of Leiria in January 1929

> The wave is rising, so the holy Dr Cruz told me yesterday. Fatima is now a source of grace not only for Portugal, but for the entire world. And if it is such now, what will happen some years hence, with the intense propaganda that is beginning to make an impact on the foreign press?[51]

President Carmona took part in the celebrations at Fatima on the twelfth anniversary of the first apparition. A month later (13 June 1929), Lucia was granted the 'Great Apparition' in a Dorothean convent at Tuy (Spain).

> '. . . it was Our Lady of Fatima, with her Immaculate Heart in her left hand, without sword or roses, but with a crown of thorns and flames. . . . Our Lady then said to me: "The moment has come in which God asks the Holy Father, in union with all the Bishops of the world, to make the consecration of Russia to my Immaculate Heart, promising to save it by this means." '[52]

Jesuit backing was crucial for Fatima's future. Confessors of the Society directed the Institute of St Dorothy in Spain and Portugal, supervising – and later editing – Lucia's correspondence,[53] some of which reached Popes Pius XI and XII. An account of the miracles by Professor Gonzaga da Fonseca,SJ,[54] of the Pontifical Biblical Institute was enthusiastically read by Jesuits, especially in France, Spain and Italy.[55]

Pius XI, who handed out Fatima picture cards to his visitors even before the cult's authorization (1930),[56] wrote to Cerejeira in 1933 that Portugal had been 'recently favoured in an extraordinary way by the Most Blessed Virgin'. This fact, in Ratti's view, would stimulate the growth of Catholic Action 'so that none of those of Our children, who, at such risk to their souls, join Socialist organizations'.[57]

LAY POPE OF FATIMA

The vestry fascism created by the 'Dictatorship of Reason and Intelligence',[58] as Salazar preferred his rule to be known, was inseparable from the new Marian shrine. According to President

Mario Soares, 'Salazarism and the Church in Portugal were intimately intertwined. ... For decades the twin powers were indistinguishable.'[59] For Dr Soares, Fatima's 'political implications are certainly beyond question'.[60] 'Dr Salazar', observed the director of the national secretariat of propaganda, 'might as well have been directing affairs of State from a sentry box or from a monk's cell.'[61] The prime minister was indeed a theopathic figure, ascribing his escape from assassination to a pact with the Virgin he made as a seminarist.[62]

Living in 'the grace of poverty',[63] Salazar was a celibate whose idea of the family – 'the purest source of the moral factors of production'[64] – embraced the whole nation. A 'mystic devoted to God and his figures'[65] whose only trip abroad took in Lourdes, he was trained for the priesthood from the age of eleven but, after taking minor orders, chose the academic cloister of Coimbra.

As dictator, he reputedly passed nights before a statue of Our Lady in his private chapel and prayed the rosary as he spoke to General Franco on the telephone.[66] Notwithstanding some Mussolinian features of the Estado Nôvo (for example, Masonry was outlawed in 1935), Salazar failed to accord to the masses the role given them in Italy, being 'neither influenced nor directed by them'.[67] The 'primacy of the spiritual',[68] especially as manifested in the armed forces,[69] was the final aim of this lay pope (for whom communism was 'the great heresy of our time'.).[70] His quasi-pontifical status was acknowledged in 1937 when indulgences were attached by the Bishop of Coimbra to novenas for 'our Chief Salazar'.[71]

Separation of Church and state was confirmed in Salazar's 'corporative and unitary' constitution of 1933,[72] though in practice religion continued to be subordinated to the regime. This was particularly evident in the missionary statute of April 1941, which stated 'The Portuguese Catholic Missions are considered institutions of imperial utility'. The year before, Pius XII – who saw a mystical significance in the fact that his episcopal ordination had taken place on 13 May 1917 and who was by now known in Portugal as 'the Pope of Fatima' – praised the Portuguese 'colonial and sacred expeditions' which 'hoped to subject the barbarians to the sweet yoke of Jesus Christ', and invoked Our Lady of Fatima in prayers for more missionary vocations.[73]

Fatima's power as a symbol was much increased by the Salazarist youth movement, the Mocidade, who paraded at the shrine, and

Portuguese Catholic Action, dedicated by Pius XI in 1933 to Christ the King and the Lady of the Cova. For every child this process of indoctrination began at primary school,[74] 'the sacred factory of souls'.[75]

The perceived threat to Portugal posed by the Spanish civil war served to consolidate the shrine's ideological position. In October 1936 the national episcopate promised Our Lady a pilgrimage to Fatima if their country were protected from the 'Red danger'.[76] The bishops accomplished their vow in May 1938, leading a crowd of half a million. In April 1940 prelates assembled there to declare war on vice and call for an 'empire of Christian virtues' which would vanquish the 'delinquency of behaviour' that was subjugating the country to 'a yoke as vile as that of the Moor'.[77]

SILENCE OF THE POPE OF FATIMA AND DEVELOPMENT OF THE CULT

Towards the end of December 1940, Sister Lucia sent a letter 'on the orders of my Spiritual Director'[78] to Pius XII, disclosing for the first time part of the 'secret' about Russia revealed to her in the visions of 1917, 1925 and 1929. Beyond urging the pope to consecrate Russia to the Immaculate Heart and institute the 'first five Saturdays' devotion, Lucia went into little detail, 'leaving it to God to provide another more favourable opportunity'.[79]

In April 1941 German, Italian and Hungarian forces occupied Yugoslavia and set up in the state of Croatia the puppet Ante Pavelic, head of the Ustaša movement, with whom the Holy See duly exchanged diplomatic representatives. A campaign of 'evangelization' was subsequently launched among the 2.2 million Christian Orthodox Serbs in Croatia. Of these, 600,000 who refused to submit to Rome were massacred with unbelievable savagery. 250,000 'converted' and around 300,000 were deported along with Jewish communities.[80] Jesuits and Franciscans are accused of participation in these policies, while the papacy, 'aware of Ustase crimes',[81] remained silent.

June 1941 was a momentous month for the message of Fatima and the closely related cult of the Sacred Heart in Falangist Spain. On the twelfth, Sister Lucia – still resident in Spain – conversed with

Mgr García y García, the influential Archbishop of Valladolid, who continued to visit her during the war.[82] On the twentieth – two days before the Nazi invasion of Russia – the nuncio, Mgr Cicognani, inaugurated in Valladolid the Sacred Heart sanctuary of the Great Promise – or 'National Temple of Expiation', the apparitional centre of the Jesuits in Spain. Exactly a week later, recruitment of Franco's Blue Division began, to augment 'Christian arms' against 'the enemies of civilization'.[83]

The Spanish volunteers – as well as other Catholic troops from Italy, Hungary, Croatia, Slovakia, Portugal and Ireland converging on the eastern front – were encouraged by a radio broadcast from the pope, who spoke of the 'consoling sight that opens the heart to great and holy expectations: the high-minded value of the defence of Christian culture and reliable hopes for its triumph.'[84] In an allusion to the purification of Russia, Pacelli said, 'As rough as the hand of the divine surgeon may appear when it pierces human flesh with the sword, still it is always only active love that directs and moves it.'[85]

Not long before the invasion, Sister Lucia received urgent orders to contribute to a new edition of Dr Galamba's *Jacinta*,[86] to be issued in time for the silver jubilee of the apparitions. On 31 August 1941 she sent to the Bishop of Leiria a fuller account of the 'secret' relating to Russia:

> When you see a night illumined by an unknown light, know
> that this is the great sign given you by God that he is about
> to punish the world for its crimes, by means of war, famine, and
> persecutions of the Church and of the Holy Father. To prevent
> this, I shall come to ask for the consecration of Russia to my
> Immaculate Heart. . . . If my requests are heeded, Russia will
> be converted, and there will be peace; if not, she will spread her
> errors throughout the world, causing wars and persecutions of the
> Church . . . various nations will be annihilated. In the end, my
> Immaculate Heart will triumph.[87]

The episcopal jubilee of Pius XII in 1942 provided Cardinal Schuster of Milan (see previous Chapter) with an opportunity to promote the Fatima visions and call for the conversion of Russia to 'Catholic unity'.[88] During the same month as the Cardinal's pastoral (April), the image of Our Lady of Fatima made its first appearance outside the sanctuary, 'conquering Lisbon' as the armed forces and youth organizations lined the streets in welcome.[89] This 'triumphal visitation' took place during a season of *The Power of Fatima* at the Teatro Nacional.[90]

In October, Pacelli made a clear allusion to Russia in his broadcast to the crowds gathered at the Cova.[91] And on 8 December 1942 he responded partially to Lucia's promptings by consecrating the world to the Immaculate Heart in St Peter's basilica. The papal act marked the hegemony of the cult of Mary in its newest form: '. . . just as the Church and entire human race were consecrated to the Heart of your Jesus, . . . they are henceforth perpetually consecrated to you, to your Immaculate Heart, O our Mother; and Queen of the World. . . .'[92] Cardinal Cerejeira expressed the hope that Fatima would be for the cult of the Immaculate Heart what Paray-le-Monial was for the Sacred Heart.

The new shrine was an ideological fulcrum in the remaining war years and a rich resource for the two surviving dictatorships after 1945. Led by the Society of Jesus, integralist forces mobilized the whole of Portugal around the latest message of Our Lady. On the feast of the Immaculate Conception in 1942, 1,461 sections of the Female League of Portuguese Catholic Action launched a 'campaign of purity' and 'crusade campaign of Fatima'.[93] During the Month of Mary (May) the following year, Catholic Youth promoted a 'week of sacrifice', which closed with a national pilgrimage to the Cova.[94] In the Month of the Rosary (October), some 5,000 workers came to Fatima for the first time after a magnificent torchlight procession in Lisbon.[95]

Towards the end of 1943 Lucia was persuaded to write down the 'third part of the secret'. The document, sealed by the Bishop of Leiria, was deposited in the Secret Archives of the Vatican.

Spain also deployed the cult of the Immaculate Heart in its 'rechristianization' programme and its 'European mission' against 'Judaism and Bolshevism'.[96] As news of heavy casualties in the 'glorious Blue Division'[97] reached western Europe, Spanish bishops praised the rosary as a means of obtaining peace.[98] Diocese after diocese from Vitoria to Malaga was consecrated to the Immaculate Heart and thousands of fliers relating the message of Fatima were scattered throughout the peninsula.

Large numbers of Spanish and Portuguese schoolchildren went through the ritual of consecration to the Immaculate Heart, using a formula composed by Pacelli himself. Numerous Catholic Action units also complying with pontifical wishes, dedicated their annual meeting in 1943 to the Heart of Our Lady. The 1944 assembly of the Spanish Mariological Society was celebrated in Fatima – 'the very same place of the manifestations of the most Pure Heart'.[99] That year, the pope extended the feast of the Immaculate Heart to the universal Church - as requested by Lucia.[100]

In May 1946 – by which time Franco's regime was internationally isolated[101] – the papal legate performed a canonical coronation of the Fatima statue[102] before great personages of the Catholic orbit[103] and a crowd of 600,000.

In the judgment of Professor Diogo Pacheco de Amorim, a leading light in the CADC, Fatima had already become 'a fact of contemporary history with a projection throughout the world. Not only is it a confirmation of the supernatural and of faith, but it is also a guarantee and testimony of the spiritual unity of the nation. And, as such, no government should ignore Fatima or disassociate itself from its patriotic significance.'[104] Echoing Antonio Sardinha, he added, 'It is through Fatima that the Portuguese of today learn to be more Portuguese.'[105]

26

POLAND AND THE CONVERSION OF RUSSIA

At once Mary appeared before him holding two crowns, one
white, the other red. She told him the white crown was for purity,
the red for martyrdom.[1]

Saint of Auschwitz: The Story of Maksymilian Kolbe

Under the 'caesaro-papism' of Nicholas II, the Russian Empire's six
million Catholics were forbidden to proselytize and their clergy cut
off from Rome. Lenin's decree of January 1918 separating church
and state (and the school from religion) seemed, in its provision of
'freedom of conscience', like a chink in the armour of Orthodox Russia. In the year of the revolution the pope granted autonomous status
to the Sacred Congregation for the Eastern Church and founded the
Pontifical Institute for Oriental Studies under Jesuit direction.

In April 1918 he ordered the prefect of the Vatican Library to
Warsaw as the first visitor apostolic for a hundred years. In the
newly-independent Poland, Mgr Ratti, who as nuncio had taken
the suggestive title of Archbishop of Lepanto, became involved in
a complex scheme to isolate the Bolsheviks through a federation of
Catholic nations in central and eastern Europe: Bavaria, Austria,
Slovakia, Bohemia, Hungary and Croatia. The mastermind of
this abortive plan was the Jesuit general Vladimir Ledochowski
(1915–42), an aristocratic Austrian Pole, who also counted on
the support of nuncio Pacelli (the future Pius XII) in Berlin.[2]
Franciscans, it was rumoured, 'were waiting at the frontiers of
Austrian Poland' to fulfil the Russian Christian's 'expectations of a
Messiah'. Bolshevism would 'pass like an evil dream'.[3]

The mystique that 'Mary' would have lent to the 'Ledochowski
Plan' is particularly clear in the case of Poland, where the
seventeenth-century vows of King Jan Casimir were still regarded
as valid. In order to repulse the Swedish and Muscovite invaders,
Jan Casimir entrusted the 'Polish Commonwealth' to the Virgin and

proclaimed her 'Queen of the Polish Crown'.[4] As the royal vows were made in Lwóv (now part of the Soviet Union) and embraced the duchies of Lithuania, Ruthenia, Prussia and so on, they form the religious cornerstone of Polish irredentism.

Impressed by Polish Marianism and 'attachment to the Church and the Supreme Pontiff',[5] Ratti witnessed in August 1920 the 'Miracle of the Vistula' – the battle on the feast of the Assumption at which Marshal Pilsudski routed the Russians against all odds, a victory attributed to the intervention of Our Lady of Czestochowa.

Once providence had put several million Russian Orthodox and Greek Uniat Christians into Polish territory, a savage crusade was launched to 'Polonize' these 'schismatics'. Churches were burnt and desecrated by Polish troops and thousands of priests arrested. The nuns of the Sacred Heart, whose Polish operation had been closed down in 1874, were welcomed back during this period.[6] Benedict XV, failing to denounce the 'Catholic terror',[7] made an important move in the Mariological sphere by conferring on the hymnographer and Orthodox saint Ephraem the Syrian the title and honours of 'Doctor of the Universal Church' (October 1920).

Della Chiesa's famed generosity was given full rein during the Volga famine of 1921. An official relief mission providing food and clothing for a million children was maintained for two years under Fr Edmund J. Walsh,SJ. Regent of the School of Foreign Service at Georgetown University (Washington), Walsh took the opportunity of entering into secret negotiations with the Soviets, liaising with the White House as well as the Vatican.[8]

Rome's proposals were hindered by Church-backed aggression from Poland (also a recipient of Vatican aid) which led to the execution in Russia of one Catholic prelate as a counter-revolutionary agent. Negotiations were finally dropped when the Soviets decided to rehabilitate the Orthodox faith through the ephemeral 'Living Church', whose hierarchy declared the regime 'the only rule in the world that achieves on earth by governmental means the ideals of the Kingdom of Heaven'.[9] The Vatican then resorted to an undercover priesthood led by Michel d'Herbigny,SJ, secretly consecrated titular bishop by Pacelli in 1926. Three years later the 'Russicum' college was founded at Rome under d'Herbigny to train ordinands for the conversion of Russia.

A major division to spring from this Ostpolitik was the Militia Immaculatae, which thrived during the military dictatorship of

Pilsudski (1926–35). This mixed (religious and lay) apostolate is significant as much for the continuing theological influence of the founder, St Maximilian Kolbe (1894–1941) as for its anti-Masonic inspiration and 'dynamic Catholic Marian Action'.[10]

The Knights of the Immaculate were conceived on the feast day of Marguerite Marie Alacoque in 1917 while Kolbe – favoured at the age of ten with an apparition of the Virgin[11] – was attending the Gregorian University. The immediate objective of the Franciscan student was to combat the lodges in the eternal city by means of prayer and the distribution of Miraculous Medals;[12] even today, the stated aim is the 'conversion of every person living in sin, heresy, schism and especially Freemasonry, and the growth in holiness of all persons, under the sponsorship of the BVM Immaculate'.[13] Propagation of Catherine Labouré's charm remains mandatory and anti-Masonic 'ejaculations' are encouraged.[14]

Members are ranked, like the enemy, in three 'degrees': MI–1 for ordinary members; MI–2 for activists (in recruitment, propaganda and Marian evangelization); MI–3 – 'a truly heroic degree, mainly for religious',[15] who live 'in limitless consecration and mystic union with Mary'.[16]

After his ordination in 1918 Kolbe returned to Poland to found what became the world's largest friary, with 750 brothers.[17] As early as 1922, Piux XI approved the Militia Immaculatae as a 'pious union' and five years later granted it powers of aggregation.

In 1927 – the year the Marshal gave orders for the vows of Jan Casimir to be repeated before the Madonna at Vilna in a coronation attended by ministers, diplomats, bishops and enormous crowds[18] – the Militia was given land to build Niepokalanow ('City of the Immaculate') as a centre for radio broadcasting and publishing. There were 126,000 Knights at that time and Kolbe's monthly *Rycerz Niepokalanej* (*Knights of the Immaculate*) had a circulation of 50,000.[19] By 1939 the 'little blue magazine' had attracted nearly a million subscribers,[20] with a Niepokalanow national daily reaching 250,000. This put Fr Kolbe at the head of the country's largest media enterprise.[21] In 1930 Kolbe founded a second city of the Immaculate near Nagasaki, and similar missions were established by the Franciscan knights throughout the world.[22]

Despite the fact that the Militia's publications had been accused of anti-Semitism before the Nazi invasion of Poland,[23] Kolbe was arrested by the Gestapo for suspected patriotic activities and died in August 1941 at Auschwitz on offering to take the place of a condemned Catholic. Testimonies to his serenity and evangelistic zeal among fellow prisoners were given at his beatification (1971) and canonization (1982).

Kolbe's Mariology (he was a trained theologian) is based on a literalist interpretation of utterances by the apparitions at the rue du Bac (the Miraculous Medal) and Lourdes ('I am the Immaculate Conception'). He considered the latter vision 'a confirmation of the whole Catholic faith'.[24] Influenced by Grignion de Montfort and the nineteenth-century German Matthias Scheeben, Kolbe taught that Mary is 'in a certain sense, the "incarnation" of the Holy Spirit'.[25] This realization led him to conclude, 'The Holy Spirit is the uncreated Immaculate Conception'.[26] In 'practical' devotional terms the Third Person of the Trinity and the Mother of Jesus are one.

> The Immaculata is united to the Holy Spirit so closely that we really cannot grasp this union. But we can say that the Holy Spirit and Mary are two persons who live in such intimate union that they have but one sole life.[27]

This concept seems to have paved the way for the charismatic movement within the Marian vanguard of the Church 30 years later (see chapter 35). Traditional baptism in the name of the Holy Trinity was insufficient for the Grand Knight: 'He wanted to see every person renew his baptismal promises by making an unreserved consecration to the Immaculata, thus making effective his rebirth in baptism'[28] – another idea strikingly in keeping with the obligatory 'spirit baptism' of the Neo-Pentecostals.

In the saint's theory of mediation and grace

> 'The Father acts through the Son, and the Son through the Holy Spirit; and, like a bridge between the Holy Spirit and the rest of creation we find the most perfect creature of all, the Immaculata. . . . Everything that the Holy Spirit receives from the Son, and the Son receives from the Father, the Holy Spirit gives to the Immaculata . . . all the graces we receive come to us through Mary alone. If we are unwilling to receive them from her we shall get none.'[29]

Poland also provided a 'continuation of the Sacred Heart messages':[30] the Divine Mercy devotions based on apparitions of Christ and Mary to Faustina Kowalska of the Congregation of Our Lady of Mercy between 1931 and the nun's death in 1938. Christ told her, 'I have loved Poland particularly. If she obeys my will, I will raise her up in power and sanctity. From her will come forth a spark that will prepare the world for my final coming.'[31] Sister Faustina's devotions, which involved saying the 'chaplet of Mary' and preserving homes by displaying a picture of the vision, were diffused worldwide by the Pallottine and Marian Fathers – until their suppression by John XXIII in 1959.

27

A GOLDEN HEART
FOR THE POOR:
THE BELGIAN APPARITIONS

Neuropathologists of wide experience will tell us that children
who take a delight in romancing or carrying on an elaborate
mystification are by no means rare; moreover, they are often
extraordinarily ingenious in keeping up the deception.[1]

Herbert Thurston, SJ

The last two Marian apparitions to be 'authenticated' by the Catholic
Church – chosen from a chain of visions across Belgium in the early
1930s – took place during a severe economic crisis exacerbated by
the double threat of socialism and war; they were backed by clerico-
fascists, the episcopate and the royal family. The circumstances and
development of the Virgin with the heart of gold (Beauraing) and 'the
Virgin of the Poor', as the cult at Banneaux became known officially,[2]
conform in major aspects to the paradigm in Part II.

Beauraing is a village near Dinant in the French-speaking south,
where 37 apparitions were experienced by five working-class children
(four girls and a boy) between 29 November 1932 and 3 January
1933.[3] On the first occasion Mary hovered over a railway bridge
and later appeared beside a Lourdes grotto in the garden of a
school run by the Sisters of Christian Doctrine. The vision was of
a blue-eyed *dame luisante* in a white robe. 'On her head she wore
a diadem . . . like those worn by certain Russian princesses of the
sixteenth and seventeenth centuries but without precious stones.'[4]
The crown was of an unusual design, consisting of a ring of vertical
tubes like children's crayons. The lady carried a rosary, whose
beads she told as the children recited the Hail Mary. Secrets were
imparted by the visitor, whose 'heart of gold' was visible to the seers.
Paraphrasing Our Lady of Lourdes, the apparition announced, 'I am
the Immaculate Virgin'.

On 8 December (feast of the Immaculate Conception) around 12,000 people converged on Beauraing, having read about the visions in the regional and Brussels press. Special trains brought cripples from France. Among the local VIPs who shared an enclosure with the visionaries were the mayor, magistrates, chiefs of police and *gendarmerie* as well as several doctors who monitored the children's ecstasies.

Ordered by his bishop to stay away from the site, the *curé* and rural dean, Fr Léon Lambert, encouraged the affair behind the scenes. A Redemptorist preacher, Fr Gaston Maes, arrived at the Academy of Christian Doctrine to take supernatural soundings via a crucifix and Latin incantations. Mother-Superior Théophile satisfied her own doubts by hanging a medal of St Benedict from the tree in which the Virgin had appeared. The hawthorne did not wither. 'In the name of the clergy, Holy Virgin', asked the seers, 'tell us what you want.' The reply was immediate: 'A chapel!'[5] On 23 December, when asked why she had come, the vision explained, 'So people will come here on pilgrimage'.[6] By the end of the month, up to 20,000 people a day were doing so.

Although such curative practices as the drinking of a tea brewed from the leaves of the sacred hawthorne were not calculated to promote their professional interests, the little group of doctors swelled to 80 practitioners, and the Society of St Luke of Belgian Catholic Doctors set up a special commission to study the case.[7]

A prominent physician at the site was 30-year-old Fernand Maistriaux, president of the local section of Catholic Action.[8] One reads in one of the 32 booklets and 13 full-length books to be published on the subject within two years, 'In as much as the visions multiplied, so the initial suggestion was strengthened, above all thanks to the preponderate influence of Dr Maistriaux, fervent Catholic, and the religious who surrounded the seers'.[9] Dr Maistriaux was, in fact, the first to publish an account of the apparitions,[10] completed by 21 December and printed in Louvain before the year was out. The cover of this pamphlet bears a distinctive crown and cross: the logo of REX publications, launched by Abbé Picard, chaplain-general of Youth Catholic Action, and already under the control of Léon Degrelle:[11] 'probably the most flamboyant fascist chief in all of western Europe.'[12]

Maistriaux and Degrelle (whose REX movement was to don SS uniform and join the Nazis at the eastern front) followed up their initial success with *Un Lourdes Belge? Les Apparitions de Beauraing*, published in 1933, the year two million people visited the village.[13]

Undeterred by press accusations that the nuns had engineered the sensation for commercial purposes,[14] the clergy, led by Mgr Heylen, Bishop of Namur and 'herald of the Marian cult',[15] soon dropped their 'prudent' approach. In June 1933 Heylen and Fr Lambert launched the 'Pro Maria' committee to promote the new shrine, and *La Voix de Beauraing* gave monthly news of developments. The result was a massive increase in devotion to Mary among Walloons (known to be less fervently Marian than their Flemish co-religionists).[16] Three years later, Princess Josephine, in taking the monastic veil shortly after the death of her husband, King Albert 1, presented her bridal veil to Mgr Heylen 'for the glorification of Our Lady of Beauraing'.[17]

Theological journals gave weighty coverage to the events. In part of a 79-page report with photographs, maps and diagrams, Carmelite Fr Bruno de Jésus-Marie took a sceptical view, noting the boy visionary's 'mocking look'[18] and repeating newspaper reports that the children had seen films about miracles and mysterious perfumed ladies shortly before the visions – and had read about Lourdes and Fatima.[19] Dr Etienne De Greef, professor of criminal anthropology at Louvain, and Dr Paul van Gehuchten, professor of neurology at the ancient Catholic university, were no more inclined to a supernatural explanation. The Louvain Jesuits, however, were more enthusiastic. Fr Lenain confirmed that there had been remarkable cures, 'but nothing of a strictly miraculous character'. Nevertheless, Beauraing clearly represented 'a call to prayer'.[20]

As for the political results of the apparitions, a later writer comments, 'The people of Beauraing returned to the sacraments, and the Socialists lost their grip on the district'.[21]

An epidemic of apparitions swept the Belgian countryside. In 1933 – the year Pius XI canonized the visionary of Lourdes – little 'Bernadettes' in the villages of Banneaux, Onkerzeele, Etikhove, Tubise, Rotselaer, Chaineaux and Melen claimed to have conversed with the Blessed Virgin.[22] Many of the prophecies reflected fears of an imminent invasion by Hitler, who had recently come to power. At Beauraing, the elderly Tilman Côme attracted a record crowd of 200,000 on 15 August after Mary had told him, 'Organize a great pilgrimage for my feast day. I will be there.'[23] When M. Côme was certified insane the following summer, a serious rival was removed from the village.

Although several of the new seers succeeded in drawing large crowds, only one was to enjoy the sanction of the Church. On 15 January – less than two weeks after the final apparition at Beauraing – eleven-year-old Mariette Beco, daughter of an unemployed artisan of Banneaux in the Walloon province of Liège, saw in her front garden

> a lady, dressed in a dazzling white gown which fell in soft drapes and pleats from its high round neckline. The waist was girdled with a sky-blue sash that hung in two streamers down to her left knee . . . the lady was slightly inclined to the left so that just one of her feet showed, and on this lay a golden rose . . . over her right arm hung a rosary.[24]

Asked to identify herself, the smart visitor told Mariette, 'Oh, the Virgin of the Poor'.[25] As doctors and journalists arrived to make their tests and reports, the child asked the Virgin what she wanted. 'Oh, a little chapel!' came the answer after a well-bred pause. Cures and conversions followed, crowds gathered and the socialists lost votes in the local elections. 'Banneaux is one more reminder', a post-war American promoter writes, 'in these days when the followers of Karl Marx seem to be sweeping everything before them, that our great hope – our only hope – lies in carrying out the request of Our Lady made at Fatima and other places.'[26]

Both Belgian shrines thrived during the Nazi occupation. German soldiers – and later the US airforce – made pilgrimages. Bishop Kerkofs of Liège canonically approved the cult of Banneaux in 1942 and 'the Virgin of the Poor' was exported to France, Germany, Italy, Romania, Brazil, India and the Congo, where statues and chapels were erected.[27] Bishop Heylen granted equivalent honours to Beauraing in 1943. The latter cult was instrumental in the conversion of the communist publisher of *Drapeau Rouge* in 1946. He subsequently founded the Belgian branch of the Legion of Mary.[28]

28

NATIONAL CATHOLICISM

[Primo de Rivera's] name – bound to the glorious date of the
Day of the Virgin – will remain in our history for ever, intimately
engraved on the heart of the Fatherland.[1]

Los Valores Historicos en la Dictadura Española

Neither the efforts of the Jesuits and sodalists through workingmen's
retreats and Spiritual Exercises,[2] nor Catholic Action's response to
the 'social question', nor the Ave Maria Schools could tame that
tricephalous beast even more savage than Modernism: proletarian
insurrection, republican separatism and militant anticlericalism.[3]
Nevertheless, Jesuit integralism and Marian nationalism provided
by means of doctrine, methods and style a prototype of 'the Movement' that would lead to the Spanish nationalist victory of 1939.

Loss of international prestige and deterioration of the socioeconomic order in the first years of the century paralleled the development of National Catholicism through the monarchy, army, and
that ghost of empire, the Hispanic community (see chapter 21).
The marrow of fascist mythology in Spain was constituted by these
symbols and structures – identified with and sheltered by the figure
of Our Lady.

From countless Virgins in the Spanish pantheon, Nuestra Señora
del Pilar – 'the nucleus of our nation and the expression of tenacity
and faith in our race'[4] – acquired a towering relevance during this
period. In 1908, a few weeks after the anti-Modernist Marian
congress at Saragossa (see chapter 22), the Patroness of the
Hispanic Peoples demonstrated her links with the armed forces
and former colonies: a captain-general's sash was tied round her
image and the flags of nineteen South American republics blessed
by the pope were placed before it 'in perpetuity' to a chorus
of *vivas* for '*America, España y la Virgen del Ebro*'.[5] Her cult was
consolidated in Spain in 1915 when Pope Benedict authorized a
mass to commemorate her appearance on the Saragossa column

'*en carne mortal*'. A few months later, a confraternity was established for the nobility: the Congregation of Our Lady of the Pillar and St Francis Borgia.

Under Jesuit direction,[6] Alfonso XIII (1886–1941) generously played the customary role of the Spanish crown in Marian affairs, and at a time of such religious effervescence and conflict his involvement (as that of the armed forces) became paramount. From the beginning of his reign, Alfonso sponsored Marian acts and propaganda. In 1903 he became honorary president of the Brotherhood of Our Lady of Linares, Conquistadora de Córdoba.[7] The following year he provided the crown for the canonical coronation of the Mare de Deu de Misericordia. The band honoured this Catalan image with the royal march.[8]

The corner-stone of Acción Católica, the Ignatian ACN de P (see chapter 22) was also vital to the anti-socialist/anti-secularist movement that brought about – 'with the glorious cooperation of the monarchy'[9] – the dictatorship of General Miguel Primo de Rivera, Marquis de Estella (1923–30). Through dynamic journalism and disciplined action ('circles', confederations, international networks),[10] the Propagandistas reactivated retreats and Spiritual Exercises, and popularized papal teachings emphasizing the principles of authority and tradition.

Expressions of the revival were the Eucharistic congress of 1911 in Madrid, where King Alfonso proclaimed his unconditional adherence to Rome, and the Montfortian congress of 1918 to promote the doctrine of Marian slavery. In 1919 – two years after a wave of *disturbios* broke out[11] and as Catalan demands for autonomy mounted – the king, wearing the uniform of a captain-general, consecrated to the Sacred Heart of Jesus 'Spain, the people of your inheritance and your predilection'.[12] The ceremony on the Cerro de los Angeles in Madrid was attended by representatives of Hispano-American nations which had contributed to the erection of the monument.[13] The Madrid review *Raza Española, Revista de España y America* was launched that year. A special edition covered the great 'Day of the Race' on 12 October (also the feast of Our Lady of the Pillar) and publicized royal calls to celebrate Iberian glories like the Magellan anniversary in 1920–1. Prefiguring Acción Española and the Falangist creed of Hispania (the empire of 'love and spirituality'),[14] the publication preached the moral reconquest of America and obliteration of the Black Legend. It sought the expansion of the 'spiritually homogeneous'[15] Hispanic culture and race, rejecting 'cold internationalism'.[16]

Naturally, the Society of Jesus was in the vanguard of the revivalist movement. At the end of the 'Bolshevik triennium' in Andalusia (1918–21) and after months of acute class confrontation and terrorism in Catalonia, Saragossa, and Bilbao, the Society organized a triumphal tour of the arm of Ignatius de Loyola and finger of Francisco Xavier. Carried with the Book of the Spiritual Exercises, the relics were escorted – amidst strains of the national anthem and *vivas* for the Compañía[17] – by artillery, para-military police, Marian/Eucharistic associations and workmen's guilds. The pageant was met by King Alfonso and local images of the Virgin. In Guipuzcoa, birthplace of St Ignatius, pilgrims gained plenary indulgences from Rome.

After the destruction of the Spanish army in Morocco (July 1921) and with the relics still on tour, the Holy See and ACN de P mounted a 'Great Social Campaign' as 'a dam against revolution' (April 1922).[18] Faced with unabated social and regional unrest, crown and army embarked on a programme of national 'regeneration' in September 1923 through the coup of Primo de Rivera, 'defender of our altars and our homes'.[19] During this first Spanish attempt to emulate the Duce, class struggle was 'abolished' and corporativist doctrines were introduced. Theological studies flourished, the Middle Ages and Hispanidad were extolled – and identified with each other;[20] Church authority and privileges were reinforced, and the cult of Mary went through yet another renaissance with some inquisitional traits.[21]

On the establishment of the dictatorship, the Unión Patriótica, 'neither of the right nor of the left',[22] was formed at Valladolid (Castile) – 'the cradle of the race'.[23] Headed by the General-Marquis himself, and backed by the Propagandistas[24] and affiliated groups like Democracia Cristiana, the movement soon reached every corner of the country, staging *actos de propaganda* and setting up youth sections[25] under the motto 'Patria, Religión y Monarquía'. Clearly influenced by Lusitanian integralism (see chapter 25), Unión Patriótica rejected 'the anti-Spanish past' and made the Catholic faith and crown its fulcrum. Consequently the nationalist movement of Primo de Rivera, an enthusiastic friend of Portugal,[26] was bound to have a distinctive Marian dimension. The rejuvenation of military Marianism and a frantic new Assumption campaign marked this period of colonial war and internal repression that was to end abruptly with the advent of the republic in 1931. The growing number of youth and agrarian groupings played an important role in the 'Catholic-patriotic' upsurge in which devotions to Mary and the Eucharist, as well as to the pope,[27] were central.

An increasingly militant Church and Establishment mounted an extensive programme promoting scholasticism, Catholic instruction and morality. A congress on Catholic education in Madrid (April 1924),[28] an 'ascetic week' in Valladolid (October 1924), a *campaña moralizadora* in Barcelona (January 1925), a Thomist week in Madrid (March 1925) – these were some of the first events held under military rule. The royal family's deification of Mary through numerous coronations of her statues[29] and military honours rendered her 'by the highest authorities'[30] were examples followed throughout the Iberian world, reactivating the old tradition.

Mary exercised her ancient maternal patronage over army and generals. In an official telegram on the battle of Alhucemas in 1925, Primo de Rivera reported that the historic landing in Morocco had taken place on 8 September, Day of the Virgin, whom many Spaniards, '. . . I among them, had asked for the triumph'.[31] As the Caudillo returned from Africa he paid public homage in Jeréz de la Frontera (his native town in the south) to the Virgin of Mercy, whose Morenita image was presented with a medal. Many other thanksgivings were offered at the feet of Our Lady after Alhucemas – a victory that restored Spain's 'great feeling of empire and Catholicity'.[32] A regiment arriving in Guipuzcoa at the end of 1926, for example, honoured the Basque patroness, the Virgin of Begoña.[33] The trust placed in Mary by the military was in full accordance with tradition. As Alfonso XIII told the military sodality at Toledo in 1928, 'You have the assurance that Our Lady Immaculate, who is patroness of our sodality, will never fail the Spanish infantry and will always protect it.'[34]

Marian confraternities blossomed in the 1920s, particularly in Andalusia, where a rejuvenation of Holy Week processions took place.[35] The king granted many confraternities the title of 'royal'; and the armed forces were affiliated to some as 'chief honorary brother'. The navy, for instance, was linked to the Pontifical Archconfraternity of Our Lady of the Rosary, founded in Granada in 1927.[36] Characteristic of the times was a type of Marian coporativism created by guilds (*gremios*) forming brotherhoods around particular images.[37] In 1928 the Knights (Caballeros) of Our Lady of the Pillar were instituted in Saragossa.

Freemasonry was correspondingly persecuted and anti-'Judaic-Masonic' literature circulated.[38] Spain, the 'alma mater of the Hispanic American culture', was confirmed in her universal mission as a first-rate nation.[39] It was in this context that the counter-Masonic Opus Dei emerged[40] and Jiménez Caballero wrote that Mary represented the opposite of the 'Semitic Eve' – a figure 'ignoble and fatal, mother of all the sinners'.[41]

As Primo's rule dragged on, the 'study circles' of the Propagandistas stressed papal doctrine on 'obeisance to constituted power'[42] and the Assumption campaign reached new heights through the efforts of the hierarchy and orders headed by the *Compañía* and its subsidiaries. In 1929 – the 75th anniversary of the Immaculate Conception declaration, exuberantly celebrated throughout Spain – the Marian Academy of Lérida launched a 'plebiscite movement' which collected 725,000 pro-Assumption signatures.[43] In Seville a Marian Hispano-American congress held *'apoteósicos actos de culto'*[44] and mini-conferences on a variety of topics from youth sodalities to the Immaculate Heart, demanding a pontifical ruling on the bodily ascension of Mary into heaven. As fresh disturbances broke out,[45] both government and monarch, represented by the minister of justice and Carlos Borbon, adhered to the Assumptionist vow.[46]

A striking feature of the 1920s was the activism of new Marian divisions devoted to nursing, catechism, education, and Spiritual Exercises. Virtually all of them were to prosper and expand to foreign lands; one would eventually be leaven in the economic transformation of Spain and, in as far as was possible given the historical derogation of Church power, put on the mantle of the Society of Jesus.

Among the divisions flourishing during Primo's dictatorship were the Daughters of Santa Teresa, a teaching institute based in Madrid. Approved as a pious union in 1924, the Teresianas were, in the words of their founder Pedro Poveda, 'eminently Marian'.[47] Pioneer of women's Catholic Action in universities, and one of the civil war's first martyrs, Padre Poveda's message was simple: 'Be apostles of Mary and propagate devotion to her.'[48]

Other communities developing in these years were the Work of the Visitation of Our Lady, founded in Barcelona in 1923 to care for the poor and sick, and the Sisters of Mary the Nazarene, an episcopal foundation of 1921 for reparation to the Sacred Heart in the sacrament 'in union with Mary Immaculate'.[49] The varied activities of the Marias Nazarenas included running Houses of Exercises and schools, and the diffusion of Marian literature. The Doctrine Workers of Our Lady of Dolours and the Slaves of the Most Holy Sacrament and of the Mother of God, congregations formed in 1925 in Valencia and Andalusia respectively, had similar aims and activities. A pious union with no less significant a name was formed in the same year at San Sebastian: Alliance in Jesus through Mary.[50] Other Basque foundations were the Congregation of Missionaries of the Sacred Hearts of Jesus and Mary (its task of fostering religious vocations started a few months before the fall of the monarchy) and the Mercedarian foundation of Margarita María López de Maturana, whose members reached China in 1926.[51]

In 1927 the Congregation of Dames of the Assumption of Our Lady was instituted in Burgos with the task of teaching in rural areas. The following year the Institute of Parochial Cooperators of Christ the King – charged with renewal through Loyola's Exercises – was founded in Barcelona. In the same year (1928), the ACN de P was approbated by the hierarchy as a 'work of the secular apostolate' and one of its lecturers conceived Opus Dei – on 2 October, feast of the Holy Guardian Angels – while on retreat in a Vincentian house in Madrid. According to a recent hagiography, Fr Escrivá 'implored the infallible help of the Virgin and put the hopes of the enterprise under her patronage'.[52] Mary herself was the 'foundress'.[53]

Josemaría Escrivá de Balaguer (1902–75)[54] was born in the small town of Barbastro, Aragon – deep in Carlist country – where his father kept a textile shop. At the age of two he was cured of a serious illness 'through the intercession of Our Lady of Torreciudad'.[55] A 'soul in love with Our Lady'.[56] he began his career as a protégé of Cardinal Soldevila of Saragossa, who tonsured him in 1922. After Soldevila's assassination by anarchists in June 1923 Escrivá continued his theology studies and 'placed himself in the hands of the Virgin Mary',[57] making daily visits to her Pillar, where his first mass was offered in 1925. In Madrid he read law, taught in the school of journalism run by *El Debate*, the Propagandista daily, and served as chaplain of missions to the sick in the care of the aristocratic Damas Apostólicas of the Sacred Heart, whose mother-house had been opened by the king in 1924.

Padre Escrivá recruited the first members of Opus Dei from a group of upper-class bachelors, who were already under his spiritual direction and who had adopted his habit of 'always glancing at an image of the blessed Virgin on entering or leaving a room'.[58] On the advice of the Marchioness de Onteiro, he set up a female section in 1930. Women, however, 'need not be scholars; it's enough for them to be prudent.'[59]

29

SECOND REPUBLIC AND SANTA CRUZADA

Above all, the blue shirt is Castile . . . the blue shirt of Toledo is the blue of the Alcázar . . . it is the mantle of the Virgin of the Alcázar, the blue of the Most Pure, Patroness of the Spanish Infantes, Patroness of the Alcázar, blue of the Falangist Virgin.[1]

E. Jiménez Caballero

Be Mary's and you will be ours.[2]

Mgr Escrivá

After the leftist landslide in the first elections for eight years, the Second Republic was proclaimed in Catalonia and the Basque country on 14 April 1931. Alfonso XIII went into exile the same day and a new series of persecutions began. The military Orders of Alcántara and Santiago were suppressed and their property, like the monarch's, was confiscated. The fate of the Society of Jesus – still immensely rich – and indeed of the whole clerical establishment, was plain to see. Quick to respond, the ACN de P launched Acción Nacional with a radical manifesto (7 May) and the motto 'Religion, Fatherland, Family, Order, Property'. The integralist Cardinal Segura, a close friend of the king, condemned the republic in terms that unleashed immediate anarchist violence (11 May). Around 100 convents and churches were ransacked and burnt, from Madrid to Malaga, among them Jesuit residences and libraries, and innumerable images of Our Lady belonging to confraternities.

A few weeks later, on 30 June, the Dolorosa appeared to two little shepherds in the Basque village of Esquioga in the Spanish Pyrenees. Rosary in hand and wearing a gold crown and black mantle, the apparition recurred many times while the number of seers kept growing.[3] Special trains brought pilgrims from France and all over Spain[4] as the ruthless dismantling of the monarchical-clerical state continued: abolition of religious education in state schools, repression of the Catholic press, secularization of cemeteries, the removal of religious orders from Marian shrines. . . .[5] Traditional acts of reparation were made to the Sacred and Immaculate Hearts (as will be seen)[6] and in many areas Holy Week processions were suspended. These were resumed only after the fall of the 'Jacobinical republic' in 1934 – the year the visions of Esquioga also faded away.

Almost from the beginning, the republic faced a highly active, centralized and coherent opposition[7] articulated round the eternal national symbols in which the temporal and spiritual merge. Key components of fascism had already appeared before the end of 1931: the anti-communist juntas[8] and Acción Española, a monarchist society financed by aristocrats in a close contact with Action Française. Acción Española's integralist journal became the mouthpiece of Hispanidad, the traditional *Weltanschauung* whose restoration was made the goal of the counter-revolution. The leading light in Acción Española was Ramiro de Maeztu y Whitney, for whom the 'Hispanic ideals of the sixteenth century'[9] were the most generous ever conceived. Extolled later as 'the Basque martyr of Hispanidad'[10] and 'unforgettable master of our counter-revolution',[11] Maeztu condemned the 'Humanism of Pride'[12] (i.e., Modernism), seeking salvation exclusively in the humanism of Hispanidad.

On the second page of the first issue of *Acción Española*[13] we find the appearance of Our Lady to Santiago presented as the seal of Spanish destiny. This concept was treated in depth by Zacarías de Vizcarra y Arana, a Basque priest who coined the term Hispanidad. In his article '*El Apóstol Santiago y el mundo Hispano*' (written to encourage Catholic Spain during the 'tribulations'),[14] Vizcarra expounded what has been called the 'magic theology of history' and 'magic radicalism'.[15] The Messianic nature of the Spanish Church is indissolubly linked with Mother Mary who actually 'came marvellously to Saragossa one day in mortal flesh, visited the apostle' and 'left him with a marble column'[16] as a symbol of the faith planted by him.

> 'Hispanidad is a sanctuary
> Founded on a pillar
> Which no one can break'.[17]

Thus ran the hymn of the pan-Hispanic movement.

Spain and her 'knight errant of Christ'[18] Santiago, who built the first chapel of Our Lady, must defend 'the Church of St Peter'[19] against the 'modern Moor'[20] (i.e. Jews, Masons and anticlericals). Infusing confidence in the new crusaders, Fr Vizcarra claims that the future missions of Hispanidad – the defeat of Antichrist and conquest of Constantinople for the glory of Rome – were foretold in the prophecies of the fourteenth century visionary St Bridget of Sweden and the writings of St Alonso Rodriguez (d. 1617), a Jesuit lay brother. Heralded as 'the prow of Christianity' and 'the north of humanity',[21] Hispanidad has three 'distinctive characters':[22] the 'Cross-Sword' of Santiago, the Virgin's pillar in Saragossa and the coat of arms of Spain.[23]

An early expression of Hispanidad was the Partido Nacionalista Español, formed by Jose María Albinana shortly before the fall of Alfonso XIII. Its members, acknowledged by Acción Española as 'fervent defenders of the throne'[24] and the Spanish Camelots du Roi had the cross of Santiago, patron of the *Reconquista*, as their badge.

In 1932 the clergy lost many privileges and expropriation of the grandees' estates began. Early in the year the Society of Jesus was dissolved 'to unharness education in Spain from the rosary and the perils of religious teachings',[25] as President Azaña put it. The expulsion of the Jesuits – which, according to General Franco, expressed 'the dictates of masonic lodges'[26] – provoked vigorous demonstrations in the name of the Sacred Heart, whose feast in June was celebrated with exceptional display.[27] A great propaganda offensive that mobilized the entire Catholic forces was mounted from the Jesuit church of San Ambrosio in Valladolid, site of the Sacred Heart apparitions to Padre Hoyos, whose bicentenary was celebrated the following year (1933). In the anniversary year *The Great Promise* magazine was launched[28] and on the feast day of St Marguerite Marie Alacoque (17 October), construction began on a 'national temple of expiation'.

This was the moment chosen by the vice-president of Union Monárquica, José Antonio Primo de Rivera (1903–36) to expound his doctrine of 'Falange Española' (29 October 1933). Loyal to the counter-revolution, the third Marquis de Estella described Rousseau as a 'cursed man'[29] and demanded respect for and protection of Spain's 'religious spirit, key to the best harquebuses of our history'.[30] The ideals of Unión Patriótica were revamped through a plan for the 'national resurrection'[31] of Spain as the 'right arm of Rome'.[32] Mystical and universal, the mission proclaimed was a

crusade against Moscow and Geneva, 'the false Rome'.[33] A stoical
and Loyolistic spirit was required: 'Life is militia.'[34]

At the Eucharistic congress in Buenos Aires the year after the
foundation of the Falange, the Spanish primate made Hispanidad
an official doctrine.

As Hispanidad and Falangism made headway, the thoughts
of Josemaría Escrivá were being systematized in *Consideraciones
espirituales*, a collection of maxims published in 1934.[35] His meditations on the Holy Rosary were issued in the same year. Moulded in
dangerous times, in an atmosphere pervaded by Ignatian tradition,
and with ends analogous to those of the Compañía, Escrivá's
teachings indicate a familiar Jesuitic path: the conquest of society
from the top,[36] a strict hierarchical order based on Rome and
devotion to the pope,[37] unquestioning submission to authority[38] and
smothering of the critical spirit,[39] systematic mortification of the flesh
(flagellation,[40] the wearing of a spiked garter, etc.); denigration of
women and the married state: 'Marriage is for the rank and file, not
for the officers of Christ's army.'[41]

Mary, 'a full participant in the work of our salvation',[42] is a key
piece in this system. Most revealing of Monseñor's commitment to
the Marian cult is his encouragement of the strangest of legends:
'Wear on your breast the holy scapular of Carmel. There are many
excellent Marian devotions, but few are as deeply-rooted among the
faithful and so richly blessed by the Popes. Besides, how motherly is
the Sabbatine privilege!'[43]

*   *   *

The Second Republic was composed of incongruous elements and
born under inauspicious circumstances. The Church, still with a
grip on women and non-urban sectors was able to capitalize on the
setbacks imposed by the crisis (financial, agrarian, etc.) and by deep
contradictions in the republican camp. Nevertheless, the two years
of 'reaction' since 1934 swung the electoral pendulum in February
1936 and the newly-formed Popular Front came to power.

Agrarian reform was resumed in vengeful mood and at break-neck
pace; the clerical bloc (convents, centres of ACN de P) was again
the target of assaults. Violence erupted at all levels and in every
direction. The military coup, only partially successful, led to a long
war (July 1936–March 1939) between 'the two cities'.[44] For the
insurgents – who worshipped their patroness in a kind of chivalric

cult – the struggle took the form of a ferocious Marian crusade. The Reds systematically desecrated and destroyed images and sanctuaries of Our Lady,[45] which occasionally became battlefields, as during the siege of Nuestra Señora de la Cabeza in Jaen (1937).

Thousands of Freemasons, 'separatists', leftists and trade unionists were massacred by the nationalists in this 'holiest war in history'.[46] Sometimes executed with their wives and daughters after receiving the last sacraments (the Church insisted on this right), their corpses were exposed to subdue the population. Fascist atrocities even took on a mock religious form, with victims forced to shout '*Viva Cristo Rey!*' before their death.[47] The republican forces hunted priests with dogs, shot prelates in public, tortured monks by forcing rosary beads through their eardrums and exhumed long-dead nuns for dancing partners.[48] After the carnage, a Jesuit historian wrote of 'Marian phalanxes, sacrificed by God for the Fatherland'.[49]

While Freemasonry officially defined itself as the 'antithesis of fascism',[50] a sort of counter-Masonry – exemplified by those 'loyal sons of the Virgin',[51] the Knights of the Pillar – flourished around the Marian cult. Yet an anomalous factor existed in the 'two cities' which would be of great consequence: the Basques – republican and socialist, egalitarian and philo-Masonic – remained, to a large extent, Catholic. In August 1936 the Bishop of Vitoria and Pamplona condemned the alliance with Marxism ('synthesis of all heresy'),[52] but a considerable body of the clergy in Vizcaya and Guipuzcoa remained loyal to the anti-fascist front.[53] On behalf of republican Basques, minister of justice Irujo made a declaration of the principles of universal brotherhood, social justice and equality while avowing, at the same time, his faith in Catholicism as a religion of love and fraternity.[54] According to Mgr Vizcarra (now a domestic prelate), this 'Catholic separatism' was part of 'a vast foreign conspiracy'[55] sown among the Basques by the 'diabolical cunning' of the sects.[56]

Although we have no concrete evidence that the Basque rebel church was Christocentric rather than Marian, it is significant that soon after the fall of Bilbao (June 1937) and the elimination of many priests,[57] Our Lady of Begoña was re-crowned by the highest authorities of the occupation, General Orgaz and Cardinal Gomá y Tomás, primate of Spain. Five months after the destruction of Guernica, Gomá told the defeated inhabitants of Bilbao assembled before a Sacred Heart monument, 'By special favour of the Holy Virgin, your city still stands'.[58]

The Immaculate Conception, patroness of the infantry, and the Virgin of the Pillar, patroness of the Guardia Civil and Spanish Legion, Grand Captain of the Spanish Armies and symbol of Mary's covenant with Spain, constituted the alpha and omega of the fascist forces. As a main plank of National Catholicism and 'primal and basic factor' of the Movement,[59] the military placed itself from the very beginning under Mary's protection. In confirming Santiago as patron of Spain by decree (1937), Franco invoked the apostle as the founder of the Virgin's cult.[60]

Saragossa, already the Marian capital of Spain, became an even greater centre of pilgrimage and national identity. 'For the Spanish', Cardinal Gomá asserted on the nineteenth centenary of the Virgin's journey, 'the Saragossa Pillar is the concretion of our whole supernatural system. It is the symbol of our "mystery" . . . the historical and geographical point through which we were inoculated with divine life.'[61]

Shortly after the *pronunciamiento* and an abortive attack on the shrine,[62] General Millán Astray made a 'triumphal entry'[63] into the temple of the Pillar at the head of Falangists and troops. In an emotive ceremony – during which there were shouts of 'Long Live Death! Long Live the Virgin of the Pillar!' – the General touched her imperial crown with his cap. Rogatory prayers were said before her image; fasting and penance followed.

On 8 December 1936 the feast of the Immaculate Conception was declared a 'national and obligatory' holiday. All regiments paraded through the streets and the radio broadcast a 'patriotic allocution' by the war minister. During the official ceremony soldiers laid their standards and weapons at the feet of the *Purísima* in a gesture of consecration.[64] The day of the Immaculate became 'the Day of the Crusader' too, set aside for 'Catholic spirituality' and 'reparation for the sacrileges'.[65] Echoing Fatima, Cardinal Gomá said the Immaculate had a great role to play in the making of peace. Fervent prayers to the Virgin had more power than diplomats, for Mary was 'the pacifier of the world'.[66]

Space does not permit an exhaustive description of the ceremonies staged before the surviving images of Mary. The essence of all these idiosyncratic rituals – often frantically performed with the sanguinary hymns of the Falange – was the triad of Mary, Spain

(Hispanidad) and holy war. A typical celebration was the procession in Saragossa on the Day of the Race, 1936. Every type of 'column' – from the Apostleship of Prayer to the Guardia Civil – marched with their banner and band behind a silver 'refulgent carriage' representing the advent of Our Lady to Aragón.[67] The pious youth of Catholic Action implored the Virgin ('Restorer of the Faith') to re-establish 'the imperial glory of Hispanidad'.[68]

National Catholicism's fixation on the Golden Age blossomed in poetry and compositions, as these lines addressed to the Patroness of Cadiz convey:

> Our Lady of the Rosary, as thou gavest victory to the navy
> of generalísimo John of Austria in the memorable and famous
> battle of Lepanto, do now grant the final triumph to our glorious
> Caudillo Franco and the total reconquest of the Spanish peoples.
> Spain, Blessed Virgin, is thy preferred daughter. . . . Save Spain,
> Holy Virgin. . . . Long Live the Virgin of the Rosary, Patroness
> of Cádiz, Long Live Spain![69]

The Nationalists invoked Mary's 'inexhaustible protection'[70] throughout the war. Franco's placing the 'convoy of victory' under the care of the Virgin of Africa[71] was a characteristic gesture. Virtually every Red defeat was attributed to the intercession of Mary under one title or another. Indeed, the head of the Spanish Church thought that any history of the war ought to include a chapter 'dedicated to the study of the intervention of the Mother of God in its plot'.[72] The Pillar of Saragossa was the very source of 'the divine strategy which gave us the final victory'. From this plinth – the 'master tree of resistance of our armies' – the Virgin holds sway over 'the destiny of the Fatherland'.[73]

The recovery of a shrine was a sure sign of celestial favour. On the 'reconquest' of Covadonga, the Falangist press remarked that 'From today, the Generalísimo can carry as a trophy the banner of the Holy Virgin of Covadonga'.[74] One of the most famous battles gave rise to a new devotion: Our Lady of the Alcázar, whose image in Toledo 'escorted the brave Spanish soldiers in the siege' (1936).[75] What was 'the secret key to so much heroism?' asked Cardinal Gomá: 'La Señora del Alcázar'.[76]

The prodigious part played by Mary was an object of much mirth for Spain's key ally. 'People speak of an intervention from heaven which decided the civil war in favour of Franco', observed Adolf Hitler,

'Perhaps so – but it was not an intervention on the part of the madam styled the Mother of God, who has recently been honoured with a Field-Marshal's baton, but the intervention of the German General von Richthofen and the bombs his squadrons rained from the heavens that decided the issue.'[77]

The sublimation of death and suffering through the omnipotent mother and executioner of heretics was perhaps the most extraordinary aspect of the phenomenon. The 'martyrs' were commemorated in her sanctuaries and towards the end of the war, Falange leader Serrano Suñer asked the Gran Capitana to render their blood 'fruitful'.[78] Mgr Escrivá – personally favoured with an apparition of Our Lady as he fled to France[79] – waxed lyrical on the subject of suffering: 'Blessed be pain, loved be pain, sanctified be pain!'[80] War had 'a supernatural end . . . we have to love it, as the religious should love his disciplines.'[81] Marian asceticism in the field seems not to have been uncommon. Some Blue Shirts consecrated themselves to the 'celestial Lady', as did the Tercios de Requetés de Isabel la Católica in Granada, who adopted Our Lady of Dolours as their *generalísima*. They commended their lives to her, offered her their daily privations, vowed to render public homage to her beloved image and finally, in 1939, formed a brotherhood of penitents: the Royal Confraternity of Our Lady of Dolours.[82]

Franco's speech in Saragossa on the Day of Hispanidad in 1939 eloquently expressed the significance of the Marian cult: 'If She [the Virgin of the Pillar] had not given us all energy, bravery, the spirit of sacrifice, living conscience of the past and blind faith in our future, all our armed guards would have kept vigil in vain.'[83]

Yet Mary's function was more complex, contributing to the identification and projection of *Caudillo* and *Patria*. 'Franco's smile has something of the Virgin's mantle held over sinners'[84] and 'all Spanish science and art have always been at the service of Mary'[85] are two telling messages. The Generalísimo's daughter played her part as a 'daughter of Mary'[86] and member of Catholic Action, which she joined with pomp in Burgos cathedral.[87]

Marianization was total. In April 1937 the education authorities issued detailed regulations for the worship of Mary in schools which would have delighted Padre Manjón.[88] Every establishment had to display her image (preferably the Purísima) and follow the traditional corporate devotions of May 'to foster the love of Our Lady in the hearts of the children'.[89] The daily invocation of her assistance and the greeting between teacher and pupil 'Ave María Purísima' (answer: 'Conceived without sin') were made compulsory. In March 1938 the 'National Syndicalist State' transformed Labour Day into the feast of St Joseph – an extension of the Marian cult.[90] Solid foundations had been laid for a new, glorious era of Mary in the Iberian peninsula.

30

QUEEN OF HISPANIDAD

THE MARIAN-INTEGRALIST STATE

On that happy day, the first of April 1939, Spain became Spain
again . . . able to manifest without fear her great devotion to the
sublime Patroness of Heaven and the whole of Spain, the most
holy Virgin Mary.[1]

El Culto Mariano en España

The Falangists' model of nationalism was heroic and missionary
sixteenth-century Spain.[2] 'Missionary expansion', declared Franco,
was basic to 'the task of civilizing and to the spiritual empire of
Spain.'[3] Diametrically opposed to the world of universal suffrage,
parliamentarianism and Freemasonry,[4] Spain recovered her position
as defender of the Catholic faith – that is, champion of the
prerogatives of Mary and Rome. Like the Immaculate Conception
belief in past centuries, the Assumption of Our Lady was a matter
of honour in Falangist Spain and a political objective of paramount
importance. The greatness of the Mother of God – the Holy Mother
Church – was Spain's greatness.

In 1938 the Generalísimo expressed the view that Spain and
Portugal were 'an eloquent statement of Christian civilization'.[5] In
both these *estados nuevos* Church, state and 'the Movement' would
indeed achieve a high degree of integration through the all-pervading
cult of the Virgin. Almost all public ceremonial was religious and
the ecclesiastical acquired an official character, for example when a
bishop invested Falangist youth with armbands[6] or the armed forces
celebrated the sixth anniversary of the Victory (April 1945) with a
pilgrimage organized by Jesuit 'Old Boys' and the Confederation of
Marian Congregations to the Sacred Heart sanctuary on the Cerro
de los Angeles.[7] As in former times, government and military maintained a corporate presence in Marian brotherhoods. In 1945 Franco
was named president of the Federation of Holy Week Confraternities,

and two confraternities involving the police force were established in Andalusia: Nuestra Señora de la Esperanza (Málaga) and María Santísima de la Aurora (Granada).[8]

The whole machinery of the Francoist state down to the Royal Academy of Medicine[9] was engaged in 'Marianization'. The representatives of universities and municipalities – as in the Middle Ages and Counter-Reformation – solemnly swore to lay down their lives for Marian beliefs. The ministry of education (which made Catholic doctrine compulsory in universities) was active alongside the Spanish Mariological Society in the Assumption campaign and related projects.

Escrivá's concept of 'unity of life',[10] in which asceticism and work (apostolic and productive) are one, was in perfect accordance with the ideal of Hispanidad as expressed by the president of Pax Romana and future ambassador to the Vatican: 'Today Hispanic culture is at the service of integral Catholicism.'[11]

Strict regulations governing dress and sexual behaviour complemented state censorship. As late as 1950, the primate protested to the government press chief over a mention of Balzac's centenary. As 'bad books' were subjected to inquisitorial control,[12] the divisions flooded the market with popular Mary magazines.[13]

The cult of regional patronesses was unstinted in the face of the mounting poverty and scarcities of the 1940s. The 'National Sanctuary of the Race' in Saragossa was given a marble facade and most other shrines were restored or redecorated early in the decade. New and repaired images, richly embellished, returned 'triumphally' to their altars. In Jaen, Our Lady of Linarejos was presented with a gold crown by 'the Pitchforkers of the Virgin',[14] a new confraternity; the black Madonna of Montserrat, patroness of Catalonia, received a magnificent silver throne from the people of the province. Marian brotherhoods thrived almost everywhere. For example, by the end of the decade some 6,000 families belonged to Our Lady of Begoña's confraternity in the Basque country. Countless honours springing from the military-feudal tradition were rendered to the heavenly Queen. Robes of new knights of the Sovereign Military Order of St John of Malta were blessed on the feast of the Purification of Our Lady in a ceremony conducted in the presence of the infante Don Fernando and the papal nuncio.[15]

Seville was granted a new coat of arms describing the city as '*Marianísima*'[16] and Pius XII proclaimed the Virgen de los Reyes its patroness (1947). The ancient protectress of Segovia, Nuestra Señora de Fuencisla, received the honours of captain-general from the Generalísimo himself and shortly afterwards, nuncio Cicognani pinned the insignia to her breast (1942). Nuestra Señora de la Victoria, patroness of Malaga, was canonically crowned by Cicognani the following year amidst 'artillery salutes and thousands of rockets'.[17] In Spanish Morocco in 1946 (while the victorious allies were demanding Franco's evacuation of Tangiers) the nuncio crowned Our Lady of Africa in a 'vibrant consecration of the country to Mary'.[18]

Catholic Action, that 'powerful instrument of the Church'[19] decisive in the building of both Marian states in the peninsula, was now under the vigilant direction of Mgr Vizcarra, who also commanded the Higher Institute of Religious Culture. The multitudinous Youth Catholic Action contributed massively to all public acts of National Catholicism, from the great pilgrimages to the highly-organized cult of the pope.[20] The investiture of new members was often held in shrines, where the 'Marian oath' was taken before Our Lady's image, promising to 'defend to the death' the Immaculate Conception, Assumption and 'the unique privilege of her universal mediation'.[21]

The figure of Christ remained obliterated by the exaltation of the Heart of Mary,[22] to which millions were consecrated. Young people were recruited for social work through devotion to the Immaculate, model of charity and obedience.[23] Mgr Vizcarra insisted, however, that Young Catholic Workers (JOC) should be concerned exclusively with the spiritual.[24]

The episcopate founded institutes for the development of Acción Católica,[25] in which the Propagandista Angel Herrera – ordained in 1940 and given the pallium seven years later – was also central. Among his many initiatives was the Sacerdotal Social School, later transformed into the Leo XIII Social Institute (see chapter 32). Fundamental to the 'conversion' of the workers – many of whom were still living 'under the weight of their old prejudices'[26] – were the popular missions and Spiritual Exercises. Immediately after the civil war, the Jesuits led a great apostolic movement of retreats and devotional exercises, mainly in the mining and industrial zones of the north. New congregations sprang up with those specific aims (for example the Slaves of Christ the King, Navarre, 1941); and an important centre was opened in 1941 hard by the ancient sanctuary of Covadonga (Asturias), where a large number of spiritual directors were trained as specialists in various sectors from miners to businessmen.[27] An experienced Jesuit in the field, Padre Felíz, studied techniques for 'rescuing the worker',[28] gaining enthusiastic support from the business community.

Catholic Action, closely controlled by the exclusive ACN de P[29] and the Opus Dei,[30] was crucial to this task.[31] Mgr Vizcarra reminded Acción Católica of the need to follow the Ignatian tradition: 'We are assured by the supreme authority of the Vicar of Christ of the capital importance and indubitable efficacy of the Spiritual Exercises as the instrument of sanctification for the members of Catholic Action.'[32]

As Bishop of Málaga, Herrera was an active spiritual director offering annual Exercises and monthly retreats to the provincial authorities. The Bishop of Mallorca, Mgr Juan Hervas, founded towards the end of the decade a secretive and select network whose devotional life revolved round the rosary and Blessed Sacrament: Cursillos de Cristiandad (Little Christian Courses).[33]

The Society of Jesus made a speedy recovery, creating a sixth Spanish province by mid-decade. By 1943, 22 of its 122 Houses of Exercises and over 12,000 of the total 127,682 centres of the Apostleship of Prayer were in Spain. New divisions – devoted to Mary and the Sacred Heart – emerged in this decade, mainly in the centre and north of the country. Founded mostly by priests including Jesuits,[34] many undertook social action among the poor (for example the Missionaries of Jesus, Mary and Joseph, a pious union since 1942) and a few followed the contemplative path of 'perpetual reparation' (such as the Slaves of the Most Holy Sacrament and the Immaculate Conception, a congregation dating from 1947). Some older congregations such as the nineteenth-century teaching order of Conceptionist Slaves expanded far beyond Spain. Yet none would outshine the Opus Dei, whose scope and structure were unique.

Despite fierce opposition from some ecclesiastical quarters[35] and Escrivá's failure to realize a personal ambition to become military vicar-general,[36] Opus Dei's achievements in the decade following the civil war were outstanding. This 'supernatural, spiritual organization'[37] was approved as a pious union in 1941 on the feast of St Joseph, and two years later the Sacerdotal Society of the Holy Cross was instituted within the Work. This exclusive section permitted diocesan priests, religious, bishops and even cardinals to join Opus Dei while their involvement was kept even more secret than the laity's.[38]

In the same year (1943), the institute received provisional approval from the Holy See and was granted the feast day of Mary, Mother of Fair Love. Pacelli endowed the Work with indulgences and praised its aim and spirit in an apostolic brief of 1946.[39] Shortly afterwards the constitutions – admitting married people – were authorized.[40] For Don Josemaría, now a domestic prelate residing in Rome with powerful friends,[41] 'each step in the legal itinerary of the Work has been taken under the protection of the Mother of God'.[42] By the mid-forties Opus had houses in all major Spanish cities and by the end of the decade the Roman College of the Holy Cross was training chaplains for an ambitious worldwide apostolate.

FRANCO, FATIMA AND THE ASSUMPTION

I entreat our Virgin Captain for . . . the greatness of the Hispanic world community.[43]

Francisco Franco, 12 October 1939

As leading Propagandistas toured the New World as ambassadors of Pax Romana in 1939, the Caudillo announced that in the following year Saragossa would be 'a living centre of the greatest Hispanic and universal demonstration of faith'.[44] In 1940 – nineteenth centenary of the Virgin's alighting on Spanish soil – the sacred pillar was indeed the hub of a series of remarkable expressions of Marian zeal. Apart from the large number of pilgrims and ceremonies like the 'inflammatory oath'[45] taken by 20,000 youngsters to defend the mystery of the Assumption, the Sociedad Mariológica Española (SME) was created under the protection of the Virgen Capitana with an 'absolutely secret scientific commission' to study her 'greatness and privileges'.[46] The anti-communist/anti-Masonic[47] legislation and tribunal, and the Council of Hispanidad were also established that year. Cardinal Gomá could justifiably claim, 'The Fatherland rises up again when devotion to the Virgin of the Pillar similarly revives.'[48]

Spanish involvement in World War II through the Blue Division kept the Marian-crusader spirit burning. Many volunteers, 'who lived a pious explosion of Marian devotion and, in particular, devotion to the Holy Virgin of the Pillar',[49] left for Russia directly from the shrine of Our Lady, whose 'picture-photograph' was used for proselytizing at the front.

The recently inaugurated National Sanctuary of the Great Promise – 'the Spanish Paray-le-Monial' – was another lighthouse of Hispanidad. In October 1941, when the first contingents of the Blue Division had reached the eastern front, the Archbishop of Valladolid announced a 'grand project' to be annexed to the National Sanctuary: a 'monument of the Hispanic world to the Sacred Hearts of Jesus and Mary with a centre for study and propaganda.'[50] Later in the decade he called for the inclusion in the Jesuit shrine of the patronesses of Mexico (Guadalupe) and the Philippines (Our Lady of Peace and Buen Viaje de Antipolo) – for the Great Promise embraced what Spain was in 1733, the year of the Sacred Heart revelation to Padre Hoyos.

'Virgin of the Pillar, Queen of Hispanidad' was the topic of a research contest in January 1943 to commemorate Our Lady's flight to Aragon.[51] The Royal Academy of History and Council of Hispanidad were represented on the panel and at the closing ceremony – a great 'act' presided over by the Archbishop of Saragossa and attended by all the authorities and 'hierarchies of the Movement'[52] – the audience sang the anthem of the Virgen del Pilar.

A few days later, the Argentinian bishops were appointed elder brothers of the Archconfraternity of the Apostle Santiago, whose commission was received by the minister of foreign affairs.[53] As a 'gesture of Hispanidad'[54] in March 1943, the Venezuelan government sent an image of the Virgen de la Soledad to Madrid to replace the one destroyed by 'revolutionary criminal fury'.[55] The new effigy – wearing a richly embroidered mantle – was greeted with the 'religious fervour of the crowd'[56] and escorted by the Falange and youth organizations. By the end of April 1943 – as the Axis powers withdrew from North Africa – Pius XII told the Propagandista Ruiz Giménez, president of Pax Romana, of his hope and trust in 'the peoples of Hispanidad' and 'the Caudillo and his government'.[57]

Peace through Mary's mediation, principally under her title of Immaculate, was Rome's constant message, particularly to the world of Hispanidad, a recipient of so many favours. Total abandonment to her was Catholic Action's order of the day.[58] On the Universal Day of Marian Congregations in May 1943, Catholic leadership dwelt on the bond between Church, Mary and Spain: 'The ancient glories of Spain will not perish whilst youth strengthens itself by imitating her virtues because the whole ecclesiastical tradition puts triumph in the hands of devotees of Mary.'[59]

Portentous 'acts of propaganda' emphasized the triad. In August 1943 Catholic-Falangist youth flocked in flag-bedecked trains from the shrine of the Great Promise in Valladolid to the sepulchre of Santiago at Compostela, where Franco made a triumphal entry accompanied by leaders of the Movement.[60]

As the pope called for a 'crusade'[61] and the blue battalions engaged the Russians,[62] a passion for consecrations to the Immaculate Heart – inspired by the accelerating cult of Fatima – gripped the Iberian peninsula. Mariologists from both countries analysed the 'efficacy' of the Immaculate Heart devotion[63] and, by the end of the war, the agglutinate 'cardio-Marian' devotion linked to the rosary[64] began to displace Our Lady of the Pillar and the Apostle Santiago.

In the crucial year of 1945, with the unconditional surrender of Germany (May) and external pressure mounting (even from the 'pretender' Don Juan de Borbon),[65] Franco's regime went through its most critical moments. Not yet settled into the dynamic of the cold war, the weak Spanish infrastructure seemed unable to cope with the international challenge and panic seized many. Serrano Suñer, ex-chief of the Falange, suggested dismantling the one-party system. Some concessions were made[66] and overall Falangist control of the state apparatus ceased; key jobs in education and foreign affairs were taken by prominent members of the ACN de P: less rigid, well connected through the Church and internationally more acceptable. But poverty and isolation lingered[67] and the Francoist state stepped up the old Assumption campaign and new cult of Fatima, waging war on Freemasonry and liberalism, Jews, Protestants, and communists as virulently as ever.

The Assumptionists' target – dogmatization of the 'psychosomatic'[68] translation of Mary – reinforced a strategic front: Fatima and the Immaculate Heart devotion. An infallible judgment was needed to establish that the heart of Our Lady – 'perfectly associated with the heart of Jesus Christ and throbbing in unison'[69] – has a glorious corporeal existence through all eternity.[70]

Opus Dei and ACN de P entered a phase of intense activity. In February 1945, soon after the Spanish-Lusitanian Marian congress on the Immaculate Heart in Fatima (see chapter 25) and at a turning point in the war, Escrivá was invited to the sanctuary by Sister Lucia herself,[71] with whom he maintained contact throughout his life.[72] He returned to Portugal twice that year to lay plans for 'a stable apostolate',[73] meeting bishops and Cardinal Cerejeira.

Pax Romana, the Propagandistas' vehicle of Hispanidad and integralism, also mustered far-flung support. In August 1945, when the allies excluded Spain from the United Nations, the president of Pax Romana went on tour again (to South America, the United States and England), holding well-publicized congresses in Salamanca and El Escorial the following year.

After the condemnation of Spain in early 1946 the Generalísimo entered the lists against Freemasonry in person together with his right hand, Admiral Carrero Blanco,[74] a close associate both of Catholic Action and Opus Dei. The anti-Masonic campaign was soon supplemented by one directed by Mgr Vizcarra against 'tolerance' of 'Protestant propaganda'.[75]

Hispanidad's obsession with the 'Russia will be converted' message was heightened by the Bolshevik victory over the Nazis and continuing western tension. The papacy and all its divisions were eager to crown the cycle of Mary's glories by defining her ascension. A bulky Assumptionist report[76] by Jesuits Hentrich and von Moos was published in 1945; in May - as the papal legate crowned the statue at Fatima – Pius XII issued his inquiry among bishops, *Dei Parae Virginis*. The Assumption was discussed at the annual SME assembly, and in early 1947 Franco, as 'a submissive son of Holy Church', petitioned Pacelli for the definition. He reminded the pope of Spain's defence of the Immaculate Conception and the fact that Isabel II had initiated the Assumptionist movement. 'Swollen with holy pride' by the 'Marian fervour' of his country, the Caudillo begged the Holy Father to proclaim, through his 'infallible magisterium', the 'glorious Assumption of the august Mother of God', such an act being the 'present and palpitating aspiration of the soul of Spain'.[77]

The ministry of education followed suit with a letter countersigned by the Opus Deísta head of the Council of Scientific Research which referred to the 'saving devotion to the Heart of Mary'.[78]

During the month of Mary a few weeks later 18 mayors took an Assumptionist oath before the civil governor and Archbishop of Madrid while the Virgin of Fatima processed through Spanish cities.[79] She was greeted by a ten-kilometre queue of hooting traffic as she crossed the border at Puerto de los Castaños. Churches and parishes named after her were 'innumerable'.[80]

In 1948 the pope called for universal consecration to the Immaculate Heart of dioceses, parishes and families, and the Marian congress of Madrid was honoured by the original image from Fatima – venerated by the head of state, his family and government.[81] The publicity generated by the Portuguese statuette gave the impression that 'she had invaded and sanctified with her presence all the media of diffusion of thought'.[82]

Part IV

ESCALATION OF THE MESSAGE OF FATIMA

31

OVERVIEW

America is the land of Our Lady. That is true whether we speak of America in the broad sense, as embracing the entire Western Hemisphere, or whether by America we mean our own United States. The Blessed Mother seems to have taken our section of the world under her special protection.

Don Sharkey, *The Woman Shall Conquer*, Milwaukee, 1952, p.267

BACKGROUND

With the advent of the national security doctrine at the beginning of the atomic era,[1] Mary – as exterminator of all heresies – took on extraordinary proportions in the east-west confrontation. A series of historical circumstances resulted in the Vatican's close association with US cold war warriors in aggressive Marian campaigns.

After the post-war division and fortification of Europe, around 45 million 'subjects' of the pope found themselves under communist rule. Brutal attempts to eradicate the Catholic faith were facilitated by the fact that hierarchies in eastern Europe had blessed, even figured largely in, quasi-fascist and quisling regimes. The trial of Archbishop Stepinac of Zagreb on charges of forced baptism in collaboration with Anton Pavelic, the Butcher of Croatia, provoked rallies in New York led by Cardinal Spellman (known in Moscow as 'the Archangel of Atomic War').[2] The names of other Princes of the Church – Mindszenty of Hungary, Wyszynski of Poland, Slipyj of the Urkraine – were added to a roll-call of 'dry martyrs' who spent long years in communist gaols while, in the pope's words, 'continuing to revere, beseech and love in a very special way the Blessed Virgin Mary, most loving and powerful Queen of Heaven and earth, to whose Immaculate Heart they have all been consecrated by Us'.[3]

The shrine of Our Lady of Czestochowa in Poland was raided for 'seditious literature' and in 1949 – the year NATO was created and Pius XII excommunicated all those who cooperated with the communists – a weeping Madonna in Lublin cathedral drew 100,000 pilgrims a day, some of whom clashed with armed police in the streets. As the hunger for miraculous cures spread to other Polish cities, employees of the state railways were arrested for laying on special trains, and the authorities accused the Church of provoking public disorder.[4] Communist youths were reported to have fought pilgrims in several eastern bloc countries.

Masses for the 'Church of Silence' were held in Rome every week during the Marian Year of 1954. At a 'rosary proclamation' held in a Cadiz theatre that year a Jesuit asserted that 'the pacification of the cold war' could be achieved solely through the 'interviews of celestial diplomacy' conducted at Lourdes and Fatima.[5]

Even before the loss of the faithful masses of eastern Europe a well-nigh bankrupt Vatican was coming to rely increasingly on United States funding for its global mission. For example, the radio and television orator Archbishop Fulton Sheen – national director of the Pontifical Society for the Propagation of the Faith and an ardent devotee of Mary who believed American missionaries were 'preserving for the world the view of the absolute incompatibility of Communism and civilization'[6] – raised on average $12.5 million a year for the Holy See.[7] The Knights of Columbus, working closely with Sheen, Spellman and Senator Joe McCarthy, continued to pump cash into papal charities and begged 'truth dollars' for Radio Free Europe.[8]

Together with this shift in financial bases a further demographic factor was added to the loss of European populations: Catholics were rapidly becoming the largest denomination in the US, with nearly 27 million members in 1950. And by 1964 there were more American Jesuits – over 8,000 – than the total number from Germany, France, Italy, Austria, Belgium and Holland[9] – countries that had historically supplied the Church with 'intellectuals'. Moreover, American Jesuits played an important role in the US armed forces as well as in the international mission field.[10] Geopolitical considerations and financial restraints brought old adversaries together: Catholic Spain and 'Masonic' USA signed a military pact in 1953.[11]

Not only were a large proportion of the world's Catholics located in the US and its dependency of Latin America, but the new

232

radio and TV networks were largely under American control.[12] In 1954 the Franciscan Friars of the Atonement, for example, maintained 350 domestic stations and over 300 stations overseas in collaboration with the Armed Forces Radio Service.[13] The age-old rosary devotions, now inseparable from the lurid message of Fatima, could thus penetrate the vast priestless regions of the Third World as a hard sell against 'communism'.

Shortly after the coronation of the statuette enthroned in the Chapel of Apparitions at Fatima, a replica dubbed the 'pilgrim Virgin' started out – with farewells from the princesses Maria Pia de Savoie, Isabelle d'Orléans and Malfalda de Bragança – for Spain, France, Belgium, Holland and Luxemburg.[14] In London the Portuguese ambassador, the Duke of Palmella, presented another replica of Our Lady of Fatima to Cardinal Griffin.[15] By 1950 – the year of the Assumption declaration – the pilgrim Virgin had drawn large crowds throughout the Far East, the Pacific Islands, Australia and Africa. In Cairo the image was crowned 'Queen of Egypt' as 'throngs of dissident Orthodox and Moslems' showed 'an equal reverence' towards it.[16]

The devastation of Hiroshima-Nagasaki and subsequent nuclear escalation[17] heightened the credibility of the Virgin's prophecies at Fatima (where she had appeared 'more brilliant than the sun'),[18] transforming the cult into a dark obsession for millions. Had not Our Lady spoken to the little shepherds of 'annihilating nations'? What could the 'third secret' of Fatima contain if not the assertion that unless Russia is 'converted', nuclear war will break out? As the less sophisticated pondered on these terrors, theologians spun an atomic casuistry to justify the possession and use of weapons of total destruction.[19]

In 1953 the first Soviet H-bomb was tested: faith in Mary seemed even more imperative. In his end-of-year broadcast to the Spanish people in 1954, Franco warned of the threat of Soviet weapons, which could destroy the world.

> With the hope that this hour does not come, we confide ourselves in full faith to the protection, which cannot fail us, of our holy patron and the intercession of the Immaculate Heart of Mary, to whom we consecrated our nation this year.[20]

The suppression of the 1956 Polish and Hungarian uprisings stimulated the growth of militant Marianism throughout the west.

Pius XII had followed in some measure the Ostpolitik of 'peaceful coexistence' after Stalin's death in 1953. The Soviet invasions brought the 'Church of Silence' back to the centre of the stage. The primates of both countries (Wyzsynski and Mindszenty) were to become openly associated with the Fatima cult from the 1960s onwards.

The ecumenical and irenical policies of John XXIII (1958–63) seem to have checked the Marianization of international politics, slowing the progress of mass movements like the Blue Army[21] and the Legion of Mary.[22] Apparitions at Garabandal in Spain (1961–5) can be seen as a reaction against John's détente.

His successor, Paul VI (1963–78), moved briskly in the opposite direction, resuming the traditional policy of the papacy and galvanizing Marianism and Mariology in a systematic, comprehensive and 'scientific' manner. Mary was proclaimed 'Mother of the Church' and increasingly merged with the Holy Spirit – whose presence was loudly monopolized by nascent Catholic Pentecostalism. 'Popular religiosity' was ferociously defended as the great missionary force of the age, in opposition to 'elitist' tendencies fostered by the theology of liberation (also dating from the late sixties).

Sanctuaries and visions again became the central politico-devotional platform. Montini's pilgrimage to Fatima, at the height of the Portuguese African wars, rehabilitated the shrine and sanctioned the activities of American-led integralists. In the very same year American *cursillistas* introduced the 'charismatic renewal' into Catholic parishes as a 'rekindling of the devotional Church'.[23] Working through established denominations, the miracle-hungry, tongue-speaking movement now overlaps with right-wing fundamentalism. Mary is the Catholic charismatics' 'model of strength'[24] in the battle against a common enemy: 'secular humanism'.

Against a background of growing Muslim fundamentalism Paul VI enthusiastically pursued relations with the Eastern Churches, especially the Greeks and Copts. In 1968 the latter were involved in a spectacular 'public apparition', which won a degree of 'ecumenical' approval.

The task of creating a thoroughly modern Mary was set by Paul VI, who called for a new 'psycho-sociology' of her person for the benefit of the 'modern woman'.[25] This ongoing theological facelift is now a vital arm of ecumenism. The Ecumenical Society of the Blessed

Virgin Mary was founded in Britain in 1967 under the patronage of Catholic and Anglican primates, with Orthodox representation at episcopal level. Issues of the multilingual *Ephemerides Mariologicae* in the 1970s reflected the hopes placed in Marian ecumenism as theologians struggled to produce a cult for the age: '. . . the new Marianism, transforming its ancient psychic mechanism, will make use of this new basis in attributing to Mary her just and adequate place in contemporary Christian humanity. Mary's place will be different.'[26] Although a feminist fringe expressed an interest in her ideological potential,[27] most left-wing Catholics were 'de-Marianized'.[28] But professional Mariologists became even more profound in their speculative search. In Spain, where Franco had once removed psychology from university curricula, theologians now wrote of the 'psychic personality of the Virgin Mary'.[29] Devotion to Mary was yet again the answer to 'the crisis of faith-obedience, of prayer-contemplation'. Renewal and reconciliation within the Church was 'feasible solely in Mary and with Mary'.[30]

Montini was followed – briefly – by Cardinal Luciani (John Paul I), also a keen supporter of Opus Dei[31] and the Blue Army.[32] The subsequent election, on 16 October 1978, of a conservative from the eastern bloc was greeted with a media fanfare whose exultant notes have only recently died away. So far, there has been no dogmatic advance under John Paul II, but the Marian cult and all those concomitant elements related to the flesh (priestly celibacy, virginity, sexual abstinence) and the spirit (obedience, humility, resignation) have attained an unprecedented impetus, especially in the Third World.

As in the past, strategic apparitions are giving shape and direction to political frustrations. Medjugorje (Yugoslavia) is a potential focus of tension between east and west, a symbol of the 'renewed fervor among Roman Catholics' in the communist bloc which 'parallels rapid growth of fundamentalist Protestantism in the Soviet Union and Romania'.[33] And in countries like Chile and Nicaragua stage-managed visions – endorsed by some local bishops – are symptoms of the north-south conflict.

In the midst of a global recession and with a third of the world's Catholics now living in fast-growing Latin America, Rome's eternal geopolitical and economic dilemmas have been sharpened under the former Archbishop of Cracow. His Polish nationalism plus the insolvency of the Vatican seem, at this conjuncture, to be furthering interdependence between the papacy and the temporal powers of the west – antagonizing the emergent anti-Marian progressive elements of the 'south' more than ever. Manifestations of this reality are attempts to silence 'rebel' theologians and religious, and the warm rapprochement between the Vatican and Anglo-Protestant countries. The United States established full diplomatic relations with the Holy See in 1983 – just three years after Britain had raised contact to diplomatic status (ambassadorial in 1982), an act made possible by 'the unprecedented popularity of John Paul II'.[34] The historic move towards some form of Anglican submission to 'a new style of papal leadership'[35] is even more significant.

Much has been written about the pope's concurrence with the Reagan administration, especially on Nicaragua, less perhaps about the similarities between US fundamentalism and the preaching of Wojtyla. Few seem aware that 'Born Again Catholics' figure prominently among Evangelicals, Orthodox Jews and Mormons in the Moral Majority.[36] Creationism neatly complements the defence of 'tradition' by orthodox Catholic thinking.

DEVOTIONS AND DIVISIONS

The army of Ignatius, chief custodian of 'the close and almost military unity of our Catholic people',[37] was put under the Belgian Jean-Baptiste Janssens in 1946, and progressive Jesuits gathered round Teilhard de Chardin were dispersed to the four corners of the world.[38] The neo-ultramontanism and Marian revivalism led by Pacelli and Janssens were reflected in divisions directly controlled by the Society, principally those exemplars of 'thinking with the Church',[39] the Sodalities of Our Lady, grouped in a world federation since 1953, and the Apostleship of Prayer, which claimed 38 million members in 1964.

Yet the long-term decline of the Jesuits was not reversed. Their mantle was to fall on the Opus Dei, whose numeraries and supernumeraries – tapping the world's richest diocese, Chicago, since 1949 – became even more international, opening university residences from Japan to Kenya, Germany to Brazil, by the 1960s.[40]

In the colonial and neo-colonial conflicts of the post-war period Mary's divisions fought many ideological battles against insurgents

– or potential insurgents – throughout Africa, South-East Asia and Latin America. An Americanized Mary was paraded through the Far East by the Blue Army of Our Lady of Fatima, the official apostolate of the shrine, claiming five million members by 1952 – the year Francisco and Jacinta Marto's beatification process began. In South Vietnam a warm reception was assured by President Diem, whose regime, like Salazar's, purported to be based on social encyclicals.[41] Cooperating closely with Blue Army leaders, the Legion of Mary – having been chased out of China[42] – made headway elsewhere, particularly in the Philippines,[43] Brazil and the Congo, with nine million supporters by 1964.[44]

The interlocking of networks became even more complex. The Knights of St Columbanus, for example, who entered the inter-party Dublin government in 1948,[45] forged links with the American Knights of Columbus, the Australasian Knights of the Southern Cross and South African Knights of Da Gamba, and set up in Nigeria the Knights of Blessed Murumba (1952). In 1951 the Society of St Vincent de Paul established 22 new conferences in Japan and by 1953 counted on 200,000 Brothers in 70 countries.[46] Another significant French lay association emerged in 1951: the 'Rosary Teams' of Dominican Fr Eyquem and Madame Colette Couvreur (whose efforts recall Pauline Jaricot of the Living Rosary). Dedicated to 'the well-being of the poor', the promotion of 'collective devotions', and 'the liberation of everyone', the Teams spread to Spain, Mexico, Argentina, Martinique and Vietnam. A group of Marian Anglicans formed a Team in England.[47] The Jocists (Young Christian Workers) were consecrated in 1950 to the Blessed Virgin, who, in the words of Mgr Cardijn, was 'a young worker, engaged to a worker, the wife of a worker, the mother of a worker family'.[48] Three years later, the Vatican suppressed the French 'worker-priest' movement.

The secretive[49] Little Christian Courses – linked both to the Legion of Mary[50] and the Opus Dei in Latin America[51] – were made compulsory for higher civil servants by General Onganía of Argentina, who seized power in 1966 and consecrated the nation to Our Lady of Luján three years later. In 1960 the religious front against democracy in Brazil produced a new integralist movement backed by big landowners: the Society for the Defence of Tradition, Family and Property.[52] Under the patronage of Our Lady of Fatima, imitating rituals of the military orders and providing arduous training,[53] 'TFP' has since taken the fight against Modernism to several countries in the region threatened by the 'New Church – atheistic, desacralized, egalitarian and placed at the service of communism'.[54]

Another division operating in South America is the 'Schönstatt Family',[55] recognized as a secular institute by Rome in 1948, the year the founder, Fr Josef Kentenich,[56] inspected branches in Brazil, Uruguay, Chile, Argentina, South Africa, and the USA. This complex institution grew from congregations under Pallottine and Eudist inspiration at the Marian sanctuary of Schönstatt near Coblenz (West Germany). Dedicated to a 'Marian formation of the world to Christ',[57] Schönstatt members make a 'covenant with Mary',[58] exchanging hearts and giving her a 'blank cheque' so that nothing may happen without her.[59]

Methods employed to glorify Mary in this period ranged from stamp exhibitions[60] to public gardens of her flowers,[61] from prestigious academic foundations[62] to the 'Voice of Mary' radio station in Bogotá.[63] Some promotions were fairly traditional (for example multiple indulgences attached to the Family Rosary), others novel and more in the realm of modern marketing. The Marianization of the masses was largely undertaken through the electronic media.[64] The Redemptorists, for instance, were highly active in the United States, spreading by radio the 'night exercises' in honour of Our Lady of Perpetual Succour and establishing her novena in eleven archdioceses and 43 dioceses.[65] Feature films and radio/TV broadcasts were the lifeblood of the anti-communist rosary campaigns. Devotion to the Sacred Heart – in a state of exhaustion despite Pacelli's attempts at resuscitation[66] – was urged on breakfast radio programmes and 'Sacred Heart Luncheon Clubs' for businessmen.[67]

The pope appeared for the first time in front of television cameras in 1954. Imparting the apostolic blessing to directors and technicians, Pius XII declared, 'the first developments of television in Rome have contributed to make more solemn the inauguration of the Marian Year, so may its further development contribute to the future triumphs of Jesus and Mary.'[68] The transmission of papal indulgences through electronic channels was accordingly authorized by the Sacred Apostolic Penitentiary.

The Knights of Columbus have contributed substantially to conveying Marianism and the papal cult to a global audience through TV networks as well as fulfilling traditional tasks like the maintenance of the façade of St Peter's basilica. The Order –

which has dedicated its 'second century' to the Virgin – is currently funding military vicars in Europe and the Far East[69] and 'adopting' impecunious seminarists by the hundred.[70] The 'millionth rosary' was recently given to a Brother Knight at his initiation ceremony and the 'Pilgrim Virgin-Marian Hours of Prayer' programme under various titles (Guadalupe, Perpetual Help, Czestochowa) has drawn millions of worshippers since 1980.

Canonizations of Mary's servants, consecrations, coronations of statues and other well-established means of manifesting filial love towards Our Lady crowded the fervent fifties. The most splendid as well as the swiftest process was that of Pius X,[71] beatified in 1951 and declared a saint three years later in a television ceremony which provided Pius XII with an opportunity to attack the dangerous new 'lay theology'. Grignion de Montfort attained sainthood in 1947. In 1950 St Alphonsus de Liguori became patron of confessors and moralists, and Antonio Maria Claret – to be acclaimed later in the US as patron against cancer and 'communistic godlessness'[72] – was canonized.[73]

The tendency to bathos inherent in military Marianism was exemplified in Bolivia during the first Marian Year, when the Mamita was proclaimed (after documents had been signed by the minister of justice and immigration) '*Patrona del Cuerpo Nacional de Carabineros y Policias . . . con el grado honorífico de Generala*'.[74] Innumerable congresses combined militaristic pageantry with a vast 'scientific' output on the 'rights' and 'privileges' of Mary. These picturesque seminars usually opened with a bombastic radio message from Pius XII as generals, sportsmen, and youth marched with prelates to a local shrine. They were frequently held under the auspices of the recently founded institutions whose libraries and journals catered for a growing Marian intelligentsia. During the 1950s, a golden age of Mariology, scholarly production was stimulated to around 1,000 books a year.[75]

The ancient phenomenon of weeping statues was reported from Brazil to Shanghai. The most memorable case was of a plaster image of Mary belonging to an epileptic woman in Syracuse, Sicily. High-ranking policemen who took possession of the statue testified to the *lacrimazione*,[76] which drew millions to a hastily-erected shrine in 1953 and warranted an enthusiastic mention from the pope in his radio message to the Sicilian Marian Congress. The massive pilgrimage of the nineteenth century was still the norm. Nearly five million pilgrims – including 40,000 military personnel from France and NATO[77] – visited Lourdes during the 1958 centenary of the visions. In an advance statement, Pacelli castigated 'materialism' and recalled the 'Marian favours' granted to France with a specific mention of the Miraculous Medal apparitions.[78]

Visions and other forms of supernatural sensationalism kept the inspectors of the Holy Office busier than ever. In addition to the solar experiences of Pius XII (never investigated) there were 80 unofficial apparitions between the end of the World War II and the opening of the Second Vatican Council (1962), of which half were in Italy and nearly all to children.[79] Mary's frequent cinema appearances had an impact on some visionaries. A thirteen-year-old girl from Gimigliano (Italy) confessed that a film about Lourdes had inspired her to imitate Bernadette.[80]

The apparitional fever was not without its critics. In 1951 Cardinal Ottaviani publicly called for more prudence among Marian votaries[81] and three years later, a Spanish Jesuit ironically noted, 'gusts of apparitions sweep through the Eastern and Western peoples of Europe, and the "marvellism" has flown as far as America and Asia, where it has produced a no less splendid flowering of prodigies.'[82]

Recognition that new forms of militancy were required was indicated by the transformation in 1971 of the bulk of ancient sodalities of Our Lady into 'Christian Life Communities'. The Jesuits – still the largest order with 36,000 members in 1965 – were to begin soft-pedalling the Sacred Heart devotion,[83] even folding the organ of their Apostleship of Prayer, *Messenger of the Sacred Heart*.

Twenty years later, we see Pope Wojtyla turning the Church back to the Jesuitic and Eudist devotions of the two Hearts. New versions, however, are needed 'so that people of today, with their own mentality and sensitivity, may find in it (the Sacred Heart) the true response to their questions and their expectations'.[84] A whole 'pastoral' movement headed by John Paul II still denounces the 'Jansenist temptation' of a 'dehumanized' and 'purist' piety.[85] Marian devotions are praised as the means of liberation from 'abstractions, ideologies and alienating systems'.[86] Indeed, 'without Mary', warns the Episcopal Conference of Latin America, 'the Gospel . . . is transformed into ideology, into spiritual rationalism'.[87] Love and devotion towards Mary, 'fundamental elements in Latin

American culture' in Wojtyla's view,[88] bolster the charismatic and integralist forces violently opposed to liberation theology.

The *sensus fidei* of the Church and the countless pronouncements and acts that oil the Marian machinery are wondrously presented as 'a product of a dogmatic-existential collective knowledge' of 'irrefutable value'.[89] The Marianism of the masses, founded on apparitions of 'the spokeswoman of her Son's will'[90] and on national shrines, is extolled by the pope as 'the true expression of the soul of a people.'[91]

32

THE FERVENT FIFTIES

THE POPE OF FATIMA AND THE RISE OF OPUS DEI

Everyone must put his trust in her as never before. . . . Her
shrines must be thronged, her feasts kept with solemnity. Her
Rosary must be gliding through everyone's fingers. . . . The name
of Mary, more delicious than nectar, more precious than any gem,
is to be held in the highest honour. . . . Let no one dare to utter
anything lacking in due reverence.[1]

Pope Pius XII

Having no rival on earth as a champion of the Cold War, Pope
Pius XII hoped, even after the carnage of World War II, for a final
war of 'liberation'[2] and engaged the still formidable apparatus of the
Roman Catholic Church in the struggle against communism both in
the 'east' and the convulsive 'south'. The main plank of the Vatican's
ideological offensive was an unprecedented glorification of the Virgin
Mary. Pius XII did 'more for the spread of Marian devotions than
any pope before him except perhaps Pius IX.'[3] Pio Nono, however,
could not call upon the media to publicize his supplications to the
Madonna as Pius XII did – that she 'reign over our intelligence' and
'annihilate the dark plans and the wicked work of the enemies of a
united and Christian humanity'.[4]

In contrast with his immediate predecessor, Eugenio Pacelli
descended from the 'black' aristocracy and had connections with
the 'white'. His grandfather, a banker and lawyer, was ennobled by
Pius IX, and his brother was created a prince by Victor-Emmanuel
in 1929 for his legal work on the *Conciliazione*.

An exceptionally gifted linguist, Mgr Pacelli travelled widely
both as nuncio and secretary of state (from 1930), visiting the
United States, South America, France and Hungary. As pope, he
surrounded himself with German members of the Jesuit Order,
which in 1942 obtained permission to celebrate the feast of the
'Queen of the Society of Jesus'. His reign (1939–58) was dedicated

to Our Lady of Good Counsel; and Catholic Action was declared 'under the guidance and support of the Blessed Virgin Mary'.[5]

Pacelli's declaration of the Assumption – the only infallible pronouncement ever made since the papal monopoly of dogma was established in 1870 – was the highlight of a pontificate resonant with Marian paeans. As the Cold War intensified, pressure for the dogmatization was stepped up by the Francoist state and on 1 November 1950 the bull *Munificentissimus Deus* proclaimed that Mary, like Christ, had ascended into heaven in bodily form.

At the time of the definition its author experienced, while walking in the Vatican gardens, a solar vision similar to the 'public miracle' at Fatima in 1917. The happening was revealed by papal legate Tedeshini (official cardinal protector of Opus Dei) to a wide-mouthed audience of one million in the Cova the following October.[6]

The Pope of Fatima followed up the Assumption declaration with a denunciation of 'false trends in modern teaching', including the theory of evolution. Not only did Darwinian science mock the authority of God as delegated to His Vicar, but 'such speculations are eagerly welcomed by the Communists, who find in them a powerful weapon for defending and popularizing their system of dialectical materialism'.[7]

The Holy Year of 1950 was a field day of indulgences for those who visited the Roman basilicas to pray for the pope's intentions. Among the many categories of penitents exempted from making the trip to Rome were the 'unfortunate inhabitants of those countries in which conditions prevent their journeying to the eternal city'.[8] More than 12,000 'scapular pilgrims' came to Rome in 1950–1 to celebrate the seventh centenary of the visions of Simon Stock; an apostolic letter described the Carmelite scapular as being in the 'first rank of Marian devotions'.[9] Jubilee fiestas were held in many Spanish cities; the Rev Dr Ricart affirmed at a meeting of the Sociedad Mariologica Española – 'with the maximum category of moral certainty'[10] – that the Holy Scapular of Carmel guaranteed salvation. The Spanish state's economic cooperation with the Vatican facilitated pilgrimages of its devout subjects,[11] whose cries of 'Spain for the Pope!' were echoed by Pacelli: 'And the Pope for Spain!'[12]

The early fifties saw the climax of Spanish Marian endeavours in modern times. In May 1950 Antonio Maria Claret, apostle of the Immaculate Heart and Assumption, was canonized in the presence of the Generalísimo's wife, and Madrid hosted a 'Marian-Guadalupan' congress in honour of the 'Patroness and Empress of all Latin America'. In his address to pilgrims from El Salvador and Honduras, the Caudillo declared adherence to 'the throne of the Lady' and the unity of a Hispanic brotherhood of race, language and tradition, before which 'those other forms of brotherhood are nothing'.[13]

Two years later the International Eucharistic Congress – 'last demonstration of mass National Catholicism'[14] – took place in Barcelona under the protection of Our Lady of Montserrat and with the attendance of Cardinal Spellman. Before a huge multitude, the head of state presided over a ceremony of unsurpassed militaristic piety, with all ranks paying homage to the sacrament in nocturnal adoration under Jesuit direction.

Cardinal Montini's call, in the name of the pope, for a 'scientific Mariology' found an immediate response at the congress in reflections on the 'Marian Eucharistic' theme. According to leading Spanish Mariologists, Holy Communion was 'the fruit of the Virgin', to whom we owe 'the body, the blood, the soul and the divinity of Jesus Christ'.[15] It was the Eucharist which established that 'special relationship'[16] between the Holy Virgin and priests, for Mary, the 'sacrificer priest', was their model, performing as she did 'sacrificial functions at Calvary, giving us the example of how we ought to exercise them at the altar'.[17] In response to 'the celestial manifestations and locutions of Fatima', the faithful were called upon to practise 'Eucharistic reparation' for offences committed against the Immaculate Heart.[18] Mgr Escrivá was later to elaborate on this theme: 'In his veins runs the blood of his Mother, the blood that is offered in the sacrifice of the redemption, on Calvary and in the Mass.'[19]

A few weeks after the Eucharistic congress – which provoked Catalan nationalists to unfurl their flag – Franco consecrated Spain to the Most Holy Sacrament. 'The history of our nation is inseparable from the history of the Catholic Church. Her glories are our glories and her enemies are our enemies.'[20]

Spain spawned new divisions devoted to the poor and sick: the Missionaries of Mary Immaculate (1952), Slaves of the Virgin Dolorosa (1956), Missionaries of the Sacred Heart (1957). The contemplative Secular Institute of Reparators was established in 1951 'in response to the calls of the Sacred Heart to St Marguerite Marie

Alacoque'[21] and was approved a few years later by a decree issued at Fatima. The ACN de P opened academic institutions and centres for the dissemination of pontifical social doctrine. Franco inaugurated the Propagandistas' *colegio mayor* San Pablo in 1951.[22] Opus Dei prospered at home and abroad, operating in Portugal, Ireland, France, Mexico, Argentina, Chile and the United States by 1950. On the feast of the Sacred Heart that year, definitive approbation was gained together with the unprecedented permission to recruit non-Catholics into the 'Association of Co-operators of Opus Dei'.

The fertile tree of Iberian Mariology put out a new branch: Josephology,[23] a 'science' which helped to mould Escrivanian asceticism. The chaste and industrious figure of St Joseph the Worker became central to Opus teaching as an exemplar of sanctification in the world through productive activity and another peerless model who 'obeys quickly and to the letter'.[24] Yet, as Monseñor pointed out, there was 'much he taught God's Son'.[25] Hence 'Get to know Joseph and you will find Jesus. Talk to Joseph and you will find Mary!'[26]

In 1951 – the year the Sociedad Española Josefina was founded in Salamanca[27] – Escrivá de Balaguer knelt in the Holy Family's house before the altar of Our Lady of Loreto and formally consecrated his association to the Most Sweet Heart of Mary.[28] Two years later a new Opus seminary opened: the Roman College of Holy Mary.

The first 'Marian Year' (1954) – centenary of the Immaculate Conception declaration, which happily coincided with the Work's silver jubilee – began with the bestowal of the highest papal decoration on Franco: the Supreme Order of Christ. The Generalísimo, in turn, conferred on Escrivá the Grand Cross of the Order of St Raimundo de Peñaforte, instituted in 1945.

A sarcophobic undercurrent accompanied the razzamatazz of the Virgin's year. The spiritual supremacy of celibates was upheld[29] and the faithful warned that the flesh – 'the sternest foe of the reason and of the law of the Gospel'[30] – must be mortified. Devotion to the Immaculate was stressed by Spanish theologians as 'a factor of great importance in resolving the problem of chastity'.[31] The Virgin 'has great power, if only through her example, to deaden the force of the sexual instinct. The purity of Mary is a psychological tonic of the first order for the crisis of youth.'[32]

Our Lady's earthly and celestial rule was celebrated in the new feast of the Queenship of Mary, introduced by the encyclical *Ad caeli reginam*: '. . . just as she wears the crown of queenly glory in heavenly bliss, Mary, the Virgin Mother of God, wields the sceptre of motherly love over the four quarters of the globe.'[33] In this major Marian document Pacelli refers to the 'Wonderful Madonna of Fatima', affirms that Mary was 'intimately associated' with Christ in the redemption'[34] and emphasizes her function as comptroller of indulgences: she holds 'the royal prerogative of dispensing largess from the treasury of our Divine Saviour's kingdom'. Alluding to the 'Church of Silence', the pope adds, 'Our Sovereign Lady is mistress of the time and tide of events. Beneath her maiden foot she can subdue tyranny.'

On 12 October – the day after the release of *Ad caeli reginam* and now the Day of Hispanidad as well as the feast day of the Pillar – Franco consecrated Spain to the Heart of Mary. 'We are moved, Lady,' he prayed, 'by a debt of gratitude: your smiles have illuminated the glorious paths of our history . . . your help has included miraculous apparitions to our missionaries and soldiers so that the natives might fraternize with us.'[35]

A radio message from Pius XII to the Marian congress at Saragossa on the same day reiterated the Marian vocation of Spain, 'land of most Holy Mary'.[36]

Confraternities and processions associated with a large number of shrines – some of which had been destroyed in the civil war – enjoyed a vigorous revival,[37] and 1954 saw several canonical coronations attended by the dictator, papal nuncio and government ministers.[38] Huesca province with its 17 Marian shrines was separately consecrated to the Immaculate Heart. Thanks were offered to the Virgin for Franco's regime, under which 'the love of your sons for you has returned like a splendid spring'.[39]

The climax of a year crammed with public spectacles was the coronation by Pius XII of *Salus Populi Romani*, a painting attributed to St Luke. The act, symbolizing Our Lady's temporal reign – especially over 'that portion of the Church which is persecuted and oppressed'[40] – was preceded by a long procession with Marian banners from all over the world, with a large group from the Church of Silence: 'Bohemia, Albania, Estonia, Lithuania, Bulgaria, Hungary, White Russia, Slovenia, Croatia, Vietnam, China, Korea. . . . Poland.'[41]

Since mid-century the Vatican-Madrid axis found a providential instrument in the Opus Dei, whose formidable organization and asceticism were creating a sort of Roman Calvinism which would shake off the *hidalgo* mentality.[42] Spain's entente with the US led to increasing conflict with, and an eventual purge of, insular Falangist elements antagonistic to the ACN de P and Opus alike.[43] General Franco, who was later to follow the Spiritual Exercises under Monseñor at the Pardo[44] and thought the Work's confessors were 'magnificent',[45] placed a number of its 'technocrats' in key positions in 1957[46] Accused of 'white Masonry' because of its secretiveness and growing worldwide network of investors and agents both within and outside Church structures,[47] the new pragmatic elite contributed largely to the transformation of Spanish administration and management.

Media and education were central in Opus, as they had been for the Jesuits and Propagandistas. A significant link in the Work's chain of prestigious foundations[48] was the social training centre at the academic-devotional complex of Torreciudad adjoining the ancient shrine of Our Lady in Huesca, Aragon. Already part of Escrivá's hagiography (see chapter 28), the sanctuary specialized in heart diseases,[49] with a large clientele of peasants from the region. A few years after the inclusion of its members in the cabinet, the 'Society of the Holy Cross and Opus Dei' took charge of the 'administration and cult of the image'[50] (saved from despoliation in 1936) and began the construction of a centre 'under the protection of the Virgin of Torreciudad'.[51] With three distinct areas for retreat, cultural research and social formation, the centre has two aims: to foster devotion to Mary and teach the Christian significance of work.[52] 'Tiled pictures of the joys and sorrows in the life of St Joseph'[53] line the path to the hermitage. Described as the 'material expression'[54] of Escrivá's love for Our Lady, Torreciudad is a most sophisticated Marian project: a place of retreat, penance and study without the 'eating houses' and shops of religious bric-a-brac.

The basilica in the Valle de los Caídos, that other great complex of the Francoist era, was inaugurated in a patriotic-religious act by the first Opus Dei government in 1958. Built by prisoners of war, Franco's future mausoleum was lavishly decorated with marble statues of the chief patronesses of Spain and of the three branches of the armed forces: the Purísima, Virgin of Carmel, and Our Ladies of Loreto, of Africa, of Mercy and of the Pillar. Shortly before this event – the culmination of Spanish National Catholicism – one of the last briefs of Pius XII established an abbey nearby with the revealing name of 'Holy Cross of the Valley of the

Fallen' and the purpose of 'attracting celestial benedictions upon the Spanish nation'.[55]

The appointment of an Opus Dei priest in 1960 as chief tutor to 'the Prince of Spain' (Juan Carlos de Borbon) is evidence of the Work's new hegemony – and its continuation of the Jesuit tradition. History professor at Navarre, Fr Federico Suárez was also a competent Mariologist, who believed that 'surely the best way to imitate Christ is to imitate Our Lady'.[56]

MARY AND US COUNTER-INSURGENCY FROM HOLLYWOOD TO VIETNAM

Queen of Freedom, protect America, land of the free, lovingly dedicated to the Immaculate Conception which made you free! . . . Mary struck the fatal blow at Communism at Fatima. Her message there is the way to Freedom.[57]

Marian Era

Although World War II smothered the anti-Semitic influence of Fr Coughlin's National Union for Social Justice,[58] Catholics remained in the vanguard of the anti-communist movement that led to the Un-American Activities Committee and other forms of witch-hunting in the McCarthyite era. In 1938 the episcopate warned of the 'spread of subversive teaching'[59] and it was Fr Edmund Walsh,SJ, veteran leader of the Vatican's ill-starred team in Russia, who advised the Senator (graduate of a Jesuit college in Milwaukee) to exploit the Red bogey.[60]

Among other powerful allies of McCarthy were the Knights of Columbus – 'the world's largest and strongest Catholic fraternal organization' solidly based on low-cost life insurance[61] – who called for the extirpation of communists from 'US life and economy' in 1946.[62] The following year the Knights broadcast a series of 'safeguards for America' talks on 226 radio stations.[63] Convinced that 'advertising pays the Church', the Order sponsored a $750,000 a year campaign on behalf of the American hierarchy in 1948.[64] Through their network of councils,[65] the Knights could offer vital support to Senator McCarthy and to Mgr Fulton Sheen, whose pamphlet *Communism, the Opium of the People* they distributed free.

A glance at the front page headlines of *Our Sunday Visitor* (Indiana), 'the Popular National Catholic Action Weekly', in the summer of 1951 indicates the tone of the age: 'Ex-Hater of Mary Claims He Saw Her. "You have spoken Much Against Me, Now that's Enough" She told him.[66] . . . Rosary Said in Six Languages on "I am an American" Day.[67] . . . Let's Correct Evils Which Breed Reds.'[68] In a story on Fatima the newspaper spoke of the 'gentle violence of the Immaculate Virgin Mary. . . . In plain words, Our Lady means business'.[69]

The diffusion of anti-communist propaganda went with a determination to enforce the authority of the Index of Forbidden Books,[70] on which modern European literature and philosophy were heavily represented.

During the Korean war the Knights' monthly *Columbia* vigorously promoted the Fatima cult and US Defense Bonds ('muscle behind our GI's bayonets').[71] In *Columbia's* universe, as in a medieval framework, no clear distinction was made between the sacred and the profane. Alongside full page advertisements for male corsets and dolls[72] whose 'mystic skin' latex limbs were filled with 'miracle foam rubber', readers were offered 'Blessed Virgin Nite-Lites' and baby shoe-shine kits attached to a 'traditional 8″ statue of the Madonna and Child finished in heavenly Mother of Pearl'. Holders of the third degree could order the Miraculous Medal stamped with the Columban emblem (stars and compasses set around the fasces and crossed by a sword and anchor). Another 'K of C Combination Medal' was a sterling silver scapular – 'ideal for the serviceman'.[73]

The Order became perceptibly more committed to Our Lady, giving one million dollars in 1957 for the construction of a 'Knights' Tower' at the national shrine of the Immaculate Conception as 'evidence of the undying loyalty of our members to Mary'.[74]

The most illustrious associate of the Knights of Columbus in the fifties was Francis Cardinal Spellman, reckoned to be the most powerful cleric outside the Curia. Protégé of nuncio Pacelli and Count Enrico Galeazzi (head of the Knights in Europe and Vatican bank chief), Spellman served as playground director of the Order in Rome while raising cash from American millionaires in exchange for papal honours. Receiving the red hat in 1946, the future primate was active in the hunt for Reds in the entertainment industry. And in 1950 he led a pilgrimage to Fatima as Archbishop of New York and US military vicar. His support for the Korean war and military dictatorships in Central America was surpassed only by his efforts in Vietnam – dubbed 'Spellman's War' by protesters.

The Cardinal's contribution to morale gained him invitations to Pentagon planning sessions.[75]

Under the aegis of 'the American Pope' as well as the one in Rome, an aggressive new form of lay apostolate took off, using sophisticated media and marketing techniques and projecting itself far beyond the USA into the boundless sphere of American interests and 'national security'. The Family Rosary Crusade led by Fr Patrick Peyton of the Congregation of the Holy Cross was established through a Hollywood radio programme in 1947. Featuring top names like Bing Crosby and Gregory Peck, the Virgin's show reached some 40 countries via the Armed Forces Radio Service. Peyton saw prayer as a 'commodity' which could be marketed like breakfast cereals.[76] The rosary campaign in Ottawa in 1948, backed by Cardinal Mindszenty, was a masterpiece of saturation advertising:

> the object is to make the crusade inescapable, so that even if
> a man does not read about it in his newspaper, hear it over his
> radio or in his church, or see it advertised on the street, yet he will
> discover the Family Rosary in his morning mail or find his child
> entered in a Family Rosary essay contest in school.[77]

In the same year Twentieth Century Fox released the Crusade's first film, *The Road to Peace*. Its message was 'the Family Rosary, as the solution to the problems of the day – Communism, war, divorce, oppression, intolerance, juvenile delinquency, labour strife'.[78]

The Reparation Society of the Immaculate Heart of Mary, founded by Jesuit John Ryan at Baltimore in 1946, represented a development from nocturnal adoration to a less strenuous nightly tuning in to the wireless.[79] Fr Ryan specialized in buying radio time for Mary and by 1978 had injected a quarter of a million dollars into the US advertising industry on her behalf. The apostolate produced a gimmick newsletter: *Fatima Findings* – 'the smallest newspaper on earth for the greatest cause in heaven'.[80] Holy Hours organized at such diverse places as the New York Fair and the Mexican sanctuary of Guadalupe served openly as vigils against communism.

The All Night Vigil Movement led by the Hon. Mrs Henrietta Bower in Britain was an offshoot of Fr Ryan's work. The daughter of Lord Strickland, prime minister of Malta, Mrs Bower was an indefatigable rosary agitator from Poland to New Zealand, Gozo to Zagorsk.[81]

Catholics in Britain, primed by a campaign of Fr Peyton's in 1952,[82] echoed the McCarthyite scare. The Order of the Knights of St Columba was consecrated to the Immaculate Heart of Mary at Leamington Spa on 26 September 1954, when Bishop Petit of Menevia warned of a possible communist takeover and called for a crusade to prevent it.[83] Ancient hopes that 'Mary's Dowry' would revert to the heavenly Queen were raised by a spectacular coronation of Our Lady of Willesden[84] in Wembley Stadium, preceded by 3,750 non-stop Hail Marys under the supervision of Mrs Bower. A crowd of 90,000 – regaled by a band of the Coldstream Guards, processions of the Children of Mary, RAF personnel and the Columban Knights – heard Cardinal Griffin pray that 'the chains of persecution be lifted from Peter'.[85]

The Block Rosary Lay Apostolate was inspired by a vision to a Detroit housewife in 1945. The apparition, clad in black, suggested that groups of housewives meet, block by block, to tell their beads. Bishop Stephen Woznicki explained that the movement was 'an extension of Fatima and has two extra values; it creates spiritual unity among neighbours . . . and is Our Lady's answer to the Block system of the Communists.'[86] By the sixties some 30 million block rosary leaflets had been distributed.

A less fruitful series of apparitions occurred in 1950–5 at Necadah, Wisconsin. The seer, eventually condemned by an ecclesiastical inquiry, was Mrs Mary Van Hoof, an official of My God and My Country, Inc., who claimed to have been favoured by the Queen of the Holy Rosary.[87] And in September 1956 'Our Lady of America' appeared to an anonymous nun and asked for the production of a transatlantic version of the Miraculous Medal.[88]

Another propaganda movement based on 'private revelations' (above all, those at Fatima), rosary/scapular devotions and the Eucharist ('our spiritual H-bomb') was named the Apostolate of Christian Action – a non-denominational title in order 'to reach out later on a large scale to non-Catholics'.[89] Established at Fresno, California by Redemptorist Bishop Willinger in 1956, the Apostolate aimed to 'help God and His Blessed Mother in their efforts to save this country and the world from the horrors of an atomic war, from the spread of Communism etc'.[90] Under the editorship of Stephen Oraze, *Divine Love* publications were distributed free, especially in the Third World,[91] in the struggle against 'materialism' and 'the cult of the body'.

By far the most significant of the post-war rosary associations is the Blue Army of Our Lady of Fatima[92] – founded, like the Family Rosary Crusade, by a priest who vowed to dedicate his life to Mary if she helped him to recover from a serious illness. Shortly after leaving hospital in the spring of 1947 (the year a replica of the Fatima statue was enshrined in the US embassy chapel in Moscow), the Rev. Harold V. Colgan mounted the pulpit in Plainfield, New Jersey, and proclaimed: 'Atheists have developed a Red Army to back up with armed threat their spread through the world. . . . In this parish let us be a Blue Army of Our Lady. . . .'[93]

Within days a young man called John Mattias Haffert arrived at Plainfield presbytery to offer himself as business manager of Fr Colgan's project. As owner of the Scapular Press, Haffert – who kept a schooner in the Bahamas called the *Santa María* – was able to contribute his expertise in the fields of publishing and public relations. He insisted that the venture must be based exclusively on the visions of Lucia, whom he had met the year before, becoming the only layman ever allowed to interview the well-guarded Carmelite.

Haffert's original recruitment leaflet read: 'Wear a blue ribbon or a blue string by which you will be recognized as a member of the Blue Army, fighting by prayer and penance the Red Army of Communism.' The Blue Army pin, introduced later by Colgan, took various forms: the Miraculous Medal in the USA, a blue cross in France, a blue star in Portugal and a blue heart in Britain.[94]

Membership is based on a pledge, authorized by Sister Lucia, to say the rosary daily and wear the scapular of Mount Carmel. The Blue Army votary prays 'to gain every indulgence and merit I can and I offer them, together with myself, to Mary Immaculate, that She may best apply them to the interests of Thy Most Sacred Heart.'[95]

Disseminating the message of Fatima through radio, films, books[96] and leaflets, the movement gained one million signed pledges by 1950, when Pius XII received Fr Colgan and told him, 'As world chief against Communism I bless you and all the members of the Blue Army'.[97] The Bishop of Fatima was appointed international spiritual director in 1953. Three years later – with membership standing at ten million – the statutes of the organization were approved *ad experimentum* by the Holy See and Colgan was made a domestic prelate. In the same year (1956) the pope sent Cardinal Tisserant, dean of the Sacred College, to bless the Army's 120-room international headquarters at Fatima.[98]

In the hills of north-west New Jersey the Blue Army built an extensive complex with reproductions of the Fatima sanctuary and the Holy House of Loreto. The movement dovetailed into existing campaigns of the Franciscans, the Legion of Mary, the Militia Immaculatae and other Marian organizations.[99] Fourth degree Knights of Columbus formed a guard of honour for the 'pilgrim Virgin' at its many appearances in the United States.

Two British communist renegades, Douglas Hyde and Hamish Fraser, became important supporters of the Blue Army. Converted while news editor of the *Daily Worker*,[100] Hyde declared in Lisbon in 1951, 'To end the threat of Communism, the vacuum must be filled. . . . In a word, our only hope for world peace is found in the message of Our Lady of Fatima.'[101] Fraser, a teacher who left the Scottish branch of the party in 1945, published in the Marian Year *Fatal Star*, a manifesto based on the cult of Fatima. This 'former Servant of Moscow' now taught that totalitarianism 'proceeds directly from the denial of the Immaculate Conception'[102] and that the 'rebirth of Christendom as a social reality' will come about on the 'enthronement of Mary in the hearts of the faithful'.[103]

*   *   *

The Far East was a major battlefield of post-war militant Marianism. On Mao's victory in 1949 the Legion of Mary underwent its baptism of fire as Fr Roberts, chaplain at Fu Yen Catholic University in Peking and leader of the 'Our Lady of Fatima' praesidium, realized that 'there could be only one salvation in the night of Communism . . . close union with Mary'.[104] Wherever 'the serpent had set up his anti-God rule under the banner of the hammer and sickle, She who crushes the serpent's head also appeared and set up the banner of the Legion of Mary.'[105] Many Legionaries served long sentences.

In Korea, where Cardinal Spellman distributed 100 million cigarettes and 50,000 religious medals on one trip alone,[106] Fr Matthew Strumski of the Marines 'wore out a pair of heavy boots carrying the Pilgrim Virgin up and down the land! And how many ceremonies, how many All-Night Vigils were conducted by the Blue Army at the line between North and South Korea, often with the Pilgrim Virgin statue!'[107]

Evangelized in the sixteenth century by Iberian mendicants and by the Jesuits in the next century, Vietnam had a long Marian tradition boosted under nineteenth-century French occupation by the cults of Lourdes and Perpetual Succour (the latter introduced by Redemptorists). Marianization was consolidated by the diffusion of works by Grignion de Montfort and Liguori. In 1950 Catholics – historically accused of facilitating foreign domination – were 'easily recognizable by their medals and, flowing from black or brown robes, scapulars (often richly embroidered) and a rosary round their necks'.[108] The long colonial and civil wars made 'the Christians of Indo-China have recourse to Mary more and more' according to a contemporary French Mariologist. 'Our Lady of Fatima has been welcomed and feted with fervour everywhere; the Legion of Mary is being organized. . . .'[109]

The importance of the Catholic sector – around 10 per cent of the fifteen million Vietnamese compared with some 30 per cent militant Buddhists[110] – was advanced to a stage of hegemony through the dictatorship of the Ngo family in the South from 1954 to 1963. Ngo Dinh Diem, ex-Maryknoll seminarist in New York and lifelong celibate, was a model for US counter-insurgency[111] and a protégé of Cardinal Spellman, who enlisted the aid of Joe Kennedy and Edmund Walsh (the ubiquitous Jesuit) in grooming Diem's aristocratic clan for power.[112]

As ruler of South Vietnam, Diem counted on several brothers including Thuc, Archbishop of Hue – whose diocese embraced the national shrine of the Blessed Mother at La-Vang (visited by Spellman in 1956). Diem's rule, which produced Buddhist unrest leading to his assassination, bred a system of corrupt sacerdotalism. Catholic events were celebrated with a profile denied to other faiths, though Buddhism was experiencing a revival. The whole of Vietnam was consecrated to Mary, Marian national congresses were attended by huge crowds in Saigon (1959) and La-Vang (1961), and the Legion underwent exceptional growth.[113] By 1967 the country was again under Catholic dominance with the election of Van Thieu and the appointment of the leader of Catholic Action, Nguyen-Van-Huyen, as president of the senate. Led by Col. Do Sinh Tu, who had trained at Fort Bragg in the United States, the Blue Army became an ever greater force, feeding off claims that 100,000 Vietnamese members had been martyred by the communists.[114]

A vital factor in propping up Diem was the flight of around 700,000 Catholics to the south between 1954–6 after the division of the country. This exodus was organized by Tom Dooley, acclaimed as 'the Splendid American,'[115] a naval doctor whose beatification cause came to an abrupt end in 1982 when his links with the CIA were exposed.[116] In his account of Red atrocities (including forced ejaculations of 'Increased Production' in place of the traditional 'Jesus, Mary and Joseph')[117] Lieutenant Dooley describes how 'the pride' of the Haiphong mission in the north, a statue of Our Lady of Fatima, was kidnapped by the forces of light:

> We wrapped it in an American Aid blanket which was on the jeep's floor and whisked it out to the airport. At this writing it is standing in a church built especially for the refugees, just outside Saigon. And that's how Our Blessed Lady of Fatima, with a boost from American Aid, made the passage to Freedom.[118]

Mary was simultaneously busy on behalf of US interests in Latin America. In the run-up to the 1954 CIA-directed coup in Guatemala against the government of Jacobo Arbenz (which was threatening to diminish economic control by the United Fruit Company) Bishop Constantino Luna, OFM, urged pastors to set up cells of the Blue Army in every parish.[119]

In Brazil millions saw Fr Peyton's fifteen films of the fifteen rosary mysteries.[120] The Family Rosary Crusade as well as the Legion of Mary (which operated 2,701 Brazilian praesidia in 1961)[121] joined the 'Family Marches with God for Liberty' that helped establish in 1964 the long military dictatorship.[122] The Cursillistas became influential at higher levels in Brazil during the 1950s, following a pattern seen in Venezuela and Argentina.

The Jesuits in Chile received direct financial aid from the US government[123] and, on the advice of Fr Vekemans, an alleged CIA agent, led Church opposition to Allende's unsuccessful presidential campaign of 1958. The subject of 'popular religiosity' (overwhelmingly Marian) was among the most important studies produced by the Centre for Research and Social Action set up by Vekemans.[124]

An intense revival of the Virgin's cult paralleled the revolt against colonialism that 'set Africa afire' in the fifties and sixties. The Vatican played its part in countering Soviet influence in the continent by plans to found an African university in Rome with a 'chair of atheism' – 'to train student priests in communist and anti-Christian evils'.[125] And Opus Dei set up institutions in Kenya in 1961.

While events had quickly sealed the fate of Frank Duff's 'bloodhounds of the Lord' in China, their success in Africa compensated for ground lost to Marxism in the east. In Nairobi in 1958 the beatification process of Edel Mary Quinn was opened. She was an 'Irish business girl'[126] who had served as the Legion's envoy, preparing the advent of the bellicose Montfortian Virgin throughout East Africa.[127] The future *beata* is credited with having converted 5,000 Chinese in Mauritius by organizing Block Rosaries.[128]

Nineteenth-century divisions consolidated their position in many areas. In British Basutoland (Lesotho) in Southern Africa the consecration of the territory to Virgin and Vatican by Chief Moshoeshoe was repeated by his descendant in October 1943.[129] Three years later the regent Amelia Mantsebo Seeiso travelled to Rome to formally confirm the pact while local chiefs arranged for 40,000 households to undergo family consecration. In 1949 'Our Lady of Fatima truly became Queen of Lesotho'[130] during a triumphant visit of her statue to the country after the conversion from Calvinism of an important chieftainess, Maria Fatima Makopoi Api. Tens of thousands lined the route as the pilgrim Virgin toured 35 missions (still largely under the control of Mazenod's Oblates) before taking possession of the national shrine of Ramabanta. The annual pilgrimage to Ramabanta was to become one of the most fervent in Africa[131] and the local culture so 'Fatimized' that the names of Lucia, Francis and Jacinta are widespread.[132]

The centenary of the South African mission of the Oblates of Mary Immaculate in 1952 saw a 'memorable milestone in the Church's "trek for souls" for Christ through Mary'[133] in the first national Marian congress held in Durban. An altar emblazoned with the Order's logo and topped by a 100-ft pillar supporting an eight-foot statue of Our Lady was erected on Greyville Racecourse, where Archbishop Hurley read Pius XII's proclamation that 'the most loving Virgin Mary, under the title of her Assumption into Heaven, is the Celestial Patroness of the whole of South Africa'.[134] Mgr Hurley extolled the recent dogma as a weapon against communism, 'the heresy that denies God and the soul, that reduces man to the condition of brute animal, that drags his highest aspirations in the gutter, and proclaims that the Kingdom of Heaven is on earth and consists in nothing nobler than filling every man with as much food as his neighbour. . . . Against the insidious heresy of the body there rises up the figure of Mary assumed into Heaven. . . .'[135]

Throughout the fifties the Oblates – who held key bishoprics (e.g. Johannesburg, Kimberley, Bloemfontein) – were vociferous in their attacks on 'the Creed of Anti-Christ'; they spread devotion to Our Lady of Fatima and the 'intentions' of the Apostleship of Prayer: 'that the danger of atheistic materialism in Africa be averted.'[136] The large crowds that greeted Fr Peyton when he preached the rosary crusade in South Africa in 1955 had been mobilized by the Oblates to prove that 'modern spirituality is Marian spirituality'.[137]

In the diocese of Mariannhill near Durban the 'Marian Action' movement published the magazine *Queen of the Kingdom of Christ*.

The Fatima story permeated Portuguese Africa, where primary education was still monopolized by the Catholic Church. Articles on the cult written in Lisbon were syndicated in the newspapers in Angola and Mozambique, and a regular Blue Army programme was transmitted by Radio Ecclesia in Luanda. Fatimization was also thoroughly carried out in the strategic, mineral-rich Congo – 'the very Heart of Africa' from where 'the Communists would be able to influence every African nation'.[138]

The Belgian part of this treasure-house had been offered up to Mary by a papal brief of 1891, and Leopold II, whose personal title to the vast territory was exploited by his own trading company, declared that if the enterprise proved successful, he would erect a church to Notre-Dame du Congo. The royal tycoon's vow, approved by Leo XIII, was eventually fulfilled by his successors at Leopold-ville in 1951.[139] Having received waves of Missionaries of the Sacred Heart, Redemptorists, Picpus Fathers, Dominicans, Assumptionists and Montfortians, the Congo Basin was soggy with Marianism. The Legion of Mary, which established a praesidium at Stanleyville in 1945, was operating at every mission post in the late fifties, and the Virgin of Fatima was enthroned in three cathedrals.[140]

33

JOHN XXIII AND THE REACTION AT GARABANDAL

In the past when visionaries saw the Virgin Mary they spent the rest of their lives in convents. Conchita has chosen a different form of isolation in the city of New York.

Garabandal – After the Visions, BBC, 1984

On 9 October 1958, shortly after denouncing the 'false patriotism' of Chinese Catholics,[1] the 'Pope of Fatima' died aged 82 at the summer palace of Castelgandolfo. The seemingly inexhaustible acerbity towards the communist world was soon to give way to a virtual revolution of Vatican policy, leading to unprecedented efforts at ecumenism, détente and social reform. This startling opening up to the outside world – termed *aggiornamento* (bringing up-to-date) by the new pope – found its ultimate expression in the aims of the Second Vatican Council (1962–5). The political undercurrents of this sea-change, however, were not immediately felt on the election of Angelo Cardinal Roncalli on 28 October. Although John XXIII's transparent goodness of heart was a welcome contrast to the autocratic glance and histrionic 'mysticism' of Pius XII, initially he continued the militantly anti-communist line of his predecessors. An almost lifelong conservative, Roncalli was a Marian sentimentalist too, but one whose love of peace and unity persuaded him not to indulge this pontifical weakness in the extreme manner of other popes.

Towards the end of the nineteenth century, while at the seminary of Bergamo, Roncalli kept a diary which expresses an intense Marian piety and his striving for sainthood and sexual purity. As pope, he painstakingly revised these spiritual notebooks and ordered their posthumous publication for 'souls who feel drawn to the priesthood'.[2] There is no sign in *Il Giornale Dell'Anima* (*Journal of a Soul*) of evolution, only a sedulous reproduction of tired devotions – an impression that disconcerted many of John's admirers.

A fundamental influence on the young seminarist was the secret wing of the ancient Marian sodality that dominated clerical life in the town: the Congregazione dell'Annunciazione e della Immacolata, to which he was admitted in 1895. The 'Little Rules' adopted by an inner circle of members 'bound by great secrecy' were copied out by Roncalli and disclosed for the first time by his literary executor in 1964.[3] They give a detailed picture of the Ignatian-Liguorian spirituality already described: daily visits to the Blessed Sacrament and altar of Our Lady, recitation of five decades of the rosary, an emphasis on the feasts of the Virgin and the Sacred Hearts, hourly worship of Mary in May 'with a small mortification of your choice', and so on.[4] Celibacy is in Mary's gift:

> To guard the virtue of purity you must have a great love for Mary most holy, and in her honour say three Hail Marys for yourself and your companions, offering them to her and begging her for this virtue . . . shun the company of women and of corrupt youths.[5]

The lesson on women was well learned. In his own adaptation of the Rules, Roncalli wrote, 'With women of whatever station in life, even if they are related to me or are holy women, I shall be particularly cautious. . . . Nor will I ever fix my eyes on their faces. So I will never confide in them in any way, but when I have to speak with them I will see that my speech is "dry, brief, prudent and correct".'[6] This resolution, made at the age of sixteen, was dedicated to the Virgin of Virgins. At 67 he recalled the

> edifying conversation in the Bishop's residence of Bergamo. . . . As for women, and everything to do with them, never a word, never; it was as if there were no women in the world. This absolute silence, even between close friends, about everything to do with women was one of the most profound and lasting lessons of my early years in the priesthood; and I am grateful still to the kind and illustrious man who taught me this discipline.[7]

Notwithstanding the humblest social origins,[8] Roncalli moved with apparent ease up the academic ladder in the vigilant reign of Pius X, later obtaining key diplomatic posts in the Fascist era. True, he was suspected by the Sodalitium Pianum, but he wrote to his powerful accuser, Cardinal De Lai, in June 1914:

> I can assure you that I have never read a single Modernist book, pamphlet or periodical. . . . I have always preferred to be ignorant, or at least seem ignorant, and to content myself with knowing the errors of Modernism through the pages of its opponents, rather than risk the danger of remaining enchanted or seduced by a direct vision of such errors.[9]

He showed considerable respect towards Mgr Benigni, the mastermind of the Sodalitium, who taught him Church history at the Roman Seminary, and revered Santo Papa Sarto, with whom he identified on devotional and social grounds. His 'clubs', apart from the sodality of Bergamo, were the Priests of the Sacred Heart, Priests Adorers of the Blessed Sacrament, and the Third Order of St Francis. His confessor was a Redemptorist of the Liguorian stamp and his favourite journalist, Louis Veuillot. His politics at that time can be surmised from the entry for Labour Day, 1903:

> Hail Mary! Today the working people, without religion and without God, the poor exploited by the demagogues, and the unthinking masses hold their own feasts. . . . But the faithful begin the month of Mary with their greetings to her who is the Mother of the Word.[10]

After war service as a chaplain in the medical corps, Roncalli took over the spiritual direction of the Bergamo seminary, leaving in 1924 to become president for Italy of the Papal Missions, and briefly took the chair of Patrology at the Lateran University. In 1925, with no more linguistic skills than a rudimentary knowledge of French, he was appointed apostolic visitor to Bulgaria and raised to the titular see of Areopolis. In Sofia (a strategic centre for Mussolini's imperial designs) and later as a papal diplomat in Greece and Turkey, he learned at first hand that Mary is the key to relations with the Eastern Orthodox.[11] At Constantinople he had the motto *Ad Jesus per Mariam* displayed at the entrance of his private chapel: 'These four words contain a whole volume of doctrine.'[12]

As an Italian prelate, Archbishop Roncalli was not unusual in failing to criticize fascism. On Christmas Day 1939 he privately expressed his gratitude for Mussolini's declaration of non-belligerence: '. ... we must really admit that the Duce is divinely guided to act for the good of the Italian people. I believe that the Lord wishes to reward both rulers and subjects for the peace made with the Church.'[13]

Through his contact with the Italian army, Roncalli participated in the occupation of Greece (which, in his view, remained stubbornly 'dominated by Freemasonry'),[14] though his intimacy with von Papen is believed to have helped save the lives of partisans captured by the Nazis.[15]

In 1947 – a year after celebrating pontifical high mass at La Salette as nuncio in General de Gaulle's France – his meditations dwelt on the 'spread of secularism and communism' while on retreat at Villa Manresa, the Jesuit house in Paris.[16] Six years later Pius XII raised him to the cardinalate and the patriarchal throne of Venice.

At Venice he crowned, during the Marian Year, the Madonna della Grazie of Folgaria (Trent) and the Madonna del Bosco on Lake Como, where he had gone on pilgrimage with his mother in a donkey cart many years ago. He represented Pacelli in Beirut at the national Marian congress in the same year and, in 1956, presided at the May pilgrimage in Fatima for the 25th anniversary of the consecration of Portugal to the Immaculate Heart – an occasion highlighted by the Soviet invasions of Poland and Hungary. During regional elections in Italy that year he warned his flock against the proposed alliance between Christian Democrats and Socialists – advice repeated the following Easter.[17] Seven months before the conclave, Roncalli was chosen to dedicate the vast underground basilica of St Pius X at Lourdes. According to his English biographer, however, he had refused to support the feast of the Queenship of Mary until it was proclaimed by the pope in 1954.[18] 'Patriarch Roncalli was swimming against the mariological tide. Few others allowed ecumenical considerations to check their mariological enthusiasm.'[19]

Soon after his coronation Roncalli wrote consoling letters to Cardinal Stepinac of Zagreb, to the Hungarian and Czech primates (both still in communist gaols), and to the Catholics of North Vietnam. In April 1959 he extended to the socialist parties Pius XII's ban on Catholic support for the communists. And in July he outlawed the worker-priest movement in France. The secretary of the Holy Office, Cardinal Pizzardo, explained the pope's decision in a confidential letter to the Archbishop of Paris:

> on his days of work it would be almost impossible for the
> priest to fulfil all the duties of prayer . . . the celebration of Holy
> Mass, faithful recitation of the breviary, mental prayer, visit to
> the Blessed Sacrament, and saying of the rosary.

Furthermore, the worker-priest

> finds himself plunged into a materialistic environment, harmful
> to his spiritual life and often even dangerous to his chastity, but
> he is also led, despite himself, to think like his brother workers
> on social or union matters and to take part in their quarrels; a
> frightening corruption which soon leads him to take part in the
> class struggle.[20]

The ban was reinforced with a long encyclical[21] on that 'wonderful model of priestly virtues', the Curé of Ars, whose 'voluntary affliction of his body' and obedience to the hierarchy provided fitting inspiration for pastoral labours. An encyclical on the Holy Rosary followed in September.[22] But while John's earlier messages struck an all too familiar Pacellian tone,[23] there is also a hint of the Roncalli whom curial reactionaries would later call the 'Red Pope'. By 1960 he had begun the difficult task of depoliticizing the right-wing Azione Cattolica and had rejected the long-established émigré ambassadors to the Holy See of Poland and Lithuania.

The style of Roncalli's pontificate was radically different from the start. After his famous visits to the Roman hospitals and prisons, he threw open the gates of the Vatican to leaders of non-Catholic churches and received in audience 'western' monarchs and presidents who had never before approached the Petrine throne.[24] As historic as the visit of the 'King of the Hellenes' was that of the supreme head of the Church of England, Queen Elizabeth, in May 1961. Orthodox metropolitans, the Archbishop of Canterbury and Methodist leaders all experienced that rustic Bergamasque charm that was quietly ending centuries of papal isolationism.

Not in disagreement with indications of political change in the Society of Jesus, Pope John took a sympathetic line towards the colonial and neocolonial countries. He canonized the first non-white saint of the New World, the mulatto Martin de Porres (d. 1639), an outstandingly charitable lay brother born in Peru; he placed the red biretta on the first African cardinal, Bishop Rugambwa of Tanganyika (March 1960). And in 1961 – the year Angolan insurgents began the long campaign against Portuguese imperialism – the Roncallian 'revolution' also began in earnest with the publication of Mater et Magistra, which gave incalculable impetus to his fellow Catholic Kennedy's development programme for the Third World. The encyclical unfolds a detailed argument for land reform and won its author the reputation of a 'crypto-communist' among elites in Latin America.

Invoking Our Lady of Loreto, whose shrine he had recently visited, John XXIII opened Vatican Council II on 11 October 1962. Despite misunderstandings over invitations and the notion that the gathering of 2,500 Catholic prelates was 'ecumenical', Russian Orthodox observers were present. The good will gained with the Soviet bloc secured the release of the Ukrainian Archbishop Slipyj, who had spent 18 years in gaol, and led to unhoped-for relaxations in Church–Party relations.

This thaw in the Cold War – as well as the pope's public intervention during the Cuban missile crisis of October 1962 – was acknowledged on 1 March 1963 by the award of the Balzan Peace Prize.[25] A week later Alexei Adjubei, editor of *Izvestia*, became the first Soviet official in history to enter the tiny Vatican state. Accompanied by his wife, the daughter of Nikita Krushchev, Adjubei told the pope in an emotionally charged meeting that the USSR was willing to establish diplomatic relations with the Vatican. John made a positive reply couched in biblical allusions and presented Rada Adjubei, a mother of three, with a rosary – to remind her that 'once there lived a Mother who was perfect'.[26]

Less than a month later John XXIII released his last and greatest encyclical, *Pacem in Terris*, in which he reversed not only the anti-communist policies of his predecessors but also his own stipulations: Catholics could now cooperate with Marxists in the interests of mutual welfare and world peace.[27]

John had no magic wand to disperse the less progressive elements at his court. His own secretary of state, Domenico Cardinal Tardini, had, until his death in 1961, favoured the Opus Dei even though Mgr Escrivá was personally contemptuous of the pope's peasant background and considered Vatican II a 'council of the Devil'.[28] Nevertheless, the more raucous militants of Mary lost much ground both during John's reign and in the wake of the

Council. In 1960 the pope opened Sister Lucia's letter containing the 'third secret' (due to be revealed, according to the seer) and returned it without comment to the Sacred Congregation for the Doctrine of the Faith.[29] The negative effects of his pontificate on the Portuguese cult are acknowledged: 'Blue Army development was partially retarded after 1960 by doubts concerning Fatima when the "1960 Secret" was not made public, and partially by postconciliar reaction to Marian devotions.'[30]

Sister Faustina Kowalska and Padre Pio were two more casualties of Roncalli's dislike of contemporary sensationalism. The 'mercy messages' of the Polish visionary were suppressed in 1959 and the following year the Capuchin stigmatist – soon to become spiritual director of the Blue Army – was once again the subject of a Vatican investigation.[31]

In his prayer life John did not desert the Madonna of his childhood, as the Journal amply shows. But during his short reign (ending in June 1963) he did not politicize this devotion in the traditional way. Active support for Fatima would have sabotaged his own work of reform. Yet papal backing for National Catholicism, especially in Spain, was not entirely withdrawn. In 1959 John issued a bull proclaiming Nuestra Señora de la Cabeza the Patroness of Jaén and approved the canonical coronation of her new image, which replaced one destroyed in the civil war. In 1961, during a 'Holy Marian Year' in Valencia, the pope declared Nuestra Señora de los Desamparados principal patroness of the region.[32]

Part of the reaction against the progressive mood in Rome focused on events in a mountain village in north-west Spain, where the Virgin of Mount Carmel appeared to four young girls no less than 2,000 times between 1961 and 1965. Beyond the fact that the 'ecstasies' of the seers were the first to be televised, the apparitions at San Sebastian de Garabandal in Santander province add nothing substantial to the sociological pattern and apocalyptic warnings of La Salette and Fatima – in danger of being forgotten as theologians deliberated on the need to adapt to the modern world.

On 18 June 1961 the Archangel Michael presented himself to the children – whose leader was Conchita González (12) – and announced the first visit of Mary for 2 July. The latter vision was attired in 'a white robe with a blue mantle and a crown of golden stars. Her hands are slender. There is a brown scapular on her right arm. . . . Her hair, deep nut-brown, is parted in the centre. Her face is oval-shaped, with a fine nose. Her mouth is very pretty with lips a bit full.'[33] Mary lamented the 'road to perdition' (a phrase used at La Salette) being taken by 'many cardinals, bishops and priests' and gave thinly veiled warnings of nuclear chastisement, the details of which remain a secret kept by Conchita, who now propagates Our Lady's message and the rosary from her house in New York.

The girls' confessor, Fr Luis Andreu, SJ, was granted a vision of 'the great miracle' before his death in August 1961. He appeared posthumously to his spiritual charges, teaching them to recite the Hail Mary in several languages, both dead and modern[34] – a foretaste of the glossolalia yet to enthral a considerable section of the Catholic Church.

Millions saw films made by Spanish, Italian and British networks of the classic behaviour of the visionaries during their encounters with the Virgin: wondrous looks towards the sky, running at 'unnatural speed', insensibility to candle flames and TV arc-lights, walking backwards in the dark over rocky paths, divining the whereabouts of objects blessed by the apparition.[35]

An inquiry under the Bishop of Santander was opened the following year, transmitting in secret its negative conclusions to Rome in 1967. The Holy See, however, failed to condemn the events on its own authority, with the result that Garabandal is still vigorously promoted, especially by the followers of Padre Pio, who claim the friar approved the visions. Señorita González was received by Cardinal Ottaviani, prefect of the Holy Office, when she travelled to Rome in 1966 in the company of two Spanish princesses.

The cult continues to attract ill-educated Catholics from many parts of the world, reflecting widely shared fears of nuclear war. The message of the Virgin bears a striking resemblance to the US fundamentalist scenario of 'the Rapture' (when true believers will fly up to heaven) which is followed by global destruction. Garabandal preaches a 'great miracle', a 'warning' and 'the punishment'.[36]

34

MARIAN RENAISSANCE UNDER PAUL VI

May Mary Virgin and Mother obtain for the Church, which
also is hailed as virgin and mother, to rejoice always . . . in
the faithfulness of her priests to the sublime gift of holy
virginity. . . .[1]

Pope Paul VI

The reign of Paul VI (1963–78) – a vapid figure in the gallery of
modern pontiffs – favoured the development of several lasting trends.
Although represented by the extreme right as vacillating towards
communism and capitulationist in his contact with Protestants,
Jews and Freemasons,[2] Pope Paul publicly supported the Opus
Dei[3] (despite a major financial scandal in Spain),[4] brought Fatima
back into the limelight and ruled decisively against 'artificial'
contraception.[5] His domination of the 'collegial' Council effectively
sabotaged the Roncallian experiment in decentralization[6] and his
endorsement of the 'charismatic renewal' a decade later (see next
chapter) was antithetical to Pope John's progressive social policy.

A fragile child of the Lombard gentry, Giovanni Battista Montini
was educated by Jesuits, ordained in 1920 and appointed chaplain-
general to Italian universities five years later. In 1933 he joined
the secretariat of state under Pacelli, who was to give him the see
of Milan in 1954. Montini steadfastly opposed the 'opening to the
left' in his great industrial archdiocese and in June 1963 emerged
as successor to 'Good Pope John'. The high position of his elder
brother Ludovico in the Christian Democrat Party and an intimate
friendship with Aldo Moro promised a good working relationship
with the right.

In his very first encyclical[7] Paul lunged at the old enemies of
Modernism ('an error which is still making its appearance under
various new guises') and communism ('doomed to utter destruction')
while taking 'this opportunity of expressing Our admiration for

Mary, the model of Christian perfection, the mirror of true virtue, the pride of our humanity'. As the anti-colonial struggle wore on, the pope declared Mary the 'Mother of the Church' on his sole authority in the closing session of the Vatican Council in 1965. He recommended the rosary to those nations 'subjected to uprisings, secret and treacherous warfare and outright battles'.[8] As Cardinal Spellman and the Blue Army's 'pilgrim Virgin' toured Vietnam, the people of 'eastern Asia' were given the same pontifical advice.[9]

The fear among some theologians of a post-conciliar 'Marian minimalism'[10] was shared by Paul VI, who lamented the 'profane mentality, a critical spirit'[11] concomitant with a lukewarm regard for Christ's mother. Marian science enjoyed his ardent patronage (the Marianum was authorized in 1965 to grant a diploma and doctorate in Mariology) and his own statement *Marialis cultus* (1974) provided scholars with renewed authority to combat the widespread antipathy to Marian devotions. Mariologists stressed Fatima's continuity with Lourdes and denied any contradiction between Vatican II and 'the charismatic message' of the Portuguese Virgin.[12] Both Council and apparitions were 'the most serene refutation' of 'the naturalism and secularism which perverts the Church and so many souls.'[13]

Through the policy of reviving a piety in steep decline seers like Maria Droste zu Vischering and founders like the great modern Mariologist Maximilian Kolbe found their way to the altars.[14] In beatifying the latter in 1971, Montini asserted that enthusiasm for Our Lady 'will never be too great'.[15] The Grand Knight of the Immaculate was 'among the greatest saints and the far-seeing visionaries who understood, venerated and sang of the mystery of Mary.'[16] The reputation of Padre Pio – cured of pleurisy by Our Lady of Fatima[17] – likewise soared when, within months of the conclave (whose result he had predicted), the Vatican gave the stigmatist leave to appear in public and communicate with his followers – who included Aldo Moro.[18]

Setting the papal barque once more on a Marian course did not mean a new offensive against 'the sect'. On the contrary, the Knights of Columbus formed an open alliance with the Freemasons, staging the solemn reception of Cardinal Cushing (spiritual adviser to the Kennedys)[19] at the Boston 'Fraternity' lodge in October 1965.[20] Cardinal Cody of Chicago made a similar hiistoric gesture of reconciliation. The purpose of such fraternization was, in the words of Supreme Knight John W. McDevitt, 'the spread and defense of a belief in God; the promotion of patriotism; and the safeguarding of the national morality.'[21] United, Knights and Masons would 'combat and overcome the forces whose degenerative influence is becoming a crippling menace to our way of life'.[22] The North American Jesuits enthused about 'the surprising growth of cooperation between councils of the Knights of Columbus and Masonic lodges', particularly over 'civic and social issues'.[23]

The Knights of St Columbanus followed suit by dropping their feud with the Rotary Club (an institution praised by the pope)[24] and got together with Masons and Lions International to plan joint action to reduce social conflict.[25]

In September 1964 Pope Paul returned the skull of St Andrew to the Greek Church. A mutual lifting of the ancient anathemas followed, and in 1967 the 'Western Patriarch' embraced Athenagoras, 'Ecumenical Patriarch', in the Phanar (Instanbul). In 1968 – the year Paul opened conversations with the Coptic Patriarch of Alexandria – a series of apparitions occurred in a Cairo suburb.[26] The city council demolished buildings to clear a space for up to 250,000 nightly witnesses transfixed by 'billowing red clouds of incense-smelling smoke which frequently ascended round the vision' – a description confirmed by Bishop Gregorius of the Institute of Coptic Culture and Scientific Research.[27]

> At each appearance of the Virgin, a deafening cry would ascend from the tumultuous thousands besieging the floodlit church on all sides, 'We believe in you, St Mary!' . . . Great numbers of Moslems who had been kneeling on their prayer mats and reciting verses from the Koran in praise of Mary, would raise their voices in fervent hymns to her.[28]

The Egyptian government's General Information and Complaints Department declared:

> The official investigations have been carried out with the result that it has been considered an undeniable fact that the Blessed Virgin Mary has been appearing on the Coptic Orthodox Church at Zaytun in a clear and bright luminous body, seen by all present in front of the church, whether Christian or Moslem.[29]

Both Kyrillos VI, Coptic Patriarch, and Cardinal Stephanos, head of the Copts in communion with Rome, endorsed the apparitions.[30]

Our Lady of Fatima remained the number one cult for royalty, dictators, and their wives. Supplicants at the Cova in the sixties and early seventies included Princess Fabiola of Belgium, Princess Grace of Monaco (who later cooperated with Fr Peyton on a radio rosary programme beamed at North America and the Philippines), ex-King Umberto of Italy,[31] Doña Carmen Franco, Fulgencio Batista (lately of Cuba) and Imelda Marcos, who donated her gold rosary to the sanctuary.[32]

In August 1963 the pope authorized Eugene Cardinal Tisserant, prefect of the Congregation of Oriental Churches and dean of the College of Cardinals, to represent him at the dedication of the Russian chapel in the Blue Army headquarters at Fatima,[33] and in November 1964 he renewed Pius XII's consecration of Portugal to the Immaculate Heart. The gift of a golden rose to the shrine the following May provided the now threatened regime[34] (whose chief 'often asked for Lucia's prayers for the solution of Portuguese problems')[35] with an opportunity to project itself domestically and externally. Military honours, government ministers and a huge crowd greeted the special Vatican commission at Lisbon airport; 24 bishops celebrated pontifical high mass and the Portuguese foreign minister spoke of 'the praise the Pope has showered on the Portuguese nation'.[36] Montini also sent a gold rosary to the Carmel of Coimbra for Sister Lucia.[37]

In May 1965 documents for the beatification of 'Santo Padre Cruz' were accepted by Rome and in October the 'pilgrim Virgin' touched down in Saigon, was carried down the gangway by South Vietnamese army officers and greeted by Mgr Angelo Palmas, apostolic delegate, with a papal telegram. The image travelled over 1,000 kilometres on tracks 'mined by terrorists' and processed down the Mekong in a flower-decked flotilla commanded by the vicars-general of Saigon and My-Tho. 'Highly emotional was the meeting of Our Lady with the lepers of Soc-Trang, the penitent young ladies of Vinh-Long and the refugees from Communist China.'[38] Meanwhile, the Archbishop of Saigon and other Vietnamese prelates flew to Fatima to pray for the success of the statue's visit.

The first papal visit to Fatima, on the 50th anniversary of the apparitions (1967), was preceded on 1 January by what the pope called a 'reform of the discipline of indulgences'. The quantitative element (e.g., '40 days' partial indulgence') was abolished, but all indulgences – even when transmitted by 'wireless broadcasts' – were now applicable to 'the souls in purgatory'.[39]

In February Cardinals Ottaviani and Cerejeira released the 'news' that the late Pope John had read the 'third secret'. Ottaviani, head of the Congregation for the Doctrine of the Faith, spoke glowingly of the beatification process of Lucia's cousins, and the Patriarch of Lisbon declared, 'Fatima arises in our anxious world like a beacon of hope against atheistic communism which tries to conquer the universe and destroy the Church.'[40]

On 12 May – the eve of his journey to Portugal – Montini issued *Signum Magnum*, an exhortation 'for an ever more fervid and fruitful Marian piety'. Clearly alluding to Lucia's later visions, the encyclical begins, 'The great sign which the Apostle John saw in heaven, "a woman clothed with the sun", is interpreted by the sacred Liturgy, not without foundation, as referring to the most blessed Mary, the mother of all men. . . .'

Fatima's golden jubilee – coinciding with the 'silver' of Pacelli's consecration of the world to the Immaculate Heart – was celebrated with a monster rally putting Portugal, at least in the mind of one Portuguese bishop, 'at the head of all the nations of Europe'.[41] Salazar, with his ministers and military chiefs, headed a crowd of well over a million, who formed a black roof of open umbrellas in commemoration of the 'Miracle of the Sun' as they waited for the pontiff and his entourage marshalled by the imposing Cardinal Tisserant, official protector of the Blue Army.

The Russian poet Evtouchenko was impressed by the pilgrims 'looking hopefully up at the sky'.[42] Exiled pretenders to various thrones mingled with Algerian Pieds Noirs and prelates from the United States, Latin America, the Far East, and Portuguese Africa (where napalm bombs were 'defending Portugal's way of life').[43]

'Our Lady of Fatima', declared the pope at the air base of Monte Real, 'deigns to shower on Catholic Portugal the most conspicuous gifts of spiritual and material well-being, prosperity, progress and peace.'[44]

After a mass at which the dictator shared the 'tribune of honour' at the altar with Sister Lucia and the parents of Francisco and Jacinta, Montini condemned 'new and peculiar ideologies, interpretations intent upon stripping the norms of faith of that which modern thought, often lacking in rational judgment, does not understand

and does not like.'[45] Nations where 'religious liberty is almost totally suppressed' were also censured.

The pope held Lucia's hand and 'showed her to the wildly enthusiastic crowds'.[46] And he conferred decorations on a number of policemen, including Major Silva Pais, director of the PIDE,[47] whose Lisbon headquarters contained a chapel dedicated to Our Lady and located next to the torture chamber.[48]

Few Portuguese clerics had ever criticized the regime; in the words of the native Archbishop of Conakry (Guinea-Bissau), there was 'total confusion between cross and flag'.[49] However, the Bishop of Oporto, Dom Fereira Gomez (exiled 1959) had spoken of 'trafficking with God' and other forms of 'magic' manifested at Fatima.[50] And just four days before the pope's arrival, Pragma, a group led by 22 priests, was suppressed after delivering a letter of protest to Cardinal Cerejeira.[51]

The papal visit was denounced by the Algerian government and the newspapers of Zaire.[52] One Portuguese exile wrote of 'the totalitarian exploitation of the Virgin Mary' and the 'idol' which 'averts revolts and screens murderers'.[53] From Moscow, Metropolitan Alexei of Tallin mocked Rome's plans to convert a country 'baptised in the tenth century'.[54]

Visitors streamed into Portugal in the wake of the Holy Father, and the Fatima cult expanded worldwide. In Koenigstein, West Germany, a 'Congress of the Friends of Fatima' was held in September 1968. Large pilgrimages in 1968–9 were led by the primate of Spain (where a train had recently been named 'Our Lady of Fatima'),[55] the Archbishop of Kinsangani (Congo), the Armenian Catholic Patriarch and prelates from Argentina, Brazil, and Japan. In April 1969 over 800 agents of the Portuguese Public Security Police 'implored protection from the Virgin'[56] and in September engineers and economists met to discuss 'a new politics of development'.[57]

Before the Children's International Pilgrimage in June 1970, *The Message of Fatima as Lived by Children*, a booklet by the Bishop of Leiria, was distributed to all junior schools with orders from the ministry of education that it be read each day.[58] The pedagogic package included leaflets about the pope and half a million exercise books in which pupils would describe their 'preparations for the great day of the visit to Fatima'. They were also to write letters to Paul VI, congratulating him on his sacerdotal jubilee and asking when he intended to canonize Francisco and Jacinta.

On 7 June around 200,000 children together with their teachers and the entire episcopate gathered in the sanctuary to hear a pontifical broadcast. A week later the shrine processed a pilgrimage of 800 'sick or mutilated soldiers'[59] at the request of another governmental client, the cabinet office for the ministry of the army.

Among clerical visitors during the year were Cardinal Slipyj, Archbishop-Major of the Ukrainian Church, Mgr Escrivá, Cardinal Carberry of St Louis (Missouri), the Archbishop of Goa, the Bishop of Grenada and Bishop Graber of Rensburg. Vasken I, Armenian Catholicos, brought greetings from the holy see of Etchmiadzin.

In 1972 Cardinal Mindszenty headed the October pilgrimage. Introduced by the Bishop of Fatima as a 'confessor and martyr for the faith, who bears in his flesh and soul the stigmata of the Passion of Christ', the Hungarian primate told the crowd, 'Certainly the prophecy of Fatima has overtaken my country.'[60]

The Blue Army rejoiced in the papal seal of approval: 'Between 1960 and 1967, the Apostolate of Fatima had suffered unexpected reverses in many parts of the world. The visit of the Pope to Fatima opened up a new period of development.'[61] In Portugal Montini had blessed replicas of the image[62] which were taken by the Blue Army to 21 countries. In October 1969 statues were enthroned in the cathedrals of Cairo, Addis Ababa, Nairobi, Salisbury, Beira, Lorenzo Marques, Johannesburg, Luanda, and Rabat. The following October the third 'world pilgrimage' of the Fatima image, sponsored by the Blue Army and veterans of Franco's Blue Division,[63] set out for Tunis, Israel, India, Thailand, Malaysia, Australia, Japan, Hawaii, Mexico, Ecuador, Colombia, and Florida.

The Orthodox – whose rite was 'a bridge, a door, to the conversion of Russia'[64] – received increased attention from the apostolate. John Haffert and the Bishop of Fatima called at the Phanar on their way to Moscow in 1970 and presented the Greek patriarch with a copy of the 'pilgrim Virgin'.[65] On the feast of the Apparition of Our Lady of Kazan, 21 July 1970, the icon known as 'Liberatrix and Protectress of Russia' – acquired by the Blue Army for 'a huge sum'[66] – was enshrined in the Byzantine Chapel at Fatima by Bishop Andrew Katkoff, rector of the Russicum, together with Metropolitan Emilianos Timiadis, representative of the Ecumenical Patriarchate at the World Council of Churches.[67] The ceremony coincided with the first Catholic-Orthodox seminar in Fatima.[68] Two years later Cardinal Wyszynski presented Our Lady of Kazan with a companion: a copy of the Black Madonna of Czesto-chowa. At the chapel's tenth anniversary in August 1973 the Vatican was represented by Cardinal Oddi,[69] a collaborator of the Opus Dei.

The arrival of a Blue Army statue in Vietnam led to an apparition of Our Lady in 1975 to Stephen Ho Ngoc Anh, who had been crippled by North Vietnamese doctors. The story of his cure – and subsequent total disablement by the communists – is affirmed by Mgr Vincent Tran Ngoc Thu, secretary to the apostolic delegate in Saigon.[70]

After the Portuguese revolution in 1974 official anticlerical measures were not taken despite the Church's former position as 'the dominant ideological apparatus'.[71] But the Catholic station Radio Renascença was temporarily occupied by Maoists,[72] and soldiers attacked some churches and distributed leaflets on contraception. In the clerical north the Archbishop of Braga raised the banner against the Marxist 'enemies of God' in violent demonstrations[73] which former agent Philip Agee claims were financed by the CIA.[74]

The number of pilgrims to Fatima, especially from Spain, dropped dramatically, but by 1976 was back to an annual figure of around three million.[75] In June 1975, as fears of communism mounted among the right, Lucia dos Santos was transferred to a Carmelite convent across the border.[76] She returned when elections swept the moderate socialist Mario Soares to power.

An enigmatic visitor to Fatima in these turbulent times was Metropolitan Nikodim of Leningrad and Novgorod. After celebrating a *moleben* (litany) to the Theotokos in the Byzantine Chapel on 22 May 1975, the Archbishop expressed to the Blue Army chaplain his firm belief in the apparitions.[77] The only member of the Holy Synod of Moscow to have visited the anti-communist shrine, he died of a heart attack during an audience with Pope John Paul I.[78]

35

OUR LADY OF NATIONAL SECURITY: CHARISMATICS VERSUS THEOLOGY OF LIBERATION

> The charism that is most evident in the account of Pentecost is glossolalia, in the form of a collective, harmonious speaking in tongues. . . . Mary, consequently, is the model not only for the charisms in general but specifically for the praying in tongues that is characteristic of the Pentecostal movement.[1]
>
> Canon René Laurentin

As the Roman curia was making arrangements for Paul VI's visit to Fatima, small groups of Catholic academics and university students in the United States underwent 'baptism in the Spirit' accompanied by their first hesitant utterances in 'tongues' (the phenomenon of 'glossolalia') and divine prophecy – activities historically linked with visionary experience.[2] The neo-Pentecostal movement, or 'charismatic renewal' as it is now more often called, was to develop apace alongside the Latin American theology of liberation, which found an articulate voice just a year after the charismatics had demonstrated a hitherto unsuspected command of unidentified 'languages'.

A survey of the literature of the two movements reveals irreconcilable social and political differences: a 'noticeable impulse to Marian piety',[3] emphasis on miraculous healing and the 'spiritual and psycho-hygienic value of glossolalia'[4] contrast sharply with the scriptural, critical and anti-theurgical approach of liberation theology. The Roman Charismatics have shown the potential to bring their share of the Latin American masses to a level comparable with rapid and widespread gains in the English-speaking world, and their anti-intellectual influence in the 'north', particularly in Rome, bodes ill for the scholarly 'southern' rebels.

Pentecostalism has its origin in a Kansas bible school in 1900. Christian Fundamentalism, to which 'classical' Pentecostals adhere, emerged a few years later.[5] Communities of 'holy rollers', many of them black, mushroomed in the United States in the first half of the century. One such church which was to form a bridge to the mainstream denominations is the Full Gospel Business Men's Fellowship, set up in 1953 by Demos Shakarian, grandson of the visionary founder of the Armenian Pentecostal Church (Los Angeles) and himself a seer, prophet and businessman.[6] The FGBMF formed hundreds of 'chapters' throughout the USA and in Australia, Hong Kong and Pretoria, and was the first association of classical Pentecostals to welcome members of other churches – including, by 1962, Catholic priests.

In 1958 the Episcopalian parish of St Mark's, Van Nuys, near Hollywood, received Spirit baptism and established the Blessed Trinity Society: a landmark in the transformation of a fringe, proletarian cult inviting ridicule into a major, 'respectable' and transdenominational movement, largely Republican[7] and with friends in mass entertainment[8] and big business.[9] The 'normalization' of glossolalia was an important factor in this change in public attitudes. Jean Stone, editor of *Trinity*, insisted that 'Speaking in tongues is not spooky; it's wholesome, good, clean, beautiful. We use no weird positions. . . .'[10]

Congregations in the American Lutheran Church were filled with the polyglottal spirit in 1962, the year Mother Basilea Schlink of the Evangelical Sisterhood of Mary, a Lutheran community in Darmstadt (West Germany), joined an international Council for the Charismatic Movement. Schlink's fundamentalist pamphlets on how Satan controls the Israeli peace movement[11] and videos of her declaiming apocalyptic prophecies[12] from the rocks of Patmos in flowing white robes were later promoted by the Catholic charismatics' *New Covenant* magazine.[13]

Anglicans found a charismatic leader in the curate of All Souls, Langham Place (London), and chaplain of the Oxford Street stores, the Rev. Michael Harper, who began to speak in tongues in 1963. Presbyterians in the US joined the renewal in the mid-1960s, their best-known convert being Kathryn Kuhlman, a 'veritable one-woman shrine of Lourdes',[14] whose healing sessions were relayed by closed-circuit TV to the multitudes of all faiths. By 1967 around 1,000 Presbyterian ministers in the USA and 700 Episcopalian priests claimed to have received Spirit baptism and were talking or singing in tongues.[15]

The immediate source of the Catholic charismatic renewal was the rosary-orientated Cursillos (see chapter 31), introduced in to the US in 1957 by Spanish pilots training in Texas.[16] American Cursillistas had recently adopted as a basic manual *Dedication and Leadership. Learning from the Communists* by Douglas Hyde,[17] the British devotee of Fatima. Hyde recognized that 'we are now at the beginning of a process of renewal' and 'need more Christian leaders as an answer to the trained Communist leaders'.[18]

News of a group of Catholics breaking out in glossolalia at Duquesne University, Pittsburgh, Pennsylvania, was brought by student members of the Cursillo to fellow Cursillistas at the University of Notre Dame, Indiana, in March 1967. A Notre Dame-South Bend charismatic group was immediately formed by Ralph Martin and Steve Clark, national leaders of the Cursillo, and within months similar prayer groups had sprung up on campuses throughout the country. An Opus Dei chaplain provided the first charismatic residence aat South Bend.[19] The Indiana Cursillo promptly 'dissolved in large part into the Pentecostal community'.[20] Another 'powerful influence' was the FGBMF, whose South Bend chapter president was 'a kind of spiritual godfather for the charismatic community' at Notre Dame.[21] The academics were also impressed by the 'sharing' of three Benedictine monks they met at a Full Gospel Business Men's banquet in Zion, Illinois.[22]

At the very first charismatic meeting at Notre Dame – now the international nerve-centre of the movement – a student prophesied, 'I feel moved to tell you all that what Mary promised at Fatima is really going to take place.'[23] Abbé Laurentin, who was introduced to the movement at a Mariological congress in Lisbon in August 1967, believes that Mary 'who seemed to have been shunted aside in contemporary Catholicism, has "returned" in the charismatic renewal'.[24]

Once Pentecostalism had penetrated Roman Catholicism, it spread 'far more rapidly than in any other of the established churches'.[25] Catholicism's leading role in ecumenism as well as its international projection – especially through American missionaries – contributed much to the expansion of the new cult.[26] There were 300,000 Catholic charismatics in the United States alone by 1973[27] and by early 1980 the figure was six or seven million, that is, 18 per cent of American Catholics.[28] With slogans like 'Freedom from Sin, Satan and Disease', American Jesuits, Dominicans, Benedictines, Redemptorists, Maryknoll Sisters and Oblates of Mary Immaculate planted the charismatic renewal from Bolivia (1969) to France (1971); from Puerto Rico, where it became a 'tidal wave',[29] to Korea, Thailand, Hong Kong, Vietnam and Taiwan. Countries like Brazil and Chile, which already had massive historical Pentecostal sects, were not overlooked.

International charismatic conferences at Notre Dame and other centres were mustering 11,500 delegates by June 1972. The presence of Cardinal Suenens, primate of Belgium, at the international conference at South Bend in June 1973 – when his reference to 'the role of Mary as a secret of holiness' produced a standing ovation from the 20,000 representatives[30] – marked a turning point in Vatican policy towards the phenomenon. A supporter of the Legion of Mary,[31] Suenens published a book on the 'New Pentecost' the following year. In it he devoted a chapter to Mary – 'the first charismatic'.

Glossolalia, attributed to such priestly models as the Curé of Ars and Padre Pio,[32] was dismissed by liberal Catholics as 'emotional disturbance'.[33] Suenens, however, considered the practice

a particular grace for the Church today, coming at a moment when the popular prayer life of the faithful – holy hour, novenas, rosaries, stations of the Cross etc. – has almost disappeared, leaving a void that needs to be filled.[34]

The issue of 'tongues' and the complementary gift of 'prophecy' (whereby a fellow worshipper 'intuitively' interprets the exotic utterance) did not prevent Paul VI from publicly encouraging the 'Jesus is Lord' movement in October 1973, when international leaders met in the Roman suburb of Grottaferrata. The pope's speech to participants did, however, stress the need for 'discernment'.[35] On 13 May ('Fatima Day') during the Holy Year of 1975 two meetings were in session in Rome: the International Conference on the Charismatic Renewal in the Catholic Church, and the International Marian Conference – on 'The Holy Spirit and Mary' – where Cardinal Suenens presided. Montini himself witnessed 'very low-key speaking in tongues'[36] at the charismatic conference and invoked Mary against secularization.[37] 'A current of intense spirituality pervades the world', the pope informed the College of Cardinals a month later, 'one would have to be blind not to recognize it . . . a new era is unfolding'.[38]

The reason why the Vatican was eager to take the Pentecostal movement under its wing is revealed by Notre Dame professor of theology Edward O'Connor:

> our age is preoccupied with the social gospel. Humanism, secularism and activism permeate much that is preached in the name of Christianity today. Modern men, and college youth in particular, have a difficult time with the idea of worship and prayer.[39]

According to this founder member of the renewal, youth – especially those in higher education – should direct their gaze to the 'charismatic and mystical' as seen in the lives of St Marguerite Marie Alacoque and St John Vianney – and located at 'Lourdes, Fatima, Beauraing, Banneaux. . . ."[40]

Professional theologians were quick to develop the pneumato-Marian line, concluding that the 'Marianization of Christianism' was the 'fruit of the progress of ecclesial faith . . . animated by the Holy Spirit'.[41]

GOSPEL OF THE SOUTH

The theology of liberation – according to its Peruvian founder Gustavo Gutierrez, 'an attempt to understand the faith from within the concrete historical, liberating and subversive praxis of the poor of this world'[42] – was first systematized in 1968, year of the populist military coup in Peru. Brazil had set up the Latin American model of national security rule four years earlier and two archetypes of left-wing heroism had recently fallen in action: Gutierrez's friend Fr Camilo Torres (Colombia, 1966) and the Argentinian 'Che' Guevara (Bolivia, 1967).

Unlike Christian Democracy, liberation theology seeks radical solutions. 'Latin American misery and injustice go too deep to be responsive to palliatives. Hence we speak of social revolution, not reform; of liberation, not development; of socialism, not modernization of the prevailing system.'[43] Still dominated by professional theologians (all of whom hold degrees from prestigious European faculties), this exegetical movement has antecedents in the 'new political theology' of West Germans J.B. Metz and Jurgen Moltmann (the latter a Protestant) and is inspired by a variety of figures like the pacifist Helda Pessoa Câmara, Archbishop of Recife and Olinda (Brazil), and Fr Ernesto Cardenal, poet and Sandinista minister of culture.

The liberation theologians were advisers to the Conference of Latin American Bishops (CELAM) at Medellín, Colombia, in 1968, which denounced the yoke of 'institutional violence'. Acclaimed as a regional and radical Vatican II, Medellín encouraged activism against the military dictatorships, which in turn led the right-wing to make a successful bid for control during the bishops' general assembly at Sucre, Bolivia, in November 1972. According to José Comblin, 'Since then CELAM's main ideology has been developing and maintaining a new security system against communism.'[44]

Gutierrez, chief spokesman of the movement since the publication of his book *Teología de la liberación* (Lima, 1971), sees the Vatican as an arm of imperialism.

> We have been mirroring the European church – uncritically borrowing our theology, institutions, canon law, spirituality and lifestyle . . . working free of the colonial mentality is undoubtedly one of the major tasks confronting the Christian community in Latin America.[45]

The growth of liberation theology is manifested by *comunidades eclesiales de base* of 'lower-class, grassroots people, the base of society, as opposed to the pinnacle of power in the social pyramid'.[46] In 1985 there were an estimated 150,000 'basic communities', half of them in Brazil.[47] Their attempts to secure social services (for example running water, electricity, health care), work, and human rights are preceded by Bible reading and discussion. 'The real tension', writes Fr Boff,

> exists between a Church that has opted for the people, for the poor and their liberation, and other groups in that same Church that have not made this option . . . or who persist in keeping to the strictly sacramental and devotional character of faith.[48]

The improvised rituals of the *comunidades* which 'center around the Bible and include significant regional objects or foods',[49] seem a far cry from native dances before the Marian mascots of the military (see next chapter).

With the interesting exception of Leonardo Boff, OFM, it is difficult to find more than a passing reference to Mary in liberation theology. The Franciscan rebel, however, looks to the Virgin as 'prophetic woman and liberator', a stance hard to square with such 'politico-military' solemnities as the visit of the 'pilgrim Virgin' of Fatima to São Paulo in April 1965 – which provoked a written protest from 113 of the city's priests.[50] Citing no less an authority than Maximilian Kolbe, Boff teaches,

> If Mary is spiritualized by the Third Person of the Holy
> Trinity, absolutely everything that one can attribute to the Holy
> Spirit can be attributed to Mary and vice-versa. . . . The people
> of God, always intuitive of the personal presence of the Spirit
> in Mary, attributing to her all the titles of grandeur created by
> piety, have truly entered into community with the Holy Spirit
> spiritualized in Mary.[51]

Boff's image of St Francis is equally odd for a liberationist; indeed, it is more in line with Gemelli's than Sabatier's (see chapter 24). He not only seems to accept the indulgence of the Portiuncula but sympathetically links it to the Poverello's 'gentle devotion to Mary'.[52]

The prefect of the Congregation for the Doctrine of the Faith (formerly the Holy Office), who still speaks openly of Mary as a remedy for 'heresy',[53] notes that 'precisely in that continent where the traditional Marian piety of the people is in decline, the resultant void is being filled by political ideologies'.[54] However, the Vatican has found it impossible to reject an idea as popular as 'liberation'. In a weighty statement on human rights,[55] Cardinal Ratzinger devotes the conclusion to 'the loving Virgin of the *Magnificat*'. Echoing the very man he condemns, the prefect asserts that Mary is 'the most perfect image of freedom and of the liberation of humanity and of the universe'.[56] But he clearly diverges from the Brazilian friar in his social vision, warning against 'a purely earthly plan of liberation' brought about by violence, which rejects hope – as 'extolled in the hymn to the God of mercy which the Virgin teaches us'.[57]

36

ARGENTINA AND CHILE:
BROTHER GENERALS IN MARY

this act . . . symbolizes the indestructible cohesion of this
people, who cannot be divided by differences made by castes
or social classes because they acknowledge the same patrimony
of blood, spirit and culture . . . the missions of friendly countries
represent our common American ideal and international
fraternity. . . . My Lord Cardinal, on behalf of the Government
of Chile, I hand over to you the Votive Temple of Maipú.[1]

General Augusto Pinochet

Neither military dictatorship nor militaristic Marianism is new to
South America. In recent decades, however, the armed forces in
government have given prominence to *religiosidad popular* through the
all-pervading media now at their service. This resuscitation of the old
colonial cult of Mary by the 'sub-fascist'[2] republics is underpinned
by the Vatican's devotional policy under Paul VI and John Paul II.
A strategy of this magnitude necessitates international solidarity. In
the way that Franco's Spain gave crucial support to Fatima, so the
military in Argentina and Chile reach out over the Cordillera in a
blue embrace.

Grouped in military Cursillos, Mary's servants led a succession of coups to purify Argentina[3] with a 'Jordan of blood',
as the military-vicar called the 'dirty war' against subversives.[4]
The Cursillista Lt-Gen. Onganía, who ruled from 1966 to 1970,
appointed ministers from both Opus Dei (which ran radio and TV
stations) and the Cursillo (which controlled the state information
service under General Eduardo Señorans).[5]

President Onganía's consecration of the nation to the Immaculate
Heart in November 1969 was, in the judgment of the Council of
Argentinian Ecclesiastical History, a 'transcendental event in the
religious history of the Argentinian people'[6] – and one required by
Our Lady of Fatima as the sole way to avert the divine wrath.[7]

Surrounded by 2,000 bodyguards (bombs were removed from a side altar and pulpit), the president-dictator led military, judiciary, and education authorities to the shrine of Luján. Every type of 'traditionalist' group was represented, from gauchos to Armenian Orthodox: the Association of Old Jesuit Pupils, Work of Mary, Polish Catholic Circles, Co-operators of the Sanctuary of Our Lady of Fatima. . . . Two bishops, however, stayed away in protest.[8]

'Our flag has the same colour as your tunic and mantle', the General prayed, '. . . Patroness of the Argentinian people and its military regiments; Virgin of Loreto, Patroness of the Airforce; Stella Maris, Patroness of the Navy; and Virgin of Mercy, General of our Army.'[9]

Another Cursillista, General Alejandro Augustin Lanusse, who was also a member of the Opus Dei,[10] headed a military junta between 1971 and 1973. In March 1976 General Jorge Rafael Videla, a rosary devotee,[11] took power in the name of 'God, Fatherland and Hearth'. As soldiers raided libraries and bookshops to make bonfires of 'pernicious documentation that affects the intellect and our way of being Christian',[12] a 'pious demonstration' organized by the Catholic Workers' Circles was addressed by Archbishop Aramburu of Buenos Aires on 'moral reconstruction' and the charismatic renewal.[13]

'Fascism', a former professor of military history at the Colegio Militar avers, 'diabolically decked out in an ultramontane Catholicism, has, for at least the last two decades, been the essence of the formation of senior staff of the army.'[14] According to the same source, officer cadets in 1975 prayed the 'campaign rosary' and kept pictures of Our Lady under their desk lids alongside swastikas.

In Chile – a democratic, poorer, less Catholic country[15] with a less powerful and reactionary hierarchy – the years before the coup (1973) saw the formation of Christians for Socialism, a group of 80 priests (condemned by the episcopate five months before the bombing of La Moneda). In reaction to left-wing and 'conciliar' liberal Catholicism, the 'heralds' of Tradición, Familia y Propiedad – wearing red sashes and tunics emblazoned with an 'M' and lion rampant – became a familiar sight, denouncing through loudhailers the 'prophets of atheism'[16] in power under Allende.

Two months after the coup, teams of Schönstatt missionaries launched a marketing-style campaign to promote Our Lady of Carmel, the patroness of the armed forces. They went from door to door armed with a manual giving precise instructions on how to approach families and a 'kit' containing a picture of the Virgin and a letter from her which echoed the 'conciliatory' rhetoric of the junta:

> In these days, I believe that Chile urgently needs the message of my Son. Despite the vast majority being Christians, Chileans have shown themselves incapable of forming a true society of brothers. Hate and political divisions have destroyed the unity of this dear Fatherland.[17]

An evaluation of the exercise stated that 20,000 people had been reached, many of whom had agreed to join a pilgrimage to Maipú. 'The Virgin opens doors,' the Schönstatt clergy concluded. 'She signifies a type of master-key to the heart of our people.'[18]

In February 1974 *El Mercurio*, the semi-official daily, published a prominent article[19] expressing gratitude to the Virgin 'for having liberated us from oppression and slavery' on 11 September 1973. This 'Second Independence of Chile' had been aided by 'the anguished supplications of innumerable faithful and believers who entreated protection and help from the Patroness of the Chilean nation and her armed forces. . . . A spark was needed to produce the unhoped for and providential phenomenon and that flash was the cry of the Patroness of our army which resounded in the hearts of our soldiers. . . .'

In July – less than a year before his death – Mgr Escrivá arrived in Santiago from Argentina, where he had led the rosary at Luján and prayed for the pope and the authorities of the three dictatorships of the River Plate (Argentina, Paraguay and Uruguay). During his brief visit to Chile, where Opus Dei had some 500 members,[20] including important advisers to the regime,[21] *el Padre* went to the Marian shrine of Lo Vásquez and to the Colegio Tabancura (an exclusive Opus school), where he told followers that Christ 'never spoke about politics. He always spoke as a priest and priests don't have any authority in those matters.'[22]

As Pinochet told copper miners in February 1974, the military government had allocated special funds to the construction of the shrine of Maipú (begun in 1944) in order to accomplish without further delay the 'national vow' made to the Virgin of Carmel by Bernardo O'Higgins,[23] *Padre de la Patria*. The grim 240-ft concrete tower – stark against the Andes like a colossal helmeted warrior – was inaugurated by the dictator himself at a Te Deum on 24

October attended by the Argentinian minister of defence and army commander-in-chief. Trumpets heralded the arrival of the 'Supreme Chief' of the Chilean nation, who cut a tricolour ribbon around the high altar, bestowing a piece on each member of the junta. The sanctuary's symbolism, explained Pinochet in a homily that owed much to Hispanidad (see also the quotation heading this chapter), 'has penetrated deeply the national soul, teaching that the passions, violence and threats of materialism which have provoked us will always collide with the granite bases of our Christian faith.'[24]

For Cardinal Silva Henríquez, the presidential gesture of handing over 'the House of Mary the faithful Virgin' was one 'whose significance will be recorded by history'.[25] The Chilean primate continued:

> The beauty of it is that Chile feels Mary to be essentially linked to that most precious gift: liberty! . . . She wants to educate her sons in true liberty: the liberty of the heart. Liberated from sin and all its fruits and manifestations: hate, lies, fear, division, resentment, envy, injustice, sadness . . . the presence of this Marian temple is also a triumph of liberty.[26]

His Eminence then presented a replica of the image of Our Lady of Carmel to General Pinochet, giving him a 'moving hug'.[27] On the steps of the church the General released 'a symbolic dove and simultaneously there was a discharge of gunnery'.[28]

Month of Mary celebrations that year stressed adhesion to the armed forces, 'pride of the country and most solid bastion of national sovereignty';[29] and in December a 'Day of Military Spirituality' was declared. At Maipú – now in the custody of the Schönstatt Fathers – a homily on the 'Marxist campaign against Chile' was preached before the image, surrounded by flowers and Orwellian slogans like 'Chile, country of brothers', and guarded by troops with fixed bayonets.[30] As the Chilean ministry of defence organized Holy Year devotions in barracks, Pope Paul sent a warm message for the consecration of Maipú: 'It is as if ancient and recent history', Montini wrote on 24 November 1974, '. . . had found genuine expression around the mystery of Mary.'[31]

Robed in a white cloak, Pinochet inaugurated, around the same time, the Evangelical Cathedral Temple of the Pentecostal Methodist Church in Santiago, a building also subsidized by the government.[32] Some 2,500 Evangelical clergy, whose personal link with the junta was the *carabineros* chief, General Mendoza (a classical Pentecostal), earlier expressed their loyalty to the regime and repudiated a recent United Nations censure.[33]

The country became a stamping ground for US preachers[34] as well as a venue for Pan-American Freemasonry,[35] Rotary International, ecumenical associations of 'Christian businessmen' and international Catholic military 'united today more than ever in the struggle for Christianity, Democracy and Freedom'.[36]

National Catholicism, however, remained the established creed of the armed forces. *Civico-militar* spectacles inspired by the Falange and Nazi Germany were enthusiastically reported. Front page colour splashes and newsfilm covered the blessing of sabres and 'emotive' rallies at which holy communion was taken in a circle of blazing torches symbolizing liberation from the 'Marxist cancer'. Even the 'Sacred Species' was pictured on the tip of Pinochet's tongue.[37]

Multifarious groups represented the 'national soul' at Maipú, the most colourful of which were the semi-pagan confraternities of 'Chinese' dancers ('Slaves of the Virgin') and mounted *Cuasimodistas* in outfits which ranged from traditional ponchos to Roman togas. Endless pilgrimages paid homage to the sanctuary of the armed forces: National Secretariats of Youth and Women, Catholic Action, Centres of Mothers, brotherhoods and sisterhoods of Carmel, Social Action María Auxiliadora, nurses, social workers, taxi-drivers, football fans and the Academy of Family Culture of the O'Higgins National Vow (devoted to 'abnegated activities' and teaching poor children 'the sacred duties and transcendent values of order, respect and historical tradition').[38]

On the jubilee of the coronation of Nuestra Señora del Carmen in 1976 Mgr Fresno, president of the episcopal conference and future primate, reminded the faithful at Maipú of the sacred vows to pray for the authorities and 'thus achieve the greatness of our nation in this construction we are making'.[39] Backed by a recent papal document,[40] rectors of Marian sanctuaries throughout Chile met in October to work out ways of opposing post-conciliar 'Europeanizing tendencies' that weakened popular religiosity.[41] One immediate counter to 'intellectualization' was the decoration of the original image of the Virgin of Carmel with the insignia of General in a ceremony attended by delegations of *carabineros* and other branches of the armed forces.[42]

In 1976, the 158th anniversary of the battle of Maipú was the occasion for a spiritual reunion between the Andean military regimes. General Leopoldo Galtieri, future Argentinian president, joined Chilean regiments and ministers at the sanctuary;[43] a few months later General Videla knelt before the Virgin beside Pinochet to celebrate the latter's coup.[44] In November 1976 – with a Chilean military delegation in Rome for the Holy Year – the Day of Military Spirituality was particularly splendid. As the yellow and white Vatican flag flew over the School of Subalterns, airforce general Leigh and *carabineros* general Mendoza swore loyalty to Mary in a televised ceremony and honoured her image with salvoes.[45]

The following year, support for the regime was beginning to fade even among the bishops of the Chilean Church, although this did not prevent a papal coronation of the Virgin at Maipú in 1987 (see Epilogue). In Argentina, however, the overwhelming majority of the hierarchy continued to endorse the military juntas.[46] General Videla was permitted a public prayer to Our Lady at the 1981 Marian congress in Mendoza[47] and the Falklands/Malvinas war stimulated Church-military collaboration. An image of Nuestra Señora de Luján had been enthroned in St Mary's, Port Stanley, in 1974.[48] Eight years later Argentinian officers led the evening rosary during the brief occupation.[49] The Archbishop of Bahia Blanca was delighted that everyone carried a rosary 'from the president of the Republic down to the last soldier'.[50]

In 1984 fifteen clergymen, including the papal nuncio, were accused by the National Commission on the Disappearance of Persons of direct collaboration in the repression.[51] In one concentration camp torturers who belonged to TFP and 'Falange of the Faith' gathered regularly in prayer beneath an image of the Blessed Virgin.[52]

Reaction to both the human rights trials and liberalism under Alfonsin's administration has been violent. In the church of Our Lady of Luján on 24 October 1984 some 1,500 *integristas*, including retired generals, serving officers, and cadets of the Military College, heard Fr Julio Triviño call for a 'holy war' against 'the radical synagogue'.[53]

37

THE VICAR OF MARY

No one has done more to remind the world of the truth of human dignity . . . than the special man who came to Portugal a few years ago after a terrible attempt on his life. He came to Fatima, the site of your great religious shrine, to fulfill his special devotion to Mary. . . .[1]

Ronald Reagan, Portugal, 9 May 1985

All the major objectives of the current pontificate – dedicated to the Immaculate since 1978[2] – derive ideological sap from the 'Woman-Mother – the genius of the heart'.[3] The *apparitional* basis of Marian doctrine is constantly revealed both in explicit references to Our Lady's earthly interventions and by a strenuous programme of visits to her sanctuaries throughout the world. From these sites of God's 'irruptions in the history of humanity',[4] 'Mary of Nazareth', recharged by the apostolic presence, regenerates National Catholicism and bolsters priestly celibacy and the traditional subservience of women. She represents the continuing struggle against persecution and secularism as well as against abortion and new rebellions against Rome. The whole strategy of evangelization and ecumenism takes place under her mantle. She 'dominates all history'[5] and 'all anguish for the future is replaced by the serene hope'[6] inspired by her person.

The Marian divisions are necessarily strengthened, especially the Opus Dei, guaranteed supremacy among international Catholic brotherhoods at the moment its power in Spain was undermined after Franco's death. A supporter of the *Obra* for many years before his election,[7] John Paul II has personally ordained scores of its priests[8] and placed *simpatizantes* in key curial positions.[9] Documents purporting to establish the 'heroic virtues' of Mgr Escrivá were laid before the Sacred Congregation for the Causes of Saints in May 1981 with the backing of 69 cardinals and 1,300 bishops.[10] The following year, Opus Dei obtained a unique form of semi-autonomy in becoming a 'personal prelature' – an advance no doubt facilitated by the Vatican's financial crisis.[11] Freemasonry proper, following the old pattern, was 'suddenly and formally' condemned again in 1981.[12] The Cursillo, another fruit of Spanish fascism, is endorsed as 'an instrument brought about by God to announce the Gospel in our age'.[13] The Sacerdotal Marian Movement, inspired by a vision at Fatima in 1973 to the Milanese priest Stefano Gobbi, also counts on papal support. The charismatic movement receives encouragement both directly and through the pneumato-Marian doctrine of Maximilian Kolbe.

Pilgrimages and the rosary, cornerstones of Marian devotion, are dramatically revalued and there are signs of a recrudescence of indulgences. Both the Blue Army and Opus Dei, for example, set great store by these purgatorial benefits, always a basic incentive to go on a pilgrimage or join a lay division. The Apostolic Penitentiary, yielding to bishops' requests, confirmed in 1985 that the treasure may be distributed 'live by television or radio' as this 'will greatly favour esteem for indulgences among the Christian people'.[14] American Catholics are urged to share indulgences with the 'Poor Souls' in purgatory, the balance going to 'their credit account in the Book of Life'.[15]

Born of lower middle-class parents in 1920, Karol Wojtyla acted in nationalist theatre and wrote poetry after graduating in Polish literature.[16] He was reduced to doing manual jobs during the Nazi occupation and, after ordination in 1946 and a clerical education at the Angelicum University in Rome, suffered harassment by the Stalinist regime. Between 1953 and 1978 Fr Wojtyla held the chair of ethics at the Catholic University of Lublin. Elevated to the see of Cracow in 1964, he was in conflict with the authorities as a participant in Cardinal Wyzynski's plans to repeat King Jan Casimir's vows to the 'Queen of Poland'. Second to none in his admiration for the Grand Knight of the Immaculate,[17] Fr Kolbe, whom he was to canonize in 1982, Wojtyla took the letter M as his episcopal emblem, transferring this 'logo' to the pontifical shield 24 years later together with the Montfortian motto: *Totus tuus* ('All Thine').

While scrupulously avoiding the term 'Co-Redemptrix', John Paul II's Mariology stresses the Virgin's role in salvation ('Mary, who in herself is a preparation for the final coming of the Lord, signifies the dawn of salvation for the whole world');[18] her spiritual motherhood of the Church ('. . . this woman made all hierarchy possible because she gave to the world the Shepherd and Bishop of our souls');[19] and her unique relationship with the Third Person of the Trinity. Everything can be resolved through her. She is the *Omnipotentia supplex*,[20] the Omnipotence of intercession. For Christ 'wishes to penetrate the soul of every sufferer through the heart of his holy Mother'.[21] Like the Legion of Mary, Militia Immaculatae and the Blue Army, the pope has the highest regard for Grignion de Montfort and some experts say he intends to make him a Doctor of the Church.[22] He reiterates the view of Mary as 'the Woman' of the Apocalypse[23] and she who will bruise the head of the serpent.[24]

Less than a fortnight after the conclave, the new pope left for the Marian shrine of Mentorella run by the Polish Fathers of the Resurrection on Mount Guadagnolo, 50 kilometers from Rome. 'The Rosary is my favourite prayer,' he declared. Its decades embrace 'all the facts that make up the life of the individual, the family, the nations, the Church and mankind.'[25] The Holy House of Loreto, 'an ancient and living legend', was visited in September 1979 to 're-read' its 'mysterious destiny' as a national symbol.[26] Three months later the papal chopper landed on the 'blessed soil of this Prelature of Pompei', sanctuary of the 'sweet chain' of the Holy Rosary, where the pope told members of Azione Cattolica, 'Look at Mary! Love Mary! Imitate Mary!'[27]

The age-old interconnected 'functions' of Mary in matters of sex, curial domination and geopolitics are brought vigorously into play under the Polish pontiff.

Mary is the 'Mother of Priests' and guardian of their celibacy.[28] She will help them to bear the loneliness of bachelorhood.[29] The pope invokes her in Africa as an aid to continence among the laity[30] and in the US as a champion against abortion.[31] Conversely, she will assist legitimate reproduction,[32] help women to 'carry out their marvellous calling as wives and mothers'[33] and persuade young girls to 'live in purity with the strength of soul of Bernadette'.[34] Paray-le-Monial, where Mary 'showed the Heart of your Son to Marguerite Marie' (Alacoque),[35] is another platform from which to attack abortion and divorce.

'Secularism' can be resisted only by remaining within 'the school of Mary', by listening to her voice and following her example.[36] For clergy faced with the even greater evil of 'indifferentism', the ascetical Curé, whose parish of Ars has become once more a major destination, 'remains for all countries an unequalled model both of the carrying out of the ministry and the holiness of the minister'.[37] The attention of female religious is similarly directed to the example of St Catherine Labouré[38]

The pope's first apostolic journey outside Italy – to put the 'future of evangelization in Latin America' in the hands of the Virgin of Guadalupe[39] – provides an example of how 'María' is still used to reinforce Vatican power and crush rebellion. Wojtyla's arrival in Mexico coincided with a meeting of Latin American bishops at Puebla, which he addressed in January 1979, severely criticizing the Iglesia Popular,[40] a liberationist tendency. No censure of right-wing groups was made nor was the papal voice raised on behalf of literally hundreds of priests and religious tortured and murdered in the region over the decade.

'It is said of my native country', John Paul announced in Mexico City, ' "Polonia semper fidelis". I want to be able to say also: Mexico semper fidelis, always faithful! . . . faithfulness to Marian devotion; exemplary faithfulness to the Pope . . . to the Vicar of Christ.'[41] At the shrine of the Morenita, where 60 velvet thrones seat Mexican dignitaries,[42] the pope told five million pilgrims, 'This people, and indirectly, the whole of this vast continent, lives its spiritual unity thanks to the fact that you are its Mother. . . .'[43] Praying for local vocations free of 'socio-political radicalisms'[44] and for protection against 'wars, hatred and subversion',[45] he presented Nuestra Señora de Guadalupe with a diadem. In the football stadium of Jalisco he told the crowd that Mary 'enables us to obtain the grace of true liberation'.[46] And at Monterrey, centre of the steel and chemical industries, he was greeted, almost like Leo XIII, with cries of 'the Worker Pope!'[47]

Wojtyla's pilgrimage to Chile (April 1987), marked by numerous acts in honour of Mary, began with an invocation of her as 'the memory of the Church' and 'Lady of Sea and Cordillera'.[48] Bishops were told to be 'always docile like her',[49] and shanty-house dwellers reminded that the 'Queen of Chile' is 'part of your soul and no one can wrest this heritage from you'.[50] The 'popular religiosity' rooted in the cult of Our Lady of Carmel, 'Mother of Chile' and patroness of the armed forces, was extolled as 'a real treasury of the People of God', an antidote to 'hatred and violence against life, especially that life that has been conceived but not yet born'.[51] The pope's speech at the Economic Commission for Latin America (CEPAL) was an impassioned attack on 'neo-Malthusianism' which concluded with an invocation of Guadalupe, Patroness of Lain America.[52]

For John Paul II, the Madonna is the 'Mother of Unity', whose 'motherly pedagogy' will engender 'the revival, in the present time, of true Christian values such as brotherhood, justice and peace.'[53] A 'mighty force of interior renewal',[54] she provides a link with Muslims and even animists who venerate her image beside Lake Togo. The beatification of a Zairese nun – an event particularly gratifying for dictator Mobutu, a servant of Our Lady of Fatima[55] – strengthens the Marianism of Africa's 46 million Catholics. Sister Anwarite of the Congregation of the Holy Family was murdered in 1964 clutching a statuette of Mary. 'Yes, Mary is a sign of a new world', the pope told the Zairese on the day of the Assumption, 1985. 'Mary enlightened [the new blessed's] faith, sustained it, guided it. . . .'[56]

Poland, where one may 'hear the beating of the heart of the nation in the heart of the Mother',[57] is of course pivotal in the Wojtylian Marian revival. As a high school student, Karol Wojtyla was granted 'special audiences' by the Virgin of Czestochowa at her monastery of Jasna Gora.[58] Returning as Roman Pontiff in June 1979, his paean to the Black Madonna encapsulates the notion that the Rome-Poland-Mary nexus is the foundation of civilization and hope:

> Our Lady of the Bright Mountain, Mother of the Church! Once more I consecrate myself to you 'in your maternal slavery of love': *Totus tuus* – I am all yours! I consecrate to you the whole Church – everywhere to the ends of the earth. I consecrate to you Humanity; I consecrate to you all men and women, my brothers and sisters. All the Peoples and the Nations. I consecrate to you Europe and all the continents. I consecrate to you Rome and Poland, united, through your servant, by a fresh bond of love.
>
> Mother, accept us! Mother, do not abandon us! Mother, be our guide![59]

Primate Wyzynski was delighted to see 'the power of the Queen of Poland display itself so magnificently'.[60]

The Gdansk strike of August 1980 which launched Solidarity was a landmark in the revival. Lech Walesa invariably wears a lapel badge of the Black Madonna and her shrine has been a rallying point for the banned union.[61] The pope's regular prayers to the

Polish Virgin, which have even taken the form of reports on union activities,[62] contrast sharply with his backing for Contra bishops in Nicaragua.

Poland's historical role in the defence of Christendom is central to Wojtyla's thinking. 'The profound union between Austria and Poland' which repulsed the Turk was made 'under the cloak of Mary' and has demonstrated 'her capacity to create authentic brotherhood,' he told pilgrims to Mariazell (Austria), a centre for German, Slav and Hungarian peoples.[63] The Victory of Vienna (1683) came about through Mary's mediation and the celebration of the tricentenary was 'a gift of hers to me'.[64] He presented Our Lady of Mariazell with a 'precious' rosary, consecrated a chapel to Our Lady of Jasna Gora and dedicated the nation to the Magna Mater Austriae.

Given the focus on Poland, it is hardly surprising that the papal assassination attempt – although made by an avowed fascist – was laid at the door of the KGB.[65] The outrage was immediately incorporated into a reading of history dominated by the celestial mother. 'Our Lady of Fatima has protected the Holy Father, this man so devoted to her veneration and so dedicated to the fate of the human family' commented the Vatican newspaper.[66] Why did the pope appoint the Virgin of the Cold War as his guardian rather than the Black Madonna or the healing Lady of Lourdes? His own reason – given in the Cova on 13 May 1982 – was that the attempt occurred 'in mysterious coincidence with the anniversary of the first apparition in Fatima. . . .'[67]

Wojtyla had received John Haffert of the Blue Army in 1979,[68] and the cause for the beatification of Francisco and Jacinta Marto seemed to be making exceptional headway at Rome.[69] The days before the shooting were packed with Marian events. On 3 May the solemnity of Mary, Queen of Poland, was celebrated both in the Vatican gardens and before her 'throne' in Czestochowa. Three days later the Vatican grotto of Lourdes was the site for the swearing-in of Swiss Guards. On 7 May the Holy Father greeted 3,000 children of the Living Rosary, who brought their statue of Our Lady of Fatima to the Vatican. The same day some 600 delegates to the Fourth International Leaders' Conference of the Charismatic Renewal gathered before the grotto, where they were praised for their contribution to ecumenism. A major papal speech against abortion was delivered on 10 May in St Peter's Square – three days before the attack – with supplications to 'the holiest of all mothers for every mother on this earth and for every unborn child'.[70]

At the first general audience held since the pope left Gemelli Hospital, he said,

> Could I ever forget that the event in St Peter's Square took place on the day and at the hour when the first appearance of the Mother of Christ to the poor little peasants has been remembered for over 60 years at Fatima in Portugal?[71]

Next May, 'a pilgrim among pilgrims' guarded personally by Archbishop Marcinkus, John Paul flew to Fatima with TAP, which provided port bottled in the year of his birth.[72] Despite disruptions of transport by communist-backed strikes,[73] around a million people assembled in the sanctuary on 12 May. The pope repeated that Our Lady of Fatima had saved his life. The following day – 65th anniversary of Our Lady's alighting on the holmoak – pilgrims heard that the apparitions were 'so deeply rooted in the Gospel and the whole of Tradition that the Church feels that the message imposes a commitment on her'.[74] The Fatima children 'became partners in dialogue with the Lady of the message and collaborators with her.'[75] Sister Lucia, aged 75, was granted a private audience with the pope.

Referring to that other 'mysterious coincidence' of Pius XII's episcopal ordination (13 May 1917), Wojtyla repeated Pacelli's consecration to the Immaculate Heart of 'the human race and especially the people of Russia'. He also invoked the Virgin against famine, nuclear war, 'sins against the life of man from its very beginning' (abortion and contraception) and 'the demeaning of the dignity of the children of God'[76] (communist persecution of the Church).

Meanwhile in Madrid, a few days before the pope left for Portugal, Blas Piñar, leader of the neo-fascist Fuerza Nueva, delivered a lecture on 'Mary in the history of salvation' in which he welcomed the imminent arrival in Spain of 'a Marian pope' whose recognition of Fatima had given everyone hope.[77]

In the 'Holy Year of Redemption' (1983), when pilgrimages were indulgenced, John Paul sent a message to the May crowds in Fatima, inviting them to pray 'with' and 'through' the pope.[78] In 1984 another triumph came for Sister Lucia and the 25 million-strong Blue Army built on her visions. On 24 March the 'pilgrim Virgin' arrived from Fatima and was installed in the pope's private chapel, where the Holy Father spent the night in vigil before it.[79] The next day, surrounded by banners of divisions including the Blue Army, the statuette was carried in procession before the pope in St Peter's Square. 'We have been given the joy of having with us the venerated image of Our Lady of Fatima,' the pontiff told the crowd and millions of television viewers throughout the world. 'To her goes the soul's first thought, to her the heart's first grateful sentiment.'[80] After a homily which warned that 'married love is too often profaned by excessive self-love, worship of pleasure and illicit practices against human generation', an Act of Entrustment to the Immaculate Heart of Mary of the world ('especially the peoples for which by reason of their situation you have particular love and solicitude') was made by the pope kneeling before the Portuguese image.

Wojtyla had requested the cooperation of all the bishops of the world, exactly as the Carmelite seer had demanded in 1929. The result of such a 'collegial' act, as Lucia's Great Apparition had revealed, would be the conversion of Russia. However, the project met with a lukewarm response from the world episcopate.

Two days later – as Mehmet Ali Agca prepared his allegations of Bulgarian complicity in the 1981 shooting[81] – the victim presented the Bishop of Leiria with the bullet removed from his flesh: a 'relic' to be preserved at Fatima.[82]

38

BORN-AGAIN CATHOLICS

Then we had a baby a year. I always told my husband that if we wanted to quit having babies all I had to do is take my scapular off and remove my life from the hands of Mary.[1]

formerly barren woman, Indiana, 1983

While the 53 million Catholics in the United States – the largest denomination – are no more politically homogeneous than any other group, the Marian devotees among them are controlled by 'conservative' bishops who have much in common with the New Right. Lay Catholics were prominent in the electronic networks whose propaganda helped put Reagan in the White House.[2] Terry Dolan, for instance, a leading fund-raiser through his National Conservative Political Action Committee, served on the Moral Majority board and other groupings linked up by his co-religionists, the direct mail wizards Richard A. Viguerie ('King Midas of the New Right')[3] and Paul Weyrich of the Heritage Foundation. Dolan described himself as a 'born-again Catholic' who believed in 'most of the tenets of fundamentalism'.[4]

The convergence of neo-conservatism with integralist currents in the Catholic Church needs little amplification. The aims of the Fatima-orientated Apostolate of Christian Action, for example, are clear: 'We encourage and support the activities of groups and individuals who are trying to combat Atheistic Communism; also evil and moral decay – such as abortion murders, pornography, immodesty in dress, homosexuality, contraception, divorce etc.'[5] The Blue Army officially attempts to 'influence legislation at all levels – especially at the national level – to abolish abortion'[6] and distributes pictures of the 'Mother of the Unborn', her fingernails filthy 'from scooping and digging out these precious souls from trash bins and garbage dumps'.[7]

Mary is invoked against enemies on the sex front under her title of Fatima, which subsumes the Immaculate Heart and Queen of the Holy Rosary. An extraordinary expression of this war is the 'Towering Madonna', a 32-ft representation of the Immaculate Conception. Blessed by Cardinal Krol – a key supporter of the Blue Army – the statue attracted large crowds during a year-long haul between Wilmington, Delaware (where it was completed in the summer of 1982) and its permanent site at the purpose-built Shrine to the Immaculate Heart of Mary opposite the Great American Amusement Park at Santa Clara, California. The stainless steel colossus stands guard between Silicon Valley and 'Sodom-by-the-Bay' (San Francisco), where devotion to the Miraculous Medal is keeping pace with the 'deluge of impurity'.[8] A message from the pope was read at the new sanctuary's dedication ceremony and Fr Peyton of the Family Rosary Crusade gave the address.

The 'nuclear dispensationalism'[9] of Evangelical rightists (a belief shared by President Reagan that the righteous will 'greet the Lord in the air' and be saved seconds before Armageddon)[10] is mirrored by an apocalyptic Catholic 'fundamentalism' based on accounts of apparitions as much as on literalist readings of scripture. Thus the Apostolate of Christian Action:

> before the promised triumph of the Immaculate Heart of
> Mary takes place, the present leaders of Soviet Russia will make
> one last all-out effort for world conquest, through an invasion of
> Europe and World War III; and through attacks against the
> United States from Cuba and Central America, particularly
> Nicaragua . . . there may be a limited nuclear war, and perhaps
> disturbances of nature, during which 'various nations will be
> annihilated', as foretold by Our Lady.[11]

The Blue Army also subscribes to the atomic fatalism characteristic of the religious right: 'Detente to avoid nuclear war is not possible from either a political or military viewpoint. Our Lady is the only "detente" we have left.'[12]

After a meeting between the pope and the international president of the Blue Army (Mgr Constantino Luna OFM, Bishop of Guatemala), a 'chain reaction' of rosaries swept the United States from July to December 1984.[13] Marking the official 2,000th anniversary of Mary's birth, the 'Rosaries for Peace' rallies were also supported by the Knights of Columbus, Legion of Mary and other divisions.[14] There were 'All-Night Vigils, mammoth Rallies, candlelight processions, Rosary marches, cathedral events, Pilgrim

Virgin visitations, crownings of Our Lady, Scapular enrolments, Benedictions, Masses and Holy Communions.'[15] A new devotion, the 'State Rosary', was introduced – with intercessions for each state of the union and the refrain 'America prays for America and the world'.

Vietnamese children celebrated the bimillenium of the Marian nativity by marching, in traditional yellow costumes and carrying pink umbrellas, beside a float of the Virgin of Fatima. A mass concelebrated by Archbishop Ngo Dinh Thuc, brother of the assassinated President Diem, provided their parents with 'the opportunity to meet old friends as well as compatriots in their struggle for freedom from Communist oppression'.[16]

During the 'birthday party' honouring Our Lady on 8 September Fr John Sweeney of the Immaculate Heart of Mary shrine leaned out of a crane lift to deposit behind the heart of the Towering Madonna a microfilm list of 3,000 devotees.[17]

In a special campaign issue, *Divine Love* (the organ of the Apostolate of Christian Action) ran stories on a Russian munitions depot which 'mysteriously' blew up on 13 May that year, the 'ominous Soviet military build up', and Sandinista plans to export Marxism from a new airport.[18]

In sharp contrast to Vatican support for the rosary rallies, Cardinal Ratzinger, who is official 'protector' of the Pontifical Marian Academy as well as doctrinal overlord, issued a stern condemnation of the theology of liberation: 'a perversion of the Christian message' and purveyor of such unwelcome devotions as 'a "Eucharist" transformed into a celebration of the people in struggle.'[19]

In September Mr Reagan, who has since publicly expressed his faith in the Fatima seers (see Introduction), visited the replica sanctuary of Czestochowa at Doylestown, Philadelphia, at the invitation of Archbishop Krol. 'Don't let anyone tell you we're less dedicated to peace because we want a strong America' was the president's message to the 20,000 'pilgrims' who greeted him – in this election year – with shouts of 'Four more years!'[20] The following May Bishop Luna dedicated a chapel of Our Lady of Fatima at the Doylestown shrine on the annual 'Day of Prayer for the Union of Polish Women in America'.[21] And in July 1985 the Blue Army youth leader, Fr Robert J. Fox, carried out at Fatima – with White House permission – a 'Consecration of the United States of America to the Immaculate Heart of Mary on behalf of the President and People of the US'.[22]

The Blue Army has maintained its position as the most highly organized and comprehensive of American lay divisions. Papal approval – virtually ignored by the Catholic press – is as strong as ever.[23] The relationship with the episcopate – canonical and 'obedient' – is enhanced by the support of Cardinals Krol (president of the National Conference of Catholic Bishops since 1984) and Law of Boston.[24] By 1983 some 85 bishops had appointed spiritual directors for a Blue Army group in their diocese.[25] Even the 'living saint' Mother Teresa of Calcutta has associated herself with the Blue Army on more than one occasion.[26]

In conscious imitation of communism, the Blue Army grows from cells, the first of which 'was formed by the three illiterate children to whom Our Lady appeared'.[27] Youth is a priority target. Blue Army Cadets are the basis of a programme aiming to turn out 'models of Marian modesty' with 'complete and undivided loyalty' to the Holy Father.[28] Children up to the age of 16 sign the Cadet Pledge, promising to wear the Brown Scapular, pray the rosary and learn a 'Marian catechism' until they feel ready for 'total consecration' to the Immaculate through the formula of Grignion de Montfort. Fr Fox, national spiritual director, gives advice in his 'mini-soul' column on the gaining of indulgences and avoidance of masturbation. 'Young men and women who pray the Rosary daily . . . will know that impure touching, petting and necking, passionate kissing, indecent dancing and dress, as well as impure talk, movies, magazines and television must be avoided.'[29] Cadets are to read about Dr Tom Dooley of Vietnam (see chapter 32) and Cardinal Newman – 'our heroes for March and April'. The first issues of *Hearts Aflame*, a new youth magazine, heavily promote the charismatic renewal[30] and, in fundamentalist style, repeatedly warn against the 'mere speculation'[31] of Darwin's work (the 'respectable way to push atheism',[32] which, of course, leads to communism).

Women and the large émigré and refugee communities, especially those from Eastern Europe and the Far East,[33] are other important sectors for recruitment. Blue Army chapels and sanctuaries are served by a 'consecrated corps' of nuns, the Handmaids of Mary Immaculate, founded in 1952 and approved as a pious union in the diocese of Trenton in 1977.[34] A 'prayer auxiliary' to this 'Eucharistic, Marian community' was set up for lay women in 1982.

The 'traditional' sensationalism of Blue Army devotions is revivified with the spirit of consumerism. Sponsored by the Knights of Columbus[35] and Legion of Mary, pilgrim Virgins are constantly on the road to 'Fatimize America', weeping 'human tears' and blood.[36] The 'Home Pilgrim Virgin' – 'a wonderful devotion. Why not introduce it in your parish?'[37] – leaves a miraculous scent of roses at wakes and follows a tight schedule visiting hospital wards.

Fatima devotions are being encouraged in another traditional sphere of Marian influence, the military. At the Naval Academy in Annapolis, Maryland, where over half the 'underclassmen' are Catholics, scapulars and rosaries are distributed by chaplains. In November 1985 a statue of Our Lady of Fatima was blessed in the academy chapel by Bishop Joseph Dimino, vicar-general of the military archdiocese.[38]

Devotional activity in the 'Year of Fatima – Marian Year' is concentrating on 'nights of love' before the Blessed Sacrament, acts of consecration to the Sacred Heart of Jesus and Immaculate Heart of Mary and, in association with the Legion of Mary, first five Saturday reparations – with the incentive of becoming 'a critical cog in salvation history'.[39] *Glasnost* is getting a Fatimist slant as news of a 'wave of conversions from Marx to Christ'[40] reaches the USA.

Already operating a television company called Gesu et Maria,[41] the Blue Army has been fortunate in sponsoring an ambitious feature film during the Marian Year: Richard Bennett's *A State of Emergency*, starring Martin Sheen. The story tells of a nuclear scientist converted at Fatima. According to the producer-director, the film's purpose is 'to alert a world trembling under the threat of nuclear war that Heaven has intervened and given us an alternative.'[42] John Haffert writes, '. . . our main concern was to have a motion picture to bring Fatima to millions, even to non-believers.'[43]

Pilgrimages, despite all the means of electronic mediation, remain a central goal. The 'American Fatima' in Warren County, New Jersey – also the home of the US Guardian Angel since 1982 and a replica of the Santa Casa of Loreto (Blue Army members gain an indulgence by visiting it)[44] – had a busy programme in 1987 of scapular investitures, days of 'Solidarity with the Unborn' and 'Acts of Consecration to the Two Hearts'.

The *Queen of the World* 707 ferries pilgrims to the Pontevedra convent in Spain (now owned by the Blue Army), where Lucia was granted the Great Apparition and to Fatima itself, now enjoying a touristic boom after the second papal visit.[45] Knock is now an 'option' on the Blue Army's thrice-weekly USA-Fatima 'getaway' and profits from *A State of Emergency* in Ireland will go to the shrine, in trouble since heavy investment in an airport failed to attract enough visitors.

In 1985 the World Apostolate of Fatima (an alternative name for the Blue Army, 'so vilified')[46] moved its international office from Basle to Fribourg, a noted Marian centre. In Italy, the president of the Blue Army is O.L. Scalfaro, minister of the interior.[47] The international projection of the apostolate, however, concentrates on Canada and Australia, the eastern bloc and developing countries like the Philippines. A statue given by the French Armée Bleu was enthroned in a Polish church in 1985, and in the same year Blue Army priests from the United States celebrated mass in the Warsaw church of Our Lady, Queen of the World, concluding the service with the Solidarity anthem.[48] Following Poland's lead, a 'perpetual rosary' has been said since 1985 for the Holy Father by Blue Army members in St Sulpice, Paris. This practice – to 'raise around His Holiness a veritable wall of protection'[49] – has spread to Italy and the United States.

The Blue Army in the Philippines has had the active support of Imelda Marcos and Cardinal Sin. Seven 'pilgrim Virgins' were delivered to Manila in 1985, one of which Mrs Marcos took to Moscow, where it is now enshrined in St Louis (Catholic) Church. 'When the statue was received, the congregation broke into tears of joy; Mrs Marcos also presented a beautiful gold vestment to the church, bearing an image of Our Lady of Fatima.'[50] Participants in a 'Symposium of the Two Hearts' sponsored by the Blue Army and Cardinal Sin at Fatima were received by the pope in September 1986.[51] A few days earlier, the Philippine ambassador to the Vatican had praised the event and, somewhat paradoxically, spoken of the Virgin's intervention in the recent overthrow of the Marcos regime: 'In defence of freedom and the right to express their will through the polls, the Filipino people, under the banner of Mary, fought and won a battle unprecedented in the history of Christianity.'[52]

The *Queen of the World* plane took 200 Blue Army soldiers to China in 1982 'to pray there for that nation of one billion persons under the yoke of atheistic Communism'.[53]

The practice – since 1947 – of enthroning 'pilgrim Virgins' in churches throughout the world continues without a break. In May

1986 the arrival of one of these images in County Waterford, Ireland, stimulated a 'miracle of the sun' and visions of Mary and Padre Pio.[54] The 1986 'Peace Flight' of the Blue Army took in Aruba, Caracas, Lagos, Rwanda, Sri Lanka, Malaysia, India, Egypt and Yugoslavia. A feature of the trip was the emphasis on new apparitions – at Medjugorje and in Africa.

39

VISITATIONS IN PROGRESS: NICARAGUA, YUGOSLAVIA, CHILE ·

The apparitions of Our Lady in these latter times have not only multiplied, but seem to be intensified. Mary's warnings, instructions, and requirements of the faithful . . . are becoming more concrete. Today it is a question dealing directly with the peace of the world, and Mary is giving very precise orientations about the manner in which a catastrophe could be avoided. . . .[1]

the Reverend Professor Hans Urs von Balthasar, 1985

The three cases of Marian apparitions we briefly examine here occur against very different backcloths: guerrilla war against a leftist state; a debilitated communist state in economic crisis; military rule in a context of widespread poverty and discontent. The Nicaraguan visions – backed by the Blue Army[2] – serve Pentagon plans for Central America: the 'special protectorate' of Mary (John Paul II); the Yugoslav ones further western ambitions in the 'east'; and the Chilean sensations aim to prop up a disintegrating regime. All three visitations exploit the fear of nuclear destruction.

OUR LADY OF FATIMA AND CUAPA

The Sandinista revolution of 1979 differed fundamentally from other Marxist victories: the vast majority of its supporters were Christians. As Graham Greene has noted, one of the slogans prominently displayed is 'Revolution Yes, But Christian'.[3] Indeed, a faction expresses 'dubious identifications between revolutionary processes and the kingdom of God'.[4] In one church, frescos of heroes like Augusto Sandino – from whom the party takes its name – have supplanted the statues of saints[5] and a 'popular Church' has sprung up with little reverence either from Rome or the national episcopate.[6]

The hierarchy had endorsed the Somoza dictatorship – as did Cardinal Spellman in defiance of John XXIII's orders[7] – until its overthrow was imminent. Initially welcoming the Sandinista victory, the bishops began to campaign against the revolutionaries in early 1980 with the support of the Vatican and CELAM.[8] Mgr Pablo Antonio Vega of Juigalpa, president of the episcopal conference (who has links with the Heritage Foundation[9] and the Blue Army),[10] announced Rome's suspension of the four Sandinista priest-ministers and, since his exile in July 1986, has lobbied the US Congress on behalf of the Contras.[11]

In May 1980 Our Lady of Fatima visited Mgr Vega's diocese to converse with a middle-aged sacristan who was concerned at the presence of Cubans in a literacy programme. Wearing a long, white dress and veil 'of a pale cream color with gold embroidery along the edge',[12] Mary announced to Bernardo Martínez: 'Nicaragua . . . will continue to suffer if you don't change. . . . I ask the Lord to appease His justice but, if you don't change, you will hasten the arrival of a Third World War.'[13] She demanded daily recitation of the rosary and the Eucharistic devotion of the 'first five Saturdays'. Martínez saw 'something like a movie': a vision of martyrs, Dominicans and Franciscans parading in the sky with 'luminous rosaries'.[14] An angel later advised the seer on how to liberate a friend in gaol for 'counter-revolutionary activity' and accurately prophesied the murder of a relative who refused to belief in the apparitions.

By September large crowds were addressed by Bishop Vega on the site of the visitation, which he had bought. Martínez was now guarded by church workers against alleged attempts by government agents to seduce him.

Two years later the Sandinistas seized 15 sets of films supplied by the Family Rosary Crusade through an executive of W.R. Grace & Co.,[15] a firm accused by Managua of working with the CIA.[16]

Radio Católica was temporarily closed down on government orders in 1986 when it substituted a rosary prayer for President Ortega's New Year message to 'unite all arms against American aggression'.[17] The Contras' own clandestine radio station took up the apparitions in the Marian Year – in parallel with Cardinal-primate

Obando's vigorous promotion of pilgrimages to Cuapa – and claimed the Virgin's words referred to their imminent victory.[18]

Meanwhile, the ancient image of the 'spiritual captain' of the Honduran armed forces, the Virgin of Suyapa, was kidnapped by insurgents (September 1986).

CHARISMATIC LADY OF CROATIA

In May 1981 – shortly before the attempt on the pope's life – Franciscan Tomislav Vlasic attended the International Leaders' Conference of the Charismatic Renewal in Rome. On hearing about the problems of the Catholic Church in Yugoslavia, two religious uttered in prophecy, 'Do not fear; I am sending you my Mother'.[19] One of the prophets was Briege McKenna,[20] an Irish Sister of St Clare who has since become famous as a healer and spiritual consultant to priests and cardinals, and even to the president of Brazil.[21]

On 24 June a lady in grey appeared to four young girls and two boys (aged from 10 to 18) on a hillside overlooking Medjugorje, a Croatian-speaking village in Bosnia-Hercegovina. Introducing herself as 'the Queen of Peace' she said:

> Tell all my sons and daughters, tell the world as soon as possible that I desire their conversion. . . . I will ask my Son not to punish the world but that the world be saved. . . . When God comes He will not be joking.[22]

The apparitions have continued – in a room in the church – regularly every evening up to the present.[23] '. . . the Madonna wears a white veil, and her gown is not bound at her waist but flows straight down and conceals her feet . . . a small black curl is seen on the left side of her face'.[24]

Running through the messages is an emphasis on fasting, through which 'You can avert wars: you can even suspend natural laws. . . . Real fasting is eating only bread and water'.[25] Gospa, as Our Lady is called in Croatian, also asked for rosary devotions and the formation of a charismatic prayer group.[26]

The first visions in a communist country to be promoted internationally, the case of Medjugorje displays major 'classic' characteristics (as summarized on pages 76–8). The apparition – of a 'three-dimensional type'[27] – presented glimpses of heaven and hell, and promised to entrust ten secrets to each of the children and adolescents (who, like Bernadette, demonstrated the ability to run at preternatural speed). Vanka, for example, an intellectually backward girl, was to learn about 'future world events'.[28]

Eventually denounced by the local bishop (Mostar) in the strongest terms,[29] the revelations and pilgrimages have remained effectively under the control of Croatian Franciscans, traditionally at loggerheads with the ordinary. According to Canon Laurentin, Rome removed responsibility for an inquiry from the Bishop of Mostar 'because of his enduring negative bias'.[30]

Fr Vlasic, 'spiritual director of the visionaries', writes that Our Lady told Mirjana Dragicevic (a 16-year-old to whom a demon has paid flattering compliments) that 'she could confide the secrets to any priest three days before each of them is due to be fulfilled'.[31] In fact, open air confession to the Franciscans is a central feature of 'the Medjugorje package';[32] long queues form in the fields outside the church. Another 'secret' – to be made public only on the orders of the pope – is the exact date of Mary's birthday, on which all the faithful are expected to stop work.

Public miracles have been plentiful. On 2 August 1981

> 'the same phenomenon which occurred at Fatima was seen everywhere in this locality. The setting sun revolved and drew nearer to the church. Many saw the Sacred Host in it and they saw hosts of angels with trumpets. . . . On 28th October, 1981, we saw a big flame on the mountainside where Our Lady first appeared'.[33]

On the feast of the Sacred Heart in 1982 crowds saw 'stars rotating in the sky'.[34] There has been a 'holiness explosion'[35] of cures, conversions, reconciliations and vocations. As at Garabandal, a 'warning or admonition to the world' will be given – followed by a miraculous sign on the mountain 'for the atheists'.

As tens of thousands converged on Medjugorje, the reaction of the Yugoslav League of Communists was 'quick and hostile'.[36] On 12 August 1981 the police cordoned off the 'Hill of Apparitions', strip-searched nuns, interrogated the seers and arrested several priests. Two local Franciscans were given harsh prison sentences for alleged 'cooperation with extreme Croatian émigré groups in the west'[37] (apparently the source of hagiological books on Cardinal Stepinac, whose grave in Zagreb has become the object of Croatian pilgrimages).[38] In November Fr Ferdo Vlasic, whose magazine had publicized the messages, received eight years (he was released in 1986) and his assistant Jozo Krizic was sentenced to five and a half years (reduced to two). Both journalist-monks are still forbidden to publish their work.

A campaign of ridicule was conducted by the Yugoslav media against the 'Ustasha Lady'. Branco Mikulic, regional party chief, accused 'clerico-nationalists' of trying to 'intimidate uneducated people' and 'manipulate them politically'.[39]

The election of John Paul II is said to have had a 'strong impact'[40] on Croatians and Slovenes who, like other Yugoslavs, face a crushing burden of inflation and unemployment. The produce of smallholders, who own four-fifths of the land, is subjected to the law of supply and demand, and the economic future for many families seems bleak.[41] The 'risk of a Polish-style upheaval',[42] already feared by the government in 1981, has increased and workers throughout the country have challenged party policies through strikes and protests, bringing the threat of military repression.[43] No matter how politically inconvenient the prospect of a 'Yugoslav Fatima' might seem to the Communist Party, the influx of around three million pilgrims (100,000 on feast days) by 1985[44] has created undeniable benefits for a region largely dependent on tourism. The government, 'happy to sacrifice its Marxist principles in exchange for the little income from the pilgrims' (as the Blue Army puts it),[45] has opened an information office on the site.

The worldwide television coverage[46] and business enterprise required to attract and handle such numbers are confidently based on a flood of books, some by scholars like Michael O'Carroll of the Pontifical Marian Academy, René Laurentin, the Lourdes authority, and Fr Bob Faricy,SJ, who teaches spiritual theology at the Gregorian University. Another supporter is the eminent Swiss theologian Hans Urs von Balthasar, who sees Medjugorje as 'Theodramatik'.

Fr Richard Foley, a key Jesuit promoter in Anglo-American circles, thinks a pilgrimage to the shrine is 'like visiting a film-set. For you have been programmed – through books, photos, videos and slides on the subject – to recognize the scenario and identify the cast'.[47] Medjugorje – which 'makes nonsense of the gospel according to Marx'[48] – is on 'a massive scale that even a Hollywood spectacular could not match', an 'ongoing drama' in which 'Gospa . . . is the star of the show.'[49]

Based at Farm Street, London, and in touch with the Boston 'Center for Peace', Croatian priests in Manhattan, and devotees at episcopal level in Ireland, Fr Foley has witnessed a solar miracle at Medjugorje. He believes 'Our Lady's message must not only reach out to believing Christians but to secular society at large, for there are millions of unchurched folk out there waiting for Gospa.'[50]

The Yugoslav clergy remains divided over the new sanctuary. Three successive episcopal commissions have failed to issue any clear ruling. The Vatican – conducting its own investigation through the Congregation for the Doctrine of the Faith – seems even less willing to formulate a judgment. But the pope is kept informed of developments and has sent his portrait to the seers with the dedication: 'Our Lady of Medjugorje is Queen of Peace.'[51]

African visions 'of a rare purity' (Laurentin)[52] followed hard on the events in Yugoslavia. 'Our Lady of the Word' has been appearing to eight young people at Kibeho in Rwanda since November 1981. The apparitions – apparently similar to Fatima and Medjugorje – have the backing of the local bishop, Mgr Aloys Bigirumwami, and the Blue Army, who have given the town a fully-equipped clinic.

'QUEEN OF PEACE AND GENERAL OF OUR ARMY'[53]

Catholic Church opposition to the dictatorship and the consequent increase in Protestant 'evangelism' among the armed forces have weakened military Marianism in Chile. But the relatively low profile of Our Lady among soldiers[54] has been offset by a boom in *religiosidad popular*, with new apparitions and the 'sociology' of sanctuaries.[55]

In February 1983, when clear signs of crisis and rebellion were seen throughout the country, the Immaculate, as a lingering 'luminous phenomenon', appeared on several consecutive days before a Lourdes grotto on a hill called Alto de la Luna, in the northern town of Vallenar. Neither the parish priest nor the hierarchy condemned the sensation, and the 'news' was given front-page treatment by national newspapers for a week, juxtaposed with pictures of 'seaside lovelies'. The 'undeniable graphic sequence', however, was rejected by local groups of Evangelicals and, as a commission of inquiry was set up by the Bishop of Copiapo, 'heretical vandals' attempted to destroy the 'wall of miracles'.[56]

This frustrated apparition was followed in June 1983 by one of Our Lady of Carmel in Villa Alemana, near the port of Valparaiso, which 'coincided with the first social mobilizations against Pinochet's regime'.[57] The seer, Miguel Angel Poblete, a poor orphan of 19 with epileptic, suicidal, and glossolalian tendencies, became Chile's first 'stigmatic' while transmitting anti-communist messages from Peñablanca, the 'new Mount Carmel'. The spectacular scenes, which drew crowds of up to 100,000, were attended on one occasion by Admiral José Toribio Merino, number two in the junta. The instigator of the visions, Christian Democrat sources suggest,[58] was the Fatimist TFP (see pp. 237–8 and 282).

The messages delivered 'through the mouth of Miguel Angel, el Niño' (the Child) – and published in book form by his spiritual guide, Fr Miguel Contardo, and the dermatologist Dr Alan Rojas – were a gruesome medley of La Salette, Fatima, and Garabandal, with classic strictures on public protest and 'political priests': Russia and the US will go to war and the destructive arms, instigated by Satan, will be their chastisement. . . . If we don't pray, the Red Dragon will enter Chile', the Virgin told Poblete in 'a sweet Spanish accent'.[59] 'For sure I tell you that many priests are taking many souls to perdition and that communism is in half of them.'[60] *El Monte Carmelo de Peñablanca* was published for the twelfth anniversary of the coup, September 1985, when the military vicar, Bishop José Joaquín Matte, asserted: 'Twelve years ago the rosary began to be prayed without pause and Mary made a miracle: it was the second independence of Chile.'[61]

Although the visions were condemned in November 1983 by an inquiry headed by Fr Jaime Fernández, a Schönstatt priest, who characterized el Niño as manic-depressive,[62] the Virgin of Peñablanca continued to enjoy the active support of followers with ample resources. Her messages were reproduced in cassette form and sold together with scapulars and rosaries. The apparitions counted on the glossy *Mariana*, 'the Virgin's Magazine',[63] launched in 1985, and a radio programme, Supernatural Events, which reached almost the entire country. The publicist behind both ventures was Jorge Castro de la Barra, a dynamic journalist who once used a helicopter to take listeners' letters to the new sanctuary.

Among those who openly backed Poblete was Luis Fernández, a Spanish priest linked to a company run by ex-naval officers. In 1984 the architect Alvaro Barros, a Catholic Pentecostal and firm believer in Peñablanca, published an illustrated popular history of Marian apparitions, with a foreword by Mgr Bernardino Piñera, president of the Episcopal Conference of Chile, and an epilogue by Mgr B. Cazzaro, vicar-apostolic of Aysén.[64]

Several doctors[65] attested to the ecstatic transmissions of Poblete, whose head bled as though lacerated by a crown of thorns. Accompanied by his confessor and an enigmatic American couple, he made a trip to New York towards the end of 1985, with a view to meeting Conchita of Garabandal and other visionaries.

Our Lady figured prominently in Chile during 1986. The discovery in August of a revolutionary arsenal (a few weeks before the attempt on Pinochet's life) was attributed to the orientation of the *Virgen del Carmen*. The miracle was celebrated at the Bernardo O'Higgins Military School in the presence of the dictator's wife and her 'Female Volunteers'.[66] After the failed 'magnicide' (as the assassination attempt is officially known), a full-colour leaflet circulated widely among the troops, explaining the protection given by Mary to Pinochet.

EPILOGUE

As we conclude this study, the Catholic world is halfway through the second Marian Year. The technological feat of its launch (June 1987) – with 18 satellites linking up major shrines[1] in a global electronic rosary – struck a Schönstatt priest as 'quasi-miraculous'.[2] A flame lit by the pontifical hand before the Salus Populi Romani image of Our Lady was carried to the world's sanctuaries to 'gather up the hopes and yearnings of humanity placed under Mary's motherly protection'.[3]

Pilgrimages to her shrines – treasure-houses of indulgences – are the main devotional focus. It is no coincidence that Cardinal Dadaglio, curial overlord of holy pardons, is president of the Central Committee for the Marian Year. Plenary indulgences are available for those who visit the Roman basilica of St Mary Major or an officially designated Marian shrine. The same benefits are granted for the recitation of the rosary and the hearing of the papal blessing, whether from a bishop or via the radio or television. The pope is giving regular talks on the apparitional traditions of such shrines as el Pilar (Saragossa) and does not hesitate to point out that the 'translation' of the Holy House of Nazareth (Loreto) is 'still the object of study and analysis by historians and Mariologists'.[4]

One of the reasons given for the Marian jubilee, held towards the end of the second Christian millenium, is that 'Mary appeared on the horizon of salvation history before Christ'.[5] Fourteen months of meditation on her 'cooperation' with Christ and the Church will, it is hoped, guide the faithful to the Eucharistic table via an 'authentic Marian spirituality'.[6] *Redemptoris Mater*, doctrinal base for the events, makes special mention of Grignion de Montfort's 'consecration to Christ through the hands of Mary' and, in a later document,[7]

311

Wojtyla praises Alphonsus de' Liguori's 'very special veneration for the Supreme Pontiff'; and defence of papal infallibility – a theme never far from that of Mary's prerogatives.

The authority of the pope, in fact, seems to be the outstanding motive for the jubilee. Renewed attempts to persuade Greek Orthodox leaders to submit once more to Rome are 'hinged' on the 'all holy One'[8] (Panaghia) as never before. Patriarch Dimitrios of Constantinople is demanding 'that the subject of Mariology should occupy a central position in the theological dialogue between our Churches'.[9] And for the first time in history the Patriarchs of east and west appeared together on the balcony overlooking St Peter's Square, when the pope spoke at length of a miraculous icon of the Theotokos venerated on Mount Athos – a gesture which will certainly have enraged the 'anti-popish' inhabitants of the Greek monastic republic.

Union with the Greeks is, of course, but one step from communion with the Russian Church. Yet the Ostpolitik of the Vatican is still boldly expressed through the apparitions of Fatima, 'a point of reference and illumination for our century'.[10] The Marian Year coincides with the millenium of Russian Christianity and sixth centenary of the 'baptism' of Lithuania; the much emphasized hopes of 'converting' the eastern bloc through a common devotion to the Virgin recall the mood of the Pacellian era. While Baltic nationalists protest against the Soviet takeover of Estonia, Latvia and Lithuania (and visions of the Virgin draw crowds in the Ukraine),[11] the United States is entrusted by the pope to the Immaculate Conception (16 September 1987).

This conjuncture is for the Blue Army 'a truly golden opportunity' to organize pilgrimages[12] and a 'Great Rosary Crusade'. Parishes across the United States are lined up in a First Saturday Reparations race in which winners will receive 'gold FSR status'.[13] The 1987 Marian congress held at Alexandria, South Dakota, was organized by Fr Robert Fox, the former Blue Army youth leader and founder of the Fatima Family Shrine. The apostolate's influence in the Third World has increased correspondingly. Bishop Sangu of Mbeya (Tanzania) reports that 'in this Marian Year, many wish to be members of the Blue Army'[14] and in Ecuador a military chaplain distributes thousands of rosaries and scapulars 'bestowed by our loved brothers and friends of the United States'.[15]

Epilogue

Canonizations strengthen the twin virtues of Marian devotion and obedience to Rome, where the cause of the little shepherds of Fatima is believed to be close to completion.[16] In England the pilgrimage to Walsingham has for one of its 'intentions' the canonization of Cardinal Newman; the 85 British martyrs honoured in the presence of Anglican observers (November 1987) are said to have died 'for their loyalty to the authority of the Successor of Peter, who alone is the Pastor of the whole flock'.[17] Also significant is the beatification of the Marian founder, Archbishop Jurgis Matulaitis (d. 1927), who negotiated a concordat between Lithuania and the Vatican after the military coup of 1926.[18]

Military vicariates are raised to the rank of bishopric (*Spiritual militum curae*, 21 July 1987) and the 'particularist' devotions are reactivated. The scapular of the militarized Chilean Virgin of Carmel, for example, was extolled as 'a mantle of protection' by the pope during his coronation of the image in April 1987.[19] Catholic newspapers call for a return to the cults of the Sacred Heart, Precious Blood, Miraculous Medal and St Joseph. Padre Pio is in the ascendant, especially since Wojtyla prayed at his tomb on 23 May 1987 (an event featured in the hagiographical film *Pray, Hope and Don't Worry*). A more novel form of devotion is a song, *Totally Yours*, by Dana, through which the pontiff's Montfortian motto has entered the pop charts.

The Marian dynamic will not end on the feast of the Assumption, 15 August 1988, which brings the jubilee to a close. We are witnessing the beginning of an ideological tug-of-war over the 'inescapable woman'[20] in which both conservatives and progressives will attempt to deploy her cult to their advantage. Brains are being racked to provide, in Hans Küng's words, 'a new interpretation of the figure of Mary for our time, freeing it of cliches and rigidities and thus smoothing the path for a genuinely ecumenical picture of Mary. . . .'[21]

Our Lady is going through the acutest identity crisis, but whatever new guises she may assume, her cult is likely to remain rooted in apparitions and at the service of manipulative power.

NOTES

INTRODUCTION

1 *Osservatore Romano* (weekly English edition), 2 April 1984.
2 *Weekly Compilation of Presidential Documents*, Administration of Ronald Reagan, 1985, vol. 21, no. 19.
3 For an excellent analysis of the 'polyvalent figure' of the Virgin, see M. Warner, *Alone of All Her Sex. The Myth and the Cult of the Virgin Mary*, London, 1976; also, G. Ashe, *The Virgin*, London, 1976.
4 J.M. Bover, SJ, 'L'Église et le nouvel Israël', *Maria*, (Paris), 1949, vol. 1.
5 J. Escrivá de Balaguer, *Christ is Passing By*, Dublin, 1974, p. 189.
6 R. Laurentin, *The Life of Catherine Labouré*, London, 1983, p. 258.

PART I: ORIGINS OF MILITANT MARIANISM

1 GENESIS OF THE CULT UNDER BYZANTIUM AND ROME

1 C.X.J.M. Friethoff, OP, *A Complete Mariology*, London, 1958, p. 276.
2 See G. Ashe, *The Virgin*, London, 1976; M. Warner, *Alone of All Her Sex. The Myth and the Cult of the Virgin Mary*, London, 1976.
3 Symptomatic of this fanciful trend were the supposititious epistles to the Virgin Mary of St Ignatius, Bishop of Antioch (martyred c. 107).
4 H. Chadwick, *The Early Church*, London, 1967, p. 267.
5 See S. Runciman, *The Medieval Manichee. A Study of the Christian Dualist Heresy*, Cambridge, 1947.

6 For the persistence of pagan cults and the transformation into Marian shrines of temples dedicated to goddesses, see Ashe and Warner.

7 The victim, executed on imperial orders, was Priscillian, Bishop of Avila, who was accused of gnosticism and witchcraft.

8 H. Lea, *An Historical Sketch of Sacerdotal Celibacy in the Christian Church*, Philadelphia, 1867, p. 65.

9 H. Graef, *Mary: a History of Doctrine and Devotion*, London/New York, 1963, vol. 1, p. 79.

10 Ambrose was the first authority to establish the relation between the Church and Mary. For a full account of the development of Marian ideology, see Graef, op.cit.

11 Lea, op.cit., pp. 72–3.

12 Lea says the fate of Vigilantius was obscured by invasions, op.cit., p. 76.

13 ibid., p. 45. The account of St Martin's visions has been lost. See Ashe, op.cit., p. 181.

14 It was mainly the tomb of St Peter that made the imperial city holy in Christian eyes. Rome was later to distribute the 'paste de' SS. Martiri', or 'grey Agnus Dei', made from wax and the dust of martyrs, which functioned as a relic-amulet. Unlike the Agnus Dei proper, a wax charm bearing the Lamb and pontifical arms, the martyrs' paste did not need consecration.

15 *Acts* 2: 42.

16 Graef, op.cit., p. 62.

17 ibid., p. 64.

18 L. Duchesne, *Early History of the Christian Church from its Foundation to the End of the Fifth Century*, London, 1924, vol. 3, p. 246.

19 The British Library, *The Christian Orient*, 1978, p. 36.

20 H. Lea, *A History of the Inquisition in the Middle Ages*, London, 1888, vol. 3, p. 554.

21 Graef, op.cit., p. 118.

22 The Girdle and Veil of the Theotokos were both kept at Constantinople.

23 G. Ostrogorsky, *A History of the Byzantine State*, trans. J. Hussey, Oxford, 1986 (5th English edition), p. 77.

24 Lea, *An Historical Sketch of Sacerdotal Celibacy*, op.cit.

25 In the previous century the followers of St Cyril of Alexandria had brutally murdered the neoplatonist philosopher Hypatia.

26 L. Ouspensky, *Theology of the Icon*, New York, 1978, p. 74.

27 e.g., C.N. Uspensky. See A.A. Vasiliev, *History of the Byzantine Empire: 324–1453*, Wisconsin, 1952, pp. 251-3. The 'materialist' view – to which Vasiliev does not commit himself – is rejected by C. Mango, *Byzantium. The Empire of New Rome*, London, 1980, p. 115.

28 Graef, op.cit., p. 146. The idea of Mary as refuge of the afflicted and the one who can mollify the Judge was also in circulation in the west, particularly among the Benedictines.

29 S. Runciman, *The Eastern Schism. A Study of the Papacy and the Eastern Churches during the XIth & XIIth centuries*, Oxford, 1955, p. 20.

30 Graef, op.cit., p. 154.
31 Ostrogorsky, op.cit., p. 175.
32 H. Lea, *A History of Auricular Confession and Indulgences in the Latin Church*, London, 1896, vol. 1, p. 127.
33 St Irene assumed full formal powers after ordering the blinding of her son, Constantine VI, on the day of the Assumption, 797.
34 At Rome Gregory IV (827–44) established the feast of All Saints.

2 THEOCRACY, THE RISE OF MARY, AND THE HOLY WAR

1 A. Luchaire, *Innocent III*, Paris; 1905.
2 S. Runciman, *A History of the Crusades*, Cambridge, 1962 (6th edition), vol. 1, p. 45.
3 H.E.J. Cowdrey, *The Cluniacs and the Gregorian Reform*, Oxford, 1970, pp. 110–11.
4 *Catholic Encyclopedia*, New York, 1907–12, vol. 9. The shrine, which Charlemagne is credited with visiting twice, is based on an apparition of the Virgin to a sick widow. Its representatives had the right to raise what amounted to a tax in several countries, including Spain.
5 S.Z. Ehler and J.B. Morral (eds), *Church and State Through the Centuries: A Collection of Historical Documents*, London, 1954.
6 According to Grignion de Montfort, Marino went through an annual public ritual of thrashing himself with a rope round his neck in front of an altar of Our Lady, on which he deposited a symbolic sum of money.
7 See H. Graef, *Mary: a History of Doctrine and Devotion*, London/New York, 1963. (2 vols.)
8 M. Bremond (ed.), *Le Puy et Ses Environs. Histoire de Notre-Dame du Puy. Notre-Dame de France*, Le Puy, 1897, p. 10.
9 M. Viller, F. Cavallera, J.de Guibert, SJ (eds), *Dictionnaire de Spiritualité*, Paris, 1957, vol. 3: 'Dévotion à l'Église et au Pape'.
10 Graef, op.cit., vol. 1, p. 248.
11 Alongside a large number of spurious relics many literary forgeries concerning the Marian question circulated in the Middle Ages, e.g. commentaries of the Pseudo-Jerome, Pseudo-Augustine and Pseudo-Bonaventura.
12 The first canonized saint was Bishop Ulrich of Augsburg (d. 973).
13 *Scapular*: a development of the ancient Agnus Dei. An amulet of two segments of cloth (a token of monastic garb) worn next to the skin. A wide range of colours – generally symbolizing Our Lady – represents different devotions and revelations. The power to bless and invest with a particular scapular belongs to a specific order, for example, the Black Scapular of the Seven Dolours of Mary was consecrated by the Servites. When worn by members of confraternities attached to the orders, scapulars carry indulgences.

14 Graef, op.cit., vol. 1, p. 278.
15 The Servite Cardinal Lépicier gives a classic definition: 'An indulgence may be defined as the remission before God of the penalty due to sin already forgiven, which ecclesiastical authority grants out of the treasury of the Church.' (A.H.M. Lépicier, OSM, *Indulgences: their Origin, Nature and Development*, London, 1928, p. 38.
16 A plenary indulgence was granted by Boniface VIII at the first jubilee in 1300.
17 In 1230 Gregory IX granted a plenary indulgence to those who settled in Mallorca, an island recently conquered by King James I of Aragon. (N. Paulus, *Indulgences as a Social Factor in the Middle Ages*, New York, 1922, p. 109).
18 The Order of Alcántara, also founded in the twelfth century to fight the Moor, was affiliated to Citeaux.
19 Instituto E. Florez/Consejo Superior de Investigaciones Científicas, *Diccionario de Historia Eclesiástica de España*, Madrid, 1973, vol. 3.
20 G. Vidal Tur, *Jaime I de Aragón y la Mariología Alicantina*, Alicante, 1978, p. 10.
21 A. Pujol, *Descenso de la Santísima Virgen a Barcelona*, Barcelona, 1934 (2nd edition), p. 17.
22 ibid.
23 *Maria* (Paris), 1952, vol. 2, p. 724. The Mercedarians were originally a military order created solely to rescue captives from the Moors; they later became another mendicant order.
24 *Diccionario de Historia Eclesiástica de España*, op.cit,. 1977, vol. 4.
25 *The Life and Revelations of St Gertrude*, London, 1876, p. 79.
26 The Presentation of the Heart (*Offrande de Coeur*), an image of courtly love probably from Carolingian times, is seen in the fifteenth-century tapestries of Burgundy, the birthplace of Alacoque (d. 1690).
27 *Revelations of St Gertrude*, op.cit., pp. 177–8.
28 W. James, *The Varieties of Religious Experience* (first published 1902), London, 1985, p. 337.
29 'Monarchisme Benedictin', *Maria*, 1952, vol. 2, pp. 563–4.
30 St Jean Eudes, *The Admirable Heart of Mary*, New York, 1948, p. 206.
31 The ten official virtues of the Virgin are chastity, prudence, humility, faith, piety, obedience, poverty, patience, charity and compassion.
32 J. Huizinga, *The Waning of the Middle Ages*, London, 1979, p. 26.
33 H. Lea, *A History of Auricular Confession and Indulgences in the Latin Church*, London, 1896, vol. 2, p. 131.
34 Pseudo Albert Magnus (Richard of St Laurent, d. after 245), says: 'in the sacrament of her Son we also eat and drink her flesh and blood' (quoted by Graef, op.cit., vol. 1, p. 267).
35 J. Guitton, *Great Heresies and Church Councils*, London, 1965, pp. 135 and 137.
36 S. Runciman, *The Medieval Manichee. A Study of the Christian Dualist Heresy*, Cambridge, 1947, p. 149.
37 The 'just war' theory was a product of thirteenth-century scholasticism.

38 The anti-heretical Militia of Jesus was set up in 1225 as an appendage to the Dominicans.

39 The Corpus Christi feast was also instituted in 1264 with an office composed by Aquinas. The Franciscans had established the feast of the Visitation of the Virgin in the previous year.

40 'Notre-Dame des Sept Douleurs', *Dictionnaire de Spiritualité*, op.cit., 1957, vol. 3.

41 R.W. Southern, *Western Society and the Church in the Middle Ages*, London, 1978, p. 142.

42 The spuriousness of this concession has been established. Not even the great Franciscan scholar Alexander Hales (d. 1245), a leading expert on indulgences, knew of a plenary granted in such circumstances (H. Lea, op.cit., vol. 3., p. 239).

43 W. Garratt (Chamberlain of the Holy House), *Loreto the New Nazareth and its Centenary Jubilee*, London, 1895, p. 83.

3 THE APOTHEOSIS OF MARY

1 I.A. Richter (ed.), *The Notebooks of Leonardo da Vinci*, Oxford, 1980, p. 248.

2 F. Braudel, *Civilization and Capitalism. 15th–18th Century*, trans. S. Reynolds, London, 1984, vol. 3, p. 117.

3 M. Weber, *The Sociology of Religion*, trans. E. Fischoff, Boston, 1964, p. 219.

4 The Franciscan William of Ockham, one of the greatest philosophers of the time, was associated with both the 'Spirituals' and the 'Imperialists'.

5 When Louis of Bavaria dethroned Pope John, he gave the title of Imperial Vicar to Marsilius of Padua, rebel theologian, scientist, physician, author of *Defensor Pacis* and imperial adviser.

6 Hegel and some Hegelians considered Eckhart a forerunner of Protestantism in his contempt for 'monkishness' and Mariolatry (J. Clark, *The Great Mystics*, Oxford, 1949, pp. 27–30).

7 The Angelus (The Hail Mary at the ringing of the bell for vespers), a Franciscan devotion, was introduced at Rome in 1327 by John XXII, who attached indulgences to the practice.

8 H. Graef, *Mary: a History of Doctrine and Devotion*, London/New York, 1963, vol. 1, p. 303.

9 Braudel notes that 'a shattering decline in economic life' followed the Black Death, op.cit., vol. 3, p. 117.

10 During the pontificate of Clement VI (1342–52) a tax system embracing the whole Church was imposed at the height of the plague that reduced the European population by one third.

11 Graef, op.cit., vol. 1, p. 306.

12 The Carmelites fabricated a document showing that the Order was

founded by Elijah and that its members were 'devoted to the Virgin 900 years before she was born' (H. Lea, *A History of Auricular Confession and Indulgences in the Latin Church*, London, 1896, vol. 3., p. 257).

13 ibid., p. 263.

14 Mary's message to Simon Stock (never formally canonized), which encapsulates the role the Church assigns to the Virgin, was broadened by a Dutch Carmelite in 1494: 'Behold the sign of salvation, safety in danger, the covenant of peace and of the sempiternal pact' (ibid.).

15 *Selected Revelations of St Bridget*, London, 1892, p. 16.

16 Quoted by A.H.M. Lépicier, *Indulgences: their origin, nature and development*, London, 1928, p. 318.

17 Graef, op.cit., vol. 1, pp. 309–10.

18 M. Viller, F. Cavallera, J. de Guibert, SJ (eds), *Dictionnaire de Spiritualité*, Paris, 1936, vol. 1.

19 ibid., 1953, vol. 2.

20 The mystical experiences of St Bridget and St Catherine were given little credence by certain authorities in the fifteenth century. At the Council of Constance, where the Bridgettine revelations were hotly debated, the chancellor of the Sorbonne, Gerson, deprecated the visions of ignorant women and at the Council of Basle the Spanish Dominican Torquemada once more assailed St Bridget's claims.

21 A. Poulain, SJ, *The Graces of Interior Prayer. A Treatise on Mystical Theology*, London, 1910, p. 345.

22 H. Lea, *A History of the Inquisition in the Middle Ages*, London, 1888, vol. 3, p. 599.

23 Frederick of Heilo, a friend of Thomas à Kempis (who doubted the spiritual value of pilgrimages) wrote a polemic entitled *Contra peregrinantes* (J. Huizinga, *The Waning of the Middle Ages*, London, 1979, p. 156).

24 H. Bettenson, *Documents of the Christian Church*, Oxford, 1943, p. 246.

25 A.G. Dickens, *Lollards and Protestants in the Diocese of York*, London, 1959, p. 75.

26 Graef, op.cit., vol. 1, pp. 313-14.

27 W. Garratt (Chamberlain of the Holy House), *Loreto the New Nazareth and its Centenary Jubilee*, London, 1895, p. 51.

28 The orders gravitating to Mary's images and altars were great beneficiaries of the system of indulgences.

29 John of Wesel was imprisoned as a heretic for deprecating the jubilee indulgence in 1475. Around this time in Franconia the theologian John Burkhardt (admired by Luther) denied the value of sacerdotal celibacy, 'a superstitious observance' (H. Lea, *An Historical Sketch of Sacerdotal Celibacy in the Christian Church*, Philadelphia, 1867, pp. 399–400).

30 P. Pourrat, *Christian Spirituality. The Devotions of the Middle Ages*, London, 1924, vol. 2, p. 330.

31 See M. Warner, *Alone of All Her Sex. The Myth and the Cult of the Virgin Mary*, London, 1976, chapter 20: 'Visions, the Rosary and War'.

32 Graef, op.cit., vol. 1, p. 318.

33 ibid., vol. 1, pp. 320–1.

34 Lépicier, op.cit., pp. 440–1.

35 See Instituto E. Florez/Consejo Superior de Investigaciones Científicas, *Diccionario de Historia Eclesiástica de España*, Madrid, 1975, vol. 4.

36 G. Townsend (ed.), *The Acts and Monuments of John Foxe*, New York,
1965, vol. 4, p. 172. The martyrologist affirms, 'nothing else almost
was taught or heard in the church, but only the commendation and
exaltation of the Virgin Mary' (ibid.).

37 *Encyclopedia of World Art*, New York, 1959, vol. 8, p. 408.

38 'The Republics of Sienna and Perugia went to war for the possession
of the marriage ring of the Blessed Virgin' (L. von Pastor, *The History of
the Popes from the Close of the Middle Ages*, London, 1950, vol. 5, p. 93).

39 Rev. G.E. Phillips, *Loreto and the Holy House. Its History Drawn from
Authentic Sources*, London, 1917, p. 96.

40 L. Ranke, *The History of the Popes, their Church and State, and Especially
of their Conflicts with Protestantism in the Sixteenth and Seventeenth Centuries*,
London, 1847, vol. 1, p. 306.

41 Phillips, op.cit., pp. 98–9.

42 Garratt, op.cit., p. 54.

43 Ranke, op.cit., vol. 1, p. 308.

44 Erasmus found sympathy with Emperor Charles V and had the
support of Adrian VI of Utrecht (1522–3), a pope whose attempts to
reform the curia made him very unpopular.

45 A. Gemelli, *The Franciscan Message to the World*, London, 1934, p. 120.

46 *Peace Protests! or Querela Pacis*, trans. J. Chapiro, Boston, 1950, p. 175.

47 ibid., p. 160.

48 Graef, op.cit., vol. 2, pp. 12–13 (London, 1965).

49 R.H. Tawney, *Religion and the Rise of Capitalism*, London, 1987, p. 119.

50 ibid., p. 101.

51 Gemelli, op.cit., pp. 121-2. At that time (April 1520) an effigy of the
Immaculate Conception in Valencia wept two tears of blood, an event
commemorated until modern times. (G. Vidal Tur, *Jaime I de Aragon y
la Mariología Alicantina*, Alicante, 1978, pp. 41–4).

52 The Brown Scapular is endowed with the promise that Mary will visit
its wearers in purgatory the first Saturday after their death and free
them. This privilege, shared today with recently founded divisions,
has been confirmed by several popes, including Pius XI (1922–39).

53 Phillips, op.cit., pp. 64–5. Clement VII fortified Ancona and imposed
a heavy tribute on the city.

54 A. Castro, *Aspectos del Vivir Hispánico*, Santiago (Chile), 1949, pp. 107–8.

55 ibid.

56 *Estudios Marianos*, 1973, vol. 37, p. 16.

57 *Diccionario de Historia Eclesiástica de España*, 1975, vol. 4.

58 See F.A. Yates, *Giordano Bruno and the Hermetic Tradition*, London,
1964, pp. 113–16.

59 Founded by St Francis of Paola (d. 1507) and known in Spain as the
Victorious Friars.

60 Our Lady of Candelaria, of apparitional origin, was canonically

crowned in 1889, a time when the papacy and *Hispanidad* were exalting the Queenship of Mary.

61   *Diccionario de Historia Eclesiástica de España*, 1972, vol. 1.
62   J.E. Longhurst, *Erasmus and the Spanish Inquisition: the Case of Juan de Valdés*, New Mexico, 1950, pp. 91-2.
63   Valdes, who made the first Spanish translation of the New Testament from the Greek, fled to Naples.
64   The primate of Spain, Alfonso de Fonseca, was unable to defend his secretary, the Hellenist and Erasmian Juan de Vergara, who was tried and eventually imprisoned for years by the Holy Office (see Longhurst, op.cit.).
65   M. Cuevas, SJ, *Historia de la Iglesia en México*, Mexico City, 1928, vol. 1, pp. 220–2.
66   F. Braudel, *The Mediterranean and the Mediterranean World in the Age of Philip II*, trans. S. Reynolds, London, 1982, vol. 2, p. 824.
67   F. Braudel, *Civilization and Capitalism*, op.cit., vol. 3, p. 394.
68   C. Bayle, SJ, *Expansión Misional de España*, Barcelona, 1936, p. 69.

4 IGNATIAN SPIRITUALITY AND COUNTER-REFORMATION

1   L.J. Puhl, SJ (trans.), *The Spiritual Exercises of St Ignatius Based on Studies in the Language of the Autograph*, Loyola University Press, Chicago, 1951, p. 157.
2   F. Braudel, *The Mediterranean and the Mediterranean World in the Age of Philip II*, trans. S. Reynolds, London, 1982, vol. 2, p. 938.
3   The primate of Spain, the Dominican Bartolome Carranza, spent the last seventeen years of his life in the Holy Office's dungeons on suspicion of Lutheranism.
4   See F.A. Yates, *Giordano Bruno and the Hermetic Tradition*, London, 1964.
5   Fr Maldonado, SJ, a great Spanish apologist of the Immaculate Conception, was also an expert demonologist.
6   W.V. Bangert, SJ, *A History of the Society of Jesus*, St Louis, 1972, pp. 6–7.
7   Puhl, op.cit., p. 132.
8   See H. Graef, *Mary: a History of Doctrine and Devotion*, London/New York, 1965, vol. 2.
9   *Estudios Marianos*, 1963, vol. 24, p. 231.
10   Graef, op.cit., vol. 2, pp. 29–30.
11   J.V. Bainvel, SJ, *Devotion to the Sacred Heart of Jesus. The Doctrine and its History*, London, 1924, p. 190.
12   Braudel, op.cit., vol. 2, p. 832.
13   The crib has its origin in a vision to St Cajetan (d. 1547), co-founder of the Theatines with G.P. Carafa, the future Paul IV.
14   The *Pia Opera dell'Incoronazione* became an important part of the

Capuchin Order by the beginning of the seventeenth century.

15 Jesuit plays were to be seen in the 1550s from Córdoba and Messina to Ingoldstadt.

16 Barcelona, 1665. See *Biblioteca de Jesuitas Españoles*, Madrid, 1904.

17 Seville, 1653, ibid.

18 Bangert, op.cit., pp. 315–16. The author of *Theatrum Asceticum* (1745), F. Neumayr, was also a preacher and sodality moderator.

19 M. Warner, *Alone of All Her Sex. The Myth and the Cult of the Virgin Mary*, London, 1976, p. 301.

20 Santa Teresa de Jesús, *Castillo Interior o las Moradas*, Barcelona, 1944, p. 227.

21 Francisco Borgia, Duke of Gandia and viceroy of Catalonia, and Princess Juana, sister of Philip II and regent in 1554–9, were secret members of the Compañía in its initial stages in Spain. The Duke was general of the Society in 1565–72.

22 The shrine was in Jesuit hands until the Society's dissolution in the late eighteenth century.

23 St Peter Canisius devoted a chapter in his first Mariological work (1577) to the defence of the sacred image against the blasphemous Calvinist author of *De Idolo Laurentano*. The title recalls *De Miraculis Virginis Laurentanae*, written two years earlier by a Jesuit of Loreto, Fr Riera.

24 Rev. G.E. Phillips, *Loreto and the Holy House. Its History Drawn from Authentic Sources*, London, 1917.

25 O. Torsellino, SJ, *The History of Our Blessed Lady* (reproduction of English recusant literature, 1608), London, 1976, p. 285.

26 ibid., p. 259.

27 Philipps, op.cit., pp. 108–9.

28 ibid.

29 A former Franciscan general and reformer, Sixtus V dedicated his first million silver scudi (deposited in the castle of St Angelo) to 'the Holy Virgin, the Mother of God and to the holy Apostles Peter and Paul' (L. Ranke, *The History of the Popes, their Church and State, and Especially of their Conflicts with Protestantism in the Sixteenth and Seventeenth Centuries*, London, 1847, vol. 1, p. 352).

30 W. Garratt (Chamberlain of the Holy House), *Loreto the New Nazareth and its Centenary Jubilee*, London, 1895, p. 61. As custodians of the House of Nazareth, the Jesuits produced quantities of apologetical and devotional works on the Holy Family, speculating even on the Seven Sorrows and Joys of St Joseph. Some of these writings exercised a lasting influence, like *De la Imitación de Nuestra Señora* by F. Arias, published at Valencia in 1588 and translated into many languages down the centuries.

31 Gregory XIII's bull of canonical erection of the Sodality of Our Lady, *Omnipotentis Dei*, 5 December 1584. The Sodality of the Annunciation is acknowledged here as the primary unit to which all other sodalities must be aggregated.

32 E. Mullan, SJ, *The Sodality of Our Lady Studied in the Documents*, London, 1912, p. 159. For the influence and social composition of Our Lady's

Sodality in Catholic Germany, see the interesting study by R. Po-Chia Hsia, *Society and Religion in Münster, 1535–1618*, Yale, 1984.
33 Mullan, op.cit., p. 100.
34 ibid., pp. 3–4.
35 *Maria* (Paris), 1952, vol. 2, p. 965.
36 Mullan, op.cit., p. 109.
37 M. García, 'La actitud de entrega o donación personal a María', *Estudios Marianos*, 1973, vol. 37.
38 St John Berchmans, SJ (d. 1621), was one of the first to sign the vow in his own blood before the Blessed Sacrament.
39 An outstanding apostle of the 'slavish' devotion was the Spanish Augustinian Bartolome de los Ríos, founder of the Ave Maria Slaves (Brussels, 1625), a confraternity formed round the miraculous image of Our Lady of Good Success.
40 The Company of Mary (or Order of Notre-Dame) and Order of St Ursula of the Blessed Virgin, for example, were established with Jesuit help. The spiritual direction of the Visitation Order – founded by the sodalist St Francis de Sales – was soon taken over by the Society.
41 See M.C. Jacob, *The Radical Enlightenment: Pantheists, Freemasons and Republicans*, London, 1981.

5 SPANISH POWER AND MARIAN COLONIZATION

1 J. de Aranaz, *El Cetro de la Fe Ortodoxa, María Santíssima en su Templo Angélico y Apostólico del Pilar*, Saragossa, 1723.
2 The Edict of Nantes (1598) gave the Calvinists only a limited recovery from the Massacre of St Bartholomew (1572) and the Counter-Reformation advance.
3 F. Braudel, *Civilization and Capitalism. 15th-18th Century*, trans. S. Reynolds, London, 1984, vol. 3, p. 414.
4 J. Miley, *The History of the Papal States from their Origin to the Present Day*, London, 1850, vol. 3, p. 488.
5 M.A. de Bunes, *Los Moriscos en el Pensamiento Histórico*, Madrid, 1983.
6 L. Cardaillac, *La Polémique antichrétienne des morisques ou l'opposition de deux communautés*: 1492–1640, Montpellier, 1973.
7 See the Koran, chapter 19: 'Maryam'. For the position of Mary in Islam's hierarchy of holy women, see R.J. McCarthy, SJ, 'Mary in Islam', in A. Stacpoole (ed.), *Mary's Place in Christian Dialogue*, London, 1982.
8 See C. Bayle, SJ, *Santa María en Indias. Devoción a Nuestra Señora de los Descubridores, Conquistadores y Pobladores de América*, Madrid, 1929; R. Vargas, SJ, *Historia del Culto de María en Ibero América y sus Imágenes y Santuarios Mas Celebrados*, Madrid, 1956.
9 Vargas, op.cit., vol. 1, pp. 71–3.
10 E. Mullan, SJ, *The Sodality of Our Lady Studied in the Documents*, London,

1912, p. 158.

11 In 1582 the Council of Lima made the Salve Regina compulsory on Saturdays in all churches; in 1585 the Mexican Provincial Council made the feast of the Immaculate Conception compulsory.

12 *Historia General de las Cosas de Nueva España*, quoted by J. Lafaye, *Quetzalcóatl and Guadalupe, the Formation of Mexican National Consciousness 1531–1813*, trans. B. Keen, Chicago, 1976, p. 217.

13 On the connection between Guadalupe and the mother goddess Tonantzin, and on St Thomas-Quetzalcóatl, see Lafaye, op.cit.

14 For the development of the cult of Our Lady of the Pillar in Spain (not dealt with by Lafaye), see chs 22, 28, 29, and 30.

15 Braudel, op.cit., vol. 3, p. 395.

16 Vargas, op.cit., vol. 1, p. 288.

17 S. Clissold, *The Saints of South America*, London, 1972, p. 90.

18 F.W. Faber, *The Saints and Servants of God*, London, 1847, p. 151.

19 Clissold, op.cit., p. 136. The Lily had a 'wardrobe of hair-shirts' and 'a whole armoury of scourges' (ibid., p. 126).

20 I. Vásquez, OFM, *Las Negociaciones Inmaculistas en la Curia Romana durante el Reinado de Carlos II de España*, Madrid, 1957; I. Iparraguirre, SJ, 'Pareceres encontrados sobre la definibilidad de la Inmaculada en el siglo 17' *Estudios Eclesiásticos* (revista trimestral de la Compañía de Jesús en España), 1954, vol. 28, no. 110–11.

21 Bunes, op.cit.

22 H. Lea, *A History of the Inquisition in Spain*, New York, 1906, vol. 4, p. 359.

23 A. Astrain, *Historia de la Compañía de Jesús en la Asistencia de España*, Madrid, 1916, p. 131.

24 *De Inmaculata B.V. Dei Genitricis Mariae Conceptione*, Seville, 1617, quoted in *Estudios Marianos*, 1984, vol. 49, p. 206.

25 Most 'Slaves' were organized in large confraternities like the one founded at Valladolid in 1610 by Antonio Alvarado, a Benedictine whose body has remained incorrupt.

26 *Estudos Marianos*, 1964, vol. 25, pp. 186–7. There seems to be an arcane link between the Marian cult and bullfighting, which could perhaps explain Pius V's attempts to ban the sport. One of the first bullrings in Spain is located within the shrine of Our Lady of Virtues.

27 Astrain, op.cit., p. 135.

28 See I. Bengochea, 'Vidas de la Virgen María en la España del siglo 17', *Estudios Marianos*, 1984, vol. 49.

29 T.D. Kendrick, *Mary of Agreda: the Life and Legend of a Spanish Nun*, London, 1967, pp. 85–6.

30 A Franciscan superior's view of Mary as a mature woman (ibid., pp. 4–5).

31 J. de Oliveira Dias, SJ, 'Notre-Dame dans la Piété Populaire Portugaise', *Maria* (Paris), 1958, vol. 4.

32 In 1670 the revelations were published in Madrid by the Franciscans as *The Mystical City of God*.

33 During the seventeenth century the number of religious and clerics

doubled while the population shrank by a third. By 1660 there were some 200,000 clerics in Spain.

34 In 1619 Saragossa vowed at the feet of the Virgin of the Pillar to defend the Immaculate Conception and in 1640 resolved to commemorate annually Mary's journey to Spain. Two years later la Pilar was proclaimed patroness of the city.

35 Aranaz, op.cit.

36 Rev. J.S. Stone, *The Cult of Santiago: Traditions, Myths and Pilgrimages. A Sympathetic Study*, London, 1927, p. 93.

37 See C. Hill, *Intellectual Origins of the English Revolution*, Oxford, 1965, chapter 2: 'London Science and Medicine'.

6 THE GRAND SIÈCLE

1 *The Admirable Heart of Mary*, New York, 1948, p. 115.

2 'For the young male, continence is impossible' wrote the unfortunate Parson Grandier in his secret treatise on sacerdotal celibacy. Accused of witchcraft and indecency by the 'possessed' Ursulines, he was burned alive in 1634. See A. Huxley, *The Devils of Loudun*, London, 1952. For the persistence of concubinage and adultery among priests, see J. Lea, *An Historical Sketch of Sacerdotal Celibacy*, Philadelphia, 1867.

3 H. Bremond, *A Literary History of Religious Thought in France*, London, 1928–36, vol. 3, p. 154.

4 L. Blond, *Notre-Dame des Victoires et le Voeu de Louis XIII*, Paris, 1938.

5 M. Vloberg, 'Le voeu de Louis XIII', *Maria* (Paris), 1958, vol. 5. We have not been able to consult G. de Paris, OMC, *Les Bénédictines du Calvaire, le P. Joseph du Tremblay et le Voeu de Louis XIII*, Paris, 1938.

6 H. Graef, *Mary: a History of Doctrine and Devotion*, London, 1965, vol. 2, p. 39.

7 L-M. Grignion de Montfort, *A Treatise on the True Devotion to the Blessed Virgin*, trans. F.W. Faber, London, 1863, p. 117.

8 P. Pourrat, *Christian Spirituality*, London, 1927, vol. 3, p. 370.

9 R.J. Gleeson, OMI, *Devotion to the Immaculate Heart of Mary*, Dublin, 1936, p. 4.

10 C. Flachaire, *La Dévotion à la Vierge dans la Littérature Catholique au commencement du XVIIᵉ siècle*, Paris, 1916.

11 *The Admirable Heart of Mary*, op.cit., pp. 10–11.

12 ibid., p. 40.

13 P. Herambourg, *Saint John Eudes, a Spiritual Portrait*, Dublin, 1960.

14 We should recall, however, that the heart was such a powerful fetish that a secularized version of the cult arose during the Revolution. After Marat's assassination revolutionaries erected 'an altar to the heart of Marat the Incorruptible'. (A. Soboul in S. Wilson (ed.), *Saints and Their Cults. Studies in Religious Sociology, Folklore and History*, Cambridge, 1985, pp. 221–2.

15 J. Carroll Cruz, *The Incorruptibles: A Study of the Incorruption of the Bodies of Various Catholic Saints and Beati*, Rockford, Il., 1977.
16 ibid.
17 See F.A. Yates, *The Rosicrucian Enlightenment*, London, 1972.
18 M. Viller, F. Cavallera, J. de Guibert, SJ, (eds), *Dictionnaire de Spiritualité*, Paris, 1953, vol. 2: 'Congrégations secrètes'.
19 ibid.
20 ibid.
21 By this time Freemasonry was already in existence in England. The first recorded Masonic initiation was in 1641. See Yates, op.cit.
22 Count H. Bégouen, introduction to A. Auguste, *La Compagnie du Saint-Sacrement à Toulouse. Notes et Documents*, Paris, 1913, p. 4.
23 R. Allier, *La Cabale des Dévots 1627–1666*, Paris, 1902. Olier himself founded a secret society, la Compagnie de la Passion.
24 Doubtless the AA of the College of Clermont (founded c. 1643) had some connection with the infallibility thesis produced there a few years later.
25 In his *Traité des Abus de la Critique en Matière de Religion* (Paris, 1710) De Laubrussel denounced 'la raison géométrique' as the kernel of the Jansenist spirit. See P. Huffer, *La Dévotion à Marie au Déclin du XVIIᵉ siècle*, Paris, 1938, p. 59.
26 Letter 9 is particularly germane to our subject. The erudite Jesuit Théophile Raymund had just published his *Scapulare Partheno-Carmeliticum* (Lyons, 1653), a famous apology of the magic garment then under attack.
27 *The Secret Policy of the Jansenists and the Present State of the Sorbon, Discovered by a Doctor of That Faculty*, London, 1667.
28 *New Catholic Encyclopedia*, New York, 1967–79.
29 A. Huxley, *Grey Eminence, a Study in Religion and Politics*, London 1944.
30 M. Molinos, *Guía Espiritual*, 1675. Translated into English in 1688, this work was greatly appreciated among Quakers and other Non-conformists.
31 L. von Pastor, *The History of the Popes*, London, 1957, vol. 23, p. 444.
32 J.V. Bainvel, SJ, *Devotion to the Sacred Heart of Jesus. The Doctrine and its History*, London, 1924, p. 343.
33 The devotion was chiefly one of gesture: 'To look lovingly at the medal of the Heart of Jesus and Mary, kiss the crucifix. . . .' See *Historia de los Ejercicios de S. Ignacio, Evolución en Europa durante el Siglo 17*, Bibliotheca Instituti Historici Soc. Iesu, Rome, 1973, vol. 36.
34 D. Van Kley, *The Jansenists and the Expulsion of the Jesuits from France: 1757–1765*, New Haven/London, 1975, p. 36.
35 H. Daniel-Rops, *The Church in the Eighteenth Century*, London, 1964, p. 29.
36 For example, Our Lady of Kevelaer appeared to a pedlar in 1642, giving birth to yet another popular shrine.
37 *The Pope's Bull, condemning the New Testament, with Moral Reflections; Done by Father Quesnel, the Present Luther of France*, London, 1714, proposition 60.

38 ibid., propositions 79–85.
39 ibid., proposition 84.
40 Adam Widenfelt, *Wholesome Advices from the Blessed Virgin to her Indiscreet Worshippers*, London, 1687.
41 ibid., p. 1.
42 ibid., pp. 1–2.
43 *Maria* (Paris), 1956, vol. 4, p. 486.
44 For all its importance, Paray-le-Monial was not the only stage chosen by the Sacred Heart. Visions and 'exchange of hearts' were experienced by a score of nuns in seventeenth-century France (see Bainvel, op.cit.). An interesting case was that of Jeanne Perraud (d. 1676) of the Third Order of St Augustine, who had a vision very similar to Alacoque's. She also understood that the devotion 'would be the most complete refutation of Jansenism' (H. Bremond, op.cit., vol. 3, p. 495).
45 G. Tickell, SJ, *The Life of Blessed Margaret Mary*, London, 1869, p. 104.
46 ibid., p. 135.
47 ibid., p. 173.
48 L. Verheylezoon, SJ, *Devotion to the Sacred Heart*, London, 1955, p. xxvi.
49 Tickell, op.cit., p. 143. By emphasizing adoration of the host, Christ was effectively contradicting Arnauld's treatise *De la Fréquente Communion* (1643).
50 Verheylezoon, op.cit., p. xxvii.
51 See C. Oman, *Mary of Modena*, London, 1962.
52 Verheylezoon, op.cit., pp. 200–1.
53 ibid., p. xxv.
54 Fr Croiset, another Jesuit and a close collaborator of the visionary, imagined the Heart of Mary as a sort of filter: the Heart of Jesus 'admits only extremely pure souls' while 'the Heart of Mary purifies' (Verheylezoon, op.cit., p. 256).
55 But while the Spanish mystic languished in a Roman dungeon, the Jansenists in Brussels – so it is said – laid a chain of secret societies all over Europe.
56 Bainvel, op.cit., p. 31.
57 ibid., p. 27.
58 ibid., pp. 24–5.
59 ibid., p. 295.
60 González did not receive support for his assault on probabilism, which he considered the source of moral laxity. His *Short Treatise on the Correct Use of Probable Opinions* was printed secretly in 1691 and Innocent XII (1691–1700) confiscated the entire edition. See W.V. Bangert, SJ, *A History of the Society of Jesus*, St Louis, 1972, pp. 274–9.
61 M. Jacob, *The Radical Enlightenment: Pantheists, Freemasons and Republicans*, London, 1981, p. 144.
62 *De Ingeniorum Moderatione in Religionibus Negotio*, 1714.
63 English edition, Dublin, 1789, p. 207.
64 ibid., pp. 210–12.
65 Jacob, op.cit., pp. 150–1.

66   The first public act of raparation and consecration to the Sacred Heart took place during the Marseilles plague in 1720.
67   'A secular priest', *Blessed Louis-Marie Grignion de Montfort and His Devotion*, London, 1892, vol. 1, p. 55.
68   The candidate for consecration to Christ 'by the hands of Mary' states: 'I praise and glorify Thee for that Thou hast been pleased to submit Thyself to Mary, Thy Holy Mother, in all things, in order to make me Thy faithful slave through her' (*A Treatise on the True Devotion to the Blessed Virgin*, trans. F.W. Faber, London, 1863, pp. 190–1).
69   'Secular priest', op.cit., p. 414.
70   The *Panoplia Mariana* (1720) by the Dominican J.B. van Ketwigh also preached devotion to Mary as a prerequisite of salvation and 'a sign of eternal predestination' (Graef, op.cit., vol. 2, pp. 68–70); and Théophilus Raymund, SJ, called the scapular of Our Lady 'a sign of predestination' (H. Lea, *A History of Auricular Confession and Indulgences in the Latin Church*, London, 1896, vol. 3, p. 267).
71   Having collapsed in the pulpit one day, he was found to be wearing against his chest 'a very sharp rasp in the shape of a heart' ('Secular priest', op.cit., p. 258).
72   ibid., p. 255.
73   *Treatise on the True Devotion to the Blessed Virgin*, London, 1962; p. 16.
74   ibid., pp. 12–13.
75   ibid., p. 17.
76   ibid., p. 21.
77   ibid., pp. 190–4. 'Jesus is wholly in Mary and Mary is wholly in Jesus . . . it would be easier to separate the light from the Sun than to separate Mary from Jesus' (ibid., p. 180).
78   A manuscript of *The True Devotion* was unearthed and identified as from the hand of Montfort in 1842.
79   J.M. Hupperts, 'S. Louis-Marie de Montfort et sa spiritualité mariale', *Maria*, 1954, vol. 3, p. 258.
80   P. Hebblethwaite, 'The Mariology of three popes', *The Way Supplement*, 1984, no. 51.

7 MARIAN CRISIS AND JESUIT COLLAPSE

1   T. Besterman (ed. & trans.), *Philosophical Dictionary* (first published 1764), London, 1979, p. 386.
2   M. Jacob, *The Radical Enlightenment: Pantheists, Freemasons and Republicans*, London, 1981, p. 241.
3   Jacob, op.cit.
4   The Sacred Heart's promise – 'I shall reign in Spain' – to Fr Hoyos, SJ, at Valladolid marked the inception of the cult in Iberia.
5   *Estudios Marianos*, 1945, vol. 4, pp. 455–6.

6   D. Van Kley, *The Jansenists and the Expulsion of the Jesuits from France: 1757–1765*, New Haven/London, 1975, p. 225.

7   Salamanca University, under Jesuit control, rejected a department of mathematics in 1761 as being a subject 'fraught with dishonour' (D. Mitchell, *The Jesuits*, London, 1980, p. 174).

8   Liguori's opuscule on infallibility (1745) has been lost but his two long dogmatic treatises on the Immaculate Conception and papal infallibility, which were inserted in his *Moral Theology* (first edition, 1748), enjoyed wide circulation.

9   A. Berthe, *Life of St Alphonsus de Liguori: Bishop and Doctor of the Church, Founder of the Congregation of the Most Holy Redeemer*, Dublin/London, 1906, vol 1, p. 387.

10 ibid., pp. 285 and 520. 'Alphonsus used to wear painful cilices, take the discipline to blood and use every possible device to afflict his body' (ibid., p. 54).

11 The injuries he inflicted on himself did not dispel his horror of death. 'When these fears torment me my only refuge is to cling to the Madonna' (ibid., pp. 668–9).

12 F. Braudel, *Civilization and Capitalism. 15th-18th Century*, trans. S. Reynolds, London, 1982, vol. 2, p. 293.

13 H. Lea, *A History of Auricular Confession and Indulgences in the Latin Church*, London, 1896, vol. 2, pp. 366–7.

14 Sister Maria Celeste Crostarosa (whose body has remained incorrupt) received divine communications in 1725 and 1731 concerning the rule, habit, spirit and founder of the new congregation. See Berthe, op.cit., vol. 1, pp. 65 and 82–3.

15 Rev. R.A. Coffin (ed.), *The Glories of Mary*, London, 1868, p. 116.

16 ibid., pp. 381–2.

17 Liguori lists a number of papal concessions to those who recite the Litany of Loreto, kiss the habit of a religious, etc. ibid., pp. 524–6.

18 When 'temptations against purity' assail us, it is useful, says Liguori, to kiss or press to our heart the rosary or scapular, or to look at an image of the Blessed Virgin (ibid., pp. 523–4).

19 ibid., p. 521.

20 ibid.

21 A few years before Maria Celeste's visions, St Paul of the Cross (d. 1775) saw Our Lady of Dolours clothed in black and with a heart on her tunic, an emblem later adopted by the Passionists, which he founded.

22 This wonder took place at Foggia (1732 and 1745), St Giorgio in Salerno (1738) and Amalfi (1756), a 'pagan city' lost to 'the unbridled love of pleasure' (Berthe, op.cit., vol. 1, p. 519).

23 ibid., p. 280.

24 In March 1746 St Alphonsus made a will naming Mary as 'universal heir' (ibid., p. 284).

25 Braudel, op.cit., p. 264.

26 Official lodges were established in France (1721) and Spain (1728). In Lisbon and Rome Freemasonry was introduced in 1735. The first

of many papal condemnations followed three years later.

27 Freemasonry in Spain, however, had a rather sporadic existence in the eighteenth century. See J. Ferrer, *La Masonería Española in el Siglo XVIII*, Madrid, 1974; *Masonería, Iglesia, Ilustración*, Madrid, 1976–77 (4 vols); *El Conde de Aranda: Mito y Realidad de un Político Aragonés*, Saragossa, 1978 (2 vols).

28 See Jacob, op.cit.

29 See J. Ferrer, *Los Archivos Secretos Vaticanos y la Masonería*, Caracas, 1976.

30 Ferrer, *La Masonería Española*, op.cit., pp. 116–17. St Leonard, a specialist in penitents' processions and stations of the cross, founded the Congregation of Lovers of Jesus and Mary and many confraternities, including the Archconfraternity of the Sacred Heart in Rome, which had 1,700 subordinate affiliates in 1743.

31 *Della regolata devozioni dei Cristiani*.

32 *Invincible Marian Wall against the Blows of a Muratorian in Disguise* by the Franciscan Domingo de S. Pedro de Alcantara was published in 1747.

33 *The Glories of Mary*, op.cit., p. 520.

34 Ferrer, *El Conde de Aranda*, op.cit., vol. 1, p. 160.

35 See A. Weld, SJ, *The Suppression of the Society of Jesus in the Portuguese Dominions*, London, 1877.

36 R. Laurentin, *Maria* (Paris), 1954, vol. 3, p. 15.

37 W.V. Bangert, SJ, *A History of the Society of Jesus*, St. Louis, 1972, p. 302.

38 N. von Hontheim, auxiliary bishop of Trier, published in 1763 under the pseudonym Justinus Febronius *Constitution of the Church and the Legitimate Power of the Roman Pontiff*. This work, swiftly translated into major languages and circulated widely, denied the legitimacy of papal claims on historical grounds and called for the return of episcopal authority and frequent general councils.

39 *Christianae Reipublicae* ('On the dangers of anti-Christian writings'), 25 November 1766.

40 In *The Truth of Faith* (1767) St Alphonsus states that the pope's judgement is infallible in all questions concerning faith or morals, a claim repeated in his *Anti-Febronius* (1768).

41 Berthe, op.cit., vol. 1, p. 436.

42 *Inscrutabile* ('on the problems of the pontificate'), 25 December, 1775.

43 Even in Spain there was an attempt to curb certain aspects of the cult. A decree of 1773 dissolved the confraternities of Nuestra Señora de la Cabeza and banned pilgrimages to the shrine, but Carlos III was forced to withdraw these measures the following year.

44 Pius VI's secretary of state, Cardinal Pallavicini, protested, 'If priests can marry, the papal hierarchy falls, the pope loses respect and supremacy . . .' (O. Chadwick, *The Popes and the European Revolution*, London, 1981, p. 439).

45 C.A. Bolton, *Church Reform in Eighteenth-Century Italy. The Synod of Pistoia, 1786*, The Hague, 1969, p. 40.

46 ibid., pp. 50–1.

47 ibid., pp. 55.

48 ibid., p. 104.

8 MARIAN RESISTANCE IN THE REVOLUTION AND FIRST EMPIRE

1 *Maria*, Paris, 1954, vol. 3, p. 325.

2 H. Daniel-Rops, *The Church in the Eighteenth Century*, London, 1964, p. 297.

3 J.V. Bainvel, SJ, *Devotion to the Sacred Heart of Jesus. The Doctrine and Its History*, London, 1924, pp. 320–1. Ferdinand VII of Spain and his family also made a vow to the Sacred Heart during their exile.

4 H.L. Hughes, *The Catholic Revival in Italy, 1815–1915*, London, 1935, p. 125.

5 M. Agulhon, *Pénitents et Francs-Macons de l'ancienne Provence. Essai sur la Sociabilité Méridionale*, Paris, 1968.

6 The Santa Casa was seized by Napoleon in 1797 and the image sent to Paris to be displayed among 'bizzare monuments of superstition' in the Bibliothèque Nationale. It was returned eventually on the insistent requests of Pius VII.

7 J. Burnichon, SJ, *La Compagnie de Jésus en France. Histoire d'un Siècle 1814–1914*, Paris, 1914, vol. 1, p. 119.

8 Fr A.M. Windisch, *The Marianist Social System According to the Writings of William Joseph Chaminade* (doctoral thesis), Fribourg, 1964, p. 3.

9 At least seven provincial Congrégations were formed in Delpuits' lifetime: those of Lyons, Bordeaux, Langres, Toulouse, Grenoble, Nantes and Rennes.

10 De Maistre represented the King of Sardinia at St Petersburg in 1803. An ex-pupil of the Jesuits and former Mason, he once proposed that Freemasonry be used to achieve Christian unity under Rome.

11 *Hell Opened to Christians*, a seventeenth-century book by the Jesuit Pinamonti, was reprinted in 1807 with vivid illustrations.

12 Liguori's *Visits to the Most Blessed Sacrament and the Blessed Virgin Mary* (1745) was reprinted in hundreds of editions, popularizing worship of Mary through the host exposed.

13 A. Rayez, SJ, 'Dévotion et mystique mariales du Père de Clorivière', *Maria*, 1954, vol. 3, p. 319.

14 The Redemptorists in Poland, and the Paccanarists universally, were disbanded in 1808.

15 The three basic grades were Associate of Charity, Squire and Knight Hospitaller. The unit corresponding to a lodge was the 'banner'. Each of the nine members of the supreme body commanded a military division.

PART II THE SIÈCLE DE MARIE

9 OVERVIEW

1 Quoted by a religious of the mother-house of the Sisters of Charity, *Bernadette of Lourdes* (*La Confidente de l'Immaculée*) Nevers, 1926, pp. 183–4.

2 E. Lafond, *La Salette, Lourdes, Pontmain: voyage d'un croyant*, Paris, 1872, p. viii.

3 J. Bowring, *Observations on the State of Religion and Literature in Spain made during a Journey through the Peninsula in 1819*, London, 1819, pp. 7–9.

4 E. Berenson, *Populist Religion and Left-wing Politics in France, 1830–52*, Princeton, 1984, p. 72. However, Berenson ignores the Marian cult.

5 In 1789 Rome appointed a former Jesuit as archbishop of Baltimore (Maryland), the first diocese in the newly independent United States.

6 The first North American vision of Mary took place in 1840, inspiring the foundation of St Mary's, a town in Ohio.

7 For example, the Missionaries of La Salette (arrived Connecticut, 1892), Marist Fathers (after 1854), Oblates of Mary Immaculate (Oregon, 1847), Sisters of the Holy Humility of Mary (Ohio, 1864).

8 The Jesuits, for example, numbered 1,344 in 1900, with 6,920 students enrolled in their schools.

9 A. Lépicier, *Indulgences: their Origin, Nature and Development*, London, 1895, p. 340.

10 At the 1910 International Eucharistic Congress (Montreal) Mgr A. Lépicier read a pioneering paper: *Relations de la Très Sainte Vierge avec le Très Saint Sacrament*.

11 In 1876 Rome condemned the belief that Mary was conceived without the involvement of Joachim.

12 T. Cranny, SA, *Father Paul: Apostle of Unity*, New York, 1965, p. 92. This title was adopted by a group of Episcopalian Brothers in New York led by Fr Paul Wattson. At the turn of the century, after Mary had appeared three times to them, the community defected to Rome as Franciscan Friars of the Atonement.

13 E. Mullan, SJ, *The Sodality of Our Lady Studied in the Documents*, London, 1912, p. 70.

14 *New Catholic Encyclopedia*, New York, 1967–79.

15 ibid. See G. Lee, *The Life of the Venerable F. Libermann, a Pioneer of the African Missions* (first published 1911), London, 1937.

16 Under Libermann's rule, the Society merged in 1848 with the eighteenth-century Congregation of the Holy Ghost to form the 'Congregation of the Holy Ghost under the Protection of the Immaculate Heart of Mary'.

17 Rev. E.J. Robinson, *The Mother of Jesus Not the Papal Mary*, Wesleyan Conference Office, London, 1875, p. 389.

18   E. Bergh, SJ, 'Les congrégations féminines des XIXe et XXe siècles', *Maria*, 1954, vol. 5.

10 RESTORATION AND THE MYSTICISM OF AUTHORITY

1   J. Burnichon, SJ, *La Compagnie de Jésus en France. Histoire d'un Siècle: 1814–1914*, Paris, 1914, vol. 1, p. 2.
2   G. Flaubert, *Madame Bovary* (first published 1857), trans. A. Russell, London, 1984, p. 48.
3   C.E. Schomöger, CSSR, *The Life of Anne Emmerich* (first published 1870), Illinois, 1967, vol. 1, p. 127.
4   ibid., p. 131.
5   ibid., p. 36.
6   Quoted by A. Lebrun, *Throne and Altar. The Political and Religious Thought of Joseph de Maistre*, Ottawa, 1965, pp. 139–40. *Réflexions sur le Protestantisme dans ses rapports avec la Souveraineté* was first published in Turin in 1798.
7   ibid.
8   *The Pope*, London, 1850, pp. 366–7.
9   ibid., p. 122.
10   ibid., p. 369.
11   ibid., p. 213.
12   *Bull for Re-establishment of the Order of Jesuits (Sollicitudo Omnium Ecclesiarum)*, August 1814.
13   D. Mitchell, *The Jesuits, a History*, London, 1980, p. 223.
14   A. Berthe, *Life of St Alphonsus de Liguori*, Dublin/London, 1906, vol. 2, p. 668.
15   E. Weber, SAC, *Vincent Pallotti: An Apostle and Mystic*, New York, 1963, p. 77.
16   ibid., p. 78.
17   Pallotti carried an image of the 'Mother of Divine Love' with him, a Madonna and Child each holding their heart. Mounted in a little portable case, this image worked wonders and became known in Rome as the Image of Miracles. (ibid., pp. 133–4).
18   The most successful one was Italian, Sisters Adorers of the Most Precious Blood, headed by the Blessed Maria de Mattias. Under the protection of the Russian princess Zena Wolkonska, the congregation established 65 schools in the peninsula in 32 years, mainly for the poor. But much of the society's property was lost during the process of disclericalization and unification.
19   Berthe, op.cit., vol. 2, pp. 680–1.
20   *New Catholic Encyclopedia*, New York, 1967–79.
21   W.V. Bangert, SJ, *A History of the Society of Jesus*, St Louis, 1972, pp. 433-5.

22 *Lettere Apostoliche della Santita di N.S. Papa Pio Settimo*, 1821.
23 C. Cantù, *Gli Eretici d'Italia*, Turin, 1867, vol. 3, p. 609.
24 E. Berenson, *Populist Religion and Left-wing Politics in France, 1830–1852*, Princeton, 1984, p. 102.
25 *Ubi Primum*, 5 May 1824.
26 *Quod hoc ineunte*, 24 May 1824.
27 Nearly half the reduced number of pilgrims to Rome were from Naples and Sicily; only a few visitors came from outside Italy.
28 *Caritate Christi urgente nos*, 25 December 1825.
29 X. Levrier, *La Croix Miraculeuse de Migne: coincidences remarquables*, Poitiers, 1913.
30 R. Magraw, *France 1815–1914, the Bourgeois Century*, London, 1983, pp. 28 and 39.
31 G. Dupeux, *French Society, 1789–1970*, London, 1972, pp. 101–2.
32 *Annual Register*, 1819, pp. 172–3.
33 Leo XII, allocution *Dirae liborum*, 26 June 1827.
34 Schools and orphanages multiplied through the missionary activity of such pioneers as St Elizabeth Bichier des Anges and St Andrew Fournet (Daughters of the Cross), St Émilie de Rodat (Congregation of the Holy Family), St Émilie de Vialar (Sisters of St Joseph of the Apparition), St Mary Magdalen Postel (Sisters of the Christian Schools of Mercy), St Euphrasia Pelletier (Institute of the Good Shepherd).
35 M. Agulhon, *Marianne into Battle: Republican Imagery and Symbolism in France, 1789–1880*, London, 1981.
36 St Louis Grignion de Montfort, *Treatise on the True Devotion to the Blessed Virgin*, London, 1962, p. 179.
37 A.M. Windisch, *The Marianist Social System according to the writings of William Joseph Chaminade* (doctoral thesis) Fribourg, 1964, p. 204.
38 Supporting this 'method' is a 'system of virtues' based on submissiveness: distrust of self, humility, modesty, self-abnegation, etc. See the graphic representation of the Method by Windisch, op.cit.
39 ibid., p. 203.
40 *New Catholic Encyclopedia*, op.cit.
41 Windisch, op.cit., p. 206.
42 ibid.
43 ibid., p. 8.
44 ibid., p. 3.
45 ibid., p. 60.
46 Marianist Fathers were to play an important role as spiritual directors and chaplains. For example, a priest of the Society of Mary was one of the confessors of the visionary of Lourdes.
47 *Catholic Encyclopedia*, New York, 1907–1912.
48 *Life and Spirit of J.B.M. Champagnat, Priest and Founder of the Little Brothers of Mary, by One of his First Disciples*, London, 1887.
49 ibid., p. 320.
50 As Max Weber described the 'fervent Mariolatry' of St Bernard

in *The Sociology of Religion* (first published 1922), trans. E. Fischoff, Boston, 1964, p. 160.

51 *Life and Spirit of J.B.M. Champagnat*, op.cit., p. 289.

52 ibid.

53 A Marist Father was the first Vicar Apostolic of West Oceania (New Zealand, Friendly Islands, Navigator Islands, Gilbert and Marshall Islands, Fiji, New Caledonia, New Guinea, Solomon and Caroline Islands).

54 *Catholic Encyclopedia*, op.cit.

55 T. Dawson, OMI, (ed.) *Sketches of the Life of Mgr de Mazenod*, Dublin, 1914, pp. 46–7.

56 Berthe, op.cit., vol. 2, pp. 681–2.

57 *Catholic Encyclopedia*, op.cit.

58 ibid.

59 P. Saunders, *Moshoeshoe. Chief of the Sotho*, London, 1975, p. 271.

60 A. Latreille et al., *Histoire du Catholicisme en France: la Période Contemporaine*, Paris, 1962, p. 24.

61 All these dignitaries are believed to have been Chevaliers de la Foi.

62 G. de Grandmaison, *La Congrégation (1801–30)*, Paris, 1889, p. 178.

63 *Catholic Encyclopedia*, op.cit.

64 L. Verheylezoon, SJ, *Devotion to the Sacred Heart*, London, 1955, p. 105.

65 *Cenacle:* the 'upper room' in which the Last Supper was held.

66 M.J. Maurin, *Pauline Jaricot, Foundress of the Association for the Propagation of the Faith and of the Living Rosary* (first published 1881), London, 1905, pp. 176–7.

67 ibid., p. 201.

68 ibid., pp. 127–8.

69 After a private audience with the Holy Father in 1835 Jaricot went to Naples to obtain a cure from St Philomena's tomb for her 'malignant fever'. Her health restored, she brought back to France 'a large relic of the martyr, enclosed in a lifesize statue dressed in royal robes' (Maurin, op.cit., p. 179). The benefits provided by this idol were to be shared with Vianney.

70 The reputation of the Curé was such that his soutane was attacked by relic-hunters armed with scissors. See Abbé A. Monnin (former assistant of Père Vianney), *The Curé of Ars* (first published 1862), London, 1924, p. 387.

71 The *cabaret* (tavern or café) was seen everywhere as a great enemy of religious life, a centre of anticlerical sociability (J. Sperber, *Popular Catholicism in Nineteenth-Century Germany*, Princeton, 1984), and the 'locus of debauchery and decadence' (Berenson, op.cit., p. 149) through which peasants attempted to fight the 'moral and ideological hegemony of the rural nobility' (ibid., p. 151).

72 For example, the seers Catherine Labouré of the Miraculous Medal, Bernadette of Lourdes, Vincent Pallotti, M.S. Barat, P.J. Eymard, Paola Frassinetti.

11 THE MIRACULOUS MEDAL

1 Quoted by Lady Cecil Kerr, *The Miraculous Medal as revealed to Saint Catherine Labouré*, Catholic Truth Society, London, c. 1984 (first published 'on date unknown'), p. 14.

2 J.V. Bainvel, SJ, *Devotion to the Sacred Heart of Jesus: the Doctrine and its History*, London, 1924, pp. 27–8.

3 Jean Guitton, *Manifestation of Mary*. Compare *Epiphany, Manifestation of Christ*.

4 René Laurentin, *The Life of Catherine Labouré*, London, 1983, p. 62.

5 The organ in question was enshrined in Lyons at the time.

6 Laurentin, op.cit., p. 66.

7 Lady Georgiana Fullerton, *The Miraculous Medal. Life and Visions of Catherine Labouré, Sister of Charity*, London, 1880, p. 13.

8 Laurentin, op.cit. p. 71.

9 ibid.

10 Kerr, op.cit., p. 7.

11 Fullerton, op.cit., p. 23. In fact, the Archbishop's successor, Mgr Affre, was killed during the June Insurrection, 1848.

12 Laurentin, op.cit., pp. 75–6.

13 B. St John, *The Blessed Virgin in the Nineteenth Century: Apparitions, Revelations, Graces*, London, 1903, p. 11.

14 Fullerton, op.cit., p. 23.

15 ibid., p. 27.

16 Laurentin, op.cit., p. 81.

17 E.E.Y. Hales, *Revolution and Papacy 1769–1846*, London, 1960, p. 265.

18 H. Hearder, *Italy in the Age of the Risorgimento, 1790–1870*, Longman History of Italy, vol. 6, London, 1983, p. 107.

19 Modena, Parma, Perugia. A few months later, 7,000 Carbonari invaded the city of Naples.

20 Gregory XVI expelled the Jews from Bologna in 1836.

21 An almost identical medal was struck ten years earlier to the design of Fr Charles Nerinckx, a Belgian who fled Europe during the French Revolution. His medal served as seal for the Sisters of Loretto, the first native order in the United States.

22 Laurentin, op.cit., p. 96.

23 The Virgin was deployed in the pacification of the new subjects of imperial France. Soon after the capitulation of Algiers (July 1830), the first French bishop of that city was given by the Sodality of Our Lady a bronze statue depicting the Immaculate Conception. 'It was the express desire of the donors that this dark-hued statue should be considered the Protectress of the Mohammedans and the negroes' (Z. Aradi, *Shrines of Our Lady Around the World*, New York, 1954, p. 125).

24 St John, op.cit., p. 33.

25 M. Aladel (Prêtre de la Mission), *La Médaille Miraculeuse, Origine, histoire, diffusion, résultats*, Paris, 1879, pp. 355–6.

26 Fullerton, op.cit., p. 80.
27 ibid., p. 158.
28 ibid., p. 88.
29 M.J. Maurin, *Pauline Marie Jaricot, Foundress of the Association for the Propagation of the Faith and of the Living Rosary*, London, 1905 (first published 1881), pp. 150–2.
30 Laurentin, op.cit., p. 13.
31 Kerr, op.cit., p. 14.
32 Quoted by Laurentin, op.cit., p. 134.
33 St John, op.cit., p. 17.
34 H. Lea, *A History of Auricular Confession and Indulgences*, vol. 3, p. 499.
35 *Dictionnaire de Spiritualité*, Paris, 1936, vol. 1, pp. 558–99.
36 F. Maurel, *Christian Instruction in the Nature and Use of Indulgences*, Dublin, 1885, pp. 202-3.
37 In addition to plenary indulgences for saying Paters and Aves, members enjoyed such local extras as the 40-day indulgence granted by Cardinal Manning of Westminster for devoutly ejaculating 'Blessed be Mary! Blessed be Mary Immaculate! Blessed be Mary our Model!'
38 *Form of Association for Children of Mary in the World*, London, 1872.
39 *Guide des Associés de l'Archiconfrèrie du Très-Saint Immaculé Coeur de Marie*, Paris, 1847. In Paris alone there were 640, 259 associates (ibid., p. 21).
40 Fullerton, op.cit., p. 126.
41 W. James, *The Varieties of Religious Experience* (first published 1902), London, 1985, p. 256.
42 Founded in Paris in 1843, with many branches in Europe and the Holy Land. In 1855–61, Ratisbonne was at the centre of two far-reaching cases of congregations holding Jewish minors against the will of their parents – scandals exacerbated by the pope's seizure of the Mortara baby from its parents in Bologna in 1858 after illegal baptism by a servant. For the Bluth and Linnerviel Affairs, see J. Maurain, *La Politique Ecclésiastique du Second Empire, 1852–1869*, Paris 1930, pp. 443, 446, 533 and 574–6.
43 Fr Ricardo Rabanos, 'La Inmaculada de la Medalla Milagrosa', *Estudios Marianos*, 1955, vol. 16, p. 418.
44 Catherine's apparitional life continued sporadically, however, with visions of the cross during the 1848 revolution and one of the Virgin during the Paris Commune.
45 Laurentin, op.cit., Calendar: 18 July 1873. The anniversary of Mary's first appearance to Sister Catherine.

12 CATHOLIC ACTION, MARIAN ACTION

1 A.J. Dunn, *Frederic Ozanam and the Establishment of the Society of St Vincent de Paul*, London, 1913, p. 18.

2 Out of the 90 bishops appointed between 1815 and 1830, 70 were aristocrats (G. Dupeux, *French Society, 1789–1970*, London, 1972, p. 99). The situation was reversed after the revolution of 1830: out of the 72 bishops appointed over the next 18 years, only 10 were of noble birth (A. Dansette, *Religious History of Modern France*, Edinburgh/London, 1961, vol. 1, p. 227).

3 In 1830 bourgeois Protestantism experienced a vigorous revival (see M. Agulhon, *The Republic in the Village*, Cambridge, 1982).

4 *Mirari vos*, 15 August (Day of the Assumption) 1832.

5 *Quo graviora*, 4 October 1833.

6 Technological and economic progress now allowed the production of cheap newspapers which reached even the peasantry in their *cabarets*.

7 E. Berenson, *Populist Religion and Left-wing Politics in France, 1830–1852*, Princeton, 1984, p. 49.

8 In *Le Vrai Christianisme* (1846) Étienne Cabet proposed the development of Christian communism in America; and the Saint-Simonian Pierre Leroux asserted in *Démocratie et Christianisme* (1848) that the vital spirit of Christianity had been 'snuffed out' by papal rule and the clergy (Berenson, op.cit., p. 40).

9 A term which now begins to be used and is inextricable from the movement centred on the populist figure of Jesus.

10 R. Laurentin, *The Life of Catherine Labouré*, London, 1983, p. 95.

11 E. O'Connor, SJ, *The Secret of Frederick Ozanam, Founder of the Society of St Vincent de Paul*, Dublin, 1953, p. 50.

12 *Manual. Society of St Vincent de Paul*, London, 1981, p. 24.

13 *Manual* (20th edition), Dublin, 1954. The 'Instructions concerning indulgences' cover 14 pages.

14 See G. de Grandmaison, *La Congrégation (1801–30)*, Paris, 1889, pp. 368–70. Not only was Ozanam's mentor and first president of the Society, Emmanuel-Joseph Bailly, an ex-Congréganiste, but his brother, Mgr Alphonse Ozanam, was also of Fr Ronsin's 'meeting'.

15 Dunn, op.cit., pp. 28–9.

16 E. Mullan, SJ, *The Sodality of Our Lady Studied in the Documents*, London, 1912, p. 157.

17 J. Maurain, *La Politique Ecclésiastique du Second Empire, 1852–1869*, Paris, 1930, p. 119.

18 ibid., p. 120.

19 In 1860 there were 1,549 conferences in France alone, with 100,000 members and a budget of five million francs (Maurain, op.cit., p. 555).

20 M.L. Brown, *Louis Veuillot: French Ultramontane Catholic Journalist and Layman, 1813–1883*, North Carolina, 1977, p. 285. Veuillot was converted to Catholicism under Jesuit influence after a visit to Rome and Loreto in 1838, described in *Rome et Lorette* (1841).

21 M. Viller, F. Cavallera, J. de Guibert, SJ, (eds), *Dictionnaire de Spiritualité*, Paris, 1957, vol. 3, p. 1746.

22 M.J. Maurin, *Pauline Jaricot, Foundress of the Association for the Propagation of the Faith and of the Living Rosary* (first published 1881), London, 1905, p. 146.

23 The Bambina Sisters were later (1855) to offer Mary 'three silver keys, bound by a ring of gold: the key of hearts, the key of graces and the key of Paradise' (Pope John Paul II, address to the 22nd general chapter of the Order, 30 March 1987).

24 J. Gaynor, *The Life of St Vincent Pallotti*, Netherlands, 1962, p. 84.

25 Lady Georgiana Fullerton, *The Miraculous Medal*, London, 1880, p. 91.

26 By 1880 there was an international network of over 17,000 associations in honour of the Immaculate Heart with a total membership of 25 million (B. St John, *The Blessed Virgin Mary in the Nineteenth Century*, London, 1903, p. 94). Ten years later the number of confraternities had risen to 19,000 with 30 million members (L. Verheylezoon, SJ, *Devotion to the Sacred Heart*, London, 1955, p. 246).

27 Under the command of the Jesuit general, there were 35 million members in 1955 and the official organ, *The Messenger of the Sacred Heart*, appeared in 40 languages.

28 Verheylezoon, op.cit., p. 261.

29 ibid., p. 264. The morning offering is: 'Divine Heart of Jesus, through the Immaculate Heart of Mary, I offer thee the prayers and works, joys and sufferings of this day, in reparation of our offences. ... I offer them to thee especially for the intentions recommended by our Holy Father the Pope.'

30 ibid., p. 365.

31 H. Ramière, SJ, *The Book of the Apostleship of Prayer* (first published 1861), London, 1891, pp. 108–10.

32 ibid.

33 ibid., p. 180.

34 ibid., pp. 113–114.

35 ibid., p. 255.

36 H. Ramière, *Le Règne Social du Coeur de Jésus*, Toulouse, 1892, p. 145.

13 LA SALETTE: MODEL OF THE MODERN SHRINE

1 W.J. Fortier, Missionary of La Salette, *Our Lady of La Salette*, London, 1931, pp. 50–1.

2 W. Ullathorne, Archbishop of Birmingham, *The Holy Mountain of La Salette* (first published 1854), New York, 1942, p. 89.

3 *Manuel de l'Archiconfrérie de Notre-Dame Réconciliatrice de la Salette*, Toulouse, 1863, p. 15.

4 M. Agulhon, *The Republic in the Village: the People of the Var from the French Revolution to the Second Republic*, Cambridge, 1982, p. 103. 'It was

one of the ways in which disobedience to the clergy . . . penetrated even to the most remote villages' (ibid.).

5 *Manuel*, op.cit., pp. 18–20.

6 J. Maurain, *La Politique Ecclésiastique du Second Empire, 1852–1869*, Paris, 1930, pp. 164–5.

7 *Constituionnel*, 2 February 1847, reproduced by J. Stern, *La Salette. Documents authentiques: dossier chronologique integral*, Rome, 1980, doc. 84.

8 *National*, 20 February 1847, ibid., doc. 83.

9 *Patriote des Alpes*, 9 January 1847, ibid., doc. 60.

10 Fortier, op.cit., p. 44. Indulgences of 100 days were offered for such ejaculations as 'Thou who dost condemn so severely our lusts and the shameful pleasures of the world' and 'Thou who, after the example of Jesus, dost heal every infirmity' (ibid., p. 50).

11 Ullathorne, op.cit., p. 166.

12 Approved by Leo XIII in 1890, the Missionaries of La Salette were dispersed by the French government in 1901 and subsequently spread throughout the world (Italy, Belgium, Poland, Switzerland, USA, England, Canada, Madagascar, Brazil, Burma, Argentina), setting up seminaries and private schools.

13 Ullathorne, op.cit., p. 188.

14 A. Monnin (former assistant priest at Ars), *The Curé of Ars*, (first published 1862), London, 1924, p. 365.

15 ibid., chapter XXXV: 'The Venerable Curé of Ars and La Salette'.

16 ibid.

17 Maurain, op.cit., p. 167.

18 ibid., note on p. 166. Mélanie was put in a convent and strictly supervised.

19 ibid., p. 795.

20 D. Flanagan, 'An Ecumenical Future for Roman Catholic Theology of Mary', in A. Stacpoole,OSB, (ed.), *Mary's Place in Christian Dialogue*, London, 1982.

21 E. Lafond, *La Salette, Lourdes, Pontmain: voyages d'un croyant*, Paris, 1872, p. 104.

22 Monnin, op.cit., p. 365.

23 K. Rahner, *Visions and Prophecies*, London, 1963, p. 61.

24 For the complete French text, see R. Griffiths, *The Reactionary Revolution. The Catholic Revival in French Literature 1870–1914*, London, 1966, appendix.

25 Huysmans, a former dabbler in the aesthetic satanism described in his 'decadent' masterpiece *Là-bas*, wrote an unfinished novel about La Salette but put aside the manuscript in 1893 for fear of damaging the Church, in which he had become a Benedictine oblate. Bloy, another convert, whose story *Celle qui pleure* (1908) was inspired by the shrine, supported 'absolute theocracy'.

26 See Père Bruno de Jésus-Marie,OCD, *Satan*, London, 1951, p. 263; and Griffiths, op. cit., for details of the distinguished Mariologist and baby-murderer Abbé J.-A. Boullan and his mentor Eugène Vintras,

visionary founder of the Carmel, a polygamous Marian sect which was revived in Poland as 'Adorers of the Most Holy Sacrament' (condemned by Pius X in *Tribus Circiter*, 5 April 1906).

14 REVOLUTION AND COALITION

1 E. Berenson, *Populist Religion and Left-wing Politics in France, 1830–1852*, Princeton, 1984, p. 101.
2 The house of the Society of the Sacred Heart at Loreto (restored to Jesuit hands by Gregory XVI) was menaced by Carbonari.
3 One of the declared aims of 'Young Italy', founded by Mazzini in 1831, was 'the destruction of all the aristocracy of the priesthood and the introduction of a simple parish system' (letter of Mazzini, quoted by H. Hearder, *Italy in the Age of the Risorgimento, 1790–1870*, London, 1983, p. 186).
4 See Berenson, op.cit.
5 ibid., p. 42.
6 ibid., pp. 204–5.
7 *Le Christ Républicain*, 8 June 1848, no. 1.
8 Berenson, op.cit., p. 206.
9 In the prosperous phase that followed, donations and legacies were abundant. The registered acquisitions of female congregations, for example, increased during the years 1852–60 from 15 million to 25 million francs. The number of male religious jumped from 9,136 in 1856 to 17,676 in 1861 (J. Maurain, *La Politique Ecclésiastique du Second Empire, 1852–1869*, Paris, 1930, p. 75). The total number of authorized ecclesiastical establishments in 1861 reached the figure of 71,557 (A. Latreille et al., *Histoire du Catholicisme en France, la Période Contemporaine*, Paris, 1962, vol. 3, p. 317).
10 The industrial-urban development of France (localized mainly in the north) lagged behind Britain in 1850 – by 67,000 horse-power to 500,000 (Braudel and Labrousse (eds), *Histoire Économique et Sociale de la France*, 1976, tome 3: 'L'Avènement de l'ère industrielle', vol. 2, p. 447).
11 Maurain, op.cit., pp. 55–6.
12 M. Agulhon, *The Republic in the Village*, Cambridge, 1982, pp. 286–7.
13 Maurain, op.cit., p. 13.
14 Louis Napoleon declared himself Emperor in 1852.
15 J.V. Bainvel, SJ, *Devotion to the Sacred Heart of Jesus. The Doctrine and its History*, London, 1924, p. 305.
16 A. Dansette, *Religious History of Modern France*, Edinburgh/London, 1961, vol. 1, p. 278.
17 The first stone of the monument was laid on 10 December 1854, feast day of Our Lady of Loreto and just two days after the Immaculate Conception declaration.

18 J. Burnichon, SJ, *La Compagnie de Jésus en France*, Paris, 1914, vol. 3, pp. 543-4.

15 SECOND REVIVAL: MARY IN THE EUCHARIST

1 Rev. M. Dempsey, *Champion of the Blessed Sacrament, St Peter Julian Eymard*, New York (no date, after 1962), p. 257.
2 The greatest Spanish saint of the nineteenth century, Claret had a vision of the Virgin and Child in 1862. A forerunner of Catholic Action in his country, he pitted Mary against 'the sect'. Among his prolific Marian writings is *La Virgen del Pilar y los Francmasones*. See N. García, 'La dévotion à la très S.V. dans la Congrégation des Missionaires Fils du Coeur Immaculé de Marie', *Maria* (Paris), 1954, vol. 3.
3 Above all, indulgences related to Marian devotions, for example, for the invocation of the Virgin under the title of Our Lady of the Blessed Sacrament. In 1851, at the request of the Jesuit general, 40 days were granted for 'ejaculating' at the time of temptation 'O my Queen, my Mother'.
4 J. Sperber, *Popular Catholicism in Nineteenth-Century Germany*, Princeton, 1984, pp. 64–5.
5 ibid., p. 60.
6 By mid-century, one third of the major colleges in France were run by Jesuits.
7 J. Maurian, *La Politique Ecclésiastique du Second Empire, 1852–1869*, Paris, 1930, p. 318. Like the secret societies, which sometimes functioned as mutual benefit organizations, the clerical institutions attracted large numbers with similar schemes. The Society of St Francis Xavier in Toulouse, for example, had two million workers affiliated to it by mid-century.
8 *Catholic Encyclopedia*, New York, 1907–12.
9 Sperber, op.cit., pp. 76–7.
10 ibid. This study of German Catholicism shows the growing political centrality of Mary and the clergy in the post-revolutionary years (1850–70), confirming our contention of a correlation between Marianism and ecclesiastical absolutism.
11 See 'La spiritualité mariale de Mère Marie Véronique', *Maria*, 1954, vol. 3.
12 ibid., p. 519.
13 ibid., p. 527.
14 ibid., pp. 523–4.
15 L. Verheylezoon, SJ, *Devotion to the Sacred Heart*, London, 1955, p. 268.
16 In 1857 Claret became confessor both to St Maria Micaela of the Blessed Sacrament and her friend, Queen Isabel, a great patroness of Marian confraternities.

17 P. Suau, SJ, *The Life of Mother Mary of Jesus, Baroness d'Hooghvorst*, London, 1913, pp. 87–90.
18 A. Calvet, SJ, *Life of Father Paul Ginhac*, London, 1914.
19 Abbé C. Sylvain, *Life of the Rev. Fr Hermann* (first published 1880), New York, 1925, p. 211.
20 One of the few musical compositions after his conversion was a ditty that began: 'I swear it, I belong to Mary' (ibid., p. 229).
21 ibid., p. 72.
22 'La dévotion mariale et la congrégation des prêtres du Saint-Sacrament', *Maria*, 1954, vol. 3; see also *Estudios Marianos*, 1953, vol. 13: 'La SV y la Eucaristia'.
23 *Le R.P. Pierre Julien Eymard, Documents sur sa Vie et ses Vertus*, Postulateur de la Cause, Paris, 1899, p. 76.
24 M. Williams, *The Society of the Sacred Heart*, London, 1979. Tamisier organized the First Eucharistic Congress (Lille, 1881).
25 Dempsey, op.cit., p. 258.
26 F.A. Beck (trans.), *Assumptionist Spirituality, a Synthesis of the Teaching of Fr E. d'Alzon*, London, 1933, pp. 16–17.
27 *The Augustinians of the Assumption: their Foundation, Spirit and History*, Maison de la Bonne Presse, Paris, 1930, p. 13.
28 Beck, op.cit., p. 23.
29 ibid.
30 ibid., pp. 40–1.
31 The Archconfraternity of the Assumption for the Conversion of the East bore the emblem of the Theotokos.
32 R. Cooke, OMI, (ed.), *Sketches of the Life of Mgr de Mazenod*, Dublin, 1914, p. 160.
33 The Oblates of Mary Immaculate also established missions in working-class areas of Liverpool (1850) and Leeds (1857).
34 *Popery, the Inquisition and the Jesuits* (pamphlet), London, 1851, p. 110.
35 One of the celebrated Carmelite's achievements in London was to persuade convicted murderers to wear Mary's scapular on the gallows.

16 TRIUMPH OF THE IMMACULATE CONCEPTION

1 *Ubi primum*, 2 February 1849.
2 Liberty of conscience was withheld in Pius's constitution of March 1848 and non-Catholics (including some 12,000 Jews in Rome) were explicitly denied civil rights.
3 *Qui pluribus*, 9 November 1846.
4 ibid.
5 ibid.
6 ibid.

7   A. Gemelli,OFM, *The Franciscan Message to the World*, London, 1936, p. 213.
8   *Ubi primum*, issued at Gaeta, Naples, op.cit.
9   *Nostis et nobiscum*, 8 December 1849.
10 ibid.
11 It is claimed that of the 620 replies to the Holy Father's inquiry only four – including Archbishop Sibour of Paris – opposed the definition.
12 *Civiltà Cattolica* was founded after the revolution of 1848–9 by Carlo Curci (1810–1891). Dismissed by Pius for supporting religious toleration, Curci was eventually expelled from the Society of Jesus for his opposition to Temporalism and his writings were placed on the Index.
13 According to the Rev. Dr Moss, 'this devotional system . . . was the real cause of the definition of the Immaculate Conception'. (C.B. Moss, *The Old Catholic Movement*, London, 1964, p. 175).
14 Passaglia became involved in an intense campaign against the territorial claims of the pope. As in the case of his fellow dissident Curci, his writings were banned by Rome.
15 *Exultavit cor nostrum*, 21 November, 1851.
16 E. Lafond, *Lorette et Castelfidardo. Letters d'un pèlerin*, Paris, 1862, p. 202.
17 Bull of 1852, quoted by W. Garratt (Chamberlain of the Holy House), *Loreto the New Nazareth and its Centenary Jubilee*, London, 1895.
18 ibid., pp. 64–5.
19 ibid., p. 346.
20 E.E.Y. Hales, *Pio Nono – a Study in European Politics and Religion in the Nineteenth Century*, London, 1956, p. 148.
21 *Irish Ecclesiastical Record*, 1904, vol. XV, p. 499.
22 R. Cooke, OMI, *Sketches of the Life of Mgr de Mazenod*, Dublin, 1914, pp. 238–9.
23 Bull *Ineffabilis Deus*, 8 December 1854.
24 *Irish Ecclesiastical Record*, op.cit.
25 Cooke, op.cit.
26 *Irish Ecclesiastical Record*, op.cit.
27 A. Sabatier, *The Religions of Authority and the Religion of the Spirit*, London, 1904, pp. 134–5.
28 B. Llorca, SJ, 'La Autoridad eclesiastica y el dogma de la Inmaculada Concepción', *Estudios Eclesiasticos*, July/December, 1954, p. 321.
29 B. Croce, *History of Europe in the Nineteenth Century*, London, 1965, p. 191.
30 F.J. Sheen, *The World's First Love*, Dublin, 1953, pp. 133–5.

17 LOURDES: THE SEAL OF PAPAL INFALLIBILITY

1   *Fulgens corona*, 8 September 1953.

2 C.C. Martindale, SJ, *Bernadette of Lourdes*, Catholic Truth Society, London, undated, p. 5.

3 E. Zola, *Lourdes*, London, 1894, p. 93. The novel is the first of the trilogy *Les Trois Villes* (Lourdes, Rome, Paris). The hero is a priest who abandons Catholicism.

4 Martindale, op.cit., p. 14.

5 The cave of Massabielle traditionally formed part of the ninth century 'domain' of the nearby sanctuary of Notre-Dame du Puy. Shrines whose origins are found in apparitions crowded the district: Notre-Dame de Héas, de Bourisp, de Poueylahun, de Nestès, de Bétharram, de Garaison (ibid., p. 4).

6 'I am the Immaculate Conception.'

7 L.-M. Cross, SJ, and M. Olphe-Galliard, SJ, *Lourdes 1858. Témoins de l'Événement*, Paris, 1957, p. 265.

8 See 'Lettre du Préfet Massy au procureur impérial Dutour', R. Laurentin, *Lourdes. Documents authentiques*, Paris, 1957, vol. 2, pp. 335–6.

9 J. Maurain, *La Politique Ecclésiastique du Second Empire, 1852–1869*, Paris, 1930, p. 233.

10 In contrast to the sympathetic treatment in the *Univers*, the secular press vigorously attacked any idea of a miracle. *Le Siècle* spoke of 'a vast conspiracy obviously organized by the clerical party against any advance of the human spirit' (quoted by M. de Saint-Pierre, *Bernadette and Lourdes*, London, 1954, p. 144).

11 Martindale, op.cit., p. 32.

12 A religious of the Mother-house, Sisters of Charity of Nevers, *Bernadette of Lourdes*, Nevers, 1926, p. 82.

13 A nineteenth-century sceptic writes, 'In France alone, miraculous waters are to be reckoned by the hundreds. Consequently both La Salette and Lourdes are far less distinguished by their sources than by the method in which they have been turned to profit' (P. Parfait, *Pilgrimage Notes – A Complement to M. Zola's 'Lourdes'*, London, 1895, p. 122).

14 Saint-Pierre, op.cit., p. 213.

15 ibid., pp. 142–3.

16 Martindale, op.cit., p. 42. Satan also interrupted Bernadette's conversation with the vision on February 19 (1858) by means of 'a tumult of sinister voices' (a religious of the Mother-house, op.cit., p. 38).

17 Saint-Pierre, op.cit., p. 83.

18 Zola, op.cit., p. 472.

19 F. Duhoureau, *Saint Bernadette of Lourdes, a Saint of the Golden Legend*, London, 1934, p. 260.

20 B. St John, *The Blessed Virgin in the Nineteenth Century: Apparitions, Revelations and Graces*, London, 1903, pp. 4–5.

21 E. Lafond, *La Salette, Lourdes, Pontmain: voyage d'un croyant*, Paris, 1872, pp. 194–6.

22 A religious of the Mother-house, op.cit., pp. 54-5.

23 C. Lattey, SJ, *Clergy Review*, 1948, Vol.XXIX, no. 5., pp. 327–8.

18 INFALLIBILITY: DEATH-KNELL OF COALITION AND TEMPORALISM

1 Cardinal Pecci, Bishop of Perugia, *The Temporal Power of The Holy See. A Pastoral for Lent*, Dublin, 1860, pp. 6–7.
2 E. Lafond, *Lorette et Castelfidardo. Lettres d'un pèlerin*, Paris, 1862, p. vii.
3 See Pius IX, *Nullis certe verbis*, 19 January 1860.
4 P. Huguet, *Les Gloires de Pie et les Grandes Fêtes de Roma en 1867*, Paris/Brussels, 1867, ch. VI: 'Les nouveaux croises', p. 162.
5 J. Powell, *Two Years in the Pontifical Zouaves*, London, 1871, p. 298.
6 By 1867 General Herman Kanzler, a Bavarian, was commander-in-chief.
7 Powell, op.cit., p. 14.
8 Mgr Besson, Bishop of Nîmes, *Xavier de Mérode, Minister and Almoner to Pius IX, Archbishop of Melitinensis: His Life and Works*, London, 1887, p. 147.
9 Count Anatole de Ségur on the death of Mizael de Pas, quoted by Count Lafond, op.cit., p. 321.
10 ibid., p. 310.
11 Powell, op.cit., p. 58.
12 Lafond, op.cit., p. 367.
13 ibid., p. 344.
14 Besson, op.cit., p. 153.
15 Lafond, op.cit., p. 339.
16 ibid., p. 357.
17 J. Maurain, *La Politique Ecclésiastique du Second Empire, 1852–1869*, Paris, 1930, p. 456.
18 ibid., pp. 451–2.
19 The entire community emigrated to the United States in 1864.
20 For example, fleurs-de-lis were exhibited in Corpus Christi processions.
21 The 18 apparitions at Lourdes were authenticated by the French hierarchy in February 1862.
22 Bishop Pie of Poitiers, a leading ultramontanist, re-established the procession of the Holy Prepuce. Lost in the sixteenth century, the foreskin was discoverd by Ursuline nuns in 1856.
23 The Association of Reparation was consecrated in 1865 at Paray-le-Monial.
24 A religious of the Mother-house, Sisters of Charity of Nevers, *Bernadette of Lourdes*, Nevers, 1926, pp. 91–3.
25 ibid.
26 *Catholic Encyclopedia*, New York, 1907–12.

27 Maurain, op.cit., p. 430. Between three and four million francs a year was raised in this way (ibid., p. 431). In the 1860s the pope was funding a front against the Garibaldians in Sicily in the 'Brigands' War' – in which Bourbon, clerical and peasant elements united against the administration of a liberalized Naples (H. Hearder, *Italy in the age of the Risorgimento, 1790–1870*, Longman History of Italy, vol. 6, London, 1983, pp. 240–1).

28 Powell, op.cit., p. 6.

29 C.S. Phillips, *The Church in France: 1848–1907*, London, 1936, pp. 116–17.

30 *Syllabus of the principal errors of our time, which are censured (by) our Most Holy Lord, Pope Pius IX*, 8 December 1864, no. 80.

31 ibid., section iv.

32 L. von Ranke, *The History of the Popes during the Last Four Centuries*, London, 1908, vol. 2, p. 551.

33 E.C. Butler, *The Vatican Council*, London, 1930: schema 'de Ecclesia Christi'.

34 Constitution *Pastor Aeternus*, 13 July 1870, Chapter III.

35 H. Küng, *Infallible?*, London, 1971, p. 96.

36 A. Sabatier, *The Religions of Authority and the Religion of the Spirit*, London, 1904, pp. 134–5.

37 Letter of Pius IX to Fr J. Jacques, 5 January 1870.

38 Rev. Nicholson, *The Adoration of Christ. Refutation of the heresies taught by Cardinal Manning*, London, 1897, p. 167.

39 I. von Döllinger, *letter addressed to the Archbishop of Munich*, London, 1871, p. 11.

40 M.L. Brown, *Louis Veuillot: French Ultramontane Catholic Journalist and Layman, 1813–1883*, North Carolina, 1977, p. 329.

41 Although barely represented at the Council, the Portuguese Church built a temple in Braga in honour of the definition of papal infallibility; the Portuguese Jesuit provincial Carlos João Rademaker wrote poems praising the Immaculate Conception and infallibility dogmas.

42 Quoted by F. Parkinson Keyes, *The Grace of Guadalupe*, London, 1951, p. 139.

43 See A.B. Hasler, *Pius IX: Infallibility and the First Vatican Council*, London, 1977; *How the Pope Became Infallible, Pius IX and the Politics of Persuasion*, New York, 1981.

44 *Pastor Aeternus*, op.cit.

45 ibid. The anti-infallibilists had appealed through the historian Lord Acton to the British government. Although Irish interests precluded any diplomatic move, the British Establishment viewed with distaste the prospect of Pius IX's 'pro-theosizing himself', as *The Times* sarcastically put it (23 July 1870).

46 Phillips, op.cit., p. 154.

47 The treaty was repudiated by an imperial rescript of Franz-Josef, advised by his former tutor, Cardinal von Rauscher, who left Rome before the voting on the infallibility constitution. In 1874 Pius IX threatened the emperor with excommunication over the

latter's friendly relations with the pope's rival, the king of Italy (E. Cranckshaw, *Fall of the House of Habsburg*, London, 1963).

48 J. Sperber, *Popular Catholicism in Nineteenth-Century Germany*, Princeton, 1984, p. 239.

49 ibid. Popular 'defence of religion' between 1871–3 often took the form of demonstrations at Marian shrines (ibid., p. 224) and Catholic polemicists characteristically saw the hand of the Masons in the action of the Iron Chancellor (ibid., pp. 217–20).

50 C.B. Moss, *The Old Catholic Movement*, London, 1964, p. 235.

51 H.L. Hughes, *The Catholic Revival in Italy: 1815–1915*, London, 1935, p. 102.

52 ibid., p. 97.

53 Quoted by P. Brocardo, 'Culte Marial dans la Famille Salesienne', *Maria*, 1954, vol. 3, pp. 450–1.

54 G. Bonetti, *St John Bosco's Early Apostolate*, London 1934, p. 2.

55 H.C. Lea, *Sacerdotal Celibacy*, London, 1867, p. 562.

56 *Maria*, op.cit., p. 452.

57 J. Soll et al., *La Virgen de los tiempos dificiles*, Madrid, 1984, p. 44.

58 ibid., p. 45.

59 *The Messenger of the Sacred Heart*, June 1870.

19 THE NATIONAL VOW AND MARIAN CORPORATIVISM

1 Quoted by Lady Georgiana Fullerton, *The Miraculous Medal*, London, 1880, p. 157.

2 N. de Saint-Pierre, *Bernadette and Lourdes*, London, 1954, p. 102.

3 B. St John, *The Blessed Virgin in the Nineteenth Century*, London, 1903, pp. 83–4.

4 A. Rhodes, *The Power of Rome in the Twentieth Century: the Vatican in the Age of the Liberal Democracies, 1870–1922*, London, 1983, p. 28.

5 C.S. Phillips, *The Church in France: 1848–1907*, London, 1936, pp. 178–9.

6 A. Dansette, *Religious History of Modern France*, Edinburgh/London, 1961, vol. 1, pp. 333.

7 E.E.Y. Hales, *Pio Nono, a study in European politics and religion in the nineteenth century*, London, 1956, p. 326.

8 J.V. Bainvel, SJ, *Devotion to the Sacred Heart of Jesus. The Doctrine and its History*, London, 1924, p. 323.

9 *Etsi multa luctuosa*, 21 November 1873. That year the Jesuit general was driven from Rome by the Piedmontese, and the short-lived Spanish First Republic – liberal and anticlerical – was established.

10 Bainvel, op.cit., p. 308.

11 *Catholic Encyclopedia*, 1911: 'Sodalities'.

12 L. Verheylezoon, *Devotion to the Sacred Heart: Object, Ends, Practice, Motives*, London, 1955, p. 206. In 1877 the Scapular of the Sons of the Immaculate Heart of Mary provided a new design symptomatic of

those troubled times: a burning heart growing from a lily and pierced with a sword.

13 Leo XIII called devotion to the Sacred Heart 'the most excellent form of religion'.

14 In the Jesuit stronghold of Marseilles, 10,000 families went through the ritual between 1882 and 1886 (Verheylezoon, op.cit., pp. 134–5).

15 E. Lafond, *La Salette, Lourdes, Pontmain: voyage d'un croyant*, Paris, 1872, pp. xiii–xiv.

16 *La Grande Encyclopedie*, Paris, 1887–1902, vol. 22, pp. 678–9.

17 *The Month*, October, 1909.

18 Maison de la Bonne Presse, *The Augustinians of the Assumption, their Foundation, Spirit and History*, Paris, 1930, p. 100.

19 *Catholic Encyclopedia*, New York, 1907–1912.

20 *Augustinians of the Assumption*, op.cit., p. 107.

21 *Pèlerin's* editor, Fr Vincent de Paul Bailly (founder of *La Croix*) was to inveigh against Zola during the Dreyfus affair (see p. 151).

22 *Augustinians of the Assumption*, op.cit., p. 106.

23 Saint-Pierre, op.cit., p. 178.

24 J. and M. Lough, *An Introduction to Nineteenth-Century France*, London, 1978, p. 142.

25 A. Debidour, *L'Église Catholique et l'État en France: sous la troisième république (1870–1906)*, Paris, 1906, vol. 1, p. 162.

26 P. Parfait, *Pilgrimage Notes – a complement to M. Zola's 'Lourdes'*, London, 1895, p. 241.

27 A year later, among the first foreigners to enter the grotto in groups were the Americans, whose bishops had declared Mary Immaculate 'Protectress of the United States' in 1846. American Catholics were to become a vital source of finance and propaganda for European visions.

28 *Pèlerin*, 23 December 1876, quoted by Parfait, op.cit.; p. 55.

29 W. Ullathorne, Archbishop of Birmingham, *The Holy Mountain of La Salette* (first published 1854), New York, 1942, p. 185.

30 Lafond, op.cit., p. 260.

31 St John, op.cit., p. 367.

32 ibid. p. 358. The last sentence was 'underlined by a broad gold stroke'.

33 T.A. Kselman, *Miracles and Prophecies in Nineteenth-Century France*, New Jersey, 1983, p. 124.

34 M.L. Brown, *Louis Veuillot: French Ultramontane Catholic Journalist and Layman, 1813–1883*, North Carolina, 1977, p. 385.

35 Kselman, op.cit., pp. 116–19.

36 St John, op.cit., p. 411.

37 H.M. Gillett, *Famous Shrines of Our Lady*, London, 1949, vol. 1, p. 236.

38 Cure by exorcism was an ancient practice at shrines, dating from at least the sixth century in Gaul. See P. Brown, *The Cult of the Saints. Its Rise and Function in Latin Christianity*, London, 1981, p. 111.

39 Gillett, op.cit., vol. 1, p. 230.

40 Verheylezoon, op.cit., p. 207.

41 *The Tablet*, 15 February 1879.

42 Fullerton, op.cit., p. 228.
43 Extracts from Fr Cavanagh's diary printed in the *Weekly News* (Dublin) give details of 600 or more cures. The newspaper is the sole source for the seers' depositions, an ecclesiastical report having been lost.
44 *Weekly News*, 29 May 1880.
45 On 14 February 1880 the *Weekly News* printed, on the same page as the depositions, an advertisement for Mr E. Soloman's lanterns which created 'Ghosts, Aerobatic, magic visions and other novelties'.
46 *Weekly News*, 7 August and 25 September 1880.
47 Letter *Cum Dei Filius*, to the Bishop of Puy, 3 September 1877.
48 Their disciple Hyacinthe de Gailhard-Bancel was instrumental in setting up the Catholic Union of Rural France (1884) and organized retreats for farm-workers.
49 Letter *Gratissima ad Nos*, 21 January 1891.
50 *Quod apostolici*, 28 December 1878.
51 By mid-century, life expectancy in Lille was 24. The city's 26,000 textile workers lived in cellars submerged in filth and disease (see R. Magraw, *France 1815–1914, The Bourgeois Century*, London, 1983, p. 181).
52 See Dansette, op.cit., vol. 2, pp. 120–1.
53 In Aachen, Germany, there was, according to a parish priest writing in 1871, 'a beautiful death benefit society attached to the Brotherhood of Mary, a Marianic league', where members practised 'harmless wordly tunes so that the filthy songs may be eventually banished from factories and workshops' (quoted by J. Sperber, *Popular Catholicism in Nineteenth-Century Germany*, Princeton, 1984, p. 21).
54 Dansette, op.cit., vol. 1, p. 341.

20 POPE OF THE ROSARY AND THE SOCIAL QUESTION

1 'Ad Beatam Virginem Marian', translated by H.T. Henry, *Poems, Charades, Inscriptions of Pope Leo XIII*, New York, 1902, p. 151.
2 E. Soderini, *Leo XIII, Italy and France*, London, 1935, p. 25. Count Soderini, official biographer of Leo XIII, was an eye-witness of the riot.
3 *Dall'alto dell'Apostolico seggio*, 15 October 1890.
4 *Nobilissima Gallorum gens*, 8 February 1884.
5 *The Catholic Press*, London, 31 December 1887. Immediately after this homage Cardinal Langenieux of Reims organized a pilgrimage of reparation to the eternal city for 10,000 workmen.
6 A fresh papal condemnation of Bruno was read from the pulpits, depicting him once more as a charlatan whose 'own writings condemn him of a degraded materialism' (J. Lindsay, Introduction to *Giordano Bruno: Cause, Principle and Unity*, Essex (UK), 1962).
7 According to Professor Küng, this term (meaning official doctrine) 'has no basis either in Scripture or in older tradition, but was a modern

introduction in connection with the doctrine of infallibility of Vatican 1 and the distinction between the Church teaching and the Church taught' (*Infallible?*, London, 1971, pp. 182–3).

8   The Pontifical Academy of St Thomas Aquinas in Rome and a Thomist chair at Louvain were founded under Leo's auspices. The encyclical *Aeterni Patris* (4 August 1879) urges the restoration of the philosophy of St Thomas in harmony with modern science and thought, and the extension of its influence to social science.

9   The office and mass of the Most Pure Heart of Mary composed by St Jean Eudes was eventually approved with modifications by the Congregation of Rites in 1885, not long after a group of cardinals initiated a vast movement promoting consecrations to the Immaculate Heart (see A. Luis, CSSR, 'Historia de la Consagración al Corazón de María', *Estudios Marianos*, 1945, vol. 4, p. 466).

10   The beatification process of Anne Emmerich was introduced at Rome in 1892, and Leo even attempted to reactivate the cause of the Franciscan visionary María de Agreda, sealed by papal decree in 1773.

11   The first Marian congress was held at Lyons in 1900, during a period of anticlericalism in France.

12   The 'Marianum' in Rome was reopened in 1895.

13   A. Fremantle (ed.), *The Papal Encyclicals in Their Historical Context: the Teachings of the Popes*, New York, 1956, p. 166.

14   See apostolic letter *Testem benevolentiae*, January 1899.

15   As an expression of the Capuchin Franciscan restoration of the 1880s we see the establishment in Rome of the Franciscan Missionaries of Mary and the Franciscan Sisters of the Sorrowful Mother (the latter dedicated to Our Lady of Sorrows).

16   A. Gemelli,OFM, (ed.), *The Franciscan Message to the World*, London, 1934, p. 216.

17   *Laetitiae sanctae*, 8 September 1893. Leo celebrates the famous 'rosary battle' of Lepanto in one of his longer Latin verses, 'Our Lady's Rosary - a prayer for help' (1895).

18   De Maistre had said in *Du Pape*: 'We have just seen the social state shaken to its foundations because there has been too much liberty in Europe and there has not been enough religion.'

19   *Dall'alto dell'Apostolico seggio*, op.cit.

20   *Immortale Dei*, 1 November 1885.

21   ibid. Luigi Taprelli, SJ (1793–1862), associate of Civiltà Cattolica and an influential Thomist, had argued that civil government originates in an extension of paternal power through the patriarchal head of groups of families.

22   *Graves de communi*, 18 January 1901.

23   ibid.

24   *Spesse volte*, 5 August 1898.

25   ibid.

26   ibid.

27   As Severino Aznar, leader of the Christian Democrats in Spain, called Vicent. See *Diccionario de Historia Eclesiástica de España*, vol. 4.

28 See E.F. Regatillo, *Un Marques Modelo: el Siervo de Dios Claudio López Bru*, Santander, 1950. The Marquis's process of beatification has been opened in Rome.

29 In 1876, Enrique de Ossó y Cervelló (1840–96), another forerunner of Catholic Action, headed a pilgrimage of 8,000 Spaniards to Rome for the month of the Rosary.

30 *Recuerdos del viaje a Roma. Peregrinación Nacional Obrera*, Barcelona, 1894, p. 94.

31 ibid.

32 In 1894 Countess Maria-Teresa Ledochowska, on instructions from the pope, founded in Austria the Sodality of St Peter Claver to support African missions and the liberation of slaves.

33 *Laetitiae sanctae*, op.cit.

34 ibid.

35 *Superiore anno*, 20 August 1884.

36 Leo XIII is believed to have had a vision of the Archangel Michael in 1887.

37 *Revista Catolica de Filipinas*, Manila, 30 July 1890.

38 The seven visionary founders of the Servites were canonized in 1888.

39 H.M. Gillett, *Famous Shrines of Our Lady*, London, 1952, vol. 1, p. 176.

40 ibid.

41 H. Lea, *A History of Auricular Confession and Indulgences in the Latin Church*, London, 1896, vol. 3, p. 540.

42 In 1897 the Congregation of Rites approved the form of the ceremony 'Ritus Servandus in Coronation Imaginis B.V.M.'.

43 See Soderini, op.cit., p. 102.

44 Leo XIII, quoted by Rev. G.E. Phillips, *Loreto and the Holy House*, London, 1917, pp. 155–6.

45 V. Olivares Biec (Royal Brotherhood of Our Lady of the Pillar), *Peregrinación a NS del Pilar de Zaragoza*, Madrid, 1880.

46 A. Eliseo de Manaricua, *Santa María de Begoña en la Historia Espiritual de Vizcaya*, Bilbao, 1950. Three years later, in 1903, when Our Lady of Begoña was proclaimed Patroness of Vizcaya by Rome, the socialists again opposed the celebrations as 'a new provocation of the reactionaries' (ibid., p. 468).

47 J. Bertrán Borrás, *NS de Misericordia y Su Santuario de Reus*, Reus, 1954.

48 *Annum Sacrum*, 25 May 1899.

49 According to Professor Bainvel, 'Leo XIII has shown us that in the Sacred Heart we were given a new *labarum*; new pictures have appeared in which the cross and the Heart are combined with the inscription *In hoc signo vinces*' (J.V. Bainvel, *Devotion to the Sacred Heart of Jesus*, London, 1924, p. 316). Numerous seventeenth century works on the Sacred Heart were reprinted by the Jesuits in the 1890s.

50 Secretary of State Cardinal Merry del Val wrote in 1905, 'It was, in fact, principally through the intervention of Mary Droste zu Vischering that this twentieth century opened under the happy

auspices of the Sacred Heart' (Abbé L. Chasle, *Sister Mary of the Divine Heart*, London, 1907, p. xii).

51 Sister Lucia of Fatima. See Parts III and IV.

21 JEWS, PROTESTANTS AND MASONS: 'ENEMIES OF OUR LADY'

1 *Revista Católica de Filipinas* (*semanario religioso, científico, literario y de conocimientos útiles*), Manila, 26 December 1889.

2 E. Mullan, SJ, *The Sodality of Our Lady Studied in the Documents* (third edition, first in English), London, 1912, p. 70.

3 *Humanum genus*, 20 April 1884. The encyclical is one of 173 curial documents against secret societies issued in Leo's pontificate.

4 ibid.

5 E. Soderini, *Leo XIII, Italy and France*, London, 1935, p. 102.

6 *Custodi di quella fede*, 8 December (feast of the Immaculate Conception) 1892.

7 ibid.

8 *Humanum genus*, op.cit.

9 P.J. Lyonnard, SJ, *L'Apostolat de la Souffrance ou les Victimes volontaires pour les Besoins actuels de l'Eglise et des nations, surtout des nations Catholiques de l'Europe*, Paris, 1866, p. 324.

10 ibid., pp. 270–1.

11 For example, anchor, sextant and compasses. The dress uniform of the Knights consisted of felt hat with ostrich feathers, scarlet cloak and sword. See C.J. Kauffman, *Faith and Fraternalism: The History of the Knights of Columbus 1882–1982*, New York, 1982.

12 P. Ginhac, SJ, in 1878. Quoted by A. Calvet, SJ, *Life of Father P. Ginhac*, London, 1914, pp. 220–1.

13 Letter dated 12 October (Day of Our Lady of the Pillar) 1890. Reproduced in *Revista Catolica de Filipinas*, 14 December 1890.

14 R. Vargas, SJ, *Historia del Culto de María en Iberoamérica y des Sus Imagenes y Santuarios más Celebrados*, Madrid, 1956, vol. 2, pp. 70–2. In 1900 the Plenary Concilium of Latin America dealt with Freemasonry.

15 M. Cuevas, SJ, *Historia de la Iglesia de México*, Mexico City, 1928, vol. 5, pp. 415.

16 Grand Lodge of Free and Accepted Masons of the Philippines, *Aguinaldo. The Mason and the Revolution*, Manila, 1969.

17 Rev. A. Coleman,OP, *The Friars in the Philippines*, Boston, 1899, pp. 104 and 112.

18 Memorial of the Philippine Friars to the Spanish Government (1898), quoted by Coleman, op.cit., pp. 73–6.

19 *La Iglesia Filipina Independiente*, Manila, no. 2: 18 October 1903.

20 ibid.

20 ibid.

21 P.S. de Achutegai, SJ, and M.A. Bernad, SJ, *Religious Revolution in the Philippines. Life and Church of Gregorio Aglipay 1860–1960*, Manila, 1960, vol. 1, p. 258.

22 *La Iglesia Filipina Independiente*, no. 2, op.cit.

23 Achutegai and Bernad, op.cit., p. 296.

24 A. Cowan, *The X-Rays in Freemasonry*, London, 1904, p. 166.

25 A. Latreille et al., *Histoire du Catholicisme en France, la Période Contemporaine*, Paris, 1962, vol. 3, p. 386.

26 Countess de Courson, 'The French Freemasons and their work'. *The Month*, September 1905.

27 ibid.

28 M. Agulhon, *The Republic in the Village*, Cambridge, 1982, p. 109.

29 Illustrative of the situation was the collapse of the Catholic bank Union Générale (1882), which set out to challenge the Rothschilds (A. Cobham, *A History of Modern France*, London, 1965, vol. 3, p. 31).

30 A. Berthe, *Life of St Alphonsus de Liguori: Bishop and Doctor of the Church, Founder of the Congregation of the Most Holy Redeemer*, London and Dublin, 1906, vol. 2, pp. 727–8.

31 A. Dansette, *Religious History of Modern France*, Edinburgh/London, 1961, vol. 2, p. 52.

32 Quoted by R.L. Hoffman, *More than A Trial. The Struggle over Captain Dreyfus*, New York, 1980, pp. 83–4.

33 *Le Testament d'un Antisémite*, Paris, 1894, p. 424.

34 L. Fry, *Leo Taxil et la Franc-Maçonnerie: lettres inedites publiées par les Amis de M. Jouin*, Chatou, 1934, p. 8.

35 'Le Péril Judeo-Maçonnique', *Revue Internationale de Sociétés Secrètes*, 1925, vol. 3, part 5, p. 31.

36 E. Jouin, *Les Protocols des Sages de Sion*, Paris, 1934.

37 'Les Fidèles de la Contre-Église. Les Maçons', *Revue Internationale de Sociétés Secrètes*, 1921, vol. 3; appendix: 'Les Juifs et la Papauté'.

38 Société Saint-Augustin, *Judaïsme et Franc-Maçonnerie, La Franc-Maçonnerie est-elle d'origine juive?*, Bruges and Lille, 1887.

39 *L'antijuif* (Défendre tous les Travailleurs. Combattre tous les Spéculateurs), 23 October 1898.

40 ibid., 21 August 1898.

41 An even earlier attack was *Le Juif, le Judaïsme et la Judaïsation des peuples chrétiens*, published in 1869 by Gougenot des Mouisseaux, Commander of the Order of Pius IX.

42 Mgr Léon Meurin, SJ, archévêque de Port-Louis, *La Franc-Maçonnerie – Synagogue de Satan*, Paris, 1893, p. 7.

43 ibid., p. 200.

44 ibid., p. 11.

45 ibid., p. 218.

46 For a synopsis, see A.E. Waite, *Devil-Worship in France or the Question of Lucifer etc.*, London, 1896, p. 99.

47 L. Taxil, *Histoire Illustrée du Clergé et des Congrégations*, Paris, 1885, vol. 1, pp. 73 and 113.

48 Fry, op.cit., p. 427.

49 J.A. Ferrer Benimeli, *Masonería, Iglesia y Ilustración*, Madrid, 1976–7.

50 H.C. Lea, *Leo Taxil, Diana Vaughan et l'Église Romaine. Histoire d'une mystification*, Paris, 1901, pp. 22-3.

51 *Civiltà Cattolica*, 1896, vol. 46. Quoted in *Encyclopedia Judaica*, vol. 5.

52 Le Figaro, 16 May 1896. Reproduced by Colette Becker (ed.), *L'Affaire Dreyfus. La Vérité en marche*, Paris, 1969, pp. 57–62.

53 J.N. Moody (ed.), *Church and Society. Catholic Social and Political Thought and Movements 1789–1950*, New York, 1953, p. 156.

54 Dansette, op.cit., vol. 2, p. 180. Père du Lac, a Paris headmaster who had converted Drumont to Catholicism, directed the chief of army staff. Aristocratic military men were prominent in the anti-Masonic movement.

55 The total circulation of *La Croix* (including provincial editions) was over half a million. In 1911, the Assumptionists' newspapers in France had combined sales of four million.

56 E. Cahm, *Politics and Society in Contemporary France, 1789–1971, a Documentary History*, London, 1972, pp. 93–4.

57 *La Faute de l'Abbé Mouret* (1875).

58 Quoted by R. Ternois, *Zola et Son Temps*, Paris, 1961, p. 148.

59 *Lourdes*, London, 1894, preface, p. x.

60 J. Hellman, *Simone Veil, an Introduction to her Thought*, London, 1982.

61 St Joan was later to inspire the Order of Jeanne d'Arc at Berkeley, California, for daughters and sisters of master Masons. Four degrees were designated Myriam, Deborah, Mary and Jeanne d'Arc.

62 R. Sanson, *Revue d'Histoire Moderne et Contemporaire*, 1973, vol. 20.

63 M. Warner, *Joan of Arc. The Image of Female Heroism*, London, 1983, p. 252.

64 See 'L'hommage de la France et de l'Empire à Jeanne d'Arc', *Action Française*, 12 May 1942, front page lead.

65 *The Times*, 24 September 1910.

66 *The Universe*, London, 30 September 1910.

67 A. Rhodes, *The Power of Rome in the Twentieth Century*, London, 1983, p. 186. While it is difficult to find in the international and religious press the exact words used in the alleged insult, it is most likely that Nathan had referred to the doctrine of the Immaculate Conception.

68 Pius X, *Ad diem illum laetissimum* (on the Immaculate Conception), 2 February 1904.

22 THE MODERNIST HERESY

1 J. Lewis May, *Father Tyrrell and the Modernist Movement*, London, 1932, p. 194.

2 *La Croix* passed into the hands of the Lille industrialist P. Féron-Vrau (see p. 138).

3 *The Tablet*, 13 December 1902 (Letter to the editor).

4   A. Dansette, *Religious History of Modern France*, Edinburgh/London, 1961, vol. 2, p. 197.
5   Pius X, *Vehementer Nos*, 11 February 1906.
6   ibid.
7   A. Poulain, SJ, *The Graces of Interior Prayer, a Treatise on Mystical Theology*, London, 1910, pp. 346–7.
8   ibid.
9   T.A. Kselman, *Miracles and Prophecies in Nineteenth Century France*, New Brunswick, New Jersey, 1983, p. 140.
10 A. Debidour, *L'Église Catholique et l'État en France: sous la troisième république (1870–1906)*, Paris, 1906, p. 197.
11 ibid., pp. 307–8.
12 Official pilgrimages alone brought at least three million visitors to Lourdes during Leo's reign.
13 F. Pisani, *Il ne faut pas fermer Lourdes*, Paris, 1906, pp. 11–12.
14 That very year Pius X proclaimed Our Lady of Guadalupe 'Principal Patron of Latin America'. Pius XI would extend her patronage to the Philippines in 1935.
15 These years saw the emergence of great corporations and Leninism, skyscrapers and cubist art, psychoanalysis and the theory of relativity.
16 G.Tyrrell, *Medievalism – a Reply to Cardinal Mercier*, London, 1908, p. 182.
17 Rev. A. MacDonald, *The Holy House of Loreto, a Critical Study of Documents and Traditions*, New York, 1913, p. 324.
18 *Catholic Encyclopedia*, New York, 1907–12, vol. 10.
19 N. García Garcés, 'El movimiento asuncionista en España, *Estudios Marianos*, Madrid, 1947, vol. 6.
20 *Modernism: What It Is and Why It Was Condemned*, London, 1908.
21 ibid.
22 In 1905 bishops were authorized to decide if Catholics under their jurisdiction might participate in political life.
23 Lewis May, op.cit., p. 221.
24 *Church and the Future*, quoted in *Catholic Dictionary of Theology*, London, 1972, vol. 3, p. 290.
25 *Medievalism*, op.cit., p. 181.
26 E. Mullan, SJ, *The Sodality of Our Lady Studied in the Documents*, London, 1912, p. 175.
27 Canonized in 1954 for his unusual humility, simplicity and goodness, Pius X was known to lend his socks to those afflicted with disorders of the feet (P. Johnson, *A History of Christianity*, London, 1976, p. 469).
28 Chicago, 1910.
29 On assuming the tiara in 1903, Sarto bestowed an indulgence of 300 days on all who kiss the scapular of St Dominic, on one side of which is pictured the saint and on the other the Blessed Reginald receiving the Order's habit from the hands of the Virgin. In December 1910 the Holy Office authorized a 'scapular medal', which bore the image of the Sacred Heart of Jesus on one side and that of His Mother on the reverse.

30 *New Catholic Encyclopedia*, New York, 1967–79.

31 L. Verheylezoon, *Devotion to the Sacred Heart: Object, Ends, Practice, Motives*, London, 1955, p. 135.

32 ibid., p. 137.

33 The work of the Enthronement and the Consecration of Families (the latter was under Jesuit management) differed little and spread in harmony, aided by *The Messenger of the Sacred Heart*, published in 26 languages by 1912.

34 Mullan, op.cit., p. 170. Among the Marian periodicals founded in the early years of the century were: *Sodalis Marianus* (Cracow, 1901), *Stella Matutina* (Rome, 1904), *Maria-Congregacio* (Hungary, 1907), *El Correo Mariano* (Palma, 1907), *Lo Pensament Maria* (Catalonia, 1907), *Estrella del Mar* (São Paolo, 1909).

35 *Pope Pius X on Social Reform: Fundamental Regulation of Christian Popular Action*, Catholic Truth Society, London, 1910, pp. 7–8.

36 *Il fermo proposito*, 11 June 1905.

37 *Ad diem illum laetissimum*, 3 February 1904.

38 ibid.

39 A religious of the Mother-house of the Sisters of Charity of Nevers, *Bernadette of Lourdes (La Confidente de l'Immaculée)*, trans. J.H. Gregory, London, 1926, p. 194.

40 ibid.

41 The Sodality of Our Lady was previously governed by the rules of 1855.

42 Mullan, op.cit., pp. 32–3.

43 ibid., p. 107.

44 N. García Garcés, op.cit.

45 Mullan, op.cit., p. 174.

46 R. Vargas, SJ, *Historia del Culto de María en Iberoamérica y de Sus Imágenes y Santuarios Más Celebrados*, Madrid, 1956, vol. 1, pp. 150–4.

47 Presbítero D.A. Magana Soria y General de Artillería M. de la Sala Valdes, *Crónica de las Solemnes Fiestas que se Celebraron en Zaragoza con motivo del fausto suceso de la Coronación Canónica de la Imagen de N.S. del Pilar* etc., Saragossa, 1906.

48 ibid., p. 153.

49 *Annual Register*, London, 1906, p. 349.

50 In the charge of Capuchins, the sanctuary specialized in 'Eucharistic-Marian devotion' (*Diccionario de Historia Eclesiastica de España*, Madrid, 1975, vol. 4: 'Santuarios').

51 *Estudios Marianos*, 1950, vol. 10, p. 194.

52 ibid.

53 ibid.

54 M. Clark, *Modern Italy: 1871–1982*, London, 1984, p. 147.

55 ibid.

56 Cardinal Billot, quoted by J.V. Bainvel, SJ, *Devotion to the Sacred Heart of Jesus. The Doctrine and its History*, London, 1924, p. 331.

57 Rev. G.E. Phillips, *Loreto and the Holy House*, London, 1917, pp. 156–7.

58 *Notre-Dame de Lorette*. Chevalier had earlier published a polemic against the Turin Shroud.

59 Phillips, op.cit.

60 P. Palmer, SJ, *Mary in the Documents of the Church*, London, 1953, p. 96, note 7.

61 E. Nolte, *Three Faces of Fascism: Action Française, Italian Fascism, National Socialism*, London, 1965, p. 64.

62 H. Jedin (ed.), *History of the Church*, London, 1981, vol. 9, p. 476.

63 ibid.

64 Nolte, op.cit., p. 138. Action Française was not condemned by Rome until 1926. Pius XI continued to communicate with Maurras (through the Carmelites of Lisieux) and the movement's newspaper was removed from the Index shortly after the pope's death (1939) as a result of measures initiated by him. Maurras, who denounced resistance fighters in his newspaper during Vichy, was later sentenced to life imprisonment and *dégradation nationale*. He died in 1952, reconciled to the Church.

65 Few details on the operation of the Sodalitium Pianum are known beyond the fact that it used pseudonyms and codes.

66 Chanoine Sauvetre, *Un Bon Serviteur de l'Église, Mgr Jouin, Protonotaire Apostolique, Curé de Saint-Augustin (1844–1932)*, Paris, 1936, pp. 204–5.

67 Letter *Notre charge apostolique*, to French bishops, 25 August 1910.

68 ibid.

69 Letter *Egregie vos*, to Jean Lerolle, 22 February 1907.

70 With the Brief *Inter Catholicos Hispaniae* (1906), Pius X approved the integralist docrine formulated by the Jesuits in *Razón y Fe*.

71 Among the string of congregations founded towards the end of the century in Spain were the Sisters of the Blessed Virgin Mary (Albacete, 1891), the Missionaries of the Sacred Hearts of Jesus and Mary (Baleares, 1891), the Slaves of Mary Immaculate, Protectress of Workers (Valencia, 1892), the Missionaries of the Blessed Sacrament and Mary Immaculate (Granada, 1896) and the Daughters of the Immaculate Heart of Mary (Lerida, 1899).

72 Un maestro de dichas escuelas, *Vida de Don Andres Manjón y Manjón*, Patronato de las Escuelas del Ave María, 1946, p. 118.

73 ibid.

PART III

23 OVERVIEW

1 B. Mussolini, *My Autobiography*, London, 1939, p. 306.

2 *Palabras del Caudillo: 1937–42*, Madrid, 1943, pp. 147–9.

3   'Salazar e Nossa Senhora', *Voz da Fatima*, 13 February 1971.
4   *Ingravescentibus malis* (on the rosary), 29 September 1937.
5   Even in England the cult was reactivated. A new image was enthroned in 1921 in Walsingham parish church and regular pilgrimages were revived. Ten years later, 'England's Nazareth' was rebuilt along the lines of Loreto.
6   Mussolini, op.cit., p. 287.
7   Vicomte L. de Poncis, *Le Portugal Renaît*, Paris, 1936, p. 55.
8   Speech by Franco in Portugal, May 1938. *Palabras del Caudillo*, op.cit., p. 19.
9   R. Vargas, SJ, *Historia del Culto de María*, Madrid, 1956 (4th edition), vol. 2, p. 246.
10   ibid., pp. 87–9.
11   Fr J.M. Elias, *Copacauana-Copacabana*, Tarija (Bolivia), 1981, pp. 133–6.
12   Inspired by the Belgian example, the parade had a strong military flavour and was presented as 'the most important spectacle celebrated in the Republic'. The press spoke of 'the need to utilize all moral forces in order to save our civilization,' See *El Murcurio* (Santiago), 17, 18 and 19 December 1926.
13   More than half the Latin American countries went through some sort of revolution between 1930 and 1931 (the inaugural year of the Second Spanish Republic).
14   Vargas, op.cit., p. 318.
15   The para-military green-shirted Integralists, who attempted a coup against President Vargas, were founded in 1933 by Plinio Salgado, a writer with a marked affection for flowery Virgins, especially Our Lady of Fatima. See his *Geographia Sentimental*, Rio de Janeiro, 1937, chapter 'Canção de Maio', and *A Mulher no Seculo XX*, Oporto, 1946, p. 155.
16   C.J. Kauffman, *Faith and Fraternalism: the History of the Knights of Columbus, 1882–1982*, New York, 1982, p. 298.
17   Pius XI, *Iniquis afflictisque*, 18 November 1926.
18   J.A. Meyer, *The Cristero Rebellion. The Mexican Peoples between Church and State 1926–1929*, Cambridge, 1976, p. 37.
19   ibid., p. 197.
20   Mussolini recalled the Italian ambassador in October 1937.
21   L. Blond, *Notre-Dame des Victoires et le Voeu de Louis XIII*, Paris, 1938; see also M. Christian, *Notre-Dame de France: le Voeu de Louis XIII à la Sainte Vierge. Une page religieuse de notre histoire nationale, 1638–1938*, Paris, 1938.
22   *Catholic Times*, London, 29 July 1938.
23   *The Protest of Pope Pius XI* (letter to Cardinal Pompili, vicar-general of Rome, 2 February 1930), Catholic Truth Society, 1930.
24   R.A. Graham, SJ, *The Pope and Poland in World War Two*, London, 1968, p. 16.
25   J.V. Bainvel, SJ, *Devotion to the Sacred Heart of Jesus. The Doctrine and its History*, London, 1924, p. 333. For the case of a conscripted Cistercian who prayed to the 'Good Holy Virgin' every time he

'pressed the trigger', see M.E. Boylan, O. Cist.R, *A Mystic Under Arms*, Cork, 1945.

26 Bainvel, op.cit., p. 334.
27 L. Verheylezoon, SJ, *Devotion to the Sacred Heart*, London, 1955, p. 140.
28 *Catholic Herald*, London, 13 September 1924.
29 *Estudios Marianos*, 1953, vol. 13, p. 173.
30 *Ingravescentibus malis*, op.cit.
31 ibid.
32 *The Catholic Society Circular*, London, 1920, vol. 1, no. 7.
33 ibid.
34 A.M. Lépicier, *The Mystery of Love: 30 considerations on the Blessed Eucharist, with examples*, London, 1925, p. 93.
35 *Manual of the Children of Mary*, trans. from the French by a Vincentian Father, London, 1938, p. 112.
36 M.S. Segovia Morón, *Aspiraciones para comulgar en Compañía de la Santísima Virgen*, 1926.
37 Lépicier, op.cit., p. 88.
38 J.C.H. Aveling, *The Jesuits*, London, 1981, p. 349.
39 *Ecclesia*, Madrid, 10 July 1943.
40 *With the Sacred Heart of Mary. Twelve Meditations by the Religious of the Sacred Heart of Mary*, Dublin, 1948, p. 10.
41 *Manual of the Children of Mary*, op.cit., p. 56.
42 A. Ayfre, 'La Vierge Marie et le cinéma', *Maria*, Paris, 1957, vol. 5.
43 After 1930 non-Catholic entertainment in the US was under the censorious spotlight of the Legion of Decency, which demanded 'self-denial in the theatre'. For Bishop Fulton Sheen, 'Eros is Thanatos. Sex is Death'. (*The World's First Love*, Dublin, 1953, pp. 133–5).
44 *Catholic Times*, 14 October 1938.
45 '. . . Even though some of their books may be interesting or unobjectionable.' (T.I. Mulcahy, SJ, *Official Manual of the Sodality of Our Lady in Ireland*, Dublin, 1934, pp. 70–1).
46 A.J. Dunn, *Frederic Ozanam and the Establishment of the Society of St Vincent de Paul*, London, 1913, p. 55.
47 P. Levilliot, *Annales d'Histoire Économique et Sociale*, May 1977, no. 45, p. 312.
48 G. Bonetti,SC, *St John Bosco's Early Apostolate*, London, 1934, p. 506.
49 For example, the Franciscan Missionary Sisters of the Immaculate Conception (Brazil, 1910), the Franciscan Handmaids of the Most Pure Heart of Mary (USA, 1916), the North American Federation of the Third Order of St Francis (1921) and the Franciscan Missionaries of the Divine Motherhood (England, 1935).
50 E. Bolster (Sister M. Angela of the Sisters of Mercy), *The Knights of St Columbanus*, Dublin, 1979, p. 20. The author, given access to the Order's archives, claims this is the first history of the Knights.
51 ibid., p. 33.
52 ibid., p. 45.
53 ibid., p. 78.
54 ibid., p. 67.

55 P.C. Hoelle, 'The Legion of Mary'. *Marian Era*, Chicago, 1962, vol. 3, p. 71.

56 L. Ó. Broin, *Frank Duff, a biography*, Dublin, 1982, p. 107.

57 ibid., p. 106. Duff was a lay adviser at the Second Vatican Council.

58 The *praesidium* is 'the unit of charity and secrecy' (*Official Handbook of the Legion of Mary*, Dublin, 1953, p. 233); 'It is treachery to repeat outside what is learned at the Praesidium meeting' (ibid., p. 232).

59 F. Duff, *Walking with Mary*, Glasgow, 1956, p. 240.

60 *Official Handbook*, op.cit., p. 57. While Mary's statuette presides at every meeting, the Legion also venerates St Joseph, 'head of the Holy Family' and symbol of patriarchal authority.

61 ibid., p. 98.

62 ibid., p. 83.

63 Mgr Suenens, auxiliary Bishop of Malines, 'Spiritualité et rayonnement de la Légion de Marie', *Maria*, 1954, vol. 3.

64 C. Hallack, *The Legion of Mary*, London, 1941, p. 127.

65 ibid., p. 137.

66 M. Williams, *The Society of the Sacred Heart*, London, 1967, p. 225.

67 Daniel A. Lord, SJ, *A Call to Catholic Action*, New York, 1935, vol. 1, p. 81.

68 C.W. Ferguson, *Fifty Million Brothers*, New York, 1937, p. 303.

69 Kauffman, op.cit., pp. 256–8.

70 In 1920 a Joan of Arc museum was planned in France as an 'instructive and moralizing influence upon the young' (*Catholic Times*, 6 November 1920).

71 *Le Journal de la Grotte de Lourdes*, 10 August 1941, 92nd year, no. 31.

72 Aveling, op.cit., p. 349.

73 H. Graef, *Mary: a History of Doctrine and Devotion*, London, 1964, vol. 1, pp. 274–5.

74 ibid., p. 266.

75 ibid., p. 269.

76 ibid., p. 267.

77 Clément Dillenschneider, *La Mariologie de S. Alphonse de Liguori. Sources et synthèse doctrinale*, Fribourg, 1934.

78 Rev. R. Gleeson, *Devotion to the Immaculate Heart of Mary*, Dublin, 1936, p. 7.

24 ROME RESURRECTED

1 D.A. Binchy, *Church and State in Fascist Italy*, Dublin, 1941, p. 100.

2 *How the 'Roman Question' was settled, explained by the Pope himself*, Catholic Truth Society, London, 1929.

3 G.A. Williams, *Antonio Gramsci* collected edition of the three special issues of *New Edinburgh Review*, undated, p. 66.

4   Q. Hoare (ed.), *Gramsci, the Lyons Congress, January 1926, Gramsci's Political Writings: 1921–26*, London, 1977, p. 396.
5   Filippo Crispolti, *Pio IX, Leone XIII, Pio X, Benedetto XV. Ricordi Personali*, Milan, 1932.
6   Don Sturzo, leader of the PPI, had been general-secretary of Catholic Action and joint membership of the two bodies was normal.
7   Allocution to the Roman Nobility, 5 January 1921. Led by Princess Giustiniani Bandini, the ladies of Italian Catholic Action formed an 'Apostolate of the Cradle' and 'Wardrobe of the Poor'; they awarded a trophy to 'the Herald of the Pope' chosen in a catechetical contest.
8   The papacy adopted a pacifistic stance. See *Ad beatissimi*, 1 November 1914.
9   Apostolic Letter *Inter Sodalitia* ('to the Sodality of Our Lady of a Happy Death'), 22 March 1918.
10   Fr Gilbert,OFM, Cap., *Our Lady of Loreto. Patroness of Aviators*, Birmingham, 1943.
11   ibid. Fr Gilbert, a British RAF chaplain, explains that the choice 'was not made merely because her house flew through the air, but particularly for these two reasons: her powerful intercession and her wonderful example'.
12   García Garcés, 'La Santísima Virgen nuestra madre y nuestra madre la santa iglesia católica', *Estudios Marianos*, 1965, vol. 26.
13   See encyclical *Fausto appetente die* on St Dominic (29 June 1921), which refers to the rosary victories over the Albigenses and the Turk.
14   *Sacra Propediem* (on the Third Order of St Francis), 6 January 1921.
15   Brief *Praestantes animi laudes*, March 1918.
16   See, for example, Cardinal Gasparri's letter to Mgr Jouin of 20 June 1919, reproduced on the cover of *Revue Internationale de Sociétés Secrètes* throughout the '20s.
17   *New Catholic Encyclopedia*, New York, 1967–79.
18   ibid.
19   Agostino Gemelli,OFM, MD, *Psychoanalysis Today*, New York, 1955, p. 139. For a critical life of this dynamic Franciscan, whose interests ranged from vivisection to training military pilots, see G. Cosmacini, *Gemelli: il Machiavelli di Dio*, Milan, 1987.
20   R.A. Webster, *Christian Democracy in Italy 1860–1960*, London, 1961, pp. 156–60.
21   *Sacra Propediem*, op.cit., Sabatier's *Vie de St François* (1894), an assault on sacerdotalism and Jesuitism, was placed on the Index.
22   Sabatier's research on Franciscan documents had conclusively shown the spuriousness of the Portiuncula indulgence.
23   A. Gemelli, *The Franciscan Message to the World*, London, 1934, p. 58.
24   'Il viaggio trionfale della Vergine di Loreto nella gloria del suo santuario' and 'La festa della Madonna a Loreto', *Osservatore Romano*, 9 September 1922.
25   'Gloria di fede romana alla Vergine che parte in trionfo per Loreto', *Osservatore Romano*, 8 September 1922.
26   'Politica a Loreto', ibid.

27   Gramsci, quoted by Q. Hoare, op.cit., p. 396.
28   Peter C. Kent, *The Pope and the Duce*, New York, 1981, p. 5.
29   Ernst Nolte, *Three Faces of Fascism: Action Française, Italian Fascism, National Socialism*, London, 1965, p. 163.
30   J. Barnes, 'Fascism and the Catholic Church'. *Dublin Review*, 1924, vol. 175, no. 350.
31   'Nel XXV anniversario di Regno', *L'Idea Nazionale*, Rome, 7 June 1925.
32   Shortly after the March on Rome, the national press carried caricatures of Masons as well as the pope's message calling for a 'riconciliazione con l'Italia' (*L'Idea Nazionale*, 24 December 1922). In February 1923 the Fascist Grand Council ruled that Freemasonry was 'incompatible' with party membership. For the Jewish situation, see M. Michaelis, *Mussolini and the Jews*, Oxford, 1978.
33   Carlo Falconi, *The Popes in the Twentieth Century*, London, 1967, p. 132.
34   Fr August Bernard Hasler, *How the Pope Became Infallible. Pius IX and the Politics of Persuasion* (Introduction by Hans Küng), New York, 1981, p. 253.
35   P. Hughes, *Pope Pius the Eleventh*, London, 1937, p. 41.
36   *Galliam Ecclesiam Filliam Primo genitam*, 2 March 1922.
37   *Ubi Arcano Dei Consilio*, 23 December 1922. Pius established an Ave Maria school in Rome.
38   *Studiorem ducem*, 29 June 1923.
39   *Ubi Arcano Dei Consilio*, op.cit.
40   *L'Idea Nazionale*, 19 May 1925.
41   Although Freemasonry was initially close to Mussolini (Nolte, op.cit., p. 259), Masons were massacred by Blackshirts and lodges plundered in 1925 (Daniel Ligou (ed.), *Dictionnaire Universel de la Franc-Maçonnerie*, Paris, 1974, p. 674).
42   *L'Idea Nazionale*, 17 May 1925.
43   *Quas primas*, 11 December 1925.
44   Hoare, op.cit., p. 402.
45   *Miserentissumus Redemptor*, 8 May 1928.
46   ibid.
47   *Mortalium animos* ('on fostering true religious unity'), 6 January 1928.
48   Binchy, op.cit., p. 190.
49   Treaty, arts 1–3.
50   ibid., art. 8.
51   Concordat, art.1. A portion of the £8 million settlement provided by the Lateran agreement was indirectly invested in the pilgrimage business through French railways.
52   Concordat, art. 27.
53   Concordat, arts 13 and 15.
54   Concordat, art. 36. For the text of the Lateran agreement, see John F. Pollard, *The Vatican and Italian Fascism 1929–32*, Cambridge 1985: appendix.
55   Binchy, op.cit., p. 323.

56 *Divini illius magistri* ('on Christian Education of Youth'), 31 December 1929.

57 *Non abbiamo bisogno*, 29 June 1931.

58 The future Pope Pius XII succeeded Gasparri in 1930.

59 *Annali del Fascismo*, September 1931.

60 Minute by Mussolini on his meeting with the pope on February 11, 1932, quoted by Peter C. Kent, op.cit., appendix. The *Osservatore Romano* favourably compared the 'Carta del lavoro' (Fascist legislation on labour relations) with *Rerum novarum*, which continued to be the doctrinal basis for social action.

61 *Caritate Christi compulsi* ('on the troubles of our time: a call to prayer and penance), 3 May 1932.

62 ibid.

63 'Il santuario di Loreto nella gloria di una nuova vita', *Civiltà Cattolica*, 1938, anno 89, vol. 3.

64 *Dizionario Mussoliniano*, 1939: '*Roma e il nostro punto di partenza edi riferimento; e il nostro simbolo, il nostro mito*' (Mussolini, April 1922).

65 *Ubi Arcano Dei Consilio*, op.cit.

66 Cardinal Schuster's lecture to mark the occasion was publicized by the 'School of Mystical Fascism of Milan'. See G. de Rossi dell'Arno, *Pio XI e Mussolini*, Rome, 1954 (first edition), p. 135.

67 E. Jiménez Caballero, *La Nueva Catolicidad*, Madrid, 1933 (2nd edition), p. 120.

68 Nolte, op.cit., p. 79.

69 Rossi dell'Arno, op.cit.

70 Cardinal Rocca, Archbishop of Bologna, October 1935, quoted by Rossi dell'Arno, op.cit., p. 68.

71 Bishop Santino Margaria of Civita Castellana, December 1935, ibid., pp. 76–7.

72 Bishop Pasquale dell'Isola of Sarmo and Cava Lettera, December 1935, ibid., pp. 90–1. The Coptic Abuna (Archbishop) Petros was publicly executed in 1936 and hundreds of monks were massacred by the Italians.

73 Bishop Lojacono of Ariano, December 1935, ibid., p. 86.

74 Bishop Cazzani of Cremona, October 1935, ibid., pp. 81–2.

75 Archbishop Marini of Amalfi, November 1935, ibid., p. 70.

76 S. Neill, *A History of Christian Missions*, London, 1979, p. 423.

25 PATRONESS OF THE ESTADO NÔVO: OUR LADY OF FATIMA AND DR SALAZAR

1 Hugh Kay, *Salazar and Modern Portugal*, London, 1970, p. 81.

2 Fr L. Kondor (ed.), *Fatima in Lucia's Own Words* (translated by Dominican Nuns of Perpetual Rosary), Fatima, 1976, p. 118.

3 R.A.H. Robinson, 'The religious question and the Catholic revival in Portugal, 1900–1930', *Journal of Contemporary History*, 1977, vol. 12, p. 348.

4 ibid., p. 351. See also Costa's doctoral thesis, *A Igreja e a Questão Social*, Coimbra, 1895, on 'sordid Jesuitry'.

5 See F. Gribble, *Royal House of Portugal*, London, 1915; *HRH the Duke of Oporto, Memoirs*, anon., with permission of his wife, HRH the Princess of Bragança, London, 1921.

6 See D.L. Wheeler, *Republican Portugal, A Political History 1910–1917*, Wisconsin, 1978.

7 ibid., p. 68. The worst brutality was, in fact, to come in Russia in 1929–34 and 1937.

8 Daniel Ligou (ed.), *Dictionnaire Universel de la Franc-Maçonnerie*, Paris, 1974: article on Portugal.

9 Dr A. Iraizoz y de Villar, *El Apóstol de la Democracia Portuguesa, Sebastian de Magalhaes Lima*, Gran Logia de la Isla de Cuba, Havana, 1929, p. 11.

10 A British protest was led by Adeline, Duchess of Bedford, and the Earl of Lytton. See E.M. Tennison, *Will England Save Portugal? Our Hereditary Obligations, 1373–1914*, London, 1914.

11 L.W. Henderson, *Angola: Five Centuries of Conflict*, London, 1979, p. 145.

12 V. de Bragança-Cunha, *Revolutionary Portugal (1910–1936)*, London, 1938, p. 105.

13 *Ordem Nova*, the organ of Lusitanian Integralism, proclaimed itself '. . . counter-revolutionary, reactionary, Catholic, Apostolic and Roman, monarchist, intolerant and intransigent. . .' Antonio de Figueiredo, *Portugal: Fifty Years of Dictatorship*, London, 1975, p. 57.

14 Conde de Santibañez del Rio, 'El Integralismo Lusitano', *Action Española*, 1932, no. 14, p. 146.

15 ibid.

16 Ramiro de Maeztu, preface to the first Spanish edition of *La Alianza Peninsular* (1930).

17 Sardinha, *La Alianza Peninsular*, Segovia, 1939, pp. 38–9.

18 ibid.

19 ibid.

20 ibid.

21 're-aportugarse'.

22 Marcello Caetano, who took over from the comatose Salazar in 1968, edited *New Order* (see note 13) while reading law at Lisbon.

23 *Grande Enciclopedia Portuguesa e Brasileira*, Lisbon/Rio de Janeiro, 1945, vol. 26: 'Salazar', p. 680.

24 ibid., vol. 6, p. 459: 'Centro Academico de Democracia Cristã'.

25 *Estudos, Bodas de Ouro de CADC, Revista de Cultura e Formacão Catolica*, Orgão do CADC, Coimbra, 1951, p. 665.

26 ibid., p. 659.

27 C.C. Martindale, SJ, *The Message of Fatima*, London, 1950, p. 69.

28 Kondor, op.cit., p. 55.

29 ibid., p. 62.
30 ibid.
31 ibid., p. 156.
32 Aventino de Oliveria, *Fátima*, Missionarios de Consolata, Fatima, 1978.
33 Luce Laurand, *Father Francisco da Cruz, the Apostle of Charity*, Lisbon, 1972, p. 52, Pius XI referred to Fr Cruz as 'the Lusitanian Saint'.
34 C.C. Martindale, SJ, *What Happened at Fatima*, Catholic Truth Society, London, 1981, p. 4.
35 J.C.H. Aveling, *The Jesuits*, London, 1981, pp. 245–6.
36 *Soul*, organ of the Blue Army of Our Lady of Fatima in the US and Canada, special issue, 1982.
37 *A Monarquia, Diario Integralista da Tarde*, 9 December 1917. Our view of the immediate instrumentalization of the visions by militaristic/clerical forces is shared by several authors, e.g. João Ilharco, *Fátima Desmascarada, a verdade historia acerca de Fátima: documentada com provas*, Coimbra, 1971.
38 'Piété populaire Portugaise', *Maria*, 1958, vol. 5, p. 633.
39 Paulo Siebertz, *A Macconaria na Luta Pelo Poder*, Oporto, 1945, p. 438.
40 'Piété populaire Portuguaisé', op.cit.
41 *Brotéria* (journal of the Portuguese Province), 1946, vol. XLIII.
42 For example, literacy campaigns (the Virgin had instructed Lucia to read and write): see Padre Moreira das Neves, 'Nossa Senhora quer que se aprenda a ler e a escrever', *Escola Portuguesa, Boletim de Accão Educativa*, Lisbon, 1957, ano XXIII, no. 1142, p. 718. The theme of the 1987 Children's Pilgrimage was: 'To contemplate like Francisco – to love like Jacinta' (*Seers of Fatima*, Bulletin for the causes of beatification of Francisco and Jacinta, 1987, no. 3/4).
43 Francisco, whose 'exquisite' death took place in April 1919, was devoted to the 'hidden Jesus' (i.e. the Eucharist) and the person of the pope. His sister, who died just before her tenth birthday, is extolled for her mortification and prophetic condemnations of liberalism: 'Fashion will offend Our Lord very much . . . Priests must be very pure. Disobedience of priests and religious to their superiors gravely displeases Our Lord; pray for rulers; the sins that cause most people to go to hell are those of the flesh', etc.
44 The Opera di Santa Dorotea (Liguria, 1838) undertook education in the Papal States and fought Freemasonry in north-east Brazil in the 1870s.
45 Visconde de Montelo, *Os episódios maravilhosos de Fátima*, Guarda, 1921.
46 *A Monarquia*, 8 March, 1922.
47 Kondor, op.cit., p. 195.
48 'Piété populaire Portugaise', op.cit., p. 630.
49 Michael Harsgor, *Portugal in Revolution*, The Washington Papers, no. 32, Georgetown, 1976, p. 4.
50 A. de O. Salazar (26 May, 1936), *Doctrine and Action: Internal and Foreign Policy of the New Portugal, 1928–1939*, London, 1939, p. 285.
51 'The Fatima diocesan process', *Seers of Fatima*, 1983, no. 3/4.

52 Kondor, op.cit., pp. 199-200. Compare the conditions, images and messages of the apparition with that of St M.M. Alacoque in seventeenth-century France (see Part I).

53 See Padre A.M. Martins, SJ, *Cartas da Irma Lucia*, Oporto, 1979 (second edition).

54 The first of many editions of Fr Fonseca's *Le Meraviglie di Fatima* was published by Propaganda Mariana, Casale Montferrato in 1931. The first English account of the visions was a translation of this, *The Wonders of Fatima*, Bombay, 1933.

55 Aveling, op.cit., p. 353.

56 M. de Faria, *Assunção de N. Senhora, Estudo Historico-Dogmatico*, Braga, 1954, p. 353.

57 Letter *Ex officiosis litteris*, to Cardinal Cerejeira, 10 November 1933.

58 *Doctrine and Action*, op.cit., p. 83.

59 Mario Soares, *Portugal's Struggle for Liberty*, London, 1971. p. 114. The integralist nature of the state is seen in the extraordinary range of literature – from Zola to Updike – banned under Salazar. See *Livros Proibidos no Regime fascista*, Comissão do Livro Negro Sobre o Regime fascista, Lisbon, 1981.

60 Soares, op.cit., p. 82.

61 Antonio Ferro, *Salazar. Portugal and Her Leader*, London, 1939. p. 116.

62 'Salazar e Nossa Senhora', *Voz da Fátima*, 13 February 1971.

63 Quoted by Kay, op.cit., p. 73.

64 *Salazar – Prime Minister of Portugal SAYS*. Two hundred thoughts selected from the writings of the leader of the Portuguese Recovery, Lisbon, undated (c. 1938), p. 42.

65 Gerald Bauer, quoted by Ferro, op.cit., p. 116.

66 *Voz da Fátima*, op.cit.

67 Ferro, op.cit., p. 77.

68 F.C.C. Egerton, *Salazar, Rebuilder of Portugal*, London, 1943, p. 11.

69 'The basis of their organization and life is spiritual' (Salazar SAYS, op.cit., p. 63).

70 *Doctrine and Action*, op.cit., pp. 208–9.

71 Silas Cerqueira, 'L'Église et la dictature portugaise', *Revue Française de Science Politique*, 1973, vol. XXIII, no. 3, p. 484.

72 Section X, art. 45.

73 *Saeculo exteunte octavo*, 13 June 1940.

74 Figueiredo, op.cit., p. 156.

75 *Salazar SAYS*, op.cit., p. 42.

76 *Civiltà Cattolica*, 1942, vol. IV.

77 J.M. Lourenco, *Situação Juridica de Igreja em Portugal*, Coimbra, 1943, p. 464.

78 *Carta enviada a Pio XII*, Tuy, 2 December 1940, Martins, op.cit., p. 57.

79 Kondor, op.cit., p. 102.

80 See Derek Holmes, *The Papacy in the Modern World*, London 1981, p. 160; David Mitchell, *The Jesuits, A History*, London, 1980, p. 270; *Martyrdom of the Serbs*, documents issued by the Serbian Eastern Orthodox Diocese for USA and Canada, 1944.

81 Carlo Falconi, *The Silence of Pius XII*, London, 1965, p. 301. Falconi, a laicized priest who made an investigation of the Croatian holocaust, concludes, 'in order not to compromise the German advance in the East Pius XII kept silence about all the crimes committed against civilians by the Nazis and their allies . . .' (*The Popes in the Twentieth Century*, London, 1967, p. 256).

82 Martins, op.cit., Introduction, pp. 22–6.

83 *El Alcázar*, Madrid, 27 January 1943.

84 Hansjakob Stehle, *Eastern Politics of the Vatican*, 1917–1979, Ohio, 1981, p. 208.

85 ibid.

86 The first edition of *Jacinta. Florinhas da Fátima. Episódios inéditos das aparições de Nossa Senhora* by Dr Jose Galamba de Oliveira came out in May 1938.

87 Kondor, op.cit., p. 104.

88 Quoted by J.M. Alonso,CMF, *História da Literatura sobre Fátima*, Fatima, 1967, p. 29.

89 *Diario de Lisboa*, 7 April 1942.

90 ibid., 2 April 1942.

91 Rt Rev. W.J. Doheny and Rev. J.P. Kelly, *Papal Documents on Mary*, Milwaukee, 1954, p. 203.

92 ibid., p. 204.

93 *Ecclesia*, Madrid, 20 February 1943.

94 ibid., 22 April 1943.

95 ibid., 13 November 1943.

96 *El Alcázar*, 27 January 1943.

97 ibid.

98 *Ecclesia*, 16 October 1943.

99 Letter to the pope from the Spanish Mariological Society. See 'Naturaleza, historia y eficacia de la devoción al corazón de María', *Estudios Marianos*, 1945, vol. 4.

100 *Carta enviada a Pio XII*, Martins, op.cit., p. 59.

101 J. Tusell, *Franco y los católicos. La política interior española entre 1945 y 1957*, Madrid, 1984, p. 154.

102 The crown contained 950 diamonds, 313 pearls, 17 rubies, 14 emeralds and 269 turquoises.

103 For example, the Duchess of Barcelona, wife of Don Juan, exiled heir to the Spanish throne.

104 *Brotéria*, December 1946, op.cit., p. 660.

105 ibid.

26 POLAND AND THE CONVERSION OF RUSSIA

1 D. Dewar, *Saint of Auschwitz: the story of Maksymilian Kolbe*, London, 1982, p. 17.

2 D. Mitchell, *The Jesuits, A History*, London, 1980, p. 254.

3　F. McCullagh, 'The Catholic Church in Russia today', *Blackfriars*, Oxford, 1923, vol. 4, no. 42.

4　M. Helm-Pirgo, *Virgin Mary, Queen of Poland*, Polish Institute of Arts and Sciences in America, New York, 1957, p. 21.

5　Carlo Falconi, *The Popes in the Twentieth Century*, London, 1967, p. 174.

6　M. Williams, *The Society of the Sacred Heart, History of a Spirit 1800–1975*, London, 1978, p. 209.

7　Mitchell, op.cit.

8　ibid.

9　Sir Steven Runciman, *The Orthodox Churches and the Secular State* (Sir Douglas Robb Lectures), Auckland, 1971, p. 85. Fr Walsh estimated that 1,800,000 died in the religious persecutions, including 28 archbishops and 1,400 priests (*Catholic Herald*, 13 September 1924).

10　F.M. Kalvelage, 'Knight of the Immaculate', *Marian Era*, Chicago, 1966, vol. 7, p. 82.

11　Dewar, op.cit., p. 17.

12　*Marian Era*, op.cit.

13　*All You Need to Know to Be a Knight!* US leaflet, c. 1985.

14　*Marytown, National Center, Knights of the Immaculate*, US leaflet, c. 1985.

15　Dewar, op.cit., p. 39.

16　*The Knights of the Immaculata Movement*, US leaflet, c. 1985.

17　*Osservatore Romano*, weekly English edition, 28 December 1972.

18　*Madonna*, Dublin, October 1927. There were 600 Polish sodalities of Our Lady in 1928.

19　Dewar, op.cit., p. 7.

20　Cardinal Wojtyla, Archbishop of Cracow, quoted by Fr H.M. Manteau-Bonamy,OP, *Immaculate Conception and the Holy Spirit. The Marian Teachings of Father Kolbe*, Kenosha, Wisconsin, 1977, p. xxii.

21　Pope Paul VI, ibid., p. x.

22　In France, Belgium, Switzerland, West Germany, Italy, Spain, Portugal, Malta, Mexico, South America, Canada, USA, Australia and New Zealand.

23　Dewar, op.cit., p. 7.

24　Conference, February 1938, quoted by Manteau-Bonamy, op.cit., p. 75.

25　Conference, 5 February 1941, ibid., p. 50.

26　Written on the day of his arrest, 17 February 1941, ibid., p. xxxiii. Sergius Bulgakov, the émigré Orthodox theologian, had expressed a very similar idea several years earlier: 'In the Virgin there are united Holy Wisdom and the Wisdom of the created world, the Holy Spirit and the human hypostasis.' (*The Orthodox Church*, London, 1935, p. 139).

27　Conference, 27 June 1936, quoted by Manteau-Bonamy, op.cit.

28　ibid., p. 108.

29　ibid., p. 121.

30　Rev J. Chrosciechowski, *The Devotion to the Divine Mercy*, Mass., 1957, p. 113.

31　ibid., p. 123.

27 A GOLDEN HEART FOR THE POOR:
THE BELGIAN APPARITIONS

1 H. Thurston, SJ, *Beauraing and Other Apparitions. An Account of Some Borderline Cases in the Psychology of Mysticism*, London, 1934, p. 17.
2 B. de Sn.Pablo, 'Revalorización de la devoción popular a la santísima Virgen', *Estudios Marianos*, 1961, vol. 22, pp. 291-2.
3 É. de Moreau, SJ, 'Le cult mariale en Belgique', *Maria*, 1956, vol. 4, pp. 511–13.
4 L. Bouchar, *Notre-Dame de Beauraing. Récit véridique et complet des célèbres apparitions (1932–1933)*, Tournai/Paris, 1933, pp. 16–18.
5 ibid., p. 31.
6 ibid., p. 34.
7 'Che cosa succede a Beauraing?', *Osservatore Romano*, 20 December 1933.
8 C.-J. Joset, SJ, *Dossiers de Beauraing*, no. 1, Beauraing, 1981, p. 20.
9 P. Brotteaux, *Hallucinations ou Miracles? Les Apparitions d'Esquioga et de Beauraing*, Paris, 1934, p. 94.
10 Docteur Maistriaux, *Que se passe-t-il à Beauraing?*, Éditions Rex, Louvain, 1932.
11 S.J. Woolf (ed.), *Fascism in Europe*, London, 1981, p. 300. A former law student and Catholic activist, Degrelle led REX – financed by Nazis and Italian Fascists – to capture 29 per cent of the vote in the general elections of 1936. His extremism and exposure of clerical corruption resulted in a condemnation by the cardinal primate the following year.
12 S.G. Payne, *Fascism. A Reader's Guide* (ed. W. Laquer), London, 1982, p. 305.
13 D. Sharkey and J. Debergh, OMI, *Our Lady of Beauraing*, New York, 1958, p. 190.
14 G. Robert, *Le Miracle de Beauraing. Récit d'un témoin*, Courtrai, 1933, p. 21.
15 L. Wilmet, *Beauraing*, Paris, 1933.
16 *New Catholic Encyclopedia*, vol. 2: article on Belgium.
17 Joset, op.cit., p. 38.
18 'Les faits mystérieux de Beauraing', *Études Carmélitaines*, 1933, vol. 1, p. 164.
19 ibid., p. 167.
20 J.B. Lenain, SJ, 'Les Événements de Beauraing', *Nouvelle Revue Théologique*, 1933, no. 4.
21 D. Sharkey, *The Woman Shall Conquer*, Milwaukee, 1952, p. 157.
22 C.M. Staehlin, SJ, *Apariciones. Ensayo Crítico*, Madrid, 1954, p. 12; Thurston, op.cit., pp. 42–3.
23 Sharkey and Debergh, op.cit., p. 176.

24 D. Walne and J. Flory, *The Virgin of the Poor. The Apparitions at Banneaux*, Catholic Truth Society, London, 1983, p. 1.
25 ibid., p. 8.
26 Sharkey, op.cit., p. 166.
27 J. Beevers, *Virgin of the Poor*, Indiana, 1975.
28 Mgr Suenens, Évêque auxiliaire, Malines, 'Spiritualité et rayonnement de la Légion de Marie', *Maria*, 1954, vol. 3.

28 NATIONAL CATHOLICISM

1 J. Pemartín, *Los Valores Históricos en la Dictadura Española*, Madrid, 1929 (second edition), p. 153.
2 One of the chief concerns of superior-general Martín was to encourage the Spiritual Exercises among working people. In Barcelona, the *caballeros*' Sodality of the Purification and St Francis Borgia appointed a committee to run workmen's retreats and published a pamphlet: *Los Santos Ejercicios para obreros, su importancia y su organización en Barcelona* (1907).
3 The 'Tragic Week' of Barcelona (1909) which left 63 churches and convents in ruins was followed by the first congress of freethinkers in Spain (October 1910), where demands were made that the government sever relations with the Vatican and forbid all public display of religion (J.A. Ferrer Benimeli, *La Masonería en los Episodos Nacionales de Pérez Galdos*, Madrid, 1982, p. 231).
4 Padre Manjón, quoted in *Vida de Don Andrés Manjón y Manjón, Fundador de las Escuelas del Ave María, por un maestro de dichas escuelas*, Alcalá de Henares, 1946, p. 170. The Ave María Schools inculcated National Catholicism through 'Marian-patriotic' acts in which honours to Our Lady were combined with the national anthem and flag-waving. The Day of Nuestra Señora del Pilar was the official foundation date of the first Ave María school. The visitor to the school today – in Granada – will see Our Lady on her pillar dominating one of the relief maps in the playground which illustrate the 'Manjonian method'.
5 R. Vargas, SJ, *Historia del Culto de María en Iberoamérica y des Sus Imágenes y Santuarios más celebrados*, Madrid, 1956, vol. 1, p. 84. A similar expression of the Marian nature of Hispanidad was the Franciscan restoration of the shrine of Our Lady of Guadalupe in 1909 'as a common shrine for Spanish-speaking people' (*New Catholic Encyclopedia*).
6 His confessor was Fr López, SJ.
7 R. Vázquez, *La Devoción Popular Cordobesa en Sus Ermitas y Santuarios*, Córdoba, 1987, p. 32.
8 J. Bertran, *Nuestra Señora de Misericordia y su Santuario de Reus*, Reus, 1954, p. 49.
9 Pemartín, op.cit., p. 37.

10 Pax Romana, a university organization formed in these years, was vital to the dissemination of the Hispanidad creed.

11 According to Pierre Vilar, there were 13 complete crises and 30 partial ones in Spain between 1917 and 1923: *Historia de España*, Barcelona, 1985 (21st edition), p. 118.

12 *Civiltà Cattolica*, 1919, anno 70, vol. 2.

13 Dynamited at the beginning of the civil war.

14 *Raza Española*, 1919, *número extraordinario commemorativo de las glorias de la raza*, p. 81.

15 ibid., January 1919, no. 1, p. 7.

16 ibid., p. 4.

17 C. Eguía Ruíz, SJ, *Reliquias de San Ignacio de Loyola y San Francisco Javier. Su recorrido triunfal por España*, Madrid, 1924, p. 325.

18 *Diccionario de Historia Eclesiástica de España*, 1972, vol. 1, p. 145.

19 Pemartín, op.cit., p. 685.

20 Pemartín thought Spanish religiosity was 'the spiritual survival of the lifeblood (*fuerza vital*) of the Spanish Middle Ages', op.cit., p. 57; Ramiro de Maeztu, leader of Hispanidad (see p. 211) wrote that the Middle Ages were 'a lovely (*amoroso*) dream of heaven', *La Crisis del Humanismo*, Buenos Aires, 1916, p. 41.

21 A woman was sent to prison in 1926 for maintaining that Mary had other children besides Jesus (R. Carr, *Spain 1808–1975*, Oxford 1982, p. 112).

22 Pemartín, op.cit., p. 61.

23 ibid.

24 The leading Propagandista, lawyer, and innovatory journalist Angel Herrera Oria participated in the inauguration of Unión Patriótica (H. Raguer, *La Espada y la Cruz. La Iglesia 1936–39*, Barcelona, 1977, p. 18).

25 The Catholic Youth Section was given its definitive shape by ACN de P in 1925.

26 Marques de Quintanar, Conde de Santibañez del Rio, Preface to *La Alianza Peninsular*, Segovia, 1939 (2nd edition), p. xliii.

27 Cardinal-primate Segura of Toledo sponsored pilgrimages to Rome and instituted 'the Day of the Pope' – later extended to a week.

28 Padre Manjón, whose many honours included the Order of Alfonso XII, was invited by the bishops to be president of the Madrid congress, but was too ill to accept.

29 Among the images canonically crowned during Primo's rule were Nuestra Señora de la Montaña (Cáceres), del Sagrario (Toledo), de la Fuensanta (Murcia), de Guadalupe (Cáceres), de los Dolores (La Coruña), de la Antigua (Seville); Virgen de las Nievas (Ciudad Real), de Lledó (Castellón).

30 A typical example of militarized worship of Mary was the investiture of the image of the *Mare de Deu de Misericordia* in Catalonia in 1929. The statue was presented with General F. Araoz's sash, Grand Cross of Military Merit and baton, while the captain-general of the province carried the shrine's banner (J. Bertran, op.cit., p. 55).

31 Pemartín, op.cit., pp. 52–3.
32 Marques de Quintanar, Conde de Santibañez del Rio, op.cit.
33 E. de Manaricua, *Sta María de Begoña en la Historia Espitual de Vizcaya*, Bilbao, 1950, p. 476.
34 *Madonna*, Dublin, May 1928.
35 A federation of Semana Santa confraternities was established in 1927 by the hierarchy in Málaga and Granada. Many of today's prosperous brotherhoods were founded in this period, e.g., the Royal Brotherhood of Our Lady of Piety (Málaga, 1926) and the Brotherhood of St Mary of the Alhambra (Granada, 1927).
36 The original brotherhood dates from the times of the Catholic Kings.
37 For example, the Royal Confraternity of Our Lady of Hope, formed in 1928 by bank staff in Granada.
38 Mgr Jouin's edition of *The Protocols of Zion* was translated into Spanish (Madrid/Burgos, 1927) and the Marquis de la Eliseda, a prominent member of Acción Española, later wrote a laudatory commentary (*Accion Española*, 1932, no. 10). Another typical piece was *El Reino de Satanás en el Mundo en Sus relaciones con el Protestantismo y la Masonería* (anon., Palma de Mallorca, 1929).
39 Pemartín, op.cit., p. 496.
40 Secrecy (or 'discretion') is central to Opus Dei. No. 191 of the association's constitutions reads: 'No one must reveal to anyone that they themselves belong to Opus Dei.' We are indebted to Dr John Roche of Linacre College, Oxford, for this point, which appears in his unpublished manuscript *Evidence from internal documents of Opus Dei and testimony*.
41 E. Jiménez Caballero, *Los Toros, las Castañuelas y la Virgen*, Madrid, 1927, p. 153.
42 *Diccionario de Historia Eclesiástica de España*. vol. 1, p. 145.
43 *Estudios Marianos*, 1947, vol. 6, pp. 529–30.
44 ibid., 1950, vol. 10, p. 196.
45 Student discontent led General Primo de Rivera to close Madrid University in March 1929.
46 In 1926 Alfonso XIII also sent a message to the Marian congress of Covadonga expressing the hope of achieving the dogmatic definition.
47 *Estudios Marianos*, 1973, vol. 37, p. 178.
48 ibid., p. 177.
49 *Diccionario de Historia Eclesiástica de España*, Madrid, 1972, vol. 2, p. 1085.
50 The beatification process of the founder, Antonio Amundaraín Garmendia (1885–1954) was opened in 1982.
51 The beatification process of Mother Margarita María (1884–1934), founder of the Institute of Mercedarian Missionaries of Biarritz and Youth Mercedarian Missionaries (1920), was opened in the 1960s.
52 A. Vásquez de Prada, *El Fundador del Opus Dei: Mons. Josemaría Escrivá de Balaguer (1902–1975)*, Madrid, 1983, p. 114.
53 ibid., p. 116.

54 Escrivá became the Marquis de Peralta in 1968, reactivating a defunct eighteenth-century title which he later waived in favour of his brother Santiago. For Escrivá's series of name changes, see L. Carandell, *Vida y Milagros de Monseñor Escrivá de Balaguer*, Barcelona, 1975, pp. 61–6 and 83.

55 J.A. Vidal-Quadras, *Torreciudad – a Shrine to Our Lady*, Torreciudad, 1978, p. 13.

56 S. Bernal, *Msgr Josemaría Escrivá de Balaguer. A Profile of the Founder of Opus Dei*, London/New York, 1977, p. 89.

57 ibid., p. 71. For a description of the Marian sensibility of Mgr Escrivá, see J. Echevarría, *El amor a María Santísima en las enseñanzas de Monseñor Josemaría Escrivá de Balaguer*, Madrid, 1978.

58 D.M. Helming, *Footprints in the Snow. A Pictorial Biography of Josemaría Escrivá, the Founder of Opus Dei* (foreword by Malcolm Muggeridge), New York/London, 1986, p. 75.

59 *Camino*, (The Way), maxim no. 946. For a woman defector's view, see Maria Angustias Moreno Cereijo, *La Otra Cara del Opus Dei*, Barcelona, 1978.

29 SECOND REPUBLIC AND SANTA CRUZADA

1 E. Jiménez Caballero, *Camisa Azúl y Boina Colorada. Fé y Acción, Fasciculo Doctrinal*, Madrid, 1939, no. 2, pp. 33–4.

2 *Camino*, 494. (See note 35.)

3 P. Brotteau, *Hallucinations ou miracles? Les Apparitions d'Esquioga et de Beauraing*, Paris, 1934, p. 24.

4 Although the visions caused a great stir for years, the shrine of Esquioga was never authorized by the Church. The large number of people involved in the experience made it unmanageable and very soon the Jesuits turned critical. P. Laburu, SJ, argued that as a rule Our Lady chose just a few 'confidents'. Brotteau, op.cit., pp. 74–5.

5 In Salamanca, for example, the Franciscans in charge of the shrine of Nuestra Señora del Castañar had to abandon their post in 1932.

6 The seventh edition of Fr Mateo Crawley Boevey's guide to expiation, *Manuel de los Sagrados Corazones*, was issued in 1932.

7 Spanish Catholic Action, confirmed by Pius XI as the central platform of the Church (*Dilectissima nobis*, 3 June 1933), became even more closely supervised by ACN de P. Angel Herrera, the Propagandistas' president, was appointed president of the Junta Central de la Acción Católica Española in 1933.

8 Towards the end of 1931, the Juntas Castellanas de Actuación Hispánica of O. Redondo (a close collaborator of Catholic Action) agreed on a common programme with R. Ledesma's Juntas de Ofensiva Sindicalistas (JONS).

9 Introduction to the first Spanish edition of Sardinha's *La Alianza Peninsular*, 1930.

10 Z. de Vizcarra, *Vasconia Españolísima*, San Sebastián, 1939, p. 227.
11 Marqués de Quintanar, preface to the second Spanish edition of *La Alianza Peninsular,*
12 R. de Maeztu, 'El Valor de la Hispanidad', *Acción Española*, 1932, vol. 1, no. 6.
13 *Acción Española*, 1931, vol. 1, no. 1, (December 15), p. 2.
14 ibid., 1932, vol. 3, no. 16.
15 R. Morodo, *Los Orígenes Ideológicos del Franquismo: Acción Española*, Madrid, 1985, pp. 143 and 148. In his analysis, however, Morodo keeps absolute silence on the Mary myth.
16 'El Apostol Santiago . . .', op.cit., pp. 396–7.
17 Vizcarra, *Vasconia Españolísima*, op.cit., pp. 242–3.
18 Vizcarra, 'El Apostol Santiago . . .', op.cit., p. 385.
19 ibid., pp. 399–400.
20 ibid.
21 Vizcarra, *Vasconia Españolísima*, op.cit., pp. 238–9.
22 ibid., p. 237.
23 While living in Argentina, Vizcarra wrote *La Vocacion de America* (Buenos Aires, 1933) in which he established the relationship between America and the Apostle Santiago (Chapter 5), and America and Mary Immaculate (Chapter 4).
24 Morodo, op.cit., p. 63.
25 Rev. R. Walker, *An Outline History of the Catholic Church*, Dublin, 1951, vol. 2, p. 241.
26 *Catholic Times*, 20 May 1938.
27 Two months later, Sanjurjo's abortive *pronunciamiento* took place in Seville.
28 In 1934 this publication appeared as *Reinaré en España* (*I shall reign in Spain*), a title which contains the core of the Sacred Heart message of 1733.
29 '*hombre nefasto*': J.A. Primo de Rivera, 'Discurso de la fundación de Falange Española', 29 October 1933, in *Obras Completas*, Madrid, 1942, p. 17.
30 ibid., p. 25.
31 E.J. Caballero, *El Fascio*, 16 March 1933 (sole number).
32 Caballero, *La Nueva Catolicidad*, Madrid, 1933 (second edition), p. 170.
33 ibid., p. 157.
34 ibid., p. 178.
35 Published since in at least 30 languages, *Consideraciones espirituales* took on its definitive form in 1939 as *Camino* (*The Way*), which contains 999 maxims. According to the *Times Literary Supplement*, 'After *The Thoughts of Chairman Mao* and *The Communist Manifesto*, *Camino* is one of the most widely distributed and studied of modern tracts' (*TLS*, 16 April 1971).
36 '. . . it is necessary to have people of prestige who with their eyes fixed on heaven dedicate themselves to all human activities, and through these activities exercise quietly – and effectively – an apostolate of a professional character' (*Camino*, 347).

37 The founder said later, 'For me, in the hierarchy of love, the Pope comes right after the most holy trinity and our Mother the Virgin' (*Conversations with Mgr Escrivá de Balaguer*, Dublin, 1968, p. 57).

38 'Blind obedience to your superior, the way of sanctity' (*Camino*, 941). But the founder also says, 'The Blessed Virgin, our teacher in all we do, shows us . . . that obedience to God is not servile' (*Cause of our Joy*, Homily on 15 August 1961, Feast of the Assumption, Scepter booklet no. 84, 1978, p. 8).

39 There are no fewer than 19 maxims in *Camino* against the 'critical spirit'.

40 The practice of flagellation continues today, as admitted by the Prelate. See Henry Kramm's interview with Mgr Alvaro del Portillo, *New York Times*, 8 January 1984. 'Corporal mortification' is also defended by Cardinal Joseph Hoeffner, Archbishop of Cologne, who points out that the 'asceticism of Opus Dei is within a centuries-old tradition' (*Scepter Bulletin*, London, August/September, 1984, p. 18).

41 *Camino*, 28.

42 *Cause of Our Joy*, op.cit., p. 13.

43 *Camino*, 500.

44 In September 1936 Bishop Enrique Pla y Deniel, a leading figure in Catholic Action and future primate of Spain (1940–68), published *Las Dos Ciudades*, a pastoral in which the City of God was identified with the counter-revolution. The same year, the doctrine of the Two Cities (God versus the Devil, the Church versus secularism) appeared in the important work of Zacarías García Villada, SJ, *El Destino de España en la Historia Universal*, Madrid, 1936.

45 Among the shrines of the Virgin damaged during the civil war were Nuestra Señora de Atocha, NS de Valverde (Madrid), NS de la Paz and de la Nieves (Ciudad Real), NS del Castellar (Toledo), Virgen de la Peña (Huesca), NS de Montetoro (Baleares), NS de los Arcos (Gerona), NS de la Victoria (Madrid).

46 Menendez Reigada, Dominican professor of moral theology at Salamanca (*Catholic Times*, 13 May 1938).

47 Hugh Thomas, *The Spanish Civil War*, Oxford, 1961, p. 166.

48 ibid., p. 174.

49 R. García-Villoslada, *Manual de Historia de la Compañía de Jesús: 1540–1940*, Madrid, 1941, p. 558. According to sound calculations (A. Montero, *Historia de la Persecución Religiosa en España, 1936–39*, Madrid, 1961) 13 per cent of the secular priesthood and 23 per cent of religious clergy were killed.

50 The 1937 declaration of Catalonian Freemasonry, quoted by J.A. Ferrer Benimeli, *El Contubernio judeo-masónico-comunista*, Madrid, 1982, pp. 300–1.

51 *Heraldo de Aragón*, Saragossa, 3 September 1936.

52 Pastoral letter *non licet* in support of the military uprising. The Archbishop of Pamplona had earlier staged a procession with a statue of Mary.

53 A few weeks after the bombing of Guernica a group of Basque priests wrote to the pope pointing out that the Bilbao government had respected the Church.

54 Juan Tusquets, a priest in the school of Mgr Jouin, gave lectures during the war on the links between Freemasonry and separatism in Catalonia and the Basque country, suggesting that the republicans had performed Masonic rituals round the tree of Guernica in 1933. *Hoja Oficial del Lunes*, San Sebastián, 1 March 1937.

55 *Vasconia españolísima*, op.cit., p. 212. As evidence for the conspiracy, Vizcarra cites dubious Soviet-Basque correspondence; Cardinal Gomá spoke of 'Jewish agents from Russia' operating through secret societies in Spain ('Lecciones de la Guerra y Deberes de la Paz', 8 August 1939, in *Por Dios y Por España*, Barcelona, 1940, p. 237).

56 *Vasconia españolísima*, op.cit., p. 210.

57 Some were shot, others exiled or sent to concentration camps.

58 Gomá, *Por Dios y Por España*, op.cit., p. 481.

59 J. Pemartín, *Los Orígenes del Movimiento*, Burgos, 1938, p. 18.

60 Gomá, *Por Dios y Por España*, op.cit., p. 467.

61 'Significado teológico-social del centenario', *Heraldo de Aragón*, 2 January 1940.

62 When republican planes strafed the Saragossa shrine on 3 August 1936, their bombs failed to explode.

63 For a description of the event, see *Heraldo de Aragón*, 26 August 1936.

64 ibid., 8 December and 9 December 1936.

65 'Exhortación para celebrar el Día del Cruzado' (November 1938), in *Por Dios y Por España*, op.cit., p. 415.

66 ibid., p. 417.

67 *Heraldo de Aragón*, 14 October 1936. 'Blessed and praised be the hour in which most holy Mary came to Saragossa in mortal flesh' – thus an ejaculation.

68 ibid., 11 October 1936.

69 *Diario de Cádiz*, 3 October 1937.

70 *Fe. Diario de Falange Española Tradicionalista y de las JONS*, Seville, 5 October 1937.

71 The Convoy of Victory left Ceuta for the peninsula on 5 August 1936.

72 Gomá, 'Virgo Stans Super Columnan', *El Noticiero*, Saragossa, 12 October 1939.

73 ibid.

74 *Boinas Rojas. Diario de Falange Española Tradicionalista y de las JONS*, Malaga, 2 October 1937.

75 J.A. Sánchez, *El Culto Mariano en España*, Madrid, 1943, p. 26. After the surrender (October 1936), the victors carried the image of NS del Alcázar to the cathedral, where it was enshrined together with the Virgin of Sagrario, Patroness of Toledo.

76 'La Madre en las Horas Trágicas de Toledo', *El Alcázar*, Toledo, 15 August 1938.

77 *Hitler's Table Talk*, London, 1953, p. 569.

78 Serrano Suñer, minister of the interior, presented the Virgin with

a mantle embroidered with the Spanish coat of arms, 'symbol of the reconquest' (*Catholic Times*, 21 October 1938).

79 Entering a village church near the frontier at Rialp, Fr Escrivá reappeared with a rose Mary had deposited on the altar. The miracle is commemorated in a picture at Opus Dei's headquarters in Rome (Luis Carandell, *Vida y Milagros de Monseñor Escrivá de Balaguer*, Barcelona, 1975, p. 206).

80 *Camino*, 208.

81 ibid., 311.

82 The emblem of this brotherhood – still in existence – consists of a crown and the crossed arrows of the Falange, framed by laurels.

83 *Palabras del Caudillo: 1937–42*, Madrid, 1943, p. 149.

84 E.J. Caballero, *Fé y Acción, Fasciculo Doctrinal*, no. 1, 1938, p. 23.

85 Message printed in school textbooks.

86 'Un acto commovedor', *Heraldo de Aragón*, 10 December 1936.

87 On that occasion, a scroll listing the devotional acts of youth was offered to the Caudillo 'for the victory of patriot Spain' (Spanish Press Services Ltd, 28 June 1938).

88 P. Caston and J.A. Morillas, 'El Nacional-Catolicismo de Guerra 1936–1939. Estudio de la legislación religiosa', *Razón y Fe*, 1978, vol. 198, pp. 431–2.

89 *Catholic Times*, 13 May 1938.

90 B. Burkey, OFM, Cap., 'St Joseph, Husband of Mary', *Marian Era*, Chicago, 1965, vol. 6.

30 QUEEN OF HISPANIDAD

1 J.A. Sanchez Pérez, *El Culto Mariano en España*, Madrid, 1943, p. 13.

2 See J. Pemartín, *Qué es lo Nuevo? Consideraciones sobre el Momento Español Presente*, Madrid, 1940 (third edition).

3 'Declaración a un corresponsal', November 1937, Palabras del Caudillo: 1937–42, Madrid, 1943.

4 Pemartín, op.cit.

5 'Declaración a O'Seculo', May 1938, *Palabras del Caudillo*, op. cit.

6 'El Pueblo Gallego', *Diario de Falange Española Tradicionalista y de las JONS*, Vigo, 27 February 1945.

7 *Sur, Diario de Falange Española Tradicionalista y de las JONS*, Malaga, 1 April 1945; *Heraldo de Aragón*, Saragossa, 5 April 1945.

8 Both confraternities are still influential. King Juan Carlos is an Elder Brother of María Santísima de la Aurora.

9 Dr J.M. Mascaró published a piece in the journal *Clínica y Laboratorio* (March 1950) entitled 'Meditaciones a propósito de la sobrenaturalidad del embarazo y parto virginales de María'.

10 J.L. Llanes, *Aspects of the Teaching of the Founder of Opus Dei: On the Theology of Work*, Dublin 1982, p. 76.

11 J. Ruíz Giménez in 1946 as director of the Instituto de Cultura Hispánica, quoted by J. Tusell, *Franco y los Católicos*, Madrid, 1984, p. 129.

12 All literature on the Roman Index was banned.

13 For example, *Miriam* (Carmelites of Seville), *El Buen Consejo* (Augustinians), *La Purísima* (Oblates of Mary Immaculate), *El Perpetuo Socorro* (Redemptorists), *El Iris de Paz* (Sons of the Immaculate Heart of Mary), *El Pilar* (shrine of Saragossa), *Estrella del Mar* (Federation of Marian Congregations).

14 *Horquilleros de la Virgen*.

15 *El Alcázar*, Madrid, 2 February 1943.

16 *Estudios Marianos*, 1959, vol. 10, p. 220.

17 *Ecclesia* (organ of Dirección Central de la Acción Católica), Madrid, 23 January 1943.

18 *Maria*, 1958, vol. 5, p. 44.

19 *Ecclesia*, 17 July 1943.

20 A 'National Executive Committee of Homage to the Pope' coordinated celebrations, public meetings, episcopal exhortations, collections for Peter's Pence, and Te Deums.

21 *Ecclesia*, 17 April 1943.

22 For instance, the diocese of Vitoria was consecrated to the Immaculate Heart on the day of the Resurrection (*Ecclesia*, 17 April 1943).

23 Youth Catholic Action participated in the 'Campaign for Charity', visiting slums, gaols and hospitals, and attended Cursillos for the 'Worker Apostolate'. See *Ecclesia*.

24 Tusell, op.cit., p. 363.

25 The Missionary Congregation of Parochial Action (Segovia, 1942) and the Institute of Apostolate of Catholic Action (Lérida, 1949), for example, were established by bishops.

26 *Ecclesia*, 14 August 1943.

27 'Sacerdotes de toda España en los cursillos sobre Ejercicios Espirituales en Covadonga', *Ecclesia*, 31 July 1943.

28 ibid., 14 August 1943.

29 By 1951 there were still only 642 Propagandistas (G. Hermet, *Les Catholiques dans l'Espagne Franquiste*, Paris, 1980, p. 227).

30 Opus Dei/Catholic Action links were so close that in 1949 the Bishop of Madrid asked Escrivá to provide a priest to head the university youth section in the capital (S. Bernal, *Msgr Josemaría Escrivá de Balaguer. A Profile of the Founder of Opus Dei*, London/New York, 1977, p. 193).

31 A collaborator of the Society of Jesus in the Spiritual Exercises mission was the Junta Técnica Nacional de Acción Católica, whose director was Alberto Martín Artajo, a member of the Council of Propagandistas, architect of Pax Romana and foreign minister in 1945.

32 *Ecclesia*, 9 January 1943.

33 According to Hervas' manual, 'those selected must be men of well-known capabilities ... influential in their own fields ...' (quoted by D.H. Levine, *Religion and Politics in Latin America*, Princeton, 1981, p. 236).

34 Missionary Daughters of the Heart of Jesus (Granada, 1942) and Missionaries of the Sacred Heart of Jesus (Santander, 1949) were among the institutes founded by Jesuits in this decade).

35 D.M. Helming, *Footprints in the Snow. A Pictorial Biography of Josemaría Escrivá, the Founder of Opus Dei* (foreword by Malcolm Muggeridge), New York/London, 1986, p. 46.

36 Tusell, op.cit., p. 239.

37 *Conversations with Mgr Escrivá de Balaguer*, Scepter Books, Dublin, 1968, p. 63.

38 Even today officials of Opus Dei refuse to name any member of the Sacerdotal Society of the Holy Cross, though an increasing number of cardinals are open supporters.

39 *Cum Societatis*, issued on the feast of the Sacred Heart of Jesus, 28 June 1946.

40 Three basic grades were established: *numerari* – celibates of the professional class who live in residences and provide the full-time leadership (including – after a ten-year study period – the Opus priesthood); *oblati*, who have less education and social status, and live at home; *supernumerari*, who may be married and include powerful businessmen.

41 Escrivá's Italian backers included Cardinal Schuster of Milan (see chapter 24), the Duchess Virginia Sforza, and Mgr Montini, Vatican undersecretary and future Pope Paul VI.

42 Bernal, op.cit., p. 243.

43 *Palabras del Caudillo: 1937–42*, Madrid, 1943, p. 151.

44 ibid., pp. 147–8.

45 *Estudios Marianos*, 1947, vol. 6, p. 539. The Assumptionist vow was made all over the country on the Day of the Immaculate, 1940. Virtually the entire population of Huesca promised in the cathedral to defend the Assumption of Mary's universal mediation.

46 *Estudios Marianos*, 1950, vol. 10, p. 200.

47 In 1940 Pétain's government also suppressed Freemasonry in France and Algeria.

48 *El Noticiero*, Saragossa, 2 January 1940.

49 *Estudios Marianos*, 1974, vol. 38. p. 223.

50 *Diccionario de Historia Eclesiástica de Espana*, Madrid, 1975, vol. 4: 'Santuario Nacional de la Gran Promesa', p. 2353.

51 'La comemoración de la venida de la Virgen del Pilar a Zaragoza', *Ecclesia*, 9 January 1943. The anniversary was declared a holiday and shops closed in the afternoon. Even at the end of the 1960s Mariologists found it 'very fitting' to call the Virgin 'Queen and Patroness of Hispanidad' because the Christianity of Hispanidad is, in part, 'of Marian origin' (*Estudios Marianos*, 1969, vol. 32, p. 315).

52 'Fallo del concurso acerca del tema la Virgen del Pilar es Reina de la Hispanidad', *El Alcázar*, 23 January 1943.

53 'Amistad Hispano-Argentina', *Ya*, Madrid, 14 February 1943. A simultaneous Hispanidad Week in Salamanca closed with a 'fervent homage to Argentina and her government' (*Ya*, 16 February 1943),

and the Archbishop of Salta (Argentina), promoter of a congress on Hispano-American culture to be held in Buenos Aires, reciprocated with a telegram to Salamanca asking for God's blessing on Hispanidad Week (*Ya*, 14 February 1943).

54 *El Alcázar*, 29 March 1943.

55 ibid.

56 ibid.

57 'Audiencia del papa al presidente de Pax Romana', *Ecclesia*, 1 May 1943.

58 *Ecclesia*, 15 May 1943.

59 ibid., 22 May 1943.

60 ibid., 28 August 1943.

61 Towards the end of 1943, A. Martin Artajo delivered a lecture to ACN de P entitled 'The Pope calls for a Crusade'. See *Ecclesia*, 27 November 1943.

62 Having suffered heavy losses, Spain withdrew the Blue Division in 1944.

63 The fourth assembly of the Spanish Mariological Society at Fatima in July 1944 focused on the 'Nature, History and Efficacy of the Devotion to the Heart of Mary'. See *Estudios Marianos*, 1945, vol. 4.

64 See Fr M. Llanera, OP, 'La Devoción al Inmaculado Corazón de María y el Santísimo Rosario', ibid.

65 In February 1945, as the allies occupied Germany, Juan de Borbón, son of Alfonso XIII, issued the Lausanne manifesto urging Spain to abandon the fascist path and join democratic Europe with himself as king.

66 For example, the fascist salute was suppressed. See Tusell, op.cit.

67 The state of siege was lifted only in 1948, the year before American aid arrived in Spain.

68 Fr E. Sauras, OP, *Estudios Marianos*, 1947, vol. 6.

69 'Catecismo de la devoción al Corazón de María', *Estudios Marianos*, 1948, vol. 7, p. 310.

70 A Mariologist declared after the assembly at Fatima (1944), 'The physical heart always comes into the cardio-Marian devotion, united by love' (*Estudios Marianos*, 1945, vol. 4, p. 410).

71 A. Vázquez de Prada, *El Fundador del Opus Dei*, Madrid, 1983, pp. 281–2. Lucia, however, remained in Spain until May 1946, when she returned to the Dorotheans near Oporto. In March 1948 she was transferred to the Carmel at Coimbra. Escrivá became a 'great pilgrim to Fatima' (A. Cosme do Amaral, Bishop of Fatima, *Fatima and its Pilgrims*, Scepter Booklets, New York, 1979, p. 18). After La Pilar and Nuestra Señora de Torreciudad, he 'felt especially united' to the Lady of Cova (Vázquez de Prada, op.cit., pp. 368-9).

72 For this important personal link between Mgr Escrivá and the seer of Fatima, we are indebted to Mr John Horrigan, press information officer of Opus Dei in Britain. According to Mr Horrigan, Don Josemaría spoke 'pretty tough' to Sister Lucia, 'as saints can do' (to N.P., Netherhall House, Hampstead, London, 10 October 1984).

73 Escrivá's disciples crossed the border into Portugal in 1940.
74 In 1946 Franco and Carrero began an anti-Masonic column (possibly with the collaboration of Jiménez Caballero) in *Arriba*, the Madrid newspaper. The articles, under the pseudonym 'E. Boor', appeared regularly until 1951. See J.A. Ferrer Benimeli, *El Contubernio Judeo-masónico-comunista*, Madrid, 1982.
75 Tusell, op.cit., p. 132.
76 Since the Vatican Council, 113 cardinals, 300 bishops, 32,000 priests, 50,000 nuns and over eight million lay people had submitted petitions.
77 *Estudios Marianos*, 1947, vol. 6, p. 538.
78 ibid.
79 *ABC*, Madrid, 24 May 1947.
80 *Estudios Marianos*, 1950, vol. 10, p. 220.
81 ibid.
82 ibid.

PART IV

31 OVERVIEW

1 See D. Yergin, *Shattered Peace: the Origins of the Cold War and the National Security State*, New York, 1977.
2 R.I. Gannon, SJ, *The Cardinal Spellman Story*, New York, 1962, p. 351.
3 *Orientalis Ecclesias*, 15 December 1952. Stepinac – by now permanently exiled to his native parish – was given the red hat this year.
4 *Tablet* (London), 23 July 1949.
5 J.A. de Sobrino, SJ, *María y Nosotros*, Cadiz, 1956, pp. 32–3.
6 Bishop F.J. Sheen, *Missions and the World Crisis*, Milwaukee, 1963, p. 23.
7 J. Cooney, *The American Pope. The Life and Times of Francis Cardinal Spellman*, New York, 1984, p. 253.
8 *Columbia* (monthly magazine of the Knights), January 1954.
9 W.V. Bangert, SJ, *A History of the Society of Jesus*, St Louis, 1972, p. 500.
10 ibid., p. 507.
11 Admiral Carrero Blanco, archcooperator of Opus Dei, said in 1962 that the integration of Spain into NATO had been sabotaged by western politicians, 'socialists and Freemasons' (A. Viñas, *Los Pactos Secretos de Franco con EU: bases, ayuda económica, recortes de soberanía*, Madrid, 1980, p. 72).
12 Eisenhower created the International Communications Agency (ICA) in 1954. See H. Schiller, *Mass Communications and American Empire*, New York, 1969.

13 *The Lamp* (monthly organ of the Friars), January 1954.

14 M. de Saint Pierre, *J'étais à Fatima de la prière à l'outrage*, Paris, 1967, p. 140.

15 *Tablet*, 23 July 1949, p. 62.

16 ibid.

17 By 1952–3 both superpowers had tested H-bombs and in 1957 intercontinental ballistic missiles were added to their arsenals.

18 During the first atomic explosion, in the New Mexican desert, R. Oppenheimer recalled the words of Krishna: 'If the radiance of a thousand suns were to burst into the sky. . . .'

19 In *On Peace* (1971), Thomas Merton, the American Trappist, wrote, 'it is certainly legitimate for a Catholic moralist to hold in theory that a limited nuclear war, in defence, is permitted by traditional Christian moral principles'.

20 *Discursos y Mensajes del Jefe del Estado*, 1951–4, Madrid, 1955, pp. 560–2.

21 *Soul Magazine* (organ of the Blue Army), special issue, 1982, p. 26.

22 The rosary became, in the phrase of the Legion's founder, a 'victim of the false aggiornamento of Vatican II' (L.Ó. Broin, *Frank Duff, a biography*, Dublin, 1982, p. 107).

23 Rev. H. Nouwen, *Ave Maria* (US national Catholic weekly), 3 June 1967.

24 *New Covenant* (Michigan), May 1981, front cover.

25 Apostolic exhortation *Marialis Cultus*, 2 February, 1974.

26 R.P. Prentice, 'Mary in a secularized world', *Ephemerides Mariologicae*, 1977, vol. 27, pp. 145–6.

27 See, for example, A. Plogsterth, 'A May meditation on Our Lady: radical feminism and conservative Mariology', *Cross Currents*, New York, 1977, vol. 27, no. 2.

28 Andrew Greeley recognized in 1977 that 'Marian devotion seems virtually non-existent among progressive Catholics' (*The Mary Myth: or the Femininity of God*, New York, 1977, p. 12). See also 'The decline of interest in Mariology as a theological problem' in *Marian Studies*, 3–4 January 1972 (report on national convention of Mariological Society of America, San Antonio, Texas).

29 E. Llamas, 'Psicología de la V.M. a la luz de la escritura, la teología, la mística y la ciencia: la personalidad psíquica de María', *Estudios Marianos*, 1974, vol. 38.

30 Dr A. Molina Prieto, 'Funcion de la espiritualidad mariana en la renovación eclesial', ibid., 1976, vol. 40, p. 227.

31 See his eulogy in *Il Gazzettino*, Venice, 25 July 1978. English translation in *The Universe*, London, 29 September 1978.

32 See 'My meeting with Lucia by Pope John Paul I', *Soul Magazine*, July–August 1987.

33 R.T. Davies (Research Center for Religion and Human Rights in Closed Societies), *International Herald Tribune*, 21–2 December 1985.

34 *The Times* (London), 13 November 1979.

35 Archbishop of Canterbury at 1986 General Synod. Quoted in *Church Times*, 21 November 1986.

36   See *Moral Majority Report*, 15 December 1980, vol. 1, no. 15.

37   Pius XII, *Bis saeculari*, 27 September 1948.

38   J.C.H. Aveling, *The Jesuits*, London, 1981, p. 359.

39   *Bis saeculari*, op.cit.

40   Mgr Escrivá began his European tour in 1956. *Camino* was published in English as *The Way* two years later, at the time of Opus Dei's entry into Franco's government.

41   P. Gheddo, *The Cross and the Bo-Tree. Catholics and Buddhists in Vietnam*, New York, 1970, pp. 121–2.

42   See Fr L. Roberts, SVD, and Fr A. McGrath, Missionary Society of St Columba, *Mary in Their Midst. The Legion of Mary in Action in China 1948–1951*, Dublin, 1960.

43   President Magsaysay, 'in a grand gesture of practical religiosity', consecrated the Filipino people to Mary Most Holy in 1954. See *Unitas*, organ of the University of Santo Tomas, Manila, 1954, nol. 4, ano 27, special edition dedicated to the Most Holy Virgin, p. 888.

44   Around the same time, the Blue Army was claiming 25 million members.

45   Columbans took the portfolios of education, justice, social welfare and lands. By 1951 their political influence was even greater and 16 Irish bishops were Knights.

46   Rev. E. O'Connor, SJ, *The Secret of Frederick Ozanam, Founder of the Society of St Vincent de Paul*, Dublin, 1953, p. 49.

47   G. Miralles, OP, 'Un movimiento actual de espiritualidad mariana: los equipos del Rosario', *Estudios Marianos*, 1973, vol. 37.

48   M. de la Bedoyère, *The Cardijn Story*, London, 1958, p. 177.

49   M. Marcoux, *Cursillo. Anatomy of a Movement. The Experience of Spiritual Renewal*, New York, 1982, p. 54. The rosary is prominent in Cursillista spirituality.

50   D.H. Levine, *Religion and Politics in Latin America*, Princeton, 1981, p. 237; *America* (journal of the Jesuits in USA and Canada), 30 August 1975, vol. 133, no. 5.

51   J. Lemoine, 'Los cruzados del siglo XX. El Opus Dei', *Periodista de Buenos Aires*, 12–18 July 1985, no. 44.

52   Founded by Professor Plinio Correa de Oliveira, TFP has three grades: hermits, heralds and guardians.

53   R. Garcia Lupo, 'Cruzadas de Fatima en el cuartel de Caracas', *Periodista de Buenos Aires*, 24–30 November 1984.

54   *Fiducia* (organ of the Sociedad Chilena de Defensa de la Tradición, Familia y Propiedad), Santiago, January 1970.

55   The Marian Sisters of Schönstatt, numbering 28,000 in 30 nations in 1976, wear either habit or secular dress. The Marian Brothers and Ladies of Schönstatt are lay people complemented by diocesan 'Schönstatt Priests', who practise a secular profession.

56   Kentenich (1885–1968), who had been held in Dachau, was expelled from the institute after a visitation by the Holy Office – for reasons we have been unable to ascertain – and confined to Milwaukee (USA) between 1952 and 1965. Rehabilitated by Pope Paul VI,

his beatification process opened in 1975, and John Paul II calls him 'one of the great priestly figures in modern history'. For his 'patrocentric spirituality', see J. Kentenich, *Desafíos de Nuestro Tiempo*, Santiago, 1986.

57 H. Jedin (ed.), *History of the Church*, London, 1981, vol. X, pp. 329–30.

58 *Osservatore Romano*, op.cit.

59 H. Graef, *Mary: a History of Doctrine and Devotion*, London, 1965, vol. 2, p. 151. *Blankovollmacht* may also be translated 'blankchit'.

60 The majority of religious stamps featured the Virgin. See L. Ropars, 'Notre-Dame et la philatélie', *Maria*, 1958, vol. 5; and *I Francobolli dello Stato della Citta del Vaticano 1929–1976*. The Polish Madonna of Ostra Brama was chosen to commemorate the Marian Year (1954).

61 J. Cloutham, 'Gardens for Mary', *Columbia*, March 1953.

62 The International (Pontifical since 1959) Marian Academy (Rome, 1946), the Mariological Society of America (1949–50) and, in the early 1950s, the Roman College of the Holy Cross, an Opus Dei foundation for the training of clerics.

63 '. . . broadcasting only music and church services, brief announcements on the message of Fatima and the evils of communism' (*Marian Era*, 1962, vol. 3, p. 45). The Fatima cult was boosted in Colombia during the Holy Year of 1950 (Fr. A. Mesanza, OP, *Célebres Imagenes y Santuarios de Nuestra Señora en Colombia*, Chiquinquira, 1950, p. 448).

64 On 12 January 1951 Pius XII declared the Archangel Gabriel patron of workers in telecommunications.

65 'Culte marial chez les Redemptoristes', *Maria*, 1958, vol. 5.

66 'Is there a devotion more excellent than that of the Sacred Heart?' he asked in *Haurietis aguas*, 15 May 1956.

67 M. Williams, *The Society of the Sacred Heart*, London, 1967, pp. 255–6.

68 *Tablet*, 16 January 1954, p. 59.

69 Report of Supreme Knight to 103rd annual meeting of Supreme Council, *Columbia*, October 1985.

70 Nearly 400 seminarists and postulants were financially helped by the Knights in 1984 and the following year the Order contributed over $1.7 million to seminarists and seminaries.

71 The beatification process of Pio Nono, Pope of the Immaculate Conception, opened in 1954.

72 F. Royer, *St Anthony Claret: Modern Prophet and Healer*, New York, 1957, pp. 283–4.

73 Among other servants of Mary raised to the altars by Pacelli were the visionaries Gemma Galgani, an Italian stigmatic, (d. 1903) and Mariana Paredes of Quito (the 'Lily' was declared national heroine by the Constitutional Assembly of Ecuador on 30 November 1945); Pierre Chanel of the Society of Mary; Gaspar del Bufalo of the Society of the Precious Blood; Domenico Savio, pupil of Don Bosco; and Mornesse Marie Mazzarello of the Filles de Marie-Auxiliatrice.

74 Fr J.M. Elias, *Copacauana-Copacabana*, Tarija (Bolivia), 1981, p. 148.

75 T. Koehler, SM, preface to G.M. Besutti, OSM (ed.), *Biografía Mariana 1973–77*, Rome, 1980.

76 A. Ortíz Muñoz, *La Virgen ha llorado en Siracusa*, Madrid, 1954, p. 28.

77 *Tablet*, 21 June 1958, p. 588.

78 *Le Pèlerinage de Lourdes*, 2 July 1957.

79 'Estadística de apariciones marianas no reconocidas por la Iglesia', *Ephemerides Mariologicae*, 1972, vol. 22.

80 K. Rahner, *Visions and Prophecies*, London, 1963, p. 88.

81 *Osservatore Romano*, 4 February 1951.

82 C.M. Staehlin, SJ, *Apariciones. Ensayo Crítico*, Madrid, 1954, p. 11, Fellini's *La Dolce Vita* (1960), the banning of which was sought by the Vatican, contains a brilliant satire on the crowd phenomenon of apparitions of the Madonna to children.

83 Documents of the 31st General Congregation of the Society of Jesus (1965/66), Institute of Jesuit Sources, St Louis, 1977. Art. 241: 'It is no secret . . . that devotion to the Sacred Heart, at least in some places, is today less appealing to Jesuits and to the faithful in general.'

84 John Paul II, letter to superior-general of the Society of Jesus from chapel of Blessed Claude de la Colombière, Paray-le-Monial, 5 October 1986.

85 S. Foljado Florez, OSA, 'María en la conciencia del pueblo cristiano', *Estudios Marianos*, 1983, vol. 48, p. 214. The contemporary attack on 'Enlightened Catholicism' vilifies such figures of the past as Muratori, considered even today as an 'insidious adversary'. See F.S. Paucheri, *La Religiosità Popolare*, Padua, 1980.

86 Final Document of Episcopal Conference of Latin American Bishops at Puebla (Mexico), 1979, art. 301.

87 ibid.

88 Homily at national shrine of Our Lady of Aparecida, Brazil, 21 July 1980.

89 Foljado Florez, op.cit., pp. 205–6.

90 *Redemptoris Mater*, 25 March 1987.

91 Homily at shrine of Our Lady of Zapopan, Mexico, 30 January 1979.

32 THE FERVENT FIFTIES

1 *Ad caeli reginam*, 11 October, 1954.

2 C. Falconi, *The Popes in the Twentieth Century. From Pius X to John XXIII*, London, 1967, p. 268.

3 H. Graef, *Mary: a History of Doctrine and Devotion*, London, 1965, p. 146.

4 *The Tablet*, 6 November 1954, p. 456.

5 H. Jedin (ed.), *History of the Church*, London, 1981, vol. X, p. 309.

6 *The Tablet*, 20 October 1951, p. 277.

7 *Humani generis*, 12 October 1950.

8 T. Cummins, 'The jubilee of 1950', *Clergy Review*, January 1950, pp. 33–4.

9 *Maria*, Paris, 1952, vol. 2, pp. 856–60.

10 J. Ricart, 'El escapulario del Carmel, prenda de salvacion', *Estudios Marianos*, 1952, vol. 12, p. 366.

11 See J. Tusell, *Franco y los Católicos. La política interior española entre 1945 y 1957*, Madrid, 1984, p. 243.

12 ibid., p. 244.

13 F. Franco, *Textos de Doctrina Política: Palabras y escritos de 1945 a 1950*, Madrid, 1951, p. 363.

14 A. Cirici, *La Estétical del Franquismo*, Barcelona, 1977, p. 108.

15 N. García Garcés, 'Relaciones de la Virgen con la sagrada eucaristía', *Estudios Marianos*, 1953, vol. 13, pp. 35–8.

16 E. Sauras, 'María y el sacerdote', ibid., pp. 143–72.

17 ibid.

18 B. de San Pablo, 'La Reparación eucarístico-mariana', ibid., p. 188. Mary was so closely identified with the mass that the Bishop of Fatima calls the Cova da Iria 'the greatest Eucharistic centre of our country' (A. Cosme do Amaral, *Fatima and its Pilgrims*, Scepter Booklet, no. 104, New York, 1979, p. 13).

19 J. Escrivá de Balaguer, *The Eucharist: Mystery of Faith and Love* (homily on 14 April 1960), Scepter Booklet no. 44, New York, 1980, p. 15.

20 F. Franco, *Discursos y Mensajes, 1951–54. Textos de Doctrina Politica* no. 5, Madrid, 1955, p. 199.

21 *Diccionario de Historia Eclesiastica de España*, Madrid, 1972, vol. 2, p. 1203.

22 The Instituto Social Leon XIII, an important teaching centre linked, like the Propagandista School of Journalism, to the University of Salamanca, was founded in 1953 under the auspices of Bishop Herrera.

23 Its international centre today is the North American Society of Josephology, which maintains manuscripts and printed volumes at the Oratory of St Joseph in Montreal. Pius XII's legate crowned a statue of St Joseph there in 1955.

24 J. Escrivá de Balaguer, *In Joseph's Workshop* (homily given on 19 March 1963), New York, 1980, pp. 7–8.

25 ibid., p. 20.

26 ibid., p. 23.

27 About two years later it became the *Sociedad Iberoamericana de Josefología* – debating such themes as the saint's cooperation in the redemption, his paternity, marriage and virginity.

28 S. Bernal, *Msgr Josemaría Escrivá de Balaguer. A Profile of the Founder of Opus Dei*, London/New York, 1977, p. 87.

29 *Sacra virginitas*, 25 March 1954.

30 *Fulgens corona*, 8 October 1953.

31 A. Hortelano, 'La Inmaculada y la sicología', *Estudios Marianos*, 1955, vol. 15, p. 297.

32 ibid.

33 *Ad caeli reginam*, op.cit. Among the saints cited here are Ildefonsus of Toledo and Alphonsus Liguori.

34 'So just as the human race was committed to death through a virgin, it is saved by means of a Virgin.'

35 F. Franco, *Palabras del Caudillo*, Madrid, 1955, pp. 517–18.

36 *Estudios Marianos*, 1969, vol. 32, p. 317.

37 *Diccionario de Historia Eclesiastica de España*, Madrid, 1975, vol. 4: 'Santuarios'.

38 For example, at the sanctuaries of Nuestra Señora de los Remedios (Lugo), de la Salud (Guadalajara), de la Regala (Cadiz), de Puig (Valencia).

39 B. Torrellas Barcelona, *La Santisima Virgen en la Provincia de Huesca*, Huesca, 1956, pp. 176–7.

40 *The Tablet*, 5 November 1954, p. 456.

41 ibid. Two years earlier Pacelli urged the Russians to beg Mary to 'illuminate' the minds of the Kremlin rulers and consecrated their nation to the Immaculate Heart (see apostolic letter *Sacro vergente anno*, 7 July 1952).

42 Without forsaking profits and accumulation, Opus Dei combines a rigorous work ethic with an aristocratic 'detachment' from wealth. See J.L. Llanes, *Aspects of the Teaching of the Founder of Opus Dei: On the Theology of Work*, Dublin, 1982; *Detachment* (homily given by Escrivá on 4 April 1955), Scepter Booklets no. 109, New York, 1979.

43 The conflict between the ACN de P and the Falange is exhaustively treated by J. Tusell, op.cit.

44 R. de la Cierva, *Francisco Franco: Biografía histórica*, Madrid, 1982, vol. 5, note on p. 330.

45 Teniente-General Franco Salgado-Aranjo, *Mis conversaciones privadas con Franco*, Madrid, 1976, pp. 474–5.

46 Banker Mariano Navarro Rubio and economic historian Alberto Ullastres Calvo, lay members, became ministers of finance and trade respectively in Franco's sixth government (February 1957–July 1962).

47 For details of Opus Dei's power base in Spain, see J. Ynfante, *La Prodigiosa aventura del Opus Dei. Génesis y desarollo de la Santa Mafia*, Paris, 1971; D. Artigues, *El Opus Dei en España 1928–1962*, Paris, 1971.

48 The flagship was Navarre University, linked to the International Institute of Pedagogy in Rome and Castelgandolfo, and with a business faculty in Barcelona.

49 B. Torrellas Barcelona, op.cit., p. 165.

50 *Diccionario de Historia Eclesiástica de España*, op.cit., vol. 4.

51 ibid. The new shrine was not completed until July 1975, a few days after Mgr Escrivá's death.

52 ibid.

53 J.A. Vidal-Quadras, *Torreciudad, a Shrine of Our Lady*, Torrecuidad, 1978, p. 16.

54 *Diccionario de Historia Eclesiástica de España*, op.cit.

55 A. Cirici, op.cit., p. 118.

56 F. Suarez Verdaguer, *Our Lady the Virgin*, Dublin, 1959, p. 6.

57 P. Hinnebusch, 'The passing of Our Lady', *Marian Era*, Chicago, 1963, vol. 4, p. 89.

58 See J. Tull, *Father Coughlin and the New Deal*, Syracuse, 1965.
59 D.F. Crosby, SJ, *God, Church and Flag. Senator Joseph R. McCarthy and the Catholic Church, 1950–1957*, North Carolina, 1978, p. 6.
60 J. Cooney, *The American Pope. The Life and Times of Francis Cardinal Spellman*, New York, 1984, p. 219.
61 *Life Magazine*, 27 May 1957.
62 Crosby, op.cit., p. 18.
63 ibid.
64 *Columbia*, New Haven, Conn., January, 1953.
65 A Knights of Columbus council in New Orleans was named 'Our Lady of Fatima'.
66 *Our Sunday Visitor*, Indiana, 27 May 1951.
67 ibid.
68 ibid., 17 June 1951.
69 ibid., 22 July 1951.
70 See Fr E.A. Burke, *What is the Index? A Clear and Complete Explanation of the Catholic Church's Position on Reading*, Milwaukee, 1952. The Index was last issued in 1948.
71 *Columbia*, July, 1953.
72 Other periodicals advertised 'The Talking Lady of Fatima Doll' (M.E. Marty and J.G. Deedy, *The Religious Press in America*, New York, 1963, p. 79).
73 *Columbia*, November, 1954.
74 C.J. Kauffman, *Faith and Fraternalism: The History of the Knights of Columbus 1882–1982*, New York, 1982, p. 385.
75 Cooney, op.cit., p. 298.
76 P.J. Peyton, *The Ear of God*, London, 1954, p. 136.
77 ibid., p. 147.
78 ibid., p. 141.
79 A. Wirtz Domas, *Mary, U.S.A.*, Indiana, 1978, p. 290. There were, however, still 100,000 members of the Nocturnal Adoration Society in the US in 1963.
80 In 1946 Fr Stanley Matuszewski of the Society of Mary launched *Our Lady's Digest*, similar in format to *Reader's Digest*.
81 See H. Bower, *Challenge to Godlessness with Vigil, Prayer and Penance. The Story of the All Night Vigil Movement*, Britons Publishing Company, Devon, nihil obstat and imprimatur, 1973.
82 In a letter to the Archbishop of Westminster, Pacelli speaks of the need for rosary devotions to be 'inculcated into children at a young and impressionable age' through the planned campaign in Southwark and Brentwood 'under the directorship of Our beloved son, Patrick Peyton' (*Osservatore Romano*, 30 July 1952).
83 *Catholic Times*, London, 1 October 1954.
84 Mgr Escrivá visited the shrine of Willesden (London) in August 1958.
85 *The Tablet*, 9 October 1954, p. 358.
86 Wirtz Domas, op.cit., p. 289.
87 'Mary cult put under interdict', *National Catholic Reporter* (USA), 16 May 1975.

88 A. Hebert, SM, *The Tears of Mary and Fatima. Why?*, Paulina, La., 1984, p. 140.

89 First editorial of *Divine Love* (1957), reprinted in issue of 1982, vol. 25, no. 89.

90 ibid.

91 *Divine Love Newsletter*, 1986, vol. 29, no. 2: obituary of Stephen Oraze, president of the Apostolate of Christian Action.

92 See J.M. Haffert, *Dear Bishop! Memoirs of the Author Concerning the History of the Blue Army*, Washington, NJ, 1982.

93 H. Colgan, 'The Blue Army of Our Lady', *Marian Era*, 1965, vol. 6, p. 48.

94 *Blue Army Manual*, Washington, NJ, 1982, p. 6.

95 ibid.

96 For example, J. Haffert, *Russia Will be Converted*, New Jersey, 1948; T. MacGlynn, OP, *Vision of Fatima*, Boston, 1948; H. Rafferty, *Fatima and the Scapular*, Chicago, 1950; J.A. Pelletier, AA, *The Sun Danced at Fatima*, Mass., 1951; E. Dockman, *The Lady and the Sun*, Maryland, 1954.

97 M. Dias Coelho, *Exército Azul de Nossa Senhora de Fátima*, Fatima, 1956, p. 8.

98 The Blue Army HQ, with its blue onion dome and Russian Orthodox cross, is the most conspicuous building after the basilica. It also serves as an hotel for 'Fatima Jetaway' trips from the United States with an indulgence as part of the package. Pilgrims sleep in rooms with names like 'Queen of the World' and 'American Marines Killed in Korea'.

99 *Mary in the Seraphic Order*, (report of 35th annual meeting of the Franciscan Educational Conference, Watkins, Glen.) New York, 1954, pp. 417–8.

100 See D. Hyde, *I Believed. The Autobiography of a Former Communist*, London, 1951. An extraordinarily similar case of Marian conversion is that of Louis Budenz, editor of the US *Daily Worker*, who embraced the Catholic Church under the guidance of Mgr Fulton J. Sheen in 1946.

101 *Soul Magazine* (organ of the Blue Army), Washington, New Jersey, special issue, 1982.

102 H. Fraser, *Fatal Star*, Glasgow, 1954, p. 175.

103 ibid.

104 Fr L. Roberts, SVD, and Fr A. McGrath, Missionary Society of St Columba, *Mary in Their Midst. The Legion of Mary in Action in China 1948–1951*, Dublin, 1960, p. 11.

105 ibid.

106 R.I. Gannon, SJ, *The Cardinal Spellman Story*, New York, 1962, p. 382.

107 Haffert, *Dear Bishop!*, op.cit., p. 254–5.

108 G. Audigou, 'Le cult marial en Indochine', *Maria*, 1956, vol. 4, p. 1006.

109 ibid., p. 1013.

110 P. Gheddo, *The Cross and the Bo-Tree. Catholics and Buddhists in Vietnam*, New York, 1960, p. 187.

111 E.H. Methuin was among the 'new mandarins' who appreciated Diem's contribution against insurgency:

Like Lawrence of Arabia, we must start to 'preach'. Such a campaign can take the name of Moral Rearmament with its theme of absolute honesty and absolute love; or 'personalism' as Diem called his humanistic philosophy of the dignity of the person.

('Ideology and Organization in Counter Insurgency', based on a lecture at US Army Engineering School, November 1962, *Orbis* 1964, vol. 8, no. 1, pp. 112–13.)

112 Cooney, op.cit., p.241.
113 Gheddo, op.cit., pp. 121-2.
114 Haffert, *Dear Bishop!*, op.cit., chapter 26: 'Vietnam's Mission'.
115 *America* (organ of the Jesuits of the United States and Canada), 4 February 1961, vol. 104, no. 18.
116 Cooney, op.cit., p. 243.
117 T. Dooley, *Deliver Us from Evil*, in *Dr Tom Dooley's Three Great Books*, New York, 1960, p. 102.
118 ibid., p. 114.
119 J.M. Haffert, *Meet the Witnesses*, Washington, NJ, 1961, p. 119.
120 *Marian Era*, 1965, vol. 6, p. 127.
121 Jedin, op.cit., vol. X, p. 683.
122 D.B. Barrett (ed.), *World Christian Encyclopedia*, Nairobi, 1982, article on Brazil.
123 D.E. Mutchler, *The Church as a Political Factor in Latin America, with particular reference to Colombia and Chile*, USA, 1971, p. 276. Professor Mutchler was a member of the Society of Jesus between 1959 and 1967.
124 ibid., p. 17.
125 *The Star*, Johannesburg, 11 January 1961.
126 *The Tablet*, 1 November 1958.
127 An unforeseen result of Miss Quinn's labours was the creation in 1962 of the schismatic Mario Legio of Africa, with 200,000 adherents led by seven 'cardinals' and a 'pope' (*World Christian Encyclopedia*, op.cit., article on Kenya).
128 *Catholic Times*, 10 September 1954.
129 M. Ferragne, OMI, 'Basutoland, terre de Marie, et notes sur la dévotion mariale en Afrique du Sud', *Maria*, 1958, vol. 5.
130 ibid., p. 186.
131 Z. Aradi, *Shrines to Our Lady Around the World*, New York, 1954, p. 188.
132 ibid.
133 *Caritas*, missionary review of the Oblates of Mary Immaculate (South Africa), souvenir of S.A. National Marian Congress in Pictures: 'South Africa for Christ, through Mary', 1952.
134 ibid.
135 ibid.
136 See *South African Mission Herald* (continuation of *Caritas*), 1953–8.
137 H. Simoneaux, 'Mary and the sense of responsibility', *South African Mission Herald*, June 1955, p. 7.
138 Fr Gerald Mahon, superior-general of the Mill Hill Missionaries, *Catholic Herald* (London), 1 January 1965.

139 'Maria et l'Afrique', *Maria*, 1958, vol. 5.
140 L. Denis, SJ, 'Le culte marial au Congo Belge et au Ruanda-Urundi', ibid.

33 JOHN XXIII AND THE REACTION AT GARABANDAL

1 *Ad Apostolorum Principis*, 29 June 1958.
2 Quoted by Mgr L. Capovilla, secretary of John XXIII, in the introduction to *Journal of a Soul*, trans. D. White, London, 1965, p. xvii.
3 See Appendix 2 in *Journal*, op.cit.
4 A letter of 1942 to his cousin, a Franciscan Missionary Sister of Mary, suggests that Roncalli retained a belief in the spiritual benefits of flagellation (*Pope John XXIII. Letters to His Family. 1901–1962*, trans. D. White, London, 1970, p. 437).
5 In bed he placed the rosary of the Blessed Virgin round his neck to guard against involuntary and 'immodest' nocturnal movements (Resolution 8, 1897).
6 *Journal*, op.cit., p. 16, (1897).
7 ibid., p. 272, (1948).
8 The Roncalli family were poor tenant farmers.
9 G. Zizola, *The Utopia of Pope John XXIII*, trans. H. Barolini, New York, 1978, p. 311.
10 *Journal*, op.cit., p. 123.
11 P. Hebblethwaite, *John XXIII, Pope of the Council*, London, 1984, pp. 170 and 230.
12 *Letters*, op.cit., p. 417.
13 ibid., p. 367.
14 ibid., p. 436.
15 Zizola, op.cit., p. 39.
16 *Journal*, op.cit., p. 268.
17 *Tablet*, 1 November 1958, p. 380.
18 Hebblethwaite, op.cit., p. 249.
19 P. Hebblethwaite, 'The Mariology of three popes', *The Way Supplement*, 1984, no. 51, p. 59.
20 E.E.Y. Hales, *Pope John and His Revolution*, London, 1965, p. 114. One wonders why the Vatican did not see a similar danger in the case of 'officer-priests' in the army, which, in John's own words, was 'a running fountain of pollution, enough to submerge whole cities' (*Journal*, op.cit., p. 88: 1902).
21 *Sacerdoti Nostri Primordia* (on St John Vianney), 1 August 1959. Out of a total of 60 maxims collected by Roncalli as a seminarist, 12 were those of the Curé, including 'God might have created a more beautiful world, but he could not have given life to a creature more beautiful than Mary'.
22 *Grata recordata*, 26 September 1959.

23 See, for example, *Ad Petri Cathedram* (29 June 1959), in which the press and cinema are lashed for the 'deceits of error and the treacherous vices of impurity'. Most of this first encyclical, however, is devoted to a call for unity.

24 For example, the Shah of Iran, King Bhumibol of Thailand, President Sukarno of Indonesia and the Japanese prime minister.

25 The international Balzan Foundation prize committee, whose 37 members voted unanimously in favour of the pope's award, included Soviet representatives.

26 Zizola, op.cit., p. 163.

27 According to commentary by H. Waterhouse, SJ, *Pacem in Terris*, Catholic Truth Society, London, 1980, p. 44, with reference to paragraphs 157–9.

28 Dr John Roche, former executive of Opus Dei, to N.P., 19 December 1984.

29 'A propos du secret de Fatima. Allocution de Cardinal Ottaviani'. *La Documentation Catholique*, 19 March 1967, no. 1490, pp. 542–51. Ottaviani, prefect of the Congregation for the Doctrine of the Faith, claimed he also had read the secret.

30 *Soul Magazine* (organ of the Blue Army), Washington, New Jersey, special issue, 1982, p. 26.

31 Duchess of St Albans, *Magic of a Mystic. Stories of Padre Pio*, New York, 1983, chronology.

32 E. Florez (ed.), *Diccionario de Historia Eclesiástica de España*, Madrid 1975, vol. 4, article on *santuarios*.

33 *The Mystery of Garabandal*, trans. leaflet of *Centro de Difusión Mariano*, Barcelona.

34 F. Sanchez-Ventura y Pascual, *The Apparitions of Garabandal*, Detroit, 1966, p. 82.

35 A snapshot was taken of a miraculous host on Conchita's tongue. At the last apparition, on 13 November 1965, a celestial voice suggested: 'Conchita, why don't you get rid of the chewing gum and offer it up as a sacrifice for the glory of my Son?' (*The Mystery of Garabandal*, op.cit.).

36 Fr J.A. Pelletier, AA, *The Warning of Garabandal* (leaflet), Workers of Our Lady of Mount Carmel, Inc., Lindenhurst, New York, undated, Fr. Pelletier, who is associated with Assumption College, Worcester, Mass., is also the author of the leaflet *Padre Pio and Garabandal*.

34 MARIAN RENAISSANCE UNDER PAUL VI

1 *Sacerdotalis caelibatus*, 24 June 1967.

2 See Vicomte Léon de Poncis, *Judaism and the Vatican. An Attempt at Spiritual Subversion*, Britons Publishing Co., Devon, 1967.

3   The pope inaugurated the Opus Dei's ELIS technical training centre in Rome on 21 December 1965.
4   See J. Ynfante, *Un Crime sous Giscard. L'Affaire de Broglie, L'Opus Dei/Matesa*, Paris, 1981. The Matesa scandal was in 1969.
5   *Humanae vitae*, 25 July 1968.
6   According to the Dogmatic Constitution on the Church (*Lumen Gentium*) promulgated by Paul VI,
    'religious submission of mind and will must be shown in a special way to the authentic magisterium of the Roman Pontiff, even when he is not speaking ex cathedra ... his definitions, of themselves, and not from the consent of the Church, are justly styled irreformable. ...'
7   *Ecclesiam Suam*, 6 August 1964.
8   *Mense Maio*, 29 April 1965.
9   *Christi Matri*, 15 September 1966.
10 See N. García Garcés,CMF, *Estudios Marianos*, 1969, vol. 33, pp. 11–12.
11 Homily at sanctuary of Our Lady of Bonaria, Sardinia, 24 April 1970, quoted by P. Lesourd and J.-M. Benjamin, *Paul VI. 1897–1978*, Paris, 1978, p. 143.
12 B. Monsegu,CP, 'Mensajes marianos y su espiritualidad', *Estudios Marianos*, 1973, vol. 37, p. 145.
13 ibid.
14 Among foundresses canonized were Julie Billiart of Notre-Dame de Namur and Vicenta María López y Vicuña of the Congregation of Sisters of Mary Immaculate.
15 Quoted by Fr H.M. Manteau-Bonamy, OP, *Immaculate Conception and the Holy Spirit. The Marian Teachings of Father Kolbe*, Kenosha, Wi., 1977, p. xii.
16 ibid.
17 The Capuchin recovered as a helicopter carrying the Blue Army's 'pilgrim Virgin' hovered over his monastery in 1959 (A. McGregor, OCSO, *The Spirituality of Padre Pio*, San Giovanni Rotondo, 1974, p. 57).
18 M.E. Ingoldsby, *Padre Pio. His Life and Mission*, Dublin, 1984, p. 96.
19 J.F.K. was a Fourth Degree Knight and his brother Edward held the Third Degree (C.J. Kauffman, *Faith and Fraternalism: the History of the Knights of Columbus*, New York, 1982, pp. 392–4).
20 M. Riquet, SJ, 'La Franc-Maçonnerie', *La Documentation Catholique*, 2 July 1978, no. 1745, p. 638. The Catholic-Masonic dialogue continued in France but with far more caution. See 'La Franc-Maçonnerie et l'Église', *Informations Catholiques Internationales*, 15 October 1975, no. 490.
21 *America* (organ of the Jesuits of US and Canada), vol. 114, no. 12, 19 March 1966, p. 371.
22 Kauffman, op.cit., p. 406.
23 *America*, vol. 113, no. 16, 16 October 1965, p. 426.
24 'Allocution de S.S. Paul VI aux membres des Rotary Clubs d'Italie' (20 March 1965), *La Documentation Catholique*, 18 April 1965, no. 1446.

25 E. Bolster, *The Knights of St Columbanus*, Dublin, 1979, pp. 59–81. Since the reconciliation, Irish Rotary presidents have very often been Knights of St Columbanus.

26 For details of the Cairo visions and Lebanese visions in 1966 'reminiscent of the visitation at Fatima', see R. Brenton Betts, *Christians in the Arab East*, London, 1978, pp. 128–9.

27 *The Herald*, Calcutta, 25 March 1977, quoted by B.M. Billon, *Dogmas on Mary*, Devon, 1978, pp. 146–8.

28 F. Johnston, *When Millions Saw Mary*, Devon, 1980, p. 5.

29 ibid., p. 14.

30 ibid., p. 13.

31 Umberto attended the tenth anniversary celebrations of the Byzantine-Russian Chapel of the Blue Army in 1973. See photograph in *Looking East* (quarterly of Byzantine Centre), 1973, vol. 8, no. 14, p. 50.

32 *Videntes de Fatima* (bulletin for the causes of beatification of Francisco and Jacinta Marto), 1970, no. 5.

33 *Soul Magazine* (organ of the Blue Army), Washington, NJ, special issue, 1982, photograph on p. 31.

34 General Delgado, leading opponent of Salazar, was murdered by the PIDE (secret police) in 1965.

35 'Salazar e Nossa Senhora', *Voz de Fatima*, 13 February 1971.

36 *Catholic Herald* (London), 21 May 1965.

37 *Videntes de Fatima*, 1965, no. 4.

38 ibid., 1965, no. 6.

39 Mgr G. Sessolo (former Regent of the Sacred Penitentiary), *Indulgences*, Catholic Truth Society, London, 1980, p. 17.

40 'Le cinquantenaire des apparitions de Fatima', *La Documentation Catholique*, 19 March 1967, no. 1490, pp. 542–51.

41 P. Nichols, 'Storm over the pope's visit', *The Times*, 11 May 1967. On 12 May a *Times* leader criticized the cult of 'a celestial Boadicea, rallying her side in the cold war between Christianity and communism'.

42 'Avec Paul VI à Fatima', *Informations Catholiques Internationales*, 1 June 1967, no. 289.

43 *Anglo-Portuguese News*, 1961.

44 *Videntes de Fatima*, 1967, no. 3.

45 *Tablet*, 20 May 1967, p. 565.

46 ibid., pp. 548–9.

47 T. Gallagher, *Portugal – a Twentieth-Century Interpretation*, Manchester, 1983, p. 119.

48 P. Mailer, *Portugal – the Impossible Revolution*, London, 1977, p. 56.

49 Mgr R.–M. Tchidimbo, 'L'Angola de Monsieur Salazar', *Informations Catholiques Internationales*, 15 June 1967, no. 290.

50 ibid., 1 December 1970, no. 373. Among other persistent opponents were Fr Felicidade Alves (suspended by Cerejeira in May 1970), Fr Joaquim de Andrade of Angola and Dom Sebastião de Resende, Archbishop of Beira (Mozambique).

51 *Tablet*, 20 May 1967.

52 'Avec Paul VI à Fatima', *Informations Catholiques Internationales*, op.cit.

53   M. Rio, *L'Église et le Fascisme au Portugal*, Paris, 1972, pp. 38–9. The comments were made in a letter to the pope dated 2 October 1967.

54   *Informations Catholiques Internationales*, 15 June 1967, no. 290.

55   At Jaen (Andalusia) station, the traveller may admire a lamp-lit representation of the apparition done in coloured tiles: Ntra Sra de Fátima Patrona de la Hermandad Católica Ferroviaria.

56   *Videntes de Fatima*, 1969, no. 5.

57   ibid.

58   ibid., 1970, no. 3.

59   ibid., 1970, no. 4.

60   ibid., 1972, no. 5.

61   J.M. Haffert, *Dear Bishop! Memoirs of the Author Concerning the History of the Blue Army*, Washington, NJ, 1982, p. 133.

62   F. Johnston, *Fatima. The Great Sign*, Washington, NJ, 1980.

63   *Videntes de Fatima*, 1970, no. 3.

64   N.T. Elko, DD ('Bishop of Byzantine Rite'), *Can the Blue Army Stop Communism?* (leaflet), Washington, NJ, undated.

65   Haffert, op.cit.

66   Johnston, *Fatima*, op.cit., p. 139. The icon was carried into battle agains the Poles (1612), Swedes (1790) and French (1870). In 1902 the sanctuary of Kazan was plundered. A painting of Our Lady of Kazan which turned up in Poland shortly after the Russian Revolution was believed to be the original. Solly Joel, a South African millionaire, brought it to England in 1935, where it was eventually acquired by the Mitchell-Hedges family of Erleigh, Reading. See J.J. Mowatt, *The Holy and Miraculous Icon of Our Lady of Kazan*, Fatima, 1974.

67   ibid., pp. 16–17.

68   Most Rev. A. Katkoff, apostolic visitor for Russian Catholics, 'The icon of Our Lady of Kazan', *Looking East*, 1972, vol. 4, no. 10, p. 7.

69   M.S. Emilianov, 'Festive days mark tenth anniversary of Byzantine-Russian chapel in Fatima', *Looking East*, 1973, vol. 8, no. 14, pp. 23–32.

70   *Message of Our Lady of Fatima at Binh Loi* (leaflet), Washington, NJ, no date.

71   N. Poulantzas, *The Crisis of the Dictatorships. Portugal, Spain, Greece*, London, 1976, p. 104.

72   'Portugal: l'Église sort de son silence', *Informations Catholiques Internationales*, 15 July 1975, no. 484.

73   'Portugal: Catholiques et communistes s'affrontent', ibid., 1 September 1975, no. 487.

74   Interview with J.P. Faye, *Portugal. The Revolution in The Labyrinth*, London, 1976, p. 190.

75   Fr Cristino, Service of Studies and Diffusion, Fatima, to the authors.

76   *National Catholic Reporter* (USA), 4 July 1975.

77   'A Russian pilgrim in Fatima', *Looking East*, 1975, vol. 10, no. 17.

78   See D. Pospielovsky, J. Lawrence, P. Oestreicher, 'Metropolitan Nikodim remembered', *Religion in Communist Lands*, 1978, vol. 6, no. 4.

35 OUR LADY OF NATIONAL SECURITY: CHARISMATICS VERSUS THEOLOGY OF LIBERATION

1   R. Laurentin, *Catholic Pentecostalism*, London, 1977, p. 196.
2   M.T. Kelsey, *Tongue Speaking. An Experiment in Spiritual Experience*, London, 1968, p. 215. For a critical, earlier, analysis see G. Barton Cutten, *Speaking with Tongues. Historically and Psychologically Considered*, Yale, 1927.
3   E.D. O'Connor,CSC, *The Pentecostal Movement in the Catholic Church. The Definitive Study of a Dynamic Rebirth from the Standpoint of Catholic Theology*, Ave Maria Press, Indiana, 1971, p. 58.
4   W. Hollenweger, *Pentecost between Black and White. Five Case Studies on Pentecost and Politics*, Belfast, 1974, p. 89.
5   A manifesto was published in 1909 and the World Christian Fundamentalist Association was founded in 1918. The famous anti-Darwinian lawsuit against the teaching of evolution followed at Dayton, Ohio, in 1925.
6   Shakarian sponsored 'evangelistic and Pentecostal rallies, increasing in size as his business ventures became more successful' (Kelsey, op.cit., p. 87).
7   R. Quebedeaux, *The New Charistmatics. The Origins, Development and Significance of Neo-Pentecostalism*, New York, 1976, p. 10.
8   For example, Pat Boon, the crooner and Maria von Trapp, the Austrian aristocrat and singer whose life inspired *The Sound of Music*.
9   George Otis, the electronics tycoon, witnessed to the renewal in 'Rotary clubs . . . television stations, government offices, Pentagon corridors, movie studios, monasteries, universities and churches' (Quebedeaux, op.cit., p. 188).
10   Quebedeaux, op.cit., p. 152.
11   See B. Schlink, *A Cry from the Heart for Israel*, Herts. (UK), 1984, pp. 15–16.
12   The Jews' return to Israel is a precondition for the destruction of the world, a view based on a reading of the Book of Ezekiel. See B. Schlink, *Countdown to World Disaster. Hope and Protection for the Future*, British edition, 1974, p. 13.
13   *New Covenant*, edited by former leaders of the Cursillo, is published by the Word of God community at Ann Arbor, Michigan.
14   Quebedeaux, op.cit., p. 84.
15   ibid., p. 183.
16   *New Covenant*, February, 1973.
17   ibid.

18 D. Hyde, *Dedication and Leadership. Learning from the Communists*, London/ Glasgow, 1966, p. 14. The book was also issued by the University of Notre Dame Press, Indiana, in the same year.

19 O'Connor, op.cit., p. 90.

20 ibid., p. 44.

21 ibid., pp. 45–6.

22 K. and D. Ranaghan, *Catholic Pentecostals*, New York, 1969, p. 49.

23 O'Connor, op.cit., p. 56.

24 Laurentin, op.cit., p. 193.

25 O'Connor, op.cit., p. 27.

26 For details, see *New Covenant's* 'International News' column.

27 J.C. Haughey, SJ, 'Holy Spirit a ghost no longer', *America* (organ of the Jesuits of the US and Canada), 16 June 1973, vol. 128, no. 23.

28 *Catholic Herald* (London), 4 September 1981.

29 Laurentin, op.cit., p. 15.

30 L.J. Cardinal Suenens, *A New Pentecost?* (first published 1974), London, 1978, p. 210.

31 See his article 'Spiritualité et rayonnement de la Légion de Marie', *Maria*, 1954, vol. 3. The Legion's founder, however, strongly objected to charismatics' claims to 'divine gifts' (see L. Ó Broin, *Frank Duff, a Biography*, Dublin, 1982, p. 108).

32 E.D. O'Connor, *New Covenant*, January 1972; S. Tugwell, OP, *Did You Receive the Spirit?*, London, 1973, p. 67.

33 A. Greeley, *National Catholic Reporter* (USA), 2 October 1970.

34 Suenens, *A New Pentecost?*. op.cit., p. 98.

35 E.D. O'Connor, *Pope Paul and the Spirit. Charisms and Church Renewal in the Teachings of Paul VI*, Ave Maria Press, Indiana, 1978, p. 200.

36 Laurentin, op.cit., p. 23.

37 O'Connor, *Pope Paul and the Spirit*, op.cit., p. 228.

38 ibid., p. 237.

39 O'Connor, *The Pentecostal Movement in the Catholic Church*, op.cit., p. 147.

40 ibid., p. 207.

41 Dr A. Molina Prieto, 'Función de la espiritualidad mariana en la renovación eclesial', *Estudios Marianos*, 1976, vol. 40, p. 227.

42 G. Gutierrez, *The Power of the Poor in History. Selected Writings*, London, 1983, p. 37.

43 ibid., p. 45.

44 J. Comblin, *The Church and the National Security State*, New York, 1979, p. 180.

45 Gutierrez, op.cit., p. 34.

46 L. Boff, *Church Charism and Power: Liberation Theology and the Institutional Church*, London, 1985, p. 125.

47 G. Russell, 'Taming the liberation theologians', *Time*, 4 February 1985, p. 45.

48 Boff, op.cit., p. 126.

49 ibid., p. 130.

50 C. Antoine, *Church Power in Brazil*, London, 1973, p. 135.

51 L. Boff, *O Rosto materno do Deus: ensaio interdisciplinar sobre o feminino e suas formas religiosas*, Petropolis (Brazil), 1979, p. 116.
52 L. Boff, *Saint Francis. A Model for Human Liberation*, New York, 1982, p. 124.
53 J. Cardinal Ratzinger with V. Messori, *The Ratzinger Report. An Exclusive Interview on the State of the Church*, Hertfordshire (UK), 1985, pp. 104–5.
54 ibid., p. 106.
55 *Instruction on Christian Freedom and Liberation*, 22 March 1986.
56 ibid.
57 ibid.

36 ARGENTINA AND CHILE: BROTHER GENERALS IN MARY

1 *El Mercurio*, Santiago, 25 October 1974.
2 N. Chomsky and E.S. Herman, *The Washington Connection and Third World Fascism*, London, 1979.
3 There are 13,390 Cursillos in 39 Argentinian dioceses, and 2,000 praesidia of the Legion of Mary (D.B. Barrett, ed., *World Christian Encyclopedia*, Nairobi, 1982: article on Argentina).
4 J. Rosales, 'Las capellanías militares y su papel en la represión: la teología de la muerte', *Periodista de Buenos Aires*, 8–12 October 1984, no. 4.
5 J. Lemoine, 'Los cruzados del siglo XX. El Opus Dei', ibid., 14–18 July 1985, no. 44.
6 *La Prensa*, Buenos Aires, 30 November 1969.
7 *La Nación*, Buenos Aires, 1 December 1969.
8 *Informations Catholiques Internationales*, 15 December 1969, no. 350.
9 *La Nación*, op.cit.
10 Lemoine, op.cit.
11 Since his imprisonment under democracy, Videla 'spends his time reciting the rosary' (*Financial Times*, London, 11 September 1985).
12 'Quemaron textos de literatura extremista', *La Nación*, Buenos Aires, 30 April 1976.
13 ibid., 17 April 1976.
14 ex-Captain of cavalry F. Mittelbach, *Periodista de Buenos Aires*, 31 October–6 November 1986, no. 112.
15 It is estimated that 1.5 million Chileans were classical Pentecostals in 1975. The Methodist Pentecostal Church (1909) and its offshoot, Evangelical Pentecostal Church (1933) operate missions in Bolivia, Peru, and Argentina, and maintain links with the USA.
16 *Fiducia* (organ of the Sociedad Chilena de Defensa de la Tradicion, Familia y Propiedad), January 1970.

17 H. Alessandri, M., 'Experiencias misioneras en el "mes de María" ', in *Religiosidad y Fe en America Latina*, ed. M. Arias,R., Santiago, 1974, pp. 181–3. This long letter is signed 'su Madre'.
18 ibid., p. 178.
19 L. Gutierrez, 'Chile en deuda con la patrona de las FF. AA.', *El Mercurio*, 17 February 1974.
20 J.-J. Thierry, *Opus Dei. A Close-up*, New York, 1975, p. 86.
21 B.H. Smith, *The Church and Politics in Chile*, Princeton, 1982, p. 338. TFP sympathizers also obtained official posts (ibid.).
22 *El Mercurio*, 7 July 1974.
23 ibid., 19 February 1974.
24 ibid., 25 October 1974.
25 ibid.
26 ibid.
27 ibid.
28 ibid.
29 'El tradicional mes de María', ibid., 11 November 1974.
30 ibid., 7 December 1974.
31 'Pope's message to episcopate and people of Chile', *Osservatore Romano* (weekly English edition), 5 December 1974.
32 *El Mercurio*, 16 December 1974.
33 ibid.
34 For example, Rev. David Wong, leader of the 37-million member World Baptist Alliance, and Rex Humbard, whose TV show was broadcast weekly in Chile.
35 After divisions and purges (Allende was expelled by the Grand Lodge of Chile), the Craft in Chile supported the junta until 1984. See 'Masonería también por el diálogo. Declaración del Gran Maestro indica posición más decidida por la democracia', *Hoy*, Santiago, 2–8 May 1984; 'La masonería contra Pinochet', *Apsi*, Santiago, 22 September–6 October 1985.
36 'España, Brasil y Chile unidos por el cristianismo: en ceremonia de condecoración a jefes militares extranjeros', *El Mercurio*, 19 September 1975.
37 See *El Mercurio*, 12 September 1975 and 7 September 1977.
38 ibid., 14 July 1976.
39 'Homenaje a la Virgen del Carmen', ibid., 27 September 1976.
40 *Evangelii nuntiandi*, 8 December 1975.
41 *El Mercurio*, 30 October 1975.
42 'Fervor para la Virgen', ibid., 8 November 1976.
43 'Emotiva conmemoración de la gesta de Maipú', ibid., 6 April 1976.
44 'Chile no esta solo, tiene amigos' (Pinochet), ibid., 13 November 1976.
45 'Fe y Devoción en homenaje de FF. AA. a Virgen del Carmen', ibid., 24 November 1976.
46 See 'Iglesia y dictadura', *Periodista de Buenos Aires*, 22–28 September 1984, no. 2. Among notable dissidents were Monseñores Podesta (who has since left the episcopacy to marry), Novak, and Hesayne. For a fuller account of Church collaboration with the Argentinian

dictatorship, see E. Fermin Mignone, *Iglesia y Dictadura: El papel de la iglesia a la luz de sus relaciones con el régimen militar*, Buenos Aires, 1986.

47 *Catholic Herald*, London, 6 December 1985.

48 'Visita a las Malvinas. Virgen de Lujan en Puerto Stanley', *La Nación*, Buenos Aires, 23 June 1974.

49 'La presencia del clero en las Malvinas', ibid., 27 April 1982.

50 'Homilía del arzobispo de Bahia Blanca. Exhorta a luchar sin claudiciones', *La Vanguardia*, Barcelona, 4 May 1982.

51 'Informe de la CONADEP', *Periodista de Buenos Aires*, 3–9 November 1984, no. 8; 'Airadas reacciones ante la mención de Pio Laghi en el informe de la Conadep', ibid., 10–16 November 1984, no. 9. The Vatican denied the allegations and transferred the nuncio, Mgr Pio Laghi, to the United States.

52 H. Verbitsky, 'La obscena teología', ibid., 28 June–4 July 1985, no. 42.

53 ibid., 27 October–2 November 1984, no. 7.

37 THE VICAR OF MARY

1 Address before the Portuguese Assembly of the Republic, *Weekly Compilation of Presidential Documents*, 1985, vol. 21, no. 19, p. 614.

2 Homily in St Mary's Basilica, 8 December 1978: 'He entrusts to her the Roman Church, as a token and principle of all the Churches in the world . . . offers it to her as her property.'

3 Audience for Young People, 10 January 1979.

4 John Paul II, quoted by L.M. Herran, 'Pastoral de los santuarios marianos sobre la base de la religiosidad, en las enseñanzas de Juan Pablo II', *Estudios Marianos*, Salamanca, 1983, vol. 48, p. 276.

5 Address to Religious Women, Washington, 7 October 1979.

6 Letter to Maltese Bishops, September 1983.

7 P. Johnson, *Pope John Paul II and the Catholic Restoration*, London, 1982, p. 184.

8 There were around 1,200 priests among 70,000 members in 1984.

9 Some high-ranking Opus supporters (e.g., Cardinals Oddi, Baggio, Poletti, González, Koenig and Hoeffner) have also been prominent figures at Fatima. For Cardinal Silvio Oddi, prefect of the Congregation for the Clergy, 'unknown Fatima and immortal Rome vibrated in unison' (*Seers of Fatima*, 1985, no. 3/4).

10 Claims of miraculous cures of malignant diseases through the intercession of Monseñor were forwarded from Madrid in 1982–3. Other 'favours' reported from all over the world in the Opus Dei newsletter range from cures for spiders' bites to death bed conversions, help in finding jobs and property, and the inducement of pregnancies in cattle.

11 The Vatican's projected budget deficit for 1986 was $56 million (*Financial Times*, 24 October 1986).

12   *The Times*, 25 March 1981. An even sterner warning – reaffirming
      the penalty of excommunication – followed from the Sacred Con-
      gregation for the Doctrine of the Faith in 1983. See 'Declaration on
      Masonic Associations', *Osservatore Romano* (weekly English edition),
      5 December 1983.

13   Address to second international assembly of the Cursillo movement,
      May 1985.

14   Cardinal Luigi Dadaglio, Major Penitentiary, and L. de Magistris,
      Regent, 'Apostolic Penitentiary Decree', *Osservatore Romano*, 14
      December 1985.

15   T.F. Quinlivan (Oblate of Mary Immaculate), 'A better deal for
      the Poor Souls', *Homiletic & Pastoral Review*, New York, 1986,
      vol. LXXXVI, no. 10, p. 62: 'Applied to the Souls in Purgatory, a
      plenary indulgence would pay the entire debt owed by a soul detained
      there and would free it to enter heaven immediately' (ibid., p. 61).

16   For the little known about John Paul II's earlier life, see P. Hebble-
      thwaite, *The Year of Three Popes*, London, 1978.

17   See Cardinal Wojtyla's comments at the press conference held on
      the beatification of Kolbe in 1971: H.M. Manteau, OP, *Immaculate
      Conception and the Holy Spirit. The Marian Teachings of Father Kolbe*,
      Kenosha, Wi. 1977, p. xxiii.

18   Letter to Maltese Bishops, op.cit.

19   Address to Religious Women, Washington, op.cit.

20   Homily on World Day of Peace, 1 January 1984.

21   *Salvifici Doloris*, 11 February 1984 (liturgical memorial of Our Lady
      of Lourdes).

22   P. Hebblethwaite, 'The Mariology of Three Popes', *The Way Supplement*,
      1984, no. 51, pp. 63–4.

23   Homily at national basilica of Our Lady of Aparecida, Brazil,
      4 July 1980.

24   St Mary Major's, 8 December 1979: 'The Woman is already known
      to us by name. She is the Immaculate Conception.'

25   *Osservatore Romano*, 9 November 1978.

26   Homily at Loreto, 8 September 1979, quoted by S. O'Byrne, *John Paul
      II. This is Your Mother*, Athlone (Ireland), 1981, p. 90.

27   Angelus at Pompeii, 21 October 1979.

28   Letter of the Supreme Pontiff to all priests of the Church, Holy
      Thursday, 1979.

29   Homily in the Marian shrine of Mariazell, Austria, 13 September 1983.

30   Consecration to Our Lady at Togoville, August 1985.

31   Homily at national shrine of the Immaculate Conception, Washington,
      7 October 1980.

32   Homily to participants in updating course in the Billings Ovulation
      Method, Catholic University of the Sacred Heart, April 1980.

33   Angelus at Lourdes, 15 August 1983.

34   ibid.

35   Angelus at Paray-le-Monial, 5 October 1986. Addressing the nuns of
      the Visitation convent, the pope gave thanks that the Blessed Claude

de la Colombière, SJ, 'permitted Marguerite Marie to overcome her doubts and to discern the authentic inspiration of her extraordinary experience'.

36 Homily at Aparecida, Brazil, 4 July 1980.

37 Retreat at Ars for priests, deacons and seminarists, 6 October 1983.

38 The pope prayed at her tomb in the Chapel of the Miraculous Medal (rue de Bac, Paris) on 31 May 1980.

39 *John Paul II in Mexico. His Collected Speeches*, Collins, London, 1979, p. 6.

40 See G. MacCarthy, 'What really happened at Puebla', *The Month*, March 1979, vol. 12, no. 3.

41 *John Paul II in Mexico*, op.cit., p. 30.

42 H.G. Cox, 'The abduction of Our Lady', *National Catholic Reporter*, 6 January 1978.

43 *John Paul II in Mexico*, op.cit., p. 30.

44 ibid., p. 49.

45 ibid., p. 46.

46 ibid., p. 126.

47 ibid., p. 150.

48 *El Mercurio*, Santiago, 2 April 1987.

49 ibid., 3 April 1987.

50 ibid.

51 'Pope's homily in La Serena', *Osservatore Romano*, 4 May 1987.

52 *El Mercurio*, 4 April 1987.

53 Address to Salesian pupils, 5 May 1979.

54 Message to Marian congresses at Saragossa, November 1979.

55 Marshal Mobutu took his whole family and government to Fatima in July 1984. The principal church of Kinshasa is dedicated to Our Lady of Fatima (*Seers of Fatima*, 1984, no. 3/4).

56 *Osservatore Romano*, 9 September 1985.

57 Homily at Jasna Gora, 4 June 1979.

58 Farewell to Jasna Gora, 6 June 1979.

59 ibid. Text in *Osservatore Romano*, 16 July 1979.

60 ibid.

61 See, for example, 'Solidarity demo at pilgrimage', *Daily Telegraph*, 22 September 1986.

62 See, for example, 'Prayer to Our Lady of Jasna Gora', *Osservatore Romano*, 20 December 1982.

63 ibid., 26 September 1983.

64 ibid.

65 See C. Sterling, 'The plot to murder the pope', *Reader's Digest*, September 1982.

66 V. Levi, 'It was the day of Fatima', *Osservatore Romano*, 18 May 1981.

67 *The Pope Speaks*, 1982, vol. 27, p. 240.

68 See photograph in *Soul Magazine*, September/October 1983.

69 By 1981 their cause was supported by 192 cardinals and bishops (*Videntes de Fatima*, 1981, no. 1/2). Fr Molinari, SJ, was appointed postulator for the cause in Rome. Despite initial objections to the beatification of children who are not martyrs, the process has

advanced. Favours granted by the candidates include good results at school and successful lawsuits (*Seers of Fatima*, 1983, no. 5/6).

70 *Osservatore Romano*, 18 May 1981.
71 ibid., 12 October 1981.
72 M. Felix, 'Aviação commercial', *TAP Magazine*, 1982.
73 Nevertheless, hundreds of thousands greeted the pontiff in Oporto with the now familiar chant of 'The Pope of the Workers' (*Catholic Herald*, 21 May 1982).
74 *Osservatore Romano*, 17 May 1982.
75 ibid.
76 ibid., 24 May 1982.
77 *El Alcázar*, Madrid, 8 May 1982.
78 *Seers of Fatima*, 1983, no. 3/4. In October 1983 the Cardinal Patriarch of Lisbon preached at Fatima against nudist camps and pending legislation on abortion.
79 ibid., 1984, no. 1/2.
80 *Osservatore Romano*, 2 April 1984.
81 The Italian courts dismissed the case on 29 March 1986 for 'lack of evidence'.
82 *Seers of Fatima*, 1984, no. 3/4.

38 BORN-AGAIN CATHOLICS

1 Mrs Kay Beeson, 'Our Lady's Care', *Soul Magazine*, March-April 1983.
2 Born Again preachers 'raised more money for the 1980 election than the entire Democrat Party nationally' (F. Fitzgerald, *New York Review of Books*, 19 November 1981).
3 P. Deane Young, *God's Bullies. Power Politics and Religious Tyranny*, New York, 1982, p. 94. In Young's view, 'the most effective leaders of the New Right are nearly all Catholics' (ibid., p. 59).
4 Deane Young, op.cit., p. 141.
5 *Divine Love*, 1981, vol. 24, no. 2–3.
6 *Blue Army Manual*, Washington, New Jersey, 1982, p. 19.
7 *Soul Magazine*, May–June 1985.
8 *Divine Love*, 1984, vol. 27, no. 1.
9 A term used by Andrew Lang of the Christic Institute, Washington, DC: 'President quotes Armageddon ideology', *National Catholic Reporter*, 2 November 1984.
10 See H. Lindsey, *The Countdown to Armageddon*, New York, 1981.
11 *Divine Love*, 1985, vol. 28, no. 1.
12 *Soul Magazine*, May–June 1985.
13 ibid., January–February 1985.
14 ibid., March–April 1985.
15 ibid.
16 ibid.

17 *Divine Love*, 1984, vol. 27, no. 2.

18 ibid.

19 *Libertatis Nuntius*, 6 August 1984.

20 'Pilgrimage of Poles hails Reagan at shrine', *National Catholic Reporter*, 21 September 1984.

21 *Soul Magazine*, September–October 1985.

22 ibid., November–December 1985.

23 Fr John W. Smus, director of the Springfield (Mass.) division of the Blue Army received a special blessing for his work from John Paul II in 1982 'as a pledge of divine protection and graces' (*Soul Magazine*, March–April 1983).

24 *Shrine Bulletin* (Blue Army), April–May–June 1987.

25 *Soul Magazine*, November–December 1983.

26 The Albanian mother-superior of the Missionaries of Charity shared a platform with the Blue Army at the International Eucharistic Congress in Philadelphia in August 1976 (A. Wirtz Domas, *Mary, U.S.A.*, Indiana, 1978, p. 328); on 22 June 1985 she addressed a Blue Army rally in Springfield, Mass., taking as her theme abortion 'murder' and the need to turn to Mary (*Soul Magazine*, November–December 1985).

27 *Blue Army Manual*, op.cit., p. 20.

28 ibid., pp. 21–2.

29 *Soul Magazine*, May–June 1985.

30 See 'Franciscan University of Steubenville' and 'New Bishop for Diocese of Blue Army National Headquarters', *Hearts Aflame*, New Jersey, June–July 1987, 'premiere issue'.

31 C. Petrassevich, 'Abbot Mendel. The Father of Genetics', ibid., August–September 1987.

32 'Why do some people deny God's existence?', ibid.

33 A Korean language supplement to *Soul Magazine* was published in May–June 1987. The first Blue Army Hispanic Day was held on 21 September 1986. An extensive Spanish department has now opened at the Washington, NJ, headquarters.

34 A year later, on 13 May 1978, 'stigmatic' Fr Gino Burresi, Oblate of the Virgin Mary, invested the first sisters of the Congregation of Oblates of the Virgin Mary of Fatima. Servicing the shrine of Our Lady of Fatima at San Vittorino (Rome), the Oblate Sisters fight 'materialistic naturalism and anti-christianism' and the 'current errors and religious ignorance' through promotion of the rosary 'in every free minute and in every place' ('Background Notes' printed by the Order, which was approved by John Paul II in April 1979).

35 The Knights set up a $500,000 trust in 1979 for 'promoting increased devotion to Our Blessed Mother' and the preservation of the national shrine of the Immaculate Conception (C.J. Kauffman, *Faith and Fraternalism: the History of the Knights of Columbus 1882–1982*, New York, 1982, p. 419).

36 See A.J. Hebert, SM, *The Tears of Mary and Fatima. Why?* (nihil obstat and imprimatur) Paulina, La., 1984 (fourth printing). A Polish woman living in the US 'found her own Fatima statue weeping again at the

times of the assassination attempts on President Reagan and Pope John Paul II' (ibid., p. 46).

37 *Soul Magazine*, September–October 1983.
38 ibid., March–April 1986.
39 ibid., May–June 1987.
40 'Is Russia's conversion occurring now?', ibid. The Fatima apparitions are accepted by some Russian Orthodox dissidents in the Soviet Union today. See T. Goricheva, *Talking about God is Dangerous*, SCM Press, London, 1986, pp. 52–3. Goricheva also speaks about Our Lady of Fatima in Messianic nationalistic terms on the last page of her book.
41 The Fatima apostolate also counts on Mother Angelica's Eternal Word Television Network.
42 *Soul Magazine*, September–October 1985.
43 ibid., November–December 1985. The project was initially entitled *The Great Sign*.
44 *Shrine Bulletin*, op.cit. Within the complex there are also shrines to St Anne, St Joseph, the Archangel Gabriel and Padre Pio.
45 Over 130 American priests made a retreat at Fatima in 1984 under Bishop Luna, and a British group of lay people walked to Fatima in 'reparation for the two million abortions' performed in the UK in 1983.
46 J.M. Haffert, *Soul Magazine*, March–April 1987.
47 ibid., July–August 1987.
48 ibid., November–December 1985.
49 Mme Coquelard, ibid., May–June 1987.
50 ibid.
51 'Symposium on Hearts of Jesus and Mary' *Osservatore Romano*, 20 October 1986. The involvement of the Blue Army is omitted in this report. See, however, *Soul Magazine*, November–December 1986.
52 'H.E. Howard Q. Dee presents letters of credence to the pope', *Osservatore Romano*, 20 October 1986.
53 *Soul Magazine*, September–October 1982.
54 'The remarkable Marian visions at Mount Melleray', *Ireland's Eye*, July 1986, no. 67. Marian phenomena appear to be on the increase in Ireland, and at least one journalist, referring to the 'swaying Madonna' of Ballinspittle, pinpoints the political undertones (see P. Johnson, 'A wholly moving experience', *The Guardian*, 8 September 1985).

39 VISITATIONS IN PROGRESS: NICARAGUA, YUGOSLAVIA, CHILE

1 *The Seers of Fatima*, 1985, no.1/2.
2 See 'Apparitions in Nicaragua', *Soul Magazine*, September–October

1985; 'Our Lady appears in Nicaragua', ibid., November–December 1986; J.M. Haffert, 'Our Lady of Fatima has appeared in America', ibid., March–April 1987.

3   Letter to *The Tablet*, 4 January 1986.

4   C. Jerez, SJ (Provincial of Central American Provinces), 'The Church and the Nicaraguan Revolution', *Cross Currents*, 1984, vol. 34, no. 1.

5   C. Hedges, *National Catholic Reporter*, 7 September 1984.

6   The *Iglesia Popular* was denounced in the pope's *Letter to the Bishops of Nicaragua*, 6 September 1982. The apostolic letter was issued a few days after a visit to the Vatican by Mr Reagan and General Haig, who 'told the pope that they wanted to work closely with the Church to stop the spread of repression and Communist tyranny' (G. MacEoin, 'Nicaragua: a church divided', *America*, 10 November 1984, vol. 151, no. 14).

7   J. Cooney, *The American Pope. The Life and Times of Francis Cardinal Spellman*, New York, 1984, p. 279.

8   MacEoin, op.cit.

9   *Catholic Herald*, 14 March 1986.

10 Bishop Vega took part in the Hispanic Day at the Blue Army Shrine in Washington, NJ, on 21 September 1986.

11 *Catholic Herald*, 8 August 1986.

12 Mgr P.A. Vega,M., *Apparitions of Our Blessed Mother at Cuapa, Nicaragua*, World Apostolate of Fatima, Washington, NJ, 1982, p. 5.

13 ibid., p. 25.

14 ibid.

15 *National Catholic Reporter*, 20 July 1984.

16 ibid., 31 August 1984.

17 *Catholic Herald*, 10 January 1986.

18 ibid., 24 July 1987.

19 L. Rooney,SND, and R. Faricy, SJ, *Mary Queen of Peace. Is the Mother of God Appearing in Medjugorje?*, Dublin, 1984, p. 29.

20 See B. McKenna, *Miracles Do Happen*, Dublin, 1987.

21 J. Cornwell, 'Sister Briege, the priest-mender', *Observer Magazine*, 11 October 1987.

22 T. Vlasic,OFM, *Our Lady Queen of Peace – Queen of Apostles is Teaching us the Way to the Truth and Life at Medugorje, Yugoslavia*, E. Sussex, 1984 (third impression), p. 7.

23 The repetitious nature of the case is explained by Canon Laurentin: 'There is television every day. What is not repeated is submerged' (R. Laurentin, *Is the Virgin Mary Appearing at Medjugorje? An Urgent Message for the World in a Marxist Country*, Washington, DC, 1984, p. 105).

24 S. Kraljevic, *The Apparitions of Our Lady at Medjugorje, 1981–1983: An Historical Account with Interviews*, Franciscan Herald Press, Chicago, 1984, p. 57. This account was edited by Fr Michael Scanlan,

president of the Franciscan University of Steubenville (Ohio), a centre of the charismatic renewal.

25 Vlasic, op.cit., p. 7.
26 ibid., p. 13.
27 ibid., p. 6.
28 Rooney and Faricy, op.cit., p. 41.
29 Fr Tomislav Vlasic was called a 'charismatic, magician, liar and perjurer' (Fr. R. Foley, SJ, *Catholic Herald*, 7 December 1984).
30 ibid., 1 May 1987.
31 Vlasic, op.cit., p. 10.
32 Fr Foley's expression.
33 Vlasic, op.cit., p. 10.
34 ibid.
35 Another phrase of Fr Foley.
36 C. Cviic, 'A Fatima in a communist land?', *Religion in Communist Lands*, 1982, vol. 10, no. 1.
37 ibid.
38 S. Alexander, 'Archbishop Stepinac reconsidered', ibid., 1978, vol. 6, no. 2.
39 Cviic, op.cit.
40 ibid.
41 See *Financial Times* survey on Yugoslavia, 21 June 1985.
42 *The Economist*, 12 September 1981.
43 *International Herald Tribune*, 23 March 1987.
44 'Yugoslavia profits from a miracle', ibid., 21 November 1985.
45 *Soul Magazine*, November–December 1986.
46 A BBC film in February 1987 provided 'background build-up', according to a grateful Fr Foley (*Catholic Herald*, 20 March 1987).
47 ibid., 17 May 1985.
48 ibid., 8 March 1985.
49 ibid., 17 May 1985.
50 ibid., 7 February 1986.
51 Fr M. O'Carroll, CSSp, ibid., 15 February 1985.
52 'Apparitions of Our Lady in Africa', *Soul Magazine*, March–April 1986.
53 Lt.-General Santiago Sinclair, referring to Our Lady of Carmel, *El Mercurio*, Santiago, 24 August 1986.
54 See H. Lagos and A. Chacón, *La Religion en las Fuerzas Armadas y de Orden*, Santiago, 1987.
55 *Religiosidad popular* is now 'scientifically' analysed from a pastoral point of view. Commissions and journals dealing with sanctuaries as places of national identity, encounter and 'privileged places for evangelization' ('María y la nueva evangelización', *Carisma*, journal of Schönstatt movement, Santiago, June 1987, no. 22, p. 34) have been set up in various parts of the continent. *Informativo Santuarios*, produced by the Comisión Nacional Coordinadora de Santuarios (Santiago 1983) is an example of this type of pastoral study, with the aim of attracting youth and other sectors.

56 See *Las Ultimas Noticias*, Santiago, third week of February 1983.
57 'Vida y milagros de la Virgen de Peñablanca', *Apsi*, Santiago, 7–20 October 1985.
58 *Hoy*, Santiago, 16–22 November 1983.
59 Dr A. Rojas Canala and Fr M. Contardo Egana, *El Monte Carmelo de Peñablanca. Una Aparición de la Santísima Virgen en Chile*, Santiago, 1985, pp. 49 and 71. The book opens with remarks on the first apparition of Our Lady in Europe (Saragossa) and the current visions of Medjugorje and Rwanda.
60 ibid., p. 108.
61 Quoted by Lagos and Chacón, op.cit., p. 24.
62 *Analisis*, Santiago, 22 November–6 December 1983.
63 One issue carries a photograph of strands of the Virgin's hair, cut by Poblete (*Mariana*, June 1985, p. 13).
64 *Que quieres mama?*, Santiago, 1984.
65 Other doctors involved were the pediatrician Adela Frias and the dermatologist Carla Hieber, a German-born specialist who has examined the Austrian stigmatic Theresa Neumann (d. 1962).
66 *El Mercurio*, 15 August 1986.

EPILOGUE

1 Among them Fatima, Lourdes, Czestochowa, Nuestra Señora del Pilar, Knock, Mariazell, Immaculate Conception (Washington), Guadalupe (Mexico) and Luján (Argentina).
2 Padre Hernan Alessandri, *La Tercera*, Santiago, Chile, 14 June 1987.
3 *Seers of Fatima*, 1987, no.3/4.
4 Angelus, 8 December 1987.
5 *Redemptoris Mater*, 25 March 1987.
6 ibid.
7 *Spiritus Domini*, 1 August 1987, apostolic letter to the Redemptorist Order on the bicentenary of the death of St Alphonsus de' Liguori.
8 'Patriarch's homily during vespers in St Mary Major's', *Osservatore Romano*, weekly English edition, 21–28 December 1987.
9 ibid.
10 John Paul II, angelus, 26 July 1987.
11 *Catholic Herald*, 14 August 1987.
12 *Soul Magazine* (organ of the Blue Army), March–April 1987.
13 ibid., January–February 1988.
14 ibid.
15 ibid.
16 *Seers of Fatima*, 1987, no. 5/6.
17 *Osservatore Romano*, weekly English edition, 30 November 1987.
18 Matulaitis was the 'second founder' of the Congregation of Marian Clerics and founder of the Congregations of Sisters of the Immaculate Conception and Handmaids of Jesus in the Eucharist.

19 'Pope entrusts Chile to Mary. May Mary help us to preserve unity', *Osservatore Romano*, weekly English edition, 27 April 1987.
20 E.R. Carroll, O. Carm., 'The Woman come of age', *Marian Studies* (Mariological Society of America), 1985, vol. 36.
21 H. Kung and J. Moltmann (eds), *Mary in the Churches*, Edinburgh/New York, 1983, p. xi.

INDEX

413

Index

Index

Index

Blue Army of Our Lady of Fatima, 3, 234, 252–5, 270, 272–3, 296–301, 312; in Africa, 257, 307, 312; atomic fatalism of, 296; cadets of, 298; and charismatics, 298; contact with Orthodox, 272–3; in Far East, 237, 253, 300; female congregation of, 298; foundation of, 3, 252; fundamentalist approach of, 298; in Guatamala, 255; and indulgences, 252, 288, 299; link with other Marian associations, 237, 253; and mass media, 257, 299; supported by papacy, 235, 252, 296, 298; in United States, 3, 296–9, 312
Blue Division, 191, 192, 223–5, 272
Blum, Léon, 166
Boff, Leonardo, Franciscan, 279–80
Bollandists, 57
Bonaparte, Eugenie, Empress, 132
Bonaventura, St, 20
Boniface VIII, Pope, 21
book burning, 9, 20, 54, 59, 85, 282
Borbón, Carlos, Prince, 207
Borbón, Juan, Count of Barcelona, 225
Borbón y Borbón, Juan Carlos, Prince, 248
Borghese, Princess, 100
Borgia, Francis, St, 36
Borgia, Roderigo, see Alexander VI, Pope
Borromeo, Charles, St, 34, 36
Bosco, John, St, 129–31, 167
Bosco, Madonna del, Italy,
Boudon, Henri-Marie, 48
Bourg, Marie du, 99
Bower, Henrietta, 250–1
Bowring, Sir John, 71
Bragança, Mafalda de, Princess, 233
Braudel, Fernand, 36, 58
Bremond, Count and Countess of, 89
Brentano, Clement, poet, 80
Brethren of the Cross, 25
Bridget of Sweden, St, 23–4, 212
Bruillard, Philibert de, Bishop, 104
Bruno de Jésus-Marie, Carmelite, 201
Bruno, Giordano, 33, 140
Bruno of Asti, Bishop, 14
Brzozowski, Jesuit general, 82
Buddhists, 254
Bufalo, Gaspare del, St, 81–2
Bugeaud, Marshal, 94
Buonaiuti, modernist, 154
Bussy, Louis de, Jesuit, 88

Cabbala, 150
Cabeza, Nuestra Señora de la, 18, 214, 264
Caetano, Marcello, 183
Calatayud, P.A., Jesuit, 57
Calixtus III, Pope, 29–30
Calles, Plutarco, 165
Calvary, Congregation of Our Lady of, 46
Calvin, John, 28
Calvinism, 34, 46–7, 49
Calvinists, 36, 39
Câmera, Helda Pessoa, Archbishop, 279
Campbell, R.J., Revd, 154
Candelaria, Nuestra Señora de la, 30
Canisius, Peter, St, 33
canonization process as a means of promoting Marian cult, 16, 44, 55, 81, 88, 96, 140, 167, 171, 177, 186, 197, 201, 237, 239, 243–4, 254–5, 269, 272, 287, 288, 291, 313
Cantù, Cesare, 82
Capitanio, Bartolomea, St, 99
Capuchins, 29, 34
Caraman Chimay, Prince de, 137
Carberry, Cardinal, 272
Carbonari, 82–3, 182, 183
Cardenal, Ernesto, 279
Cardijn, Cardinal, 237
Carlos I, King of Portugal, 182
Carlos II, King of Spain, 45
Carlos III, King of Spain, 59
Carmel, Our Lady of, 3, 23, 282–6, 290, 307–9, 313; see also Carmelites
Carmelites, 16, 23, 28, 114, 273
Carrero Blanco, Luis, Admiral, 226
Cartellier, Fr, Curé of Grenoble, 104
Castelfidardo, battle of, 124, 125
Castro de la Barra, Jorge, 308
Cathars, 15–16, 19, 25
Catherine of Sienna, St, 24, 42
Catholic Action, 73, 99, 129, 131, 141, 142, 144, 155, 159–60, 164, 169, 171, 173, 176–9, 188–9, 192, 200, 203, 207, 216, 217, 221, 222, 224; ACN de P and Opus Dei in Spain, 160, 204, 221; and Apostleship of Prayer, 100; as bulwark against 'subversion', 142; controlled by Jesuits in France, 159; controlled by Jesuits in Spain, 142; and Fatima, 188, 190; led by nobility in Italy, 173; origin of, 129
Catholic Association of French Youth, 151, 159, 183

Index

418

Index

Index

Index

Iglesia Popular, 290, 303
Ignatius of Loyola, St, 33, 43, 205
Ildefonsus, St, 10
illuminism, 30
Immaculate Conception: apparitions of, 41, 43, 130, 135, 199; campaigns for declaration of, 43–5, 74, 116–17; confirmed at Council of Trent, 33; confraternities of, *see* confraternities; consecrations to, 111, 197; controversy of, 23–7; declaration of, 2, 72, 109, 110, 112, 116–18, 126, 207; denied by apparitions of Mary, 24, 27; 'immaculate embassy' to Rome, 43, 44; indulgences for devotion to, *see* indulgences; Missionaries of the, 153; National Shrine of (US), 249; Patroness of Latin America, 147; Patroness of Spanish Empire, 60; Patroness of Spanish Infantry, 215; Patroness of United States, 73, 248, 312; role of Joachim, 11, 43;
vow to defend, 38, 57; *see also* Immaculate Heart of Mary; Lourdes; Miraculous Medal
Immaculate Heart of Mary, 2, 18, 38, 46, 47, 66, 133, 166, 174, 177, 180, 225; apparitions of, *see* Fatima, Our Lady of; Archconfraternity of, 176; consecrations to, 1, 100, 145, 167, 170, 191–2, 227, 233, 245, 246, 251, 261, 281–2, 293, 297–8, 299; feast of, 63; Reparation Society of the, 250; reparation to, 79, 185, 211, 244; scapular of, 144, 158; shrine in California, 296; Society of, 75; Sons of the, 110; *see also* Sacred Hearts of Jesus and Mary
incorruptibility of saints, 48, 78, 90, 113; *see also* relics
Index of Forbidden Books, 32, 45, 138, 149, 155, 249; *see also* book burning; censorship
indulgences, 2, 3, 16, 17, 23, 33, 61, 72, 73, 74, 75, 89, 97, 110, 121, 129, 133, 166, 189, 205, 280, 293; applied to the dead, 30, 269–70, 288; attached to scapulars, 95, 136, 144; attacks on, 26, 28, 49, 61, 62, 97, 129, 155; confirmed by apparitions, 23; electronic transmission of, 238, 288, 311; granted for land colonization,

17; granted for Marian devotions and to confraternities, 21, 23, 26, 27, 28, 37, 40, 47, 58, 65, 78, 98, 100, 104, 117, 134, 144, 147, 156, 168, 175, 179, 223, 298, 299; granted for military purposes, 17, 26, 125; papal control of, 16, 84, 168; and papal cult, 75, 143, 243; profusion of, 25, 26, 74, 155; reform of, 36, 269–70; revival under John Paul II, 288, 311; theory of, 16, 84, 167–8; and Virgin Mary's merits, 16, 28, 84, 246; *see also* hell
infallibility, *see* papal infallibility
Innocent I, Pope, St, 8
Innocent III, Pope, 15–16, 17
Innocent IV, Pope, 20
Innocent VIII, Pope, 28
Innocent X, Pope, 42
Innocent XI, Pope, 52
Inquisition, 16, 17, 19, 20, 28, 31, 32, 40, 43, 50, 59, 71, 83, 110
Institute of the Heart of Jesus, 66; *see also* Sacred Heart of Jesus
integralism, 2, 159–60, 183, 203, 205, 219–27, 241, 286, 295
Irene, Empress, St, 11
Irish National Land League, 136
Isabel II, Queen of Spain, 110, 226
Isis, 8
Islam, 10, 11, 40, 234, 268, 291

James the Apostle, St, *see* Santiago
James, King of Aragon, 17
James II, King of England, 48, 52
James, William, 18, 96
Jan Casimir, King of Poland, 194–5, 196, 288
Jansenism, 2, 38, 49–54, 56, 59–62, 79, 82, 87, 139, 148, 154, 155, 170
Jansenius, Cornelius, Bishop, 49
Janssens, Jean-Baptiste, Jesuit general, 263
Jaricot, Pauline Marie, 89, 99
Jefferson, Thomas, 81
Jerome, St, 33
Jesuits, 31, 32–8, 39, 41–4, 46–54, 59–62, 64–6, 71, 72, 75, 76, 82, 83, 88–9, 91, 97–100, 110, 112, 115, 122, 124, 133, 139, 142, 164, 166, 171, 179, 181, 185, 186, 190, 194–5, 201, 205, 207, 219, 222, 232, 236, 242, 244, 247, 248, 253, 262, 266; and

Index

Index

Index

Loyola, Juan de, 57
Luciani, Cardinal, *see* John Paul I, Pope
Luján, Nuestra Señora de, Argentina, 237, 282, 283, 286
Luna, Constantine, Bishop, Franciscan, 255, 296
Luther, Martin, 28
Lutheranism, 29, 275; *see also* Luther, Martin
Lyons, council of, 20

McCarthy, Joseph, Senator, 232, 248
McDevitt, John W., Knight of Columbus, 267
McKenna, Briege, Sister, 304
MacMahon, Madame, 97
McQuaid, Archbishop, 170
Maes, Gaston, Redemptorist, 200
Maeztu y Whitney, Ramiro de, 211
Magalhaes-Lima, Sabastião, Freemason, 182
Magna Mater, *see* Kybele
Maipú, Chile, shrine of, 281, 283, 284, 285
Maistre, Joseph de, Count, 65, 80, 82
Miastriaux, Fernand, Dr, 200
Makapoi Api, Maria Fatima, Chieftainess, 256
Malabar Church, 76
Malagrida, Fr, Jesuit, 60
Malebranche, Nicholas de, 53
Manichaeans, 8, 11
Manjón, Andrés, Fr, 160, 217
Manning, Cardinal, 128
Mantsebo, Seeiso, Amerilia, Regent of Lesotho, 256
Manuel, King of Portugal, 181
Marcinkus, Archbishop, 293
Marcionites, 8
Marcocci, Antonio, Jesuit, 181
Marcos, Imelda, 269, 300
Margaret of Cortona, St, 20
Maria Pia of Belgium, Princess, 233
Marian Academy of Lérida, 207
Marian Action (South Africa), 257
Marian Fathers, 198
Marian oath, 221, 223, 226; *see also* Immaculate Conception, oath to defend; Votum Sanguinarium
Marian slavery, 11, 14, 38, 43, 48, 50, 54, 73; *see also* Slaves of the Virgin
Marian Year (1954), 232, 238, 245; (1987–8), 311–13

Mariana de Jesus, St, 42
Marianists (Society of Mary), 65, 85–6, 107
Marianne (French republican goddess), 85, 108,
Marianum, 267
Mariazell, Austria, shrine of, 292
Marino, Blessed, 14
Mariology, 3, 8, 9, 14, 18, 22, 33, 74, 140, 171–2, 197, 223, 234–5, 239, 244, 245, 267, 276, 288–9, 312
Marists (Society of), 85, 86, 112, 153
Martín, Luis, Jesuit general, 156, 160
Martin, Ralph, 276
Martin of Tours, St, 8–9
Martindale, C. C., Jesuit, 121
Martínez, Bernardo, seer, 303
Marto, Francisco and Jacinta, seers, 184, 186, 237, 270, 272, 292, 313
Marx, Karl, 118, 140
Mary Immaculate, Missionaries of, 244,
Mary of Agreda, *see* Agreda, Mary of
Mary of Modena, 51, 52
Mary the Nazarene, Sisters of, 207
Maryknoll Order, 254, 277
Masuccio di Salerno, 28
Mathieu, Mélanie, seer, 102–3, 105–6
Matte, Bishop José Joaquin, 308
Matthew, St, 8
Matulaitis, Jurgis, Blessed, 313
Maurain, Jean, 128
Maurras, Charles, 158–9, 183
Mazenod, Charles Eugène de, Blessed, 87, 114, 118, 167
Mazzini, Giuseppe, 107, 116, 123, 152
Mechtilde, St, 18
Medici, Cosmo de', 26
Medici, Giulio de', *see* Clement VII, Pope
Mendoza, General, 285, 286
Mercurian, Jesuit General, 35
Mérode, Xavier de, Archbishop, 121, 123
Medjugorje, Yugoslavia, 235, 304–7
Mentorella, Italy, shrine of, 289
Mercedarians, 16, 17,
Mercy, Congregation of Our Lady of, 197–8; *see also* apparitions, to Sister Faustina Kowalska
Merino, José Toribio, Admiral, 308
Methodism, 76
Metz, J. B., 279
Meurin, Léon, Archbishop, 150–1

425

Index

Index

Index

Index

Index

Index

Index

Index